ALL ART IS PROPAGANDA

BY GEORGE ORWELL

Fiction

Burmese Days

A Clergyman's Daughter

Keep the Aspidistra Flying

Coming Up for Air

Animal Farm

1984

Nonfiction

Down and Out in Paris and London

The Road to Wigan Pier

Homage to Catalonia

Facing Unpleasant Facts: Narrative Essays

ALL ART IS PROPAGANDA

Critical Essays

GEORGE ORWELL

Compiled by George Packer
With an introduction by Keith Gessen

Mariner Books / Houghton Mifflin Harcourt
BOSTON NEW YORK

First Mariner Books edition 2009

www.hmhco.com

Essays collected from *The Complete Works of George Orwell,* edited by Peter Davison, OBE, published in Great Britain in 1998 by Secker & Warburg. Grateful acknowledgement is made to Peter Davison for permission to draw from his notes.

Excerpts from "The Dry Salvages" in *Four Quartets*, copyright 1941 by T. S. Eliot and renewed 1969 by Esme Valerie Eliot, reprinted by permission of Houghton Mifflin Harcourt Publishing Company.

Excerpts from "East Coker" in *Four Quartets*, copyright 1940 by T. S. Eliot and renewed 1968 by Esme Valerie Eliot, reprinted by permission of Houghton Mifflin Harcourt Publishing Company.

Excerpt from "Spain" from *Selected Poems, Expanded Edition* by W. H. Auden, edited by Edward Mendelsohn. Used by permission of Vintage Books, a division of Random House, Inc.

Library of Congress Cataloging-in-Publication Data
Orwell, George, 1903–1950.
All art is propaganda: critical essays/by George Orwell; compiled by George Packer; with an introduction by Keith Gessen.—1st ed.
p. cm.
Includes bibliographical references.
I. Packer, George, 1960– II. Title.
PR6029.R8A626 2008
824'.912—dc22 2008012356
ISBN 978-0-15-101355-5
ISBN 978-0-15-603307-7 (pbk.)

Text set in Garamond MT
Designed by Cathy Riggs

Printed in the United States of America

16 2021
4500842056

CONTENTS

Foreword by George Packer · ix

Introduction by Keith Gessen · xvii

Charles Dickens · 1

Boys' Weeklies · 63

Inside the Whale · 95

Drama Reviews: *The Tempest, The Peaceful Inn* · 141

Film Review: *The Great Dictator* · 144

Wells, Hitler and the World State · 148

The Art of Donald McGill · 156

No, Not One · 169

Rudyard Kipling · 177

T. S. Eliot · 194

Can Socialists Be Happy? · 202

Benefit of Clergy: Some Notes on Salvador Dali · 210

Propaganda and Demotic Speech · 223

Raffles and Miss Blandish · 232

Good Bad Books · 248

The Prevention of Literature · 253

Politics and the English Language · 270

Confessions of a Book Reviewer · 287

Politics vs. Literature: An Examination of *Gulliver's Travels* · 292

Lear, Tolstoy and the Fool · 316

Writers and Leviathan · 337

Review of *The Heart of the Matter* by Graham Greene · 346

Reflections on Gandhi · 352

Notes · 363

FOREWORD

BEFORE anything else, George Orwell was an essayist. His earliest published pieces were essays; so were his last deathbed writings. In between, he never stopped working at the essay's essential task of articulating thoughts out of the stuff of life and art in a compressed space with a distinctly individual voice that speaks directly to the reader. The essay perfectly suited Orwell's idiosyncratic talents. It takes precedence even in his best-known fiction: During long passages of *1984*, the novelistic surface cracks and splits open under the pressure of the essayist's concerns. His more obscure novels of social realism from the 1930s are marked, and to some extent marred, by an essayist's explaining; and his great nonfiction books, *Down and Out in Paris and London, The Road to Wigan Pier,* and *Homage to Catalonia,* continually slip between particular and general, concrete and abstract, narration and exposition, in a way that would be alien to a storytelling purist and that defines Orwell's core purpose as a writer. As soon as he began to write something, it was as natural for Orwell to propose, generalize, qualify, argue, judge—in short, to think—as it was for Yeats to versify or Dickens to invent. In his best work, Orwell's arguments are mostly with himself.

Part of the essay's congeniality for Orwell is its flexibility. All a reader asks is that the essayist mean what he says and say something interesting, in a voice that's recognizably his; beyond that, subject matter, length, structure, and occasion are extremely variable. Orwell, who produced a staggering amount of prose over the course of a career cut short at forty-six by tuberculosis, was a working journalist, and in the two volumes of this new selection of his essays you will find book, film, and theater reviews, newspaper columns, and war reporting, as well as cultural commentary, literary criticism, political argument, autobiographical fragments, and longer personal narratives. In Orwell's hands, they are all essays. He is always pointing to larger concerns beyond the immediate scope of his subject.

Orwell had the advantage of tradition: He worked in the lineage of the English essay dating back to the eighteenth century, whose earlier masters were Samuel Johnson, Charles Lamb, and William Hazlitt, and whose last great representative was Orwell himself. Within this tradition it was entirely natural for a writer to move between fiction and nonfiction, journalism and autobiography, the daily newspaper, the weekly or monthly magazine, and the quarterly review; and between the subjects of art, literature, culture, politics, and himself. This tradition hasn't thrived in the United States. Our national literature was born with the anxieties and ambitions of New World arrivistes, and Americans have always regarded the novel as the highest form of literary art; if we recognize essays at all, it's as the minor work of novelists and poets (and yet some of the greatest modern essayists—James Baldwin and Edmund Wilson, to name two—have been Americans). As for journalism of the kind that Orwell routinely turned out, the word itself has suggested something like the opposite of literature to an American reader. The English essay comes out of a more workmanlike view of what it means to be a writer: This view locates the writer squarely within the struggles of his historical time and social place, which is where the essayist has to live.

A tradition in which the line between writer and journalist is hard to draw allows plenty of room for the characteristic qualities of the Orwell essay: his informal, direct prose style; his interest in sociological criticism that takes in both high and popular culture; his penchant for overstatement and attack; his talent for memorable sentences, especially his openings, which a journalist would call the lede: "In Moulmein, in Lower Burma, I was hated by large numbers of people—the only time in my life that I have been important enough for this to happen to me"; "Saints should always be judged guilty until they are proved innocent"; "There is very little in Eliot's later work that makes any deep impression on me"; "Dickens is one of those writers who are well worth stealing." The American critic Irving Howe wrote in his autobiography *A Margin of Hope* that when he set out to learn to write essays in the 1940s, he turned to Orwell: "How do you begin a literary piece so as to hold attention? George Orwell was masterful at this, probably because he had none of the American literary snobbism about doing 'mere journalism.'"

Orwell lived in and wrote about interesting times: war, ideological extremism, intellectual combat, dilemmas over the role of the writer in a period of partisanship and upheaval. "In a peaceful age I might have written ornate or merely descriptive books, and might have remained almost unaware of my political loyalties," he speculates in "Why I Write." "As it is I have been forced into becoming a sort of pamphleteer." If it's true, then we can be grateful for the timing of Orwell's birth, since his talent was never going to lie in updating the nineteenth-century naturalistic novel. The work Orwell started doing to pay the bills while he wrote fiction—his reviews, sketches, polemics, columns—turned out to be the purest expression of his originality. "Pamphleteer" might suggest a kind of hack, but in Orwell's case it's an essayist with a cause.

Our times are interesting in similar ways and have opened up a space for writers who are similarly capable of thinking clearly about history as it's unfolding without surrendering their grip on permanent standards of artistic judgment, political idealism, and moral decency. In other words, our age demands essayists. So it's an odd fact that even readers who know *1984* well and have read one or two of Orwell's other books are likely to be unfamiliar with the most essential Orwell. Aside from "Politics and the English Language" and perhaps "Shooting an Elephant," none of his essays are widely read, and some of the best remain almost unknown. Those American readers who have read the essays are likely to have encountered only the single-volume *A Collection of Essays,* which includes just fourteen wonderful but somewhat randomly chosen pieces—not enough to give a sense of Orwell's growth as a writer, the range and evolution of his interests.

How should one conceive a more generous edition of Orwell's essays? A strictly chronological version would function as a kind of autobiography; a division by subject matter—socialism, the Spanish civil war, England—would offer a historical primer. But for contemporary readers, the particular content of Orwell's life and times can sometimes seem dated and remote, whereas the drama of a great writer mastering a form in countless variations is always current. The two volumes of this new edition are organized to illuminate Orwell as an essayist—to show readers how he made the essay his own. In them, you'll find Orwell engaged in two different modes of writing: The essays in *Facing Unpleasant Facts* build meaning from telling a story; the essays in *All Art Is Propaganda* hold something up to critical scrutiny. The first is based on narrative, the second on analysis, and Orwell was equally brilliant at both. He wrote more narrative essays early in his career, in the 1930s, when he was drawing on his personal encounters with imperialism, poverty, and war; and more critical essays later on, in the 1940s, when his most important experiences were behind him. But he never stopped writing either kind; one of his last essays was the posthumously published account of his schooldays, "Such, Such Were the Joys." The literary problems raised and the demands imposed by these two types of essay are sufficiently different that they distinguish the essays written across Orwell's career in a more fundamental way than subject, period, or publication.

This division shows the technical difficulties of the essay in especially sharp relief. Essays seem to offer almost limitless room to improvise and experiment, and yet their very freedom makes them unforgiving of literary faults: sloppiness, vagueness, pretension, structural misshapenness, an immature voice, insular material, and the nearly universal plague of bad thinking are all mercilessly exposed under the spotlight in which the essayist stands alone onstage. There are no props, no sets, no other actors; the essayist is the existentialist of literature, and a mediocre talent will wear out his audience within a couple of paragraphs. Orwell was a technical master whose essays are so clear and coherent that they act as guides to how they were put together. You can learn most of what you need to know about the steps by which a narrative essay arrives at a larger truth out of personal experience from "Shooting an Elephant," and about the way close reading in a critical essay can open up literary and philosophical commentary from "T. S. Eliot." Orwell's essays demonstrate how to be interesting line after line. The emphasis in these collections on the two kinds of essay he wrote is directed not just at readers who want to discover or rediscover his work, but at writers who want to learn from it.

Certain essays don't fit my scheme, such as the "As I Please" columns, which appeared in the weekly *Tribune,* and Orwell's short commentaries on English cooking, sports, toads, and coal fires.

I've included these partly for the sake of their obscurity, to satisfy the aficionado along with the amateur, and partly because they show how much of life interested him. He could savor and mine the trivial and become partisan about things that have nothing to do with politics. On every subject he took up, Orwell quickly hit the target of something essential, making an insight that would occur to no other writer and would still resonate over half a century later. And it's often a short step from these slighter works to the themes of his most famous books. For example, "As I Please, 16," which sentences to death certain overused political terms, is the germ of the great essay "Politics and the English Language," which in turn crystallizes much of the intellectual content behind the nightmare vision of *1984*. Seeing the development of a writer's obsessions through his work is just one reason to read these two volumes of essays together.

A generation of students has gone to school on the banal truth that all literature is "constructed," and learned to scoff at the notion that words on the page might express something essentially authentic about the writer. The usefulness of this insight runs up against its limits when you pick up Orwell's essays. Open these books anywhere and you encounter the same voice. Orwell always sounds like Orwell: readier to fight than most writers, toughened but also deepened by hard, largely self-inflicted experience, able to zero in on what's essential about a poem or a politician or a memory, unsurprised without being cynical, principled without being priggish, direct and yet slightly reserved. It is not a clever or inventive voice, and occasionally it can sound a bit pedestrian. It doesn't seduce and exhaust you with literary dazzle; it persuades you with the strength of its prose and the soundness of its judgment. Exactly what relation this voice has to the private individual born with the name Eric Arthur Blair is unknowable. Within the confines of these pages, its integrity is consistent and enduring.

A career like Orwell's would be difficult to undertake today. There is too much specialization in writing, too little genuine independence, and not much room in the major newspapers and magazines for strongly individual essays. It was hard enough to make a living as an essay writer when Orwell was alive—in 1944, one of his most prolific years as an essayist, he earned less than six hundred pounds for his one hundred thousand words—and much harder now. Yet for any young writer willing to try, these essays don't merely survive as historical artifacts and literary masterpieces. In his openness to the world and his insistence on being true to himself, Orwell's essays show readers and writers of any era what it means to live by the vocation.

—George Packer

INTRODUCTION

By Keith Gessen

ORWELL published the essays collected here in the 1940s—and though he was just thirty-seven in 1940, this would be the last decade of his life. He had behind him four conventional "social" novels and, more significantly, three books of documentary reportage, each one better than the last, culminating in his classic account of the Spanish civil war, *Homage to Catalonia.* Gradually in the others but culminating in *Homage,* Orwell perfected his signature "plain" style, which so resembles someone speaking honestly and without pretense directly to you, and he had more or less settled on his political opinions: "Every line of serious work that I have written since 1936 has been written, directly or indirectly, *against* totalitarianism and *for* democratic Socialism, as I understand it." So he said in 1946.

But while this may have been settled, there were other matters Orwell was still working out in his mind. The subjects of these critical essays are almost all, in one way or another, things Orwell *doesn't like.* The essays are incessantly self-contradicting. First, Orwell declares that no great novel could now be written from a Catholic (or Communist) perspective; later he allows that a novel *could* be written from such a perspective, in a pinch; and then in his essay on Graham Greene he comes very near to suggesting that *only* Catholics can now write novels. At one point ("The Art of Donald McGill") he praises dirty postcards; at another he suggests that a different sort of dirty postcard ("that used to be sold in Mediterranean seaport towns") ought to be censored. In the essay on T. S. Eliot he writes that it is "fashionable to say that in verse only the words count and the 'meaning' is irrelevant, but in fact every poem contains a prose-meaning, and when the poem is any good it is a meaning which the poet urgently wishes to express. All art is to some extent propaganda." Several years later, in "The Prevention of Literature," in arguing for the idea that poetry might survive totalitarianism while prose would not, he writes that "what the poet is saying—that is, what his poem 'means' if translated into prose—is relatively unimportant even to himself." Early in the volume, which also means early in the war, he repeatedly points out that the insight of the great totalitarian ideologies (at another point, however, "smelly little orthodoxies") is that mankind needs more than simply a bit of pleasure to make life worth living. The scientific rationalist H. G. Wells, who insisted on belittling Hitler, "was, and still is, quite incapable of understanding that nationalism, religious bigotry and feudal loyalty are far more powerful forces than what he himself would describe as sanity. Creatures out of the Dark Ages have come marching into the present, and if they are ghosts they are at any rate ghosts which need a strong magic to lay them." Later in the volume, after the war, Orwell will repeatedly plead for a much more humdrum view of human life. What's particularly frustrating about these contradictions is that at each successive moment Orwell presents them in his great style, his wonderful sharp-edged plainspoken style, which makes you feel that there is no way on earth you could possibly disagree with him, unless you're part of the pansy left, or a sandal wearer and fruit-juice drinker, or maybe just a crank.

In a way I'm exaggerating, because the rightness of Orwell on a number of topics has been an albatross around his neck for sixty years. In truth, Orwell was wrong about all sorts of things. He is wrong in these essays about Eliot's "Four Quartets," a poem of more profound despair than he admits. He is howlingly wrong when he says that *Uncle Tom's Cabin* will outlive the complete works of Virginia Woolf. These are minor things. A major thing he was wrong about was the inner logic of totalitarianism: He thought a mature totalitarian system would so deform its citizenry that they would not be able to overthrow it. This was the nightmare vision of *1984*. In fact, as it turned out in Russia, even the ruling elite was not willing to maintain mature totalitarianism after Stalin's death. Other totalitarian regimes have repeated the pattern. Orwell was wrong and Orwell contradicted himself. He was more insightful about the distant dangers of Communist thought-control, in the Soviet Union, than the more pressing and durable thought-control of Western consumerism. Nor did he see the sexual revolution coming, not by a long shot; one wonders what the too-frequent taunter of the "pansy left" would have made of the fact that the gay movement was one of the most successful, because most militant, of the post-1960s liberation struggles.

But there is a deeper logic to these essays, beneath the contradictions and inevitable oversights. The crisis that Orwell was writing himself through in the 1940s was the crisis of the war and, even more confusingly, the postwar. It involved a kind of projection into the future of certain tendencies latent in the present. Throughout these essays Orwell worries about the potential Sovietization of Europe, but also the infection by totalitarian thinking of life outside the Soviet sphere—not just specific threats to specific freedoms, but to deeper structures of feeling. As the philologist Syme says to Winston Smith in *1984*: "Don't you see that the whole aim of Newspeak is to narrow the range of thought? . . . Every year fewer and fewer words, and the range of consciousness always a little smaller." If Orwell was wrong in some sense about the long-term development of totalitarianism, he was right about its deepest intellectual intentions, about the rot it wished to create at the center of thinking itself. And he was right that this rot could spread.

One solution would be to cordon off literature from life and politics entirely: This was, in some sense, the solution adopted by the writers of the previous generation—Eliot, James Joyce, D. H. Lawrence, Ezra Pound—whom Orwell calls the writers of the 1920s and we now call the high modernists. And yet Orwell did not want to make a special plea for literature; in fact, of all the writers of his time, Orwell was constitutionally the least capable of making this separation. His own writing and politics were the fruit of his specific experience—of imperialism in Burma, of the conditions in the English coal mines, of the war in Spain. He begins these essays with the insistence that "all art is propaganda" (he repeats this several times)—the expression of a particular worldview. In Dickens's case this is the worldview of a classic nineteenth-century bourgeois liberal, a worldview Orwell admires even as he sees its limitations. ("Dickens seems to have succeeded in attacking everybody and antagonizing nobody. Naturally this makes one wonder whether after all there was something unreal in his attack upon society.") In the case of boys' weeklies, it is a worldview that is in a sense incidental (precisely because they are *not* art): "These papers exist because of a specialised demand, because boys at certain ages find it necessary to read about Martians, death-rays, grizzly bears and gangsters. They get what they are looking for, but they get it wrapped up in the illusions which their future employers think suitable for them." Orwell was producing these essays contemporaneously with the great Western Marxist debates over "committed" literature, but Orwell is, to put it mildly, considerably more down to earth. In the case of the boys' weeklies he suggests some reforms: not that they become the *Daily*

Worker, but, since it's all the same to the boys so long as the death rays are present, that a more leftist perspective couldn't hurt.

For the Orwell of the early essays, the case of Henry Miller is the tough one. Because while Dickens's politics are in the end congenial enough, Miller's quietism is less so. "I first met Miller at the end of 1936, when I was passing through Paris on my way to Spain," writes Orwell. "What most intrigued me about him was to find that he felt no interest in the Spanish war whatever. He merely told me in forcible terms that to go to Spain at that moment was the act of an idiot." Orwell nonetheless went to Spain, and fought there. He was a writer who felt it was vital to let politics animate his work; Miller was the opposite. As Orwell puts it in perfect Orwell deadpan: "When *Tropic of Cancer* was published the Italians were marching into Abyssinia and Hitler's concentration-camps were already bulging. The intellectual foci of the world were Rome, Moscow and Berlin. It did not seem to be a moment at which a novel of outstanding value was likely to be written about American dead-beats cadging drinks in the Latin Quarter." And yet, as Orwell suggests, someone this unfashionable had to be working under the spell of a profound conviction. He contrasts Miller favorably to W. H. Auden, who at this time in the famous poem "Spain" was miming the thoughts of the good party man about the "necessary murder." Miller is so far removed from this sort of sentiment, so profound is his individualism and his conviction, that Orwell comes close to endorsing it—"Seemingly there is nothing left but quietism—robbing reality of its terrors by simply submitting to it. Get inside the whale—or rather, admit that you are inside the whale (for you *are*, of course)." Except Orwell doesn't really mean this. He may be inside the whale but he does not intend to stop disturbing its digestion, he does not intend to be any more quietistic—in fact, just a few months later, in one of his eccentric moods, Orwell was drawing up a scheme for the guerrilla defense of the island, in case the Germans landed, and trying to get it to the government. What he admired above all in Miller was his willingness to go against the grain of the time. While all art is propaganda, it needn't necessarily propagandize something correct. The important thing is that the writer himself believe it.

But there are certain things—here is where Orwell begins to extend and then to contradict his thinking—that you simply can't believe. "No one ever wrote a good book in praise of the Inquisition," he asserts. Is that true? At almost the exact same moment, Jean-Paul Sartre (a writer Orwell thought, incorrectly, was "full of air"), in *What Is Literature?* was writing, "Nobody can suppose for a moment that it is possible to write a good novel in praise of anti-Semitism." Is *that* true? It seems to have been a problem that leftist writers of the 1940s were going to face by sheer bluff assertion. For Orwell the number of beliefs hostile to literary production seemed to expand and expand. Eliot's "Four Quartets" is labeled "Petainist"—a fairly strong term to hurl at a long experimental poem that doesn't even rhyme. And Salvador Dalí, in "Benefit of Clergy," is a "rat." Orwell wants to chart a middle course between the philistines who would dismiss Dalí out of hand for his outrages and the aesthetes unable even to acknowledge the problem, but Orwell's own trouble is that he loathes Dalí, above all for abandoning France in its moment of danger. After asserting that the painter is more talented than most of the people who would denounce his morals, Orwell proceeds to denounce those morals, and the morals of those who enjoy Dalí's paintings.

As the war goes on, then ends, Orwell's sense of peril grows sharper, and he looks at literature in a different way. He comes to think that no matter who wins, the world will find itself split again into armed camps, each of them threatening the others, none of them truly free—and literature will simply not survive. This is the landscape of *1984* and it is also the landscape of the later essays in this volume—"The Prevention of Literature," "Politics and the English Language," "Writers and Leviathan." There is even, momentarily, a kind of hallucination, in the curious short piece "Confessions of a Book Reviewer," where some of Orwell's old interest in the starving writer crops up, now mixed with the wintry gloominess of his later years: "In a cold but stuffy bed-sitting room littered with cigarette ends and half-empty cups of tea, a man in a moth-eaten dressing gown sits at a rickety table, trying to find room for his typewriter among the piles of dusty papers that surround it . . . He is a man of 35, but looks 50. He is bald, has varicose veins and wears spectacles, or would wear them if only his pair were not chronically lost." Who is this but Winston Smith, the failed hero of *1984,* figured as a book reviewer? Or who, conversely, is Winston Smith, but a book reviewer figured as the prisoner of a futuristic totalitarian regime?

In the earlier essays Orwell sees totalitarian patterns of thought in the excuses made for Stalin by left-wing intellectuals; in the later essays he begins to see the same patterns in writers and thinkers of any political stripe who seek too much purity or too much goodness from the world. There is perhaps a biographical strain to this: widowed, tubercular, increasingly reclusive, and still brutally honest, Orwell was becoming a saint. Three of the late essays—on Leo Tolstoy, Graham Greene, and Mahatma Gandhi—deal with saints. Orwell doesn't like them. He had never particularly liked them: "If you look into your own mind, which are you, Don Quixote or Sancho Panza?" he had asked in the great essay on dirty postcards. "Almost certainly you are both. There is one part of you that wishes to be a hero or a saint, but another part of you is a little fat man who sees very clearly the advantages of staying alive with a whole skin. He is your unofficial self, the voice of the belly protesting against the soul." But back then he thought the saint at least exercised a kind of good example for the fat little man inside us; by the end of his life he seems to have thought the saint a positive evil. Anything that would interrupt the free play of the mind, its commitment to the truth of experience as it actually is rather than as one would like it to be, was an evil. And saints, it turns out, are censorious—Gandhi wanted to throw out cigarettes and meat, which was bad enough, but Tolstoy wanted to throw out Shakespeare, which was even worse.

With great doggedness, then, Orwell keeps delving into the question of literature's position in society, and what might be done to keep it alive in a time of total politics. Eventually, the middle ground he'd managed to inhabit by admiring Henry Miller, Eliot's early poetry, and that essentially apolitical masterpiece, *Ulysses,* gives way beneath him. The pressure of totalitarianism is too great, and as he begins to contemplate the brutal unresolved reality of the postwar, with its two or three warring, nuclear-armed camps (Orwell was enough of a patriot to think that Britain might not actually be subsumed by the United States), he surrenders. In "Writers and Leviathan," dated 1948, he argues that writers must ultimately separate themselves from their political work. It's a depressing essay and it ends—one wonders whether Orwell was aware of this—with an echo of the line of Auden's he so reviled: The writer capable of separating himself from his political activity will be the one who "stands aside, records the things that are done and admits their necessity, but refuses to be deceived as to their true nature." Orwell was always a realist who knew that politics was a dirty business—but he was never quite such a realist as here. The realm of freedom had finally shrunk to a small, small point, and it had to be defended. As Winston Smith says in *1984,* "Nothing was your own except the few cubic centimetres inside your skull."

It's hard not to wonder whether the pessimism of this conclusion—its separation of art and politics, after so many attempts at an integration, or at least some kind of accord—was partly a response to the art (or propaganda) Orwell was himself creating in those years. He had published *Animal Farm* in 1945; weakened by the tuberculosis that would kill him, he was writing *1984* in 1947–48. After the reception of *Animal Farm,* and with the direction *1984* was taking, it must have been clear to him on some level that the world was going to use these books in a certain way. And it did use them that way. The socialist critique of Orwell's late work seems essentially correct—they were not only anti-Stalinist but antirevolutionary, and were read as such by millions of ordinary people (a fact that Orwell, who was always curious to know what ordinary people thought, would have had to respect). It cannot be entirely a case of devious propaganda that Orwell the avowed democratic Socialist came eventually to be claimed ("stolen," as he says here of Dickens) by the Right in the Cold War; that his "social patriotism" soon reverted, in the hands of many, into simple nationalism; that it was under the banner of Orwell, a convinced anti-imperialist, that some of the best intellectuals in Britain and the United States cheered on the 2003 invasion of Iraq.

Writers write because they want to justify themselves to the world. Orwell's essays here, his final reflections on the separation of the politics of the man from the art of the man, can serve as a guide to the Orwell of the 1940s. Out of "necessity" he had chosen a position, and a way of stating that position, that would be used for years to come to bludgeon the antiwar, anti-imperialist left. That he had chosen honestly what seemed to him the least bad of a set of bad political options did not make them, in the long view of history, any better.

But what a wonderful writer he had become! That voice—once you've heard it, how do you get it out of your head? It feels like the truth, even when it's not telling the truth. It is clear and sharp but unhurried; Orwell is not afraid to be boring, which means that he is never boring. He had been shot through the throat by a sniper's bullet in 1937. A tall man, well over six feet, he was standing up in a trench at night, telling his fellow soldiers—as they later recalled—about some brothels he'd visited in Paris, when the bullet hit. It missed Orwell's esophagus by millimeters. He survived, but contemporaries report that Orwell's voice changed. It became slightly flattened and metallic. Some people found it disconcerting.

Orwell's voice as a writer had been formed before Spain, but Spain gave him a jolt—not the fighting or the injury, though these had their effects, but the calculated campaign of deception he saw in the press when he got back, waged by people who knew better. "Early in life I had noticed that no event is ever correctly reported in a newspaper," Orwell recalled, "but in Spain, for the first time, I saw newspaper reports which did not bear any relation to the facts, not even the relationship which is implied in an ordinary lie. I saw great battles reported where there had been no fighting, and complete silence where hundreds of men had been killed. . . . This kind of thing is frightening to me, because it often gives me the feeling that the very concept of objective truth is fading out of the world. After all, the chances are that those lies, or at any rate similar lies, will pass into history."

This insight reverberates through Orwell's work for the rest of his life. The answer to lies is to tell the truth. But how? How do you even know what the truth is, and how do you create a style in which to tell it? Orwell's answer is broadly consistent with the philosophical movements—of which he would have been only a little aware—of his time. There is no necessarily anterior truth; language creates it. Orwell lays out the method in "Politics and the English Language": You avoid ready phrases, you purge your language of dead metaphors, you do not claim to know what you do not know. Far from being a relaxed prose (which is how it seems), Orwell's is a supremely vigilant one. It's interesting that Orwell didn't go to college. He went to Eton, the most prestigious of the English boarding schools, but he loafed around there and, afterward, went off to Burma as a police officer. College is where you sometimes get loaded up with fancy terms whose meaning you're not quite sure of. Orwell was an intellectual and a highbrow who thought Joyce, Eliot, and Lawrence were the greatest writers of his age, but he never uses fancy terms.

These essays typically open with a very strong, flat, memorable statement: "Autobiography is only to be trusted when it reveals something disgraceful"; "Saints should always be judged guilty until they are proved innocent"; or even just, "There is very little in Eliot's later work that makes any deep impression on me." They often do a bit of summarizing—Orwell's style is perfectly adapted to dry, funny plot summary, because it often happens that if you summarize the contents of a novel straight they will sound very funny. (And much of the time Orwell means them to.) Typically, he moves on to a more general philosophical question—"Kipling is in the peculiar position of having been a by-word for fifty years. During five literary generations every enlightened person has despised him, and at the end of that time nine-tenths of those enlightened persons are forgotten and Kipling is in some sense still there." Why is that? Orwell goes on to explain that Kipling cannot be defended as a humanitarian, or nonracist, or anti-imperialist—he was clearly on the wrong side of all those questions. But then Orwell shows the vividness of Kipling's descriptions of life, the singular musicality of his "good bad poetry," and you begin to see what has allowed Kipling to endure.

You could say that Orwell was not essentially a literary critic, or you could say that he was the only kind of literary critic worth reading. He was most interested in the way that literature intersects with life, with the world, with groups of actual people. Some of the more enjoyable essays in this volume deal with things that a lot of people read and consume—postcards, detective fiction, "good bad books" (and poetry)—simply *because* a lot of people consume them. Postwar intellectuals would celebrate (or bemoan) the "rise of mass culture." Orwell never saw it as a novel phenomenon. He was one of the first critics to take popular culture seriously because he believed it had always been around and simply wanted attention. These essays are part of a deeply democratic commitment to culture in general and reading in particular.

His reading of writers who were more traditionally "literary" is shot through with the same commitment. Orwell had read a great deal, and his favorite writers were by many standards difficult writers, but he refused to appeal to the occult mechanisms of literary theory. "One's real reaction to a book, when one has a reaction at all, is usually 'I like this book' or 'I don't like it,' and what follows is a rationalisation. But 'I like this book' is not, I think, a non-literary reaction." And the "rationalization," Orwell saw, was going to involve your background, your expectations, the historical period you're living through. Orwell often launches off on fairly long digressions—like the one on A. E. Housman in "Inside the Whale"—that no other literary critic would even consider, much less get away with. But he does get away with them (more or less), because they're so clearly in the service of trying to pin down a general view of life, and history, and politics. Nothing is ever separate from anything else in Orwell, though at the same time nothing is ever allowed to overshadow the task at hand. "While I have been writing this book," he writes in the essay on Miller (the first three essays in this volume were published under the title *Inside the Whale,* in the spring of 1940), "another European war has broken out. . . . What is quite obviously happening, war or no war, is the break-up of laissez-faire capitalism and of the liberal-Christian culture." And this means we ought to read Henry Miller!

This is great, a belief in the tenacity of politics and bombs but the equally powerful tenacity of literature and personality. If we compare Orwell to his near-contemporary Edmund Wilson, who was in many senses a more sensitive critic and with whose range in literary interests and languages Orwell could not possibly compete, we see Orwell's peculiar strength. At almost the exact moment as Orwell, in early 1940, Wilson published a psychobiographical essay on Dickens in which he traced much of Dickens's later development to his brush with poverty as a young man. Orwell's treatment is much more sociological and political, and in a way less dramatic than Wilson's. Yet at one point Orwell encapsulates Wilson's argument with a remarkable concision: "Dickens had grown up near enough to poverty to be terrified of it, and in spite of his generosity of mind, he is not free from the special prejudices of the shabby-genteel." This is stark, and fair, and that "terrified" is unforgettable.

It's possible to imagine a kind of tragedy to Orwell's style. He was a writer who saw both sides to every issue, and argued with himself about them, but whose style could only come down on one side at a time. You can imagine him trapped in that style, even as he used it to slash through cant and falsehood. You can imagine him trapped in it, too, whenever he expressed a vision of what the good society should be like; for it is, finally, a destructive style, peculiarly ill suited to expressing positive visions of anything. It's a funny, brutal, dry, destructive style. One of the slightly surprising things about these essays is how funny they are—in the elegant, deadpan plot summaries, but also in the retorts. To see Orwell slash through H. G. Wells, and Dalí, and Tolstoy—and to see his glimmer of self-recognition in contemplating the work of the fantastically misanthropic Jonathan Swift—is to learn a bit of what language is still capable of.

Orwell might not have admitted, as we would automatically admit today, that there were multiple subjective truths in the world, that a writer must negotiate the various possibilities of those many truths; and still, even while we know this and Orwell didn't, he always seems to be telling *the* truth. Part of the magic is that he never speaks from a point of view that is anything but his own, while at the same time he believes that any normal unprejudiced person—the "common man," the common Englishman—would see it the same way. The belief in a common man—in his existence as well as his decency—is a profound animating principle of these essays, and Orwell rarely misses an opportunity to stress this decency, as when he undramatically notes that anti-Jewish postcards disappeared from British newsstands after the rise of Hitler in Germany. Having established the common man's existence and his decency, Orwell is empowered to speak for him. There is a doubleness then to the point of view: Orwell is telling us only what he himself has seen—in Spain, in the coal mines, in the books he's read—but he's also convinced that a whole mass of people, standing behind him, would see it the same way, if only they saw it as clearly. And his gift is to convince us that we are those ordinary people, and we see it that way, too.

You can tie yourself in knots—many leftist intellectuals have done this over the years—proving that Orwell's style is a facade, an invention, a mask he put on when he changed his name from Eric Blair to "George Orwell"; that by seeming to tell the whole story in plain and honest terms, it actually makes it more difficult to see, it *obfuscates,* the part of the story that's necessarily left out; that ultimately it rubber-stamps the status quo. In some sense, intellectually, all this is true enough; you can spend a day, a week, a semester proving it. There really are things in the world that Orwell's style would never be able to capture. But there are very few such things.

Orwell did not want to become a saint, but he became a saint anyway. For most of his career a struggling writer, eking out a living reviewing books at an astonishing rate, he was gradually acknowledged, especially after the appearance of *Homage to Catalonia* in 1938, to be a great practitioner of English prose. With the publication of *Animal Farm*—a book turned down by several of England's preeminent houses (including Eliot's Faber and Faber) because they did not want to offend Britain's ally the Soviet Union—Orwell became a household name. Then his influence grew and grew, so that shortly after his death he was already a phenomenon. "In the Britain of the fifties," the great cultural critic Raymond Williams once lamented, "along every road that you moved, the figure of Orwell seemed to be waiting. If you tried to develop a new kind of popular cultural analysis, there was Orwell; if you wanted to report on work or ordinary life, there was Orwell; if you engaged in any kind of socialist argument, there was an enormously inflated statue of Orwell warning you to go back." In a way the incredible posthumous success of Orwell has seemed one of the peculiar episodes in the cultural life of the West. He was not, as Lionel Trilling once pointed out, a genius; he was not mysterious; he had served in Burma, washed dishes in a Parisian hotel, and fought for a few months in Spain, but this hardly added up to a life of adventure; for the most part he lived in London and *reviewed books.* So odd in fact has the success of Orwell seemed to some that there is even a book, *George Orwell: The Politics of Literary Reputation,* devoted to getting to the bottom of it.

When you return to these essays, the mystery evaporates. You would probably not be able to write this way now, even if you learned the craft: The voice would seem put-on, after Orwell; it would seem deliberately "hard-boiled." But there is nothing put-on about it here, and it seems to speak, despite the specificity of the issues discussed, directly to the present. In Orwell's clear, strong voice we hear a warning. Because we, too, live in a time when truth is disappearing from the world, and doing so in just the way Orwell worried it would: through language. We move through the world by naming things in it, and we explain the world through sentences and stories. The lesson of these essays is clear: Look around you. Describe what you see as an ordinary observer—for you *are* one, you know—would see them. Take things seriously. And tell the truth. Tell the truth.

ALL ART IS PROPAGANDA

Charles Dickens

Inside the Whale, March 11, 1940

Inside the Whale and Other Essays was published in London by Victor Gollancz Ltd on March 11, 1940. It contained three essays: "Charles Dickens," "Boys' Weeklies," and "Inside the Whale."

I

Dickens is one of those writers who are well worth stealing. Even the burial of his body in Westminster Abbey was a species of theft, if you come to think of it.

When Chesterton wrote his introductions to the Everyman Edition of Dickens's works, it seemed quite natural to him to credit Dickens with his own highly individual brand of medievalism, and more recently a Marxist writer, Mr. T. A. Jackson,[1] has made spirited efforts to turn Dickens into a bloodthirsty revolutionary. The Marxist claims him as "almost" a Marxist, the Catholic claims him as "almost" a Catholic, and both claim him as a champion of the proletariat (or "the poor," as Chesterton would have put it). On the other hand, Nadezhda Krupskaya, in her little book on Lenin, relates that towards the end of his life Lenin went to see a dramatised version of *The Cricket on the Hearth,* and found Dickens's "middle-class sentimentality" so intolerable that he walked out in the middle of a scene.

Taking "middle-class" to mean what Krupskaya might be expected to mean by it, this was probably a truer judgment than those of Chesterton and Jackson. But it is worth noticing that the dislike of Dickens implied in this remark is something unusual. Plenty of people have found him unreadable, but very few seem to have felt any hostility towards the general spirit of his work. Some years ago Mr. Bechhofer Roberts published a full-length attack on Dickens in the form of a novel (*This Side Idolatry*), but it was a merely personal attack, concerned for the most part with Dickens's treatment of his wife. It dealt with incidents which not one in a thousand of Dickens's readers would ever hear about, and which no more invalidate his work than the second-best bed invalidates *Hamlet.* All that the book really demonstrated was that a writer's literary personality has little or nothing to do with his private character. It is quite possible that in private life Dickens was just the kind of insensitive egoist that Mr. Bechhofer Roberts makes him appear. But in his published work there is implied a personality quite different from this, a personality which has won him far more friends than enemies. It might well have been otherwise, for even if Dickens was a bourgeois, he was certainly a subversive writer, a radical, one might truthfully say a rebel. Everyone who has read widely in his work has felt this. Gissing, for instance, the best of the writers on Dickens, was anything but a radical himself, and he disapproved of this strain in Dickens and wished it were not there, but it never occurred to him to deny it. In *Oliver Twist, Hard Times, Bleak House, Little Dorrit,* Dickens attacked English institutions with a ferocity that has never since been approached. Yet he managed to do it without making himself hated, and, more than this, the very people he attacked have swallowed him so completely that he has become a national institution himself. In its attitude towards Dickens the English public has always been a little like the elephant which feels a blow with a walking-stick as a delightful tickling. Before I was ten years old I was having Dickens ladled down my throat by schoolmasters in whom even at that age I could see a strong resemblance to Mr. Creakle, and one knows without needing to be told that lawyers delight in Serjeant Buzfuz and that *Little Dorrit* is a favourite in the Home Office. Dickens seems to have succeeded in attacking everybody and antagonizing nobody. Naturally this makes one wonder whether after all there was something unreal in his attack upon society. Where exactly does he stand, socially, morally and politically? As usual, one can define his position more easily if one starts by deciding what he was *not.*

In the first place he was *not,* as Messrs. Chesterton and Jackson seem to imply, a "proletarian" writer. To begin with, he does not write about the proletariat, in which he merely resembles the overwhelming majority of novelists, past and present. If you look for the working classes in fiction, and especially English fiction, all you find is a hole. This statement needs qualifying, perhaps. For reasons that are easy enough to see, the agricultural labourer (in England a proletarian) gets a fairly good showing in fiction, and a great deal has been written about criminals, derelicts and, more recently, the working-class intelligentsia. But the ordinary town proletariat, the people who make the wheels go round, have always been ignored by novelists. When they do find their way between the covers of a book, it is nearly always as objects of pity or as comic relief. The central action of Dickens's stories almost invariably takes place in middle-class surroundings. If one examines his novels in detail one finds that his real subject-matter is the London commercial bourgeoisie and their hangers-on—lawyers, clerks, tradesmen, innkeepers, small craftsmen and servants. He has no portrait of an agricultural worker, and only one (Stephen Blackpool in *Hard Times*) of an industrial worker. The Plornishes in *Little Dorrit* are probably his best picture of a working-class family—the Peggottys, for instance, hardly belong to the working class—but on the whole he is not successful with this type of character. If you ask any ordinary reader which of Dickens's proletarian characters he can remember, the three he is almost certain to mention are Bill Sikes, Sam Weller and Mrs. Gamp. A burglar, a valet and a drunken midwife—not exactly a representative cross-section of the English working class.

Secondly, in the ordinarily accepted sense of the word, Dickens is not a "revolutionary" writer. But his position here needs some defining.

Whatever else Dickens may have been, he was not a hole-and-corner soul-saver, the kind of well-meaning idiot who thinks that the world will be perfect if you amend a few by-laws and abolish a few anomalies. It is worth comparing him with Charles Reade, for instance. Reade was a much better-informed man than Dickens, and in some ways more public-spirited. He really hated the abuses he could understand, he showed them up in a series of novels which for all their absurdity are extremely readable, and he probably helped to alter public opinion on a few minor but important points. But it was quite beyond him to grasp that, given the existing form of society, certain evils *cannot* be remedied. Fasten upon this or that minor abuse, expose it, drag it into the open, bring it before a British jury, and all will be well—that is how he sees it. Dickens at any rate never imagined that you can cure pimples by cutting them off. In every page of his work one can see a consciousness that society is wrong somewhere at the root. It is when one asks "Which root?" that one begins to grasp his position.

The truth is that Dickens's criticism of society is almost exclusively moral. Hence the utter lack of any constructive suggestion anywhere in his work. He attacks the law, parliamentary government, the educational system and so forth, without ever clearly suggesting what he would put in their places. Of course it is not necessarily the business of a novelist, or a satirist, to make constructive suggestions, but the point is that Dickens's attitude is at bottom not even *de*structive. There is no clear sign that he wants the existing order to be overthrown, or that he believes it would make very much difference if it *were* overthrown. For in reality his target is not so much society as "human nature." It would be difficult to point anywhere in his books to a passage suggesting that the economic system is wrong *as a system.* Nowhere, for instance, does he make any attack on private enterprise or private property. Even in a book like *Our Mutual Friend,* which turns on the power of corpses to interfere with living people by means of idiotic wills, it does not occur to him to suggest that individuals ought not to have this irresponsible power. Of course one can draw this inference for oneself, and one can draw it again from the remarks about Bounderby's will at the end of *Hard Times,* and indeed from the whole of Dickens's work one can infer the evil of *laissez-faire* capitalism; but Dickens makes no such inference himself. It is said that Macaulay refused to review *Hard Times* because he disapproved of its "sullen Socialism." Obviously Macaulay is here using the word "Socialism" in the same sense in which, twenty years ago, a vegetarian meal or a Cubist picture used to be referred to as "Bolshevism." There is not a line in the book that can properly be called Socialistic; indeed, its tendency if anything is pro-capitalist, because its whole moral is that capitalists ought to be kind, not that workers ought to be rebellious. Bounderby is a bullying windbag and Gradgrind has been morally blinded, but if they were better men, the system would work well enough—that, all through, is the implication. And so far as social criticism goes, one can never extract much more from Dickens than this, unless one deliberately reads meanings into him. His whole "message" is one that at first glance looks like an enormous platitude: If men would behave decently the world would be decent.

Naturally this calls for a few characters who are in positions of authority and who *do* behave decently. Hence that recurrent Dickens figure, the Good Rich Man. This character belongs especially to Dickens's early optimistic period. He is usually a "merchant" (we are not necessarily told what merchandise he deals in), and he is always a superhumanly kind-hearted old gentleman who "trots" to and fro, raising his employees' wages, patting children on the head, getting debtors out of jail and, in general, acting the fairy godmother. Of course he is a pure dream figure, much further from real life than, say, Squeers or Micawber. Even Dickens must have reflected occasionally that anyone who was so anxious to give his money away would never have acquired it in the first place. Mr. Pickwick, for instance, had "been in the city," but it is difficult to imagine him making a fortune there. Nevertheless this character runs like a connecting thread through most of the earlier books. Pickwick, the Cheerybles, old Chuzzlewit, Scrooge—it is the same figure over and over again, the good rich man handing out guineas. Dickens does however show signs of development here. In the books of the middle period the good rich man fades out to some extent. There is no one who plays this part in *A Tale of Two Cities,* nor in *Great Expectations*—*Great Expectations* is, in fact, definitely an attack on patronage—and in *Hard Times* it is only very doubtfully played by Gradgrind after his reformation. The character reappears in a rather different form as Meagles in *Little Dorrit* and John Jarndyce in *Bleak House*—one might perhaps add Betsy Trotwood in *David Copperfield.* But in these books the good rich man has dwindled from a "merchant" to a rentier. This is significant. A rentier is part of the possessing class, he can and, almost without knowing it, does make other people work for him, but he has very little direct power. Unlike Scrooge or the Cheerybles, he cannot put everything right by raising everybody's wages. The seeming inference from the rather despondent books that Dickens wrote in the 'fifties is that by that time he had grasped the helplessness of well-meaning individuals in a corrupt society. Nevertheless in the last completed novel, *Our Mutual Friend* (published 1864–65), the good rich man comes back in full glory in the person of Boffin. Boffin is a proletarian by origin and only rich by inheritance, but he is the usual *deus ex machina,* solving everybody's problems by showering money in all directions. He even "trots," like the Cheerybles. In several ways *Our Mutual Friend* is a return to the earlier manner, and not an unsuccessful return either. Dickens's thoughts seem to have come full circle. Once again, individual kindliness is the remedy for everything.

One crying evil of his time that Dickens says very little about is child labour. There are plenty of pictures of suffering children in his books, but usually they are suffering in schools rather than in factories. The one detailed account of child labour that he gives is the description in *David Copperfield* of little David washing bottles in Murdstone & Grinby's warehouse. This, of course, is autobiography. Dickens himself, at the age of ten, had worked in Warren's blacking factory in the Strand, very much as he describes it here. It was a terribly bitter memory to him, partly because he felt the whole incident to be discreditable to his parents, and he even concealed it from his wife till long after they were married. Looking back on this period, he says in *David Copperfield*:

> . . . it is matter of some surprise to me, even now, that I can have been so easily thrown away at such an age. A child of excellent abilities, and with strong powers of observation, quick, eager, delicate, and soon hurt bodily or mentally, it seems wonderful to me that nobody should have made any sign in my behalf. But none was made; and I became, at ten years old, a little labouring hind in the service of Murdstone & Grinby.

And again, having described the rough boys among whom he worked:

> No words can express the secret agony of my soul as I sunk into this companionship . . . and felt my hopes of growing up to be a learned and distinguished man, crushed in my bosom.

Obviously it is not David Copperfield who is speaking, it is Dickens himself. He uses almost the same words in the autobiography that he began and abandoned a few months earlier. Of course Dickens is right in saying that a gifted child ought not to work ten hours a day pasting labels on bottles, but what he does not say is that *no* child ought to be condemned to such a fate, and there is no reason for inferring that he thinks it. David escapes from the warehouse, but Mick Walker and Mealy Potatoes and the others are still there, and there is no sign that this troubles Dickens particularly. As usual, he displays no consciousness that the *structure* of society can be changed. He despises politics, does not believe that any good can come out of Parliament—he had been a Parliamentary shorthand writer, which was no doubt a disillusioning experience—and he is slightly hostile to the most hopeful movement of his day, trade unionism. In *Hard Times* trade unionism is represented as something not much better than a racket, something that happens because employers are not sufficiently paternal. Stephen Blackpool's refusal to join the union is rather a virtue in Dickens's eyes. Also, as Mr. Jackson has pointed out, the apprentices' association in *Barnaby Rudge,* to which Sim Tappertit belongs, is probably a hit at the illegal or barely legal unions of Dickens's own day, with their secret assemblies, passwords and so forth. Obviously he wants the workers to be decently treated, but there is no sign that he wants them to take their destiny into their own hands, least of all by open violence.

As it happens, Dickens deals with revolution in the narrower sense in two novels, *Barnaby Rudge* and *A Tale of Two Cities.* In *Barnaby Rudge* it is a case of rioting rather than revolution. The Gordon Riots of 1780, though they had religious bigotry as a pretext, seem to have been little more than a pointless outburst of looting. Dickens's attitude to this kind of thing is sufficiently indicated by the fact that his first idea was to make the ringleaders of the riots three lunatics escaped from an asylum. He was dissuaded from this, but the principal figure of the book is in fact a village idiot. In the chapters dealing with the riots Dickens shows a most profound horror of mob violence. He delights in describing scenes in which the "dregs" of the population behave with atrocious bestiality. These chapters are of great psychological interest, because they show how deeply he had brooded on this subject. The things he describes can only have come out of his imagination, for no riots on anything like the same scale had happened in his lifetime. Here is one of his descriptions, for instance:

> If Bedlam gates had been flung open wide, there would not have issued forth such maniacs as the frenzy of that night had made. There were men there who danced and trampled on the beds of flowers as though they trod down human enemies, and wrenched them from the stalks, like savages who twisted human necks. There were men who cast their lighted torches in the air, and suffered them to fall upon their heads and faces, blistering the skin with deep unseemly burns. There were men who rushed up to the fire, and paddled in it with their hands as if in water; and others who were restrained by force from plunging in, to gratify their deadly longing. On the skull of one drunken lad—not twenty, by his looks—who lay upon the ground with a bottle to his mouth, the lead from the roof came streaming down in a shower of liquid fire, white hot, melting his head like wax . . . But of all the howling throng not one learnt mercy from, or sickened at, these sights; nor was the fierce, besotted, senseless rage of one man glutted.

You might almost think you were reading a description of "Red" Spain by a partisan of General Franco. One ought, of course, to remember that when Dickens was writing, the London "mob" still existed. (Nowadays there is no mob, only a flock.) Low wages and the growth and shift of population had brought into existence a huge, dangerous slum-proletariat, and until the early middle of the nineteenth century there was hardly such a thing as a police force. When the brickbats began to fly there was nothing between shuttering your windows and ordering the troops to open fire. In *A Tale of Two Cities* he is dealing with a revolution which was really *about* something, and Dickens's attitude is different, but not entirely different. As a matter of fact, *A Tale of Two Cities* is a book which tends to leave a false impression behind, especially after a lapse of time.

The one thing that everyone who has read *A Tale of Two Cities* remembers is the Reign of Terror. The whole book is dominated by the guillotine—tumbrils thundering to and fro, bloody knives, heads bouncing into the basket, and sinister old women knitting as they watch. Actually these scenes only occupy a few chapters, but they are written with terrible intensity, and the rest of the book is rather slow going. But *A Tale of Two Cities* is not a companion volume to *The Scarlet Pimpernel.*[2] Dickens sees clearly enough that the French Revolution was bound to happen and that many of the people who were executed deserved what they got. If, he says, you behave as the French aristocracy had behaved, vengeance will follow. He repeats this over and over again. We are constantly being reminded that while "my lord" is lolling in bed, with four liveried footmen serving his chocolate and the peasants starving outside, somewhere in the forest a tree is growing which will presently be sawn into planks for the platform of the guillotine, etc. etc. etc. The inevitability of the Terror, given its causes, is insisted upon in the clearest terms:

> It was too much the way . . . to talk of this terrible Revolution as if it were the one only harvest ever known under the

> skies that had not been sown—as if nothing had ever been done, or omitted to be done, that had led to it—as if observers of the wretched millions in France, and of the misused and perverted resources that should have made them prosperous, had not seen it inevitably coming, years before, and had not in plain words recorded what they saw.

And again:

> All the devouring and insatiate Monsters imagined since imagination could record itself, are fused in the one realisation, Guillotine. And yet there is not in France, with its rich variety of soil and climate, a blade, a leaf, a root, a sprig, a peppercorn, which will grow to maturity under conditions more certain than those that have produced this horror. Crush humanity out of shape once more, under similar hammers, and it will twist itself into the same tortured forms.

In other words, the French aristocracy had dug their own graves. But there is no perception here of what is now called historic necessity. Dickens sees that the results are inevitable, given the causes, but he thinks that the causes might have been avoided. The Revolution is something that happens because centuries of oppression have made the French peasantry subhuman. If the wicked nobleman could somehow have turned over a new leaf, like Scrooge, there would have been no Revolution, no jacquerie, no guillotine—and so much the better. This is the opposite of the "revolutionary" attitude. From the "revolutionary" point of view the class-struggle is the main source of progress, and therefore the nobleman who robs the peasant and goads him to revolt is playing a necessary part, just as much as the Jacobin who guillotines the nobleman. Dickens never writes anywhere a line that can be interpreted as meaning this. Revolution as he sees it is merely a monster that is begotten by tyranny and always ends by devouring its own instruments. In Sidney Carton's vision at the foot of the guillotine, he foresees Defarge and the other leading spirits of the Terror all perishing under the same knife—which, in fact, was approximately what happened.

And Dickens is very sure that revolution *is* a monster. That is why everyone remembers the revolutionary scenes in *A Tale of Two Cities*; they have the quality of nightmare, and it is Dickens's own nightmare. Again and again he insists upon the meaningless horrors of revolution—the mass-butcheries, the injustice, the ever-present terror of spies, the frightful blood-lust of the mob. The descriptions of the Paris mob—the description, for instance, of the crowd of murderers struggling round the grindstone to sharpen their weapons before butchering the prisoners in the September massacres—outdo anything in *Barnaby Rudge.* The revolutionaries appear to him simply as degraded savages—in fact, as lunatics. He broods over their frenzies with a curious imaginative intensity. He describes them dancing the "Carmagnole,"[3] for instance:

> There could not be fewer than five hundred people, and they were dancing like five thousand demons . . . They danced to the popular Revolution song, keeping a ferocious time that was like a gnashing of teeth in unison . . . They advanced, retreated, struck at one another's hands, clutched at one another's heads, spun round alone, caught one another and spun round in pairs, until many of them dropped . . . Suddenly they stopped again, paused, struck out the time afresh, formed into lines the width of the public way, and with their heads low down and their hands high up, swooped scream-

> ing off. No fight could have been half so terrible as this dance. It was so emphatically a fallen sport—a something, once innocent, delivered over to all devilry. . . .

He even credits some of these wretches with a taste for guillotining children. The passage I have abridged above ought to be read in full. It and others like it show how deep was Dickens's horror of revolutionary hysteria. Notice, for instance, that touch, "with their heads low down and their hands high up," etc., and the evil vision it conveys. Madame Defarge is a truly dreadful figure, certainly Dickens's most successful attempt at a *malignant* character. Defarge and others are simply "the new oppressors who have risen on the destruction of the old," the revolutionary courts are presided over by "the lowest, cruellest and worst populace," and so on and so forth. All the way through Dickens insists upon the nightmare insecurity of a revolutionary period, and in this he shows a great deal of prescience. "A law of the suspected, which struck away all security for liberty or life, and delivered over any good and innocent person to any bad and guilty one; prisons gorged with people who had committed no offence, and could obtain no hearing"—it would apply pretty accurately to several countries to-day.

The apologists of any revolution generally try to minimise its horrors; Dickens's impulse is to exaggerate them—and from a historical point of view he has certainly exaggerated. Even the Reign of Terror was a much smaller thing than he makes it appear. Though he quotes no figures, he gives the impression of a frenzied massacre lasting for years, whereas in reality the whole of the Terror, so far as the number of deaths goes, was a joke compared with one of Napoleon's battles. But the bloody knives and the tumbrils rolling to and fro create in his mind a special, sinister vision which he has succeeded in passing on to generations of readers. Thanks to Dickens, the very word "tumbril" has a murderous sound; one forgets that a tumbril is only a sort of farm-cart. To this day, to the average Englishman, the French Revolution means no more than a pyramid of severed heads. It is a strange thing that Dickens, much more in sympathy with the ideas of the Revolution than most Englishmen of his time, should have played a part in creating this impression.

If you hate violence and don't believe in politics, the only major remedy remaining is education. Perhaps society is past praying for, but there is always hope for the individual human being, if you can catch him young enough. This belief partly accounts for Dickens's preoccupation with childhood.

No one, at any rate no English writer, has written better about childhood than Dickens. In spite of all the knowledge that has accumulated since, in spite of the fact that children are now comparatively sanely treated, no novelist has shown the same power of entering into the child's point of view. I must have been about nine years old when I first read *David Copperfield.* The mental atmosphere of the opening chapters was so immediately intelligible to me that I vaguely imagined they had been written *by a child.* And yet when one re-reads the book as an adult and sees the Murdstones, for instance, dwindle from gigantic figures of doom into semi-comic monsters, these passages lose nothing. Dickens has been able to stand both inside and outside the child's mind, in such a way that the same scene can be wild burlesque or sinister reality, according to the age at which one reads it. Look, for instance, at the scene in which David Copperfield is unjustly suspected of eating the mutton chops; or the scene in which Pip, in *Great Expectations,* coming back from Miss Havisham's house and finding himself completely unable to describe what he has seen, takes refuge in a series of outrageous lies—which, of course, are eagerly believed. All the isolation of childhood is there. And how accurately he has recorded the mechanisms of the child's mind, its visualising tendency, its sensitiveness to certain kinds of impression. Pip relates how in his childhood his ideas about his dead parents were derived from their tombstones:

> The shape of the letters on my father's, gave me an odd idea that he was a square, stout, dark man, with curly black hair. From the character and turn of the inscription, "*Also Georgiana, Wife of the Above,*" I drew a childish conclusion that my mother was freckled and sickly. To five little stone lozenges, each about a foot and a half long, which were arranged in a neat row beside their grave, and were sacred to the memory of five little brothers of mine . . . I am indebted for a belief I religiously entertained that they had all been born on their backs with their hands in their trousers-pockets, and had never taken them out in this state of existence.

There is a similar passage in *David Copperfield.* After biting Mr. Murdstone's hand, David is sent away to school and obliged to wear on his back a placard saying, "Take care of him. He bites." He looks at the door in the playground where the boys have carved their names, and from the appearance of each name he seems to know in just what tone of voice the boy will read out the placard:

> There was one boy—a certain J. Steerforth—who cut his name very deep and very often, who, I conceived, would read it in a rather strong voice, and afterwards pull my hair. There was another boy, one Tommy Traddles, who I dreaded would make game of it, and pretend to be dreadfully frightened of me. There was a third, George Demple, who I fancied would sing it.

When I read this passage as a child, it seemed to me that those were exactly the pictures that those particular names would call up. The reason, of course, is the sound-associations of the words (Demple—"temple"; Traddles—probably "skedaddle"). But how many people, before Dickens, had ever noticed such things? A sympathetic attitude towards children was a much rarer thing in Dickens's day than it is now. The early nineteenth century was not a good time to be a child. In Dickens's youth children were still being "solemnly tried at a criminal bar, where they were held up to be seen," and it was not so long since boys of thirteen had been hanged for petty theft. The doctrine of "breaking the child's spirit" was in full vigour, and *The Fairchild Family* was a standard book for children till late into the century. This evil book is now issued in pretty-pretty expurgated editions, but it is well worth reading in the original version. It gives one some idea of the lengths to which child-discipline was sometimes carried. Mr. Fairchild, for instance, when he catches his children quarrelling, first thrashes them, reciting Doctor Watts's "Let dogs delight to bark and bite" between blows of the cane, and then takes them to spend the afternoon beneath a gibbet where the rotting corpse of a murderer is hanging. In the earlier part of the century scores of thousands of children, aged sometimes as young as six, were literally worked to death in the mines or cotton mills, and even at the fashionable public schools boys were flogged till they ran with blood for a mistake in their Latin verses. One thing which Dickens seems to have recognised, and which most of his contemporaries did not, is the sadistic sexual element in flogging. I think this can be inferred from *David Copperfield* and *Nicholas Nickleby*. But mental cruelty to a child infuriates him as much as physical, and though there is a fair number of exceptions, his schoolmasters are generally scoundrels.

Except for the universities and the big public schools, every kind of education then existing in England gets a mauling at Dickens's hands. There is Doctor Blimber's Academy, where little boys are blown up with Greek until they burst, and the revolting charity schools of the period, which produced specimens like Noah Claypole and Uriah Heep, and Salem House, and Dotheboys Hall, and the disgraceful little dame-school kept by Mr. Wopsle's great-aunt. Some of what Dickens says remains true even to-day. Salem House is the ancestor of the modern "prep. school," which still has a good deal of resemblance to it; and as for Mr. Wopsle's great-aunt, some old fraud of much the same stamp is carrying on at this moment in nearly every small town in England. But, as usual, Dickens's criticism is neither creative nor destructive. He sees the idiocy of an educational system founded on the Greek lexicon and the wax-ended cane; on the other hand, he has no use for the new kind of school that is coming up in the 'fifties and 'sixties, the "modern" school, with its gritty insistence on "facts." What, then, *does* he want? As always, what he appears to want is a moralised version of the existing thing—the old type of school, but with no caning, no bullying or underfeeding, and not quite so much Greek. Doctor Strong's school, to which David Copperfield goes after he escapes from Murdstone & Grinby's, is simply Salem House with the vices left out and a good deal of "old grey stones" atmosphere thrown in:

> Doctor Strong's was an excellent school, as different from Mr. Creakle's as good is from evil. It was very gravely and decorously ordered, and on a sound system; with an appeal, in everything, to the honour and good faith of the boys . . . which worked wonders. We all felt that we had a part in the management of the place, and in sustaining its character and

> dignity. Hence, we soon became warmly attached to it—I am sure I did for one, and I never knew, in all my time, of any boy being otherwise—and learnt with a good will, desiring to do it credit. We had noble games out of hours, and plenty of liberty; but even then, as I remember, we were well spoken of in the town, and rarely did any disgrace, by our appearance or manner, to the reputation of Doctor Strong and Doctor Strong's boys.

In the woolly vagueness of this passage one can see Dickens's utter lack of any educational theory. He can imagine the *moral* atmosphere of a good school, but nothing further. The boys "learnt with a good will," but what did they learn? No doubt it was Doctor Blimber's curriculum, a little watered down. Considering the attitude to society that is everywhere implied in Dickens's novels, it comes as rather a shock to learn that he sent his eldest son to Eton and sent all his children through the ordinary educational mill. Gissing seems to think that he may have done this because he was painfully conscious of being under-educated himself. Here perhaps Gissing is influenced by his own love of classical learning. Dickens had had little or no formal education, but he lost nothing by missing it, and on the whole he seems to have been aware of this. If he was unable to imagine a better school than Doctor Strong's, or, in real life, than Eton, it was probably due to an intellectual deficiency rather different from the one Gissing suggests.

It seems that in every attack Dickens makes upon society he is always pointing to a change of spirit rather than a change of structure. It is hopeless to try and pin him down to any definite remedy, still more to any political doctrine. His approach is always along the moral plane, and his attitude is sufficiently summed up in that remark about Strong's school being as different from

Creakle's "as good is from evil." Two things can be very much alike and yet abysmally different. Heaven and Hell are in the same place. Useless to change institutions without a "change of heart"—that, essentially, is what he is always saying.

If that were all, he might be no more than a cheer-up writer, a reactionary humbug. A "change of heart" is in fact *the* alibi of people who do not wish to endanger the *status quo.* But Dickens is not a humbug, except in minor matters, and the strongest single impression one carries away from his books is that of a hatred of tyranny. I said earlier that Dickens is not *in the accepted sense* a revolutionary writer. But it is not at all certain that a merely moral criticism of society may not be just as "revolutionary"—and revolution, after all, means turning things upside down—as the politico-economic criticism which is fashionable at this moment. Blake was not a politician, but there is more understanding of the nature of capitalist society in a poem like "I wander through each charter'd street" than in three-quarters of Socialist literature. Progress is not an illusion, it happens, but it is slow and invariably disappointing. There is always a new tyrant waiting to take over from the old—generally not quite so bad, but still a tyrant. Consequently two viewpoints are always tenable. The one, how can you improve human nature until you have changed the system? The other, what is the use of changing the system before you have improved human nature? They appeal to different individuals, and they probably show a tendency to alternate in point of time. The moralist and the revolutionary are constantly undermining one another. Marx exploded a hundred tons of dynamite beneath the moralist position, and we are still living in the echo of that tremendous crash. But already, somewhere or other, the sappers are at work and fresh dynamite is being tamped in place to blow Marx at the moon. Then Marx, or somebody like him, will come back with yet more dynamite, and so the process continues, to an end we cannot yet foresee. The central problem—how to prevent power from being abused—remains unsolved. Dickens, who had not the vision to see that private property is an obstructive nuisance, had the vision to see that. "If men would behave decently the world would be decent" is not such a platitude as it sounds.

2

More completely than most writers, perhaps, Dickens can be explained in terms of his social origin, though actually his family history was not quite what one would infer from his novels. His father was a clerk in government service, and through his mother's family he had connections with both the army and the navy. But from the age of nine onwards he was brought up in London in commercial surroundings, and generally in an atmosphere of struggling poverty. Mentally he belongs to the small urban bourgeoisie, and he happens to be an exceptionally fine specimen of this class, with all the "points," as it were, very highly developed. That is partly what makes him so interesting. If one wants a modern equivalent, the nearest would be H. G. Wells, who has had a rather similar history and who obviously owes something to Dickens as a novelist. Arnold Bennett was essentially of the same type, but, unlike the other two, he was a midlander, with an industrial and Nonconformist rather than commercial and Anglican background.

The great disadvantage, and advantage, of the small urban bourgeois is his limited outlook. He sees the world as a middle-class world, and everything outside these limits is either laughable or slightly wicked. On the one hand, he has no contact with industry or the soil; on the other, no contact with the governing classes. Anyone who has studied Wells's novels in detail will have noticed that though he hates the aristocrat like poison, he has no particular objection to the plutocrat, and no enthusiasm for the proletarian. His most-hated types, the people he believes to be responsible for all human ills, are kings, landowners, priests, nationalists, soldiers, scholars and peasants. At first sight a list beginning with kings and ending with peasants looks like a mere omnium gatherum, but in reality all these people have a common factor. All of them are archaic types, people who are governed by tradition and whose eyes are turned towards the past—the opposite, therefore, of the rising bourgeois who has put his money on the future and sees the past simply as a dead hand.

Actually, although Dickens lived in a period when the bourgeoisie was really a rising class, he displays this characteristic less strongly than Wells. He is almost unconscious of the future and has a rather sloppy love of the picturesque (the "quaint old church," etc.). Nevertheless his list of most-hated types is like enough to Wells's for the similarity to be striking. He is vaguely on the side of the working class—has a sort of generalised sympathy with them because they are oppressed—but he does not in reality know much about them; they come into his books chiefly as servants, and comic servants at that. At the other end of the scale he loathes the aristocrat and—going one better than Wells in this—loathes the big bourgeois as well. His real sympathies are bounded by Mr. Pickwick on the upper side and Mr. Barkis on the lower. But the term "aristocrat," for the type Dickens hates, is vague and needs defining.

Actually Dickens's target is not so much the great aristocracy, who hardly enter into his books, as their petty offshoots, the cadging dowagers who live up mews in Mayfair, and the bureaucrats and professional soldiers. All through his books there are countless hostile sketches of these people, and hardly any that are friendly. There are practically no friendly pictures of the landowning class, for instance. One might make a doubtful exception of Sir

Leicester Dedlock; otherwise there is only Mr. Wardle (who is a stock figure—the "good old squire") and Haredale in *Barnaby Rudge,* who has Dickens's sympathy because he is a persecuted Catholic. There are no friendly pictures of soldiers (i.e. officers), and none at all of naval men. As for his bureaucrats, judges and magistrates, most of them would feel quite at home in the Circumlocution Office. The only officials whom Dickens handles with any kind of friendliness are, significantly enough, policemen.

Dickens's attitude is easily intelligible to an Englishman, because it is part of the English puritan tradition, which is not dead even at this day. The class Dickens belonged to, at least by adoption, was growing suddenly rich after a couple of centuries of obscurity. It had grown up mainly in the big towns, out of contact with agriculture, and politically impotent; government, in its experience, was something which either interfered or persecuted. Consequently it was a class with no tradition of public service and not much tradition of usefulness. What now strikes us as remarkable about the new moneyed class of the nineteenth century is their complete irresponsibility; they see everything in terms of individual success, with hardly any consciousness that the community exists. On the other hand, a Tite Barnacle, even when he was neglecting his duties, would have some vague notion of what duties he was neglecting. Dickens's attitude is never irresponsible, still less does he take the money-grubbing Smilesian[4] line; but at the back of his mind there is usually a half-belief that the whole apparatus of government is unnecessary. Parliament is simply Lord Coodle and Sir Thomas Doodle, the Empire is simply Major Bagstock and his Indian servant, the Army is simply Colonel Chowser and Doctor Slammer, the public services are simply Bumble and the Circumlocution Office—and so on and so forth. What he does not see, or only intermittently sees, is that Coodle and Doodle and all the other corpses left over from the eighteenth century *are* performing a function which neither Pickwick nor Boffin would ever bother about.

And of course this narrowness of vision is in one way a great advantage to him, because it is fatal for a caricaturist to see too much. From Dickens's point of view "good" society is simply a collection of village idiots. What a crew! Lady Tippins! Mrs. Gowan! Lord Verisopht! The Honourable Bob Stables! Mrs. Sparsit (whose husband was a Powler)! The Tite Barnacles! Nupkins! It is practically a case-book in lunacy. But at the same time his remoteness from the landowning-military-bureaucratic class incapacitates him for full-length satire. He only succeeds with this class when he depicts them as mental defectives. The accusation which used to be made against Dickens in his lifetime, that he "could not paint a gentleman," was an absurdity, but it is true in this sense, that what he says against the "gentleman" class is seldom very damaging. Sir Mulberry Hawk, for instance, is a wretched attempt at the wicked-baronet type. Harthouse in *Hard Times* is better, but he would be only an ordinary achievement for Trollope or Thackeray. Trollope's thoughts hardly move outside the "gentleman" class, but Thackeray has the great advantage of having a foot in two moral camps. In some ways his outlook is very similar to Dickens's. Like Dickens, he identifies with the puritanical moneyed class against the card-playing, debt-bilking aristocracy. The eighteenth century, as he sees it, is sticking out into the nineteenth in the person of the wicked Lord Steyne. *Vanity Fair* is a full-length version of what Dickens did for a few chapters in *Little Dorrit.* But by origins and upbringing Thackeray happens to be somewhat nearer to the class he is satirising. Consequently he can produce such comparatively subtle types as, for instance, Major Pendennis and Rawdon Crawley. Major Pendennis is a shallow old snob, and Rawdon Crawley is a thick-headed ruffian who sees nothing wrong in living for years by swindling tradesmen; but what Thackeray realises is that according to their tortuous code they are neither of them bad men. Major Pendennis would not sign a dud cheque, for instance. Rawdon certainly would, but on the other hand he would not desert a friend in a tight corner. Both of them would behave well on the field of battle—a thing that would not particularly appeal to Dickens. The result is that at the end one is left with a kind of amused tolerance for Major Pendennis and with something approaching respect for Rawdon; and yet one sees, better than any diatribe could make one, the utter rottenness of that kind of cadging, toadying life on the fringes of smart society. Dickens would be quite incapable of this. In his hands both Rawdon and the Major would dwindle to traditional caricatures. And, on the whole, his attacks on "good" society are rather perfunctory. The aristocracy and the big bourgeoisie exist in his books chiefly as a kind of "noises off," a haw-hawing chorus somewhere in the wings, like Podsnap's dinner-parties. When he produces a really subtle and damaging portrait, like John Dorrit or Harold Skimpole, it is generally of some rather middling, unimportant person.

One very striking thing about Dickens, especially considering the time he lived in, is his lack of vulgar nationalism. All peoples who have reached the point of becoming nations tend to despise foreigners, but there is not much doubt that the English-speaking races are the worst offenders. One can see this from the fact that as soon as they become fully aware of any foreign race, they invent an insulting nickname for it. Wop, Dago, Froggy, Squarehead, Kike, Sheeny, Nigger, Wog, Chink, Greaser, Yellowbelly—these are merely a selection. Any time before 1870 the list would have been shorter, because the map of the world was different from what it is now, and there were only three or four foreign races that had fully entered into the English consciousness. But towards these, and especially towards France, the nearest and best-hated nation, the English attitude of patronage was so intolerable that

English "arrogance" and "xenophobia" are still a legend. And of course they are not a completely untrue legend even now. Till very recently nearly all English children were brought up to despise the southern European races, and history as taught in schools was mainly a list of battles won by England. But one has got to read, say, the *Quarterly Review* of the 'thirties to know what boasting really is. Those were the days when the English built up their legend of themselves as "sturdy islanders" and "stubborn hearts of oak" and when it was accepted as a kind of scientific fact that one Englishman was the equal of three foreigners. All through nineteenth-century novels and comic papers there runs the traditional figure of the "Froggy"—a small ridiculous man with a tiny beard and a pointed top-hat, always jabbering and gesticulating, vain, frivolous and fond of boasting of his martial exploits, but generally taking to flight when real danger appears. Over against him was John Bull, the "sturdy English yeoman," or (a more public-school version) the "strong, silent Englishman" of Charles Kingsley, Tom Hughes and others.

Thackeray, for instance, has this outlook very strongly, though there are moments when he sees through it and laughs at it. The one historical fact that is firmly fixed in his mind is that the English won the battle of Waterloo. One never reads far in his books without coming upon some reference to it. The English, as he sees it, are invincible because of their tremendous physical strength, due mainly to living on beef. Like most Englishmen of his time, he has the curious illusion that the English are larger than other people (Thackeray, as it happened, *was* larger than most people), and therefore he is capable of writing passages like this:

> I say to you that you are better than a Frenchman. I would lay even money that you who are reading this are more than five feet seven in height, and weigh eleven stone; while a

> Frenchman is five feet four and does not weigh nine. The Frenchman has after his soup a dish of vegetables, where you have one of meat. You are a different and superior animal—a French-beating animal (the history of hundreds of years has shown you to be so), etc. etc.

There are similar passages scattered all through Thackeray's works. Dickens would never be guilty of anything of the kind. It would be an exaggeration to say that he nowhere pokes fun at foreigners, and of course, like nearly all nineteenth-century Englishmen, he is untouched by European culture. But never anywhere does he indulge in the typical English boasting, the "island race," "bulldog breed," "right little, tight little island" style of talk. In the whole of *A Tale of Two Cities* there is not a line that could be taken as meaning, "Look how these wicked Frenchmen behave!" The one place where he seems to display a normal hatred of foreigners is in the American chapters of *Martin Chuzzlewit.* This, however, is simply the reaction of a generous mind against cant. If Dickens were alive to-day he would make a trip to Soviet Russia and come back with a book rather like Gide's *Retour de l'URSS.*[5] But he is remarkably free from the idiocy of regarding nations as individuals. He seldom even makes jokes turning on nationality. He does not exploit the comic Irishman and the comic Welshman, for instance, and not because he objects to stock characters and ready-made jokes, which obviously he does not. It is perhaps more significant that he shows no prejudice against Jews. It is true that he takes it for granted (*Oliver Twist* and *Great Expectations*) that a receiver of stolen goods will be a Jew, which at the time was probably justified. But the "Jew joke," endemic in English literature until the rise of Hitler, does not appear in his books, and in *Our Mutual Friend* he makes a pious though not very convincing attempt to stand up for the Jews.

Dickens's lack of vulgar nationalism is in part the mark of a real largeness of mind, and in part results from his negative, rather unhelpful political attitude. He is very much an Englishman, but he is hardly aware of it—certainly the thought of being an Englishman does not thrill him. He has no imperialist feeling, no discernible views on foreign politics, and is untouched by the military tradition. Temperamentally he is much nearer to the small Nonconformist tradesman who looks down on the "redcoats" and thinks that war is wicked—a one-eyed view, but, after all, war *is* wicked. It is noticeable that Dickens hardly writes of war, even to denounce it. With all his marvellous powers of description, and of describing things he had never seen, he never describes a battle, unless one counts the attack on the Bastille in *A Tale of Two Cities.* Probably the subject would not strike him as interesting, and in any case he would not regard a battlefield as a place where anything worth settling could be settled. It is one up to the lower-middle-class, puritan mentality.

3

Dickens had grown up near enough to poverty to be terrified of it, and in spite of his generosity of mind, he is not free from the special prejudices of the shabby-genteel. It is usual to claim him as a "popular" writer, a champion of the "oppressed masses." So he is, so long as he thinks of them as oppressed; but there are two things that condition his attitude. In the first place, he is a south-of-England man, and a Cockney at that, and therefore out of touch with the bulk of the real oppressed masses, the industrial and agricultural labourers. It is interesting to see how Chesterton, another Cockney, always presents Dickens as the spokesman of "the poor," without showing much awareness of who "the poor" really are. To Chesterton "the poor" means small shopkeepers and servants. Sam Weller, he says, "is the great symbol in English literature of the populace peculiar to England"; and Sam Weller is a valet! The other point is that Dickens's early experiences have given him a horror of proletarian roughness. He shows this unmistakably whenever he writes of the very poorest of the poor, the slum-dwellers. His descriptions of the London slums are always full of undisguised repulsion:

> The ways were foul and narrow; the shops and houses wretched; and people half-naked, drunken, slipshod and ugly. Alleys and archways, like so many cesspools, disgorged their offences of smell, and dirt, and life, upon the straggling streets; and the whole quarter reeked with crime, and filth, and misery, etc. etc.

There are many similar passages in Dickens. From them one gets the impression of whole submerged populations whom he regards as being beyond the pale. In rather the same way the modern doctrinaire Socialist contemptuously writes off a large block of the population as "lumpenproletariat." Dickens also shows less understanding of criminals than one would expect of him. Although he is well aware of the social and economic causes of crime, he often seems to feel that when a man has once broken the law he has put himself outside human society. There is a chapter at the end of *David Copperfield* in which David visits the prison where Littimer and Uriah Heep are serving their sentences. Dickens actually seems to regard the horrible "model" prisons, against which Charles Reade delivered his memorable attack in *It is Never too Late to Mend,* as too humane. He complains that the food is too good! As soon as he comes up against crime or the worst depths of poverty, he shows traces of the "I've always kept myself respectable" habit of mind. The attitude of Pip (obviously the attitude of Dickens himself) towards Magwitch in *Great Expectations* is extremely interesting. Pip is conscious all along of his ingratitude towards Joe, but far less so of his ingratitude towards Magwitch. When he discovers that the person who has loaded him with benefits for years is actually a transported convict, he falls into frenzies of disgust. "The abhorrence in which I held the man, the dread I had of him, the repugnance with which I shrank from him, could not have been exceeded if he had been some terrible beast," etc. etc. So far as one can discover from the text, this is not because when Pip was a child he had been terrorised by Magwitch in the churchyard; it is because Magwitch is a criminal and a convict. There is an even more "kept-myself-respectable" touch in the fact that Pip feels as a matter of course that he cannot take Magwitch's money. The money is not the product of a crime, it has been honestly acquired; but it is an ex-convict's money and therefore "tainted." There is nothing psychologically false in this, either. Psychologically the latter part of *Great Expectations* is about the best thing Dickens ever did; throughout this part of the book one feels "Yes, that is just how Pip would have behaved." But the point is that in the matter of Magwitch, Dickens identifies with Pip, and his attitude is at bottom snobbish. The result is that Magwitch belongs to the same queer class of characters as Falstaff and, probably, Don Quixote — characters who are more pathetic than the author intended.

When it is a question of the non-criminal poor, the ordinary, decent, labouring poor, there is of course nothing contemptuous in Dickens's attitude. He has the sincerest admiration for people like the Peggottys and the Plornishes. But it is questionable whether he really regards them as equals. It is of the greatest interest to read Chapter XI of *David Copperfield* and side by side with it the autobiographical fragment (parts of this are given in Forster's *Life*), in which Dickens expresses his feelings about the blacking-factory episode a great deal more strongly than in the novel. For more than twenty years afterwards the memory was so painful to him that he would go out of his way to avoid that part of the Strand. He says that to pass that way "made me cry, after my eldest child could speak." The text makes it quite clear that what hurt him most of all, then and in retrospect, was the enforced contact with "low" associates:

> No words can express the secret agony of my soul as I sunk into this companionship; compared these every day associates with those of my happier childhood . . . But I held some station at the blacking warehouse too . . . I soon became at least as expeditious and as skilful with my hands, as either of the other boys. Though perfectly familiar with them, my conduct and manners were different enough from theirs to place a space between us. They, and the men, always spoke of me as "the young gentleman." A certain man . . . used to call me "Charles" sometimes in speaking to me; but I think it was mostly when we were very confidential . . . Poll Green uprose once, and rebelled against the "young-gentleman" usage; but Bob Fagin settled him speedily.

It was as well that there should be "a space between us," you see. However much Dickens may admire the working classes, he does not wish to resemble them. Given his origins, and the time he lived in, it could hardly be otherwise. In the early nineteenth century class-animosities may have been no sharper than they are now, but the surface differences between class and class were enormously greater. The "gentleman" and the "common man" must have seemed like different species of animal. Dickens is quite genuinely on the side of the poor against the rich, but it would be next door to impossible for him not to think of a working-class exterior as a stigma. In one of Tolstoy's fables the peasants of a certain village judge every stranger who arrives from the state of his hands. If his palms are hard from work, they let him in; if his palms are soft, out he goes. This would be hardly intelligible to Dickens; all his heroes have soft hands. His younger heroes—Nicholas Nickleby, Martin Chuzzlewit, Edward Chester, David Copperfield, John Harmon—are usually of the type known as "walking gentlemen." He likes a bourgeois exterior and a bourgeois (not aristocratic) accent. One curious symptom of this is that he will not allow anyone who is to play a heroic part to speak like a working man. A comic hero like Sam Weller, or a merely pathetic figure like Stephen Blackpool, can speak with a broad accent, but the *jeune premier* always speaks the then equivalent of B.B.C. This is so, even when it involves absurdities. Little Pip, for instance, is brought up by people speaking broad Essex, but talks upper-class English from his earliest childhood; actually he would have talked the same dialect as Joe, or at least as Mrs. Gargery. So also with Biddy Wopsle, Lizzie Hexam, Sissie Jupe, Oliver Twist—one ought perhaps to add Little Dorrit. Even Rachel in *Hard Times* has barely a trace of Lancashire accent, an impossibility in her case.

One thing that often gives the clue to a novelist's real feelings on the class question is the attitude he takes up when class collides with sex. This is a thing too painful to be lied about, and consequently it is one of the points at which the "I'm-not-a-snob" pose tends to break down.

One sees that at its most obvious where a class-distinction is also a colour-distinction. And something resembling the colonial attitude ("native" women are fair game, white women are sacrosanct) exists in a veiled form in all-white communities, causing bitter resentment on both sides. When this issue arises, novelists often revert to crude class-feelings which they might disclaim at other times. A good example of "class-conscious" reaction is a rather forgotten novel, *The People of Clopton,* by George Bartram.[6] The author's moral code is quite clearly mixed up with class-hatred. He feels the seduction of a poor girl by a rich man to be something atrocious, a kind of defilement, something quite different from her seduction by a man in her own walk of life. Trollope deals with this theme twice (*The Three Clerks* and *The Small House at Allington*) and, as one might expect, entirely from the upper-class angle. As he sees it, an affair with a barmaid or a landlady's daughter is simply an "entanglement" to be escaped from. Trollope's moral standards are strict, and he does not allow the seduction actually to happen, but the implication is always that a working-class girl's feelings do not greatly matter. In *The Three Clerks* he even gives the typical class-reaction by noting that the girl "smells." Meredith (*Rhoda Fleming*) takes more the "class-conscious" viewpoint. Thackeray, as often, seems to hesitate. In *Pendennis* (Fanny Bolton) his attitude is much the same as Trollope's; in *A Shabby Genteel Story* it is nearer to Meredith's.

One could divine a good deal about Trollope's social origin, or Meredith's, or Bartram's, merely from their handling of the class-sex theme. So one can with Dickens, but what emerges, as usual, is that he is more inclined to identify himself with the middle class than with the proletariat. The one incident that seems to contradict this is the tale of the young peasant-girl in Doctor Manette's manuscript in *A Tale of Two Cities.* This, however, is merely a costume-piece put in to explain the implacable hatred of Madame Defarge, which Dickens does not pretend to approve of. In *David Copperfield,* where he is dealing with a typical nineteenth-century seduction, the class-issue does not seem to strike him as paramount. It is a law of Victorian novels that sexual misdeeds must not go unpunished, and so Steerforth is drowned on Yarmouth sands, but neither Dickens, nor old Peggotty, nor even

Ham, seems to feel that Steerforth has added to his offence by being the son of rich parents. The Steerforths are moved by class-motives, but the Peggottys are not—not even in the scene between Mrs. Steerforth and old Peggotty; if they were, of course, they would probably turn against David as well as against Steerforth.

In *Our Mutual Friend* Dickens treats the episode of Eugene Wrayburn and Lizzie Hexam very realistically and with no appearance of class bias. According to the "unhand me, monster" tradition, Lizzie ought either to "spurn" Eugene or to be ruined by him and throw herself off Waterloo Bridge; Eugene ought to be either a heartless betrayer or a hero resolved upon defying society. Neither behaves in the least like this. Lizzie is frightened by Eugene's advances and actually runs away from them, but hardly pretends to dislike them; Eugene is attracted by her, has too much decency to attempt seducing her and dare not marry her because of his family. Finally they are married and no one is any the worse, except perhaps Mr. Twemlow, who will lose a few dinner engagements. It is all very much as it might have happened in real life. But a "class-conscious" novelist would have given her to Bradley Headstone.

But when it is the other way about—when it is a case of a poor man aspiring to some woman who is "above" him—Dickens instantly retreats into the middle-class attitude. He is rather fond of the Victorian notion of a woman (woman with a capital W) being "above" a man. Pip feels that Estella is "above" him, Esther Summerson is "above" Guppy, Little Dorrit is "above" John Chivery, Lucy Manette is "above" Sydney Carton. In some of these the "above"-ness is merely moral, but in others it is social. There is a scarcely mistakable class-reaction when David Copperfield discovers that Uriah Heep is plotting to marry Agnes

Wickfield. The disgusting Uriah suddenly announces that he is in love with her:

> "Oh, Master Copperfield, with what a pure affection do I love the ground my Agnes walks on!"
>
> I believe I had a delirious idea of seizing the red-hot poker out of the fire, and running him through with it. It went from me with a shock, like a ball fired from a rifle: but the image of Agnes, outraged by so much as a thought of this red-headed animal's, remained in my mind when I looked at him, sitting all awry as if his mean soul griped his body, and made me giddy . . . "I believe Agnes Wickfield to be as far above *you* (David says later on), and as far removed from all *your* aspirations, as that moon herself!"

Considering how Heep's general lowness—his servile manners, dropped aitches and so forth—has been rubbed in throughout the book, there is not much doubt about the nature of Dickens's feelings. Heep, of course, is playing a villainous part, but even villains have sexual lives; it is the thought of the "pure" Agnes in bed with a man who drops his aitches that really revolts Dickens. But his usual tendency is to treat a man in love with a woman who is "above" him as a joke. It is one of the stock jokes of English literature, from Malvolio onwards. Guppy in *Bleak House* is an example, John Chivery is another, and there is a rather ill-natured treatment of this theme in the "swarry" in *Pickwick Papers.* Here Dickens describes the Bath footmen as living a kind of fantasy-life, holding dinner-parties in imitation of their "betters" and deluding themselves that their young mistresses are in love with them. This evidently strikes him as very comic. So it is, in a way, though one might question whether it is not better for a footman even to have delusions of this kind than simply to accept his status in the spirit of the catechism.

In his attitude towards servants Dickens is not ahead of his age. In the nineteenth century the revolt against domestic service was just beginning, to the great annoyance of everyone with over £500 a year. An enormous number of the jokes in nineteenth-century comic papers deal with the uppishness of servants. For years *Punch* ran a series of jokes called "Servant Gal-isms," all turning on the then astonishing fact that a servant is a human being. Dickens is sometimes guilty of this kind of thing himself. His books abound with the ordinary comic servants; they are dishonest (*Great Expectations*), incompetent (*David Copperfield*), turn up their noses at good food (*Pickwick Papers*), etc. etc.—all rather in the spirit of the suburban housewife with one downtrodden cook-general. But what is curious, in a nineteenth-century radical, is that when he wants to draw a sympathetic picture of a servant, he creates what is recognisably a feudal type. Sam Weller, Mark Tapley, Clara Peggotty are all of them feudal figures. They belong to the genre of the "old family retainer"; they identify themselves with their master's family and are at once doggishly faithful and completely familiar. No doubt Mark Tapley and Sam Weller are derived to some extent from Smollett, and hence from Cervantes; but it is interesting that Dickens should have been attracted by such a type. Sam Weller's attitude is definitely medieval. He gets himself arrested in order to follow Mr. Pickwick into the Fleet, and afterwards refuses to get married because he feels that Mr. Pickwick still needs his services. There is a characteristic scene between them:

> "... vages or no vages, notice or no notice, board or no board, lodgin' or no lodgin', Sam Veller, as you took from the old inn in the Borough, sticks by you, come what come may ..."

> "My good fellow," said Mr. Pickwick, when Mr. Weller had sat down again, rather abashed at his own enthusiasm, "you are bound to consider the young woman also."
>
> "I do consider the young 'ooman, sir," said Sam. "I have considered the young 'ooman. I've spoke to her, I've told her how I'm sitivated, she's ready to vait till I'm ready, and I believe she vill. If she don't, she's not the young 'ooman I take her for, and I give her up vith readiness."

It is easy to imagine what the young woman would have said to this in real life. But notice the feudal atmosphere. Sam Weller is ready as a matter of course to sacrifice years of life to his master, and he can also sit down in his master's presence. A modern manservant would never think of doing either. Dickens's views on the servant question do not get much beyond wishing that master and servant would love one another. Sloppy in *Our Mutual Friend,* though a wretched failure as a character, represents the same kind of loyalty as Sam Weller. Such loyalty, of course, is natural, human and likeable; but so was feudalism.

What Dickens seems to be doing, as usual, is to reach out for an idealised version of the existing thing. He was writing at a time when domestic service must have seemed a completely inevitable evil. There were no labour-saving devices, and there was huge inequality of wealth. It was an age of enormous families, pretentious meals and inconvenient houses, when the slavey drudging fourteen hours a day in the basement kitchen was something too normal to be noticed. And given the *fact* of servitude, the feudal relationship is the only tolerable one. Sam Weller and Mark Tapley are dream figures, no less than the Cheerybles. If there have got to be masters and servants, how much better that the master should be Mr. Pickwick and the servant should be Sam Weller. Better still, of course, if servants did not exist at all—but this

Dickens is probably unable to imagine. Without a high level of mechanical development, human equality is not practically possible; Dickens goes to show that it is not imaginable either.

4

It is not merely a coincidence that Dickens never writes about agriculture and writes endlessly about food. He was a Cockney, and London is the centre of the earth in rather the same sense that the belly is the centre of the body. It is a city of consumers, of people who are deeply civilised but not primarily useful. A thing that strikes one when one looks below the surface of Dickens's books is that, as nineteenth-century novelists go, he is rather ignorant. He knows very little about the way things really happen. At first sight this statement looks flatly untrue, and it needs some qualification.

Dickens had had vivid glimpses of "low life"—life in a debtor's prison, for example—and he was also a popular novelist and able to write about ordinary people. So were all the characteristic English novelists of the nineteenth century. They felt at home in the world they lived in, whereas a writer nowadays is so hopelessly isolated that the typical modern novel is a novel about a novelist. Even when Joyce, for instance, spends a decade or so in patient efforts to make contact with the "common man," his "common man" finally turns out to be a Jew, and a bit of a highbrow at that. Dickens at least does not suffer from this kind of thing. He has no difficulty in introducing the common motives, love, ambition, avarice, vengeance and so forth. What he does not noticeably write about, however, is *work*.

In Dickens's novels anything in the nature of work happens off-stage. The only one of his heroes who has a plausible profession is David Copperfield, who is first a shorthand writer and then a novelist, like Dickens himself. With most of the others, the way they earn their living is very much in the background. Pip, for instance, "goes into business" in Egypt; we are not told what business, and Pip's working life occupies about half a page of the book. Clennam has been in some unspecified business in China, and later goes into another barely-specified business with Doyce. Martin Chuzzlewit is an architect, but does not seem to get much time for practising. In no case do their adventures spring directly out of their work. Here the contrast between Dickens and, say, Trollope is startling. And one reason for this is undoubtedly that Dickens knows very little about the professions his characters are supposed to follow. What exactly went on in Gradgrind's factories? How did Podsnap make his money? How did Merdle work his swindles? One knows that Dickens could never follow up the details of Parliamentary elections and Stock Exchange rackets as Trollope could. As soon as he has to deal with trade, finance, industry or politics he takes refuge in vagueness, or in satire. This is the case even with legal processes, about which actually he must have known a good deal. Compare any lawsuit in Dickens with the lawsuit in *Orley Farm,*[7] for instance.

And this partly accounts for the needless ramifications of Dickens's novels, the awful Victorian "plot." It is true that not all his novels are alike in this. *A Tale of Two Cities* is a very good and fairly simple story, and so in its different way is *Hard Times*; but these are just the two which are always rejected as "not like Dickens"—and incidentally they were not published in monthly numbers.* The two first-person novels are also good stories, apart

***Hard Times* was published as a serial in *Household Words* and *Great Expectations* and *A Tale of Two Cities* in *All the Year Round.* Forster says that the shortness of the weekly instalments made it "much more difficult to get sufficient interest into each." Dickens himself complained of the lack of "elbow-room." In other works, he had to stick more closely to the story [Orwell's footnote].

from their subplots. But the typical Dickens novel, *Nicholas Nickleby, Oliver Twist, Martin Chuzzlewit, Our Mutual Friend,* always exists round a framework of melodrama. The last thing anyone ever remembers about these books is their central story. On the other hand, I suppose no one has ever read them without carrying the memory of individual pages to the day of his death. Dickens sees human beings with the most intense vividness, but he sees them always in private life, as "characters," not as functional members of society; that is to say, he sees them statically. Consequently his greatest success is *The Pickwick Papers,* which is not a story at all, merely a series of sketches; there is little attempt at development—the characters simply go on and on, behaving like idiots, in a kind of eternity. As soon as he tries to bring his characters into action, the melodrama begins. He cannot make the action revolve round their ordinary occupations; hence the crossword puzzle of coincidences, intrigues, murders, disguises, buried wills, long-lost brothers, etc. etc. In the end even people like Squeers and Micawber get sucked into the machinery.

Of course it would be absurd to say that Dickens is a vague or merely melodramatic writer. Much that he wrote is extremely factual, and in the power of evoking visual images he has probably never been equalled. When Dickens has once described something you see it for the rest of your life. But in a way the concreteness of his vision is a sign of what he is missing. For, after all, that is what the merely casual onlooker always sees—the outward appearance, the non-functional, the surfaces of things. No one who is really involved in the landscape ever sees the landscape. Wonderfully as he can describe an *appearance,* Dickens does not often describe a *process.* The vivid pictures that he succeeds in leaving in one's memory are nearly always the pictures of things seen in leisure moments, in the coffee-rooms of country inns or through the windows of a stage-coach; the kind of things he notices are inn-signs, brass door-knockers, painted jugs, the interiors of shops and private houses, clothes, faces and, above all, food. Everything is seen from the consumer-angle. When he writes about Coketown he manages to evoke, in just a few paragraphs, the atmosphere of a Lancashire town as a slightly disgusted southern visitor would see it. "It had a black canal in it, and a river that ran purple with evil-smelling dye, and vast piles of buildings full of windows where there was a rattling and a trembling all day long, and where the piston of the steam-engine worked monotonously up and down, like the head of an elephant in a state of melancholy madness." That is as near as Dickens ever gets to the machinery of the mills. An engineer or a cotton-broker would see it differently, but then neither of them would be capable of that impressionistic touch about the heads of the elephants.

In a rather different sense his attitude to life is extremely unphysical. He is a man who lives through his eyes and ears rather than through his hands and muscles. Actually his habits were not so sedentary as this seems to imply. In spite of rather poor health and physique, he was active to the point of restlessness; throughout his life he was a remarkable walker, and he could at any rate carpenter well enough to put up stage scenery. But he was not one of those people who feel a need to use their hands. It is difficult to imagine him digging at a cabbage-patch, for instance. He gives no evidence of knowing anything about agriculture, and obviously knows nothing about any kind of game or sport. He has no interest in pugilism, for instance. Considering the age in which he was writing, it is astonishing how little physical brutality there is in Dickens's novels. Martin Chuzzlewit and Mark Tapley, for instance, behave with the most remarkable mildness towards the Americans who are constantly menacing them with revolvers and bowie-knives. The average English or American novelist would have had them handing out socks on the jaw and exchanging pistol-shots in all directions. Dickens is too decent for that; he sees the stupidity of violence, and also he belongs to a cautious urban class which does not deal in socks on the jaw, even in theory. And his attitude towards sport is mixed up with social feelings. In England, for mainly geographical reasons, sport, especially field-sports, and snobbery are inextricably mingled. English Socialists are often flatly incredulous when told that Lenin, for instance, was devoted to shooting. In their eyes shooting, hunting, etc., are simply snobbish observances of the landed gentry; they forget that these things might appear differently in a huge virgin country like Russia. From Dickens's point of view almost any kind of sport is at best a subject for satire. Consequently one side of nineteenth-century life—the boxing, racing, cockfighting, badger-digging, poaching, rat-catching side of life, so wonderfully embalmed in Leech's illustrations to Surtees—is outside his scope.

What is more striking, in a seemingly "progressive" radical, is that he is not mechanically minded. He shows no interest either in the details of machinery or in the things machinery can do. As Gissing remarks, Dickens nowhere describes a railway journey with anything like the enthusiasm he shows in describing journeys by stage-coach. In nearly all of his books one has a curious feeling that one is living in the first quarter of the nineteenth century, and in fact, he does tend to return to this period. *Little Dorrit,* written in the middle 'fifties, deals with the late 'twenties; *Great Expectations* (1861) is not dated, but evidently deals with the 'twenties and 'thirties. Several of the inventions and discoveries which have made the modern world possible (the electric telegraph, the breech-loading gun, india-rubber, coal gas, wood-pulp paper) first appeared in Dickens's lifetime, but he scarcely notes them in his books. Nothing is queerer than the vagueness with which he speaks of Doyce's "invention" in *Little Dorrit.* It is represented as something extremely ingenious and revolutionary, "of great importance to his country and his fellow-creatures," and it is also an important minor link in the book; yet we are never told what the "invention" is! On the other hand, Doyce's physical appearance is hit off with the typical Dickens touch; he has a peculiar way of moving his thumb, a way characteristic of engineers. After that, Doyce is firmly anchored in one's memory; but, as usual, Dickens has done it by fastening on something external.

There are people (Tennyson is an example) who lack the mechanical faculty but can see the social possibilities of machinery. Dickens has not this stamp of mind. He shows very little consciousness of the future. When he speaks of human progress it is usually in terms of *moral* progress—men growing better; probably he would never admit that men are only as good as their technical development allows them to be. At this point the gap between Dickens and his modern analogue H. G. Wells, is at its widest. Wells wears the future round his neck like a millstone, but Dickens's unscientific cast of mind is just as damaging in a different way. What it does is to make any *positive* attitude more difficult for him. He is hostile to the feudal, agricultural past and not in real touch with the industrial present. Well, then, all that remains is the future (meaning Science, "progress" and so forth), which hardly enters into his thoughts. Therefore, while attacking everything in sight, he has no definable standard of comparison. As I have pointed out already, he attacks the current educational system with perfect justice, and yet, after all, he has no remedy to offer except kindlier schoolmasters. Why did he not indicate what a school *might* have been? Why did he not have his own sons educated according to some plan of his own, instead of sending them to public schools to be stuffed with Greek? Because he lacked that kind of imagination. He has an infallible moral sense, but very little intellectual curiosity. And here one comes upon something which really is an enormous deficiency in Dickens, something that really does make the nineteenth century seem remote from us—that he has no ideal of *work*.

With the doubtful exception of David Copperfield (merely Dickens himself), one cannot point to a single one of his central characters who is primarily interested in his job. His heroes work in order to make a living and to marry the heroine, not because they feel a passionate interest in one particular subject. Martin Chuzzlewit, for instance, is not burning with zeal to be an architect; he might just as well be a doctor or a barrister. In any case, in the typical Dickens novel, the *deus ex machina* enters with a bag of gold in the last chapter and the hero is absolved from further struggle. The feeling, "This is what I came into the world to do. Everything else is uninteresting. I will do this even if it means starvation," which turns men of differing temperaments into scientists, inventors, artists, priests, explorers and revolutionaries—this motif is almost entirely absent from Dickens's books. He himself, as is well known, worked like a slave and believed in his work as few novelists have ever done. But there seems to be no calling except novel-writing (and perhaps acting) towards which he can imagine this kind of devotion. And, after all, it is natural enough, considering his rather negative attitude towards society. In the last resort there is nothing he admires except common decency. Science is uninteresting and machinery is cruel and ugly (the heads of the elephants). Business is only for ruffians like Bounderby. As for politics—leave that to the Tite Barnacles. Really there is no objective except to marry the heroine, settle down, live solvently and be kind. And you can do that much better in private life.

Here, perhaps, one gets a glimpse of Dickens's secret imaginative background. What did he think of as the most desirable way to live? When Martin Chuzzlewit had made it up with his uncle, when Nicholas Nickleby had married money, when John Harmon had been enriched by Boffin—what did they *do*?

The answer evidently is that they did nothing. Nicholas Nickleby invested his wife's money with the Cheerybles and "became a rich and prosperous merchant," but as he immediately retired into Devonshire, we can assume that he did not work very hard. Mr. and Mrs. Snodgrass "purchased and cultivated a small farm, more for occupation than profit." That is the spirit in which most of Dickens's books end—a sort of radiant idleness. Where he appears to disapprove of young men who do not work (Harthouse, Harry Gowan, Richard Carstone, Wrayburn before his reformation), it is because they are cynical and immoral or because they are a burden on somebody else; if you are "good," and also self-supporting, there is no reason why you should not spend fifty years in simply drawing your dividends. Home life is always enough. And, after all, it was the general assumption of his age. The "genteel sufficiency," the "competence," the "gentleman of independent means" (or "in easy circumstances")—the very phrases tell one all about the strange, empty dream of the eighteenth- and nineteenth-century middle bourgeoisie. It was a dream of *complete idleness.* Charles Reade conveys its spirit perfectly in the ending of *Hard Cash.* Alfred Hardie, hero of *Hard Cash,* is the typical nineteenth-century novel-hero (public-school style), with gifts which Reade describes as amounting to "genius." He is an old Etonian and a scholar of Oxford, he knows most of the Greek and Latin classics by heart, he can box with prize-fighters and win the Diamond Sculls at Henley. He goes through incredible adventures in which, of course, he behaves with faultless heroism, and then, at the age of twenty-five, he inherits a fortune, marries his Julia Dodd and settles down in the suburbs of Liverpool, in the same house as his parents-in-law:

> They all lived together at Albion Villa, thanks to Alfred . . . Oh, you happy little villa! You were as like Paradise as any mortal dwelling can be. A day came, however, when your walls could no longer hold all the happy inmates. Julia presented Alfred with a lovely boy; enter two nurses, and the villa showed symptoms of bursting. Two months more, and Alfred and his wife overflowed into the next villa. It was but twenty yards off; and there was a double reason for the migration. As often happens after a long separation, Heaven bestowed on Captain and Mrs. Dodd another infant to play about their knees, etc. etc. etc.

This is the type of the Victorian happy ending—a vision of a huge, loving family of three or four generations, all crammed together in the same house and constantly multiplying, like a bed of oysters. What is striking about it is the utterly soft, sheltered, effortless life that it implies. It is not even a violent idleness, like Squire Western's. That is the significance of Dickens's urban background and his non-interest in the blackguardly-sporting-military side of life. His heroes, once they had come into money and "settled down," would not only do no work; they would not even ride, hunt, shoot, fight duels, elope with actresses or lose money at the races. They would simply live at home in feather-bed respectability, and preferably next door to a blood-relation living exactly the same life:

> The first act of Nicholas, when he became a rich and prosperous merchant, was to buy his father's old house. As time crept on, and there came gradually about him a group of lovely children, it was altered and enlarged; but none of the old rooms were ever pulled down, no old tree was ever

> rooted up, nothing with which there was any association of bygone times was ever removed or changed.
>
> Within a stone's-throw was another retreat, enlivened by children's pleasant voices too; and here was Kate . . . the same true, gentle creature, the same fond sister, the same in the love of all about her, as in her girlish days.

It is the same incestuous atmosphere as in the passage quoted from Reade. And evidently this is Dickens's ideal ending. It is perfectly attained in *Nicholas Nickleby, Martin Chuzzlewit* and *Pickwick,* and it is approximated to in varying degrees in almost all the others. The exceptions are *Hard Times* and *Great Expectations*—the latter actually has a "happy ending," but it contradicts the general tendency of the book, and it was put in at the request of Bulwer Lytton.

The ideal to be striven after, then, appears to be something like this: a hundred thousand pounds, a quaint old house with plenty of ivy on it, a sweetly womanly wife, a horde of children, and no work. Everything is safe, soft, peaceful and, above all, domestic. In the moss-grown churchyard down the road are the graves of the loved ones who passed away before the happy ending happened. The servants are comic and feudal, the children prattle round your feet, the old friends sit at your fireside, talking of past days, there is the endless succession of enormous meals, the cold punch and sherry negus, the feather beds and warming-pans, the Christmas parties with charades and blind man's buff; but nothing ever happens, except the yearly childbirth. The curious thing is that it is a genuinely happy picture, or so Dickens is able to make it appear. The thought of that kind of existence is satisfying to him. This alone would be enough to tell one that more than a hundred years have passed since Dickens's first book was written. No modern man could combine such purposelessness with so much vitality.

5

By this time anyone who is a lover of Dickens, and who has read as far as this, will probably be angry with me.

I have been discussing Dickens simply in terms of his "message," and almost ignoring his literary qualities. But every writer, especially every novelist, *has* a "message," whether he admits it or not, and the minutest details of his work are influenced by it. All art is propaganda. Neither Dickens himself nor the majority of Victorian novelists would have thought of denying this. On the other hand, not all propaganda is art. As I said earlier, Dickens is one of those writers who are felt to be worth stealing. He has been stolen by Marxists, by Catholics and, above all, by Conservatives. The question is, What is there to steal? Why does anyone care about Dickens? Why do *I* care about Dickens?

That kind of question is never easy to answer. As a rule, an æsthetic preference is either something inexplicable or it is so corrupted by non-æsthetic motives as to make one wonder whether the whole of literary criticism is not a huge network of humbug. In Dickens's case the complicating factor is his familiarity. He happens to be one of those "great authors" who are ladled down everyone's throat in childhood. At the time this causes rebellion and vomiting, but it may have different after-effects in later life. For instance, nearly everyone feels a sneaking affection for the patriotic poems that he learned by heart as a child. "Ye Mariners of England," the "Charge of the Light Brigade"[8] and so forth. What one enjoys is not so much the poems themselves as the memories they call up. And with Dickens the same forces of association are at work. Probably there are copies of one or two of his books lying about in an actual majority of English homes. Many children begin to know his characters by sight before they can even read, for on the whole Dickens was lucky in his illustrators. A thing that is absorbed as early as that does not come up against any critical judgment. And when one thinks of this, one thinks of all that is bad and silly in Dickens—the cast-iron "plots," the characters who don't come off, the *longueurs,* the paragraphs in blank verse, the awful pages of "pathos." And then the thought arises, when I say I like Dickens, do I simply mean that I like thinking about my childhood? Is Dickens merely an institution?

If so, he is an institution that there is no getting away from. How often one really thinks about any writer, even a writer one cares for, is a difficult thing to decide; but I should doubt whether anyone who has actually read Dickens can go a week without remembering him in one context or another. Whether you approve of him or not, he is *there,* like the Nelson Column. At any moment some scene or character, which may come from some book you cannot even remember the name of, is liable to drop into your mind. Micawber's letters! Winkle in the witness-box! Mrs. Gamp! Mrs. Wititterly and Sir Tumley Snuffim! Todgers's! (George Gissing said that when he passed the Monument it was never of the Fire of London that he thought, always of Todgers's). Mrs. Leo Hunter! Squeers! Silas Wegg and the Decline and Fall-off of the Russian Empire! Miss Mills and the Desert of Sahara! Wopsle acting Hamlet! Mrs. Jellyby! Mantalini, Jerry Cruncher, Barkis, Pumblechook, Tracy Tupman, Skimpole, Joe Gargery, Pecksniff—and so it goes on and on. It is not so much a series of books, it is more like a world. And not a purely comic world either, for part of what one remembers in Dickens is his Victorian morbidness and necrophilia and the blood-and-thunder scenes—the death of Sikes, Krook's spontaneous combustion, Fagin in the condemned cell, the women knitting round the guillotine. To a surprising extent all this has entered even into the minds of people who do not care about it. A music-hall comedian can (or at any rate could quite recently) go on the stage and impersonate Micawber or Mrs. Gamp with a fair certainty of being understood,[9] although not one in twenty of the audience had ever read a book of Dickens's right through. Even people who affect to despise him quote him unconsciously.

Dickens is a writer who can be imitated, up to a certain point. In genuinely popular literature—for instance, the Elephant and Castle version of *Sweeny Todd*—he has been plagiarised quite shamelessly. What has been imitated, however, is simply a tradition that Dickens himself took from earlier novelists and developed, the cult of "character," i.e. eccentricity. The thing that cannot be imitated is his fertility of invention, which is invention not so much of characters, still less of "situations," as of turns of phrase and concrete details. The outstanding, unmistakable mark of Dickens's writing is the *unnecessary detail.* Here is an example of what I mean. The story given below is not particularly funny, but there is one phrase in it that is as individual as a fingerprint. Mr. Jack Hopkins, at Bob Sawyer's party, is telling the story of the child who swallowed its sister's necklace:

> Next day, child swallowed two beads; the day after that, he treated himself to three, and so on, till in a week's time he had got through the necklace—five-and-twenty beads in all. The sister, who was an industrious girl, and seldom treated herself to a bit of finery, cried her eyes out, at the loss of the necklace; looked high and low for it; but I needn't say didn't find it. A few days afterwards, the family were at dinner—baked shoulder of mutton, and potatoes under it—the child, who wasn't hungry, was playing about the room, when

> suddenly there was heard a devil of a noise, like a small hail storm. "Don't do that, my boy," says the father. "I ain't a-doin' nothing," said the child. "Well, don't do it again," said the father. There was a short silence, and then the noise began again, worse than ever. "If you don't mind what I say, my boy," said the father, "you'll find yourself in bed, in something less than a pig's whisper." He gave the child a shake to make him obedient, and such a rattling ensued as nobody ever heard before. "Why, damme, it's *in* the child!" said the father; "he's got the croup in the wrong place!" "No, I haven't father," said the child, beginning to cry, "it's the necklace; I swallowed it, father"—The father caught the child up, and ran with him to the hospital: the beads in the boy's stomach rattling all the way with the jolting; and the people looking up in the air, and down in the cellars to see where the unusual sound came from. "He's in the hospital now," said Jack Hopkins, "and he makes such a devil of a noise when he walks about, that they're obliged to muffle him in a watchman's coat, for fear he should wake the patients!"

As a whole, this story might come out of any nineteenth-century comic paper. But the unmistakable Dickens touch, the thing nobody else would have thought of, is the baked shoulder of mutton and potatoes under it. How does this advance the story? The answer is that it doesn't. It is something totally unnecessary, a florid little squiggle on the edge of the page; only, it is by just these squiggles that the special Dickens atmosphere is created. The other thing one would notice here is that Dickens's way of telling a story takes a long time. An interesting example, too long to quote, is Sam Weller's story of the obstinate patient in Chapter XLIV of *The Pickwick Papers.* As it happens, we have a standard of comparison here, because Dickens is plagiarising, consciously or unconsciously. The story is also told by some ancient Greek writer. I cannot now find the passage, but I read it years ago as a boy at school, and it runs more or less like this:

> A certain Thracian, renowned for his obstinacy, was warned by his physician that if he drank a flagon of wine it would kill him. The Thracian thereupon drank the flagon of wine and immediately jumped off the house-top and perished. "For," said he, "in this way I shall prove that the wine did not kill me."

As the Greek tells it, that is the whole story—about six lines. As Sam Weller tells it, it takes round about a thousand words. Long before getting to the point we have been told all about the patient's clothes, his meals, his manners, even the newspapers he reads, and about the peculiar construction of the doctor's carriage, which conceals the fact that the coachman's trousers do not match his coat. Then there is the dialogue between the doctor and the patient. " 'Crumpets is wholesome, sir,' said the patient. 'Crumpets is *not* wholesome, sir,' says the doctor, wery fierce," etc. etc. In the end the original story has been buried under the details. And in all of Dickens's most characteristic passages it is the same. His imagination overwhelms everything, like a kind of weed. Squeers stands up to address his boys, and immediately we are hearing about Bolder's father who was two pounds ten short, and Mobbs's stepmother who took to her bed on hearing that Mobbs wouldn't eat fat and hoped Mr. Squeers would flog him into a happier state of mind. Mrs. Leo Hunter writes a poem, "Expiring Frog"; two full stanzas are given. Boffin takes a fancy to pose as a miser, and instantly we are down among the squalid biographies of eighteenth-century misers, with names like Vulture Hopkins and the Rev. Blewberry Jones, and chapter headings like "The Story of the

Mutton Pies" and "The Treasures of a Dunghill." Mrs. Harris, who does not even exist, has more detail piled onto her than any three characters in an ordinary novel. Merely in the middle of a sentence we learn, for instance, that her infant nephew has been seen in a bottle at Greenwich Fair, along with the pink-eyed lady, the Prussian dwarf and the living skeleton. Joe Gargery describes how the robbers broke into the house of Pumblechook, the corn and seed merchant—"and they took his till, and they took his cashbox, and they drinked his wine, and they partook of his wittles, and they slapped his face, and they pulled his nose, and they tied him up to his bedpust, and they give him a dozen, and they stuffed his mouth full of flowering annuals to perwent his crying out." Once again the unmistakable Dickens touch, the flowering annuals; but any other novelist would only have mentioned about half of these outrages. Everything is piled up and up, detail on detail, embroidery on embroidery. It is futile to object that this kind of thing is rococo—one might as well make the same objection to a wedding-cake. Either you like it or you do not like it. Other nineteenth-century writers, Surtees, Barham, Thackeray, even Marryat, have something of Dickens's profuse, overflowing quality, but none of them on anything like the same scale. The appeal of all these writers now depends partly on period-flavour, and though Marryat is still officially a "boys' writer" and Surtees has a sort of legendary fame among hunting men, it is probable that they are read mostly by bookish people.

Significantly, Dickens's most successful books (not his *best* books) are *The Pickwick Papers,* which is not a novel, and *Hard Times* and *A Tale of Two Cities,* which are not funny. As a novelist his natural fertility greatly hampers him, because the burlesque which he is never able to resist is constantly breaking into what ought to be serious situations. There is a good example of this in the opening chapter of *Great Expectations.* The escaped convict, Magwitch, has just captured the six-year-old Pip in the churchyard. The scene starts terrifyingly enough, from Pip's point of view. The convict, smothered in mud and with his chain trailing from his leg, suddenly starts up among the tombs, grabs the child, turns him upside down and robs his pockets. Then he begins terrorising him into bringing food and a file:

> . . . he held me by the arms in an upright position on the top of the stone, and went on in these fearful terms:
>
> "You bring me, to-morrow morning early, that file and them wittles. You bring the lot to me, at that old Battery over yonder. You do it, and you never dare to say a word or dare to make a sign concerning your having seen such a person as me, or any person sumever, and you shall be let to live. You fail, or you go from my words in any partickler, no matter how small it is, and your heart and your liver shall be tore out, roasted and ate. Now, I ain't alone, as you may think I am. There's a young man hid with me, in comparison with which young man I am a Angel. That young man hears the words I speak. That young man has a secret way pecooliar to himself, of getting at a boy, and at his heart, and at his liver. It is in wain for a boy to attempt to hide himself from that young man. A boy may lock his door, may be warm in bed, may tuck himself up, may draw the clothes over his head, may think himself comfortable and safe, but that young man will softly creep and creep his way to him and tear him open. I am keeping that young man from harming of you at the present moment, with great difficulty. I find it wery hard to hold that young man off of your inside. Now, what do you say?"

Here Dickens has simply yielded to temptation. To begin with, no starving and hunted man would speak in the least like that.

Moreover, although the speech shows a remarkable knowledge of the way in which a child's mind works, its actual words are quite out of tune with what is to follow. It turns Magwitch into a sort of pantomime wicked uncle, or, if one sees him through the child's eyes, into an appalling monster. Later in the book he is to be represented as neither, and his exaggerated gratitude, on which the plot turns, is to be incredible because of just this speech. As usual, Dickens's imagination has overwhelmed him. The picturesque details were too good to be left out. Even with characters who are more of a piece than Magwitch he is liable to be tripped up by some seductive phrase. Mr. Murdstone, for instance, is in the habit of ending David Copperfield's lessons every morning with a dreadful sum in arithmetic. "If I go into a cheese-monger's shop, and buy five thousand double-Gloucester cheeses at fourpence halfpenny each, present payment," it always begins. Once again the typical Dickens detail, the double-Gloucester cheeses. But it is far too human a touch for Murdstone; he would have made it five thousand cashboxes. Every time this note is struck, the unity of the novel suffers. Not that it matters very much, because Dickens is obviously a writer whose parts are greater than his wholes. He is all fragments, all details—rotten architecture, but wonderful gargoyles—and never better than when he is building up some character who will later on be forced to act inconsistently.

Of course it is not usual to urge against Dickens that he makes his characters behave inconsistently. Generally he is accused of doing just the opposite. His characters are supposed to be mere "types," each crudely representing some single trait and fitted with a kind of label by which you recognise him. Dickens is "only a caricaturist"—that is the usual accusation, and it does him both more and less than justice. To begin with, he did not think of himself as a caricaturist, and was constantly setting into action characters who ought to have been purely static. Squeers, Micawber, Miss

Mowcher,* Wegg, Skimpole, Pecksniff and many others are finally involved in "plots" where they are out of place and where they behave quite incredibly. They start off as magic-lantern slides and they end by getting mixed up in a third-rate movie. Sometimes one can put one's finger on a single sentence in which the original illusion is destroyed. There is such a sentence in *David Copperfield.* After the famous dinner-party (the one where the leg of mutton was underdone), David is showing his guests out. He stops Traddles at the top of the stairs:

> "Traddles," said I, "Mr. Micawber don't mean any harm, poor fellow; but, if I were you, I wouldn't lend him anything."
>
> "My dear Copperfield," returned Traddles, smiling, "I haven't got anything to lend."
>
> "You have got a name, you know," said I.

At the place where one reads it this remark jars a little, though something of the kind was inevitable sooner or later. The story is a fairly realistic one, and David is growing up; ultimately he is bound to see Mr. Micawber for what he is, a cadging scoundrel. Afterwards, of course, Dickens's sentimentality overcomes him and Micawber is made to turn over a new leaf. But from then on, the original Micawber is never quite recaptured, in spite of desperate efforts. As a rule, the "plot" in which Dickens's characters get entangled is not particularly credible, but at least it makes some pretence at reality, whereas the world to which they belong is a never-never land, a kind of eternity. But just here one sees that

*Dickens turned Miss Mowcher into a sort of heroine because the real woman whom he had caricatured had read the earlier chapters and was bitterly hurt. He had previously meant her to play a villainous part. But *any* action by such a character would seem incongruous [Orwell's footnote].

"only a caricaturist" is not really a condemnation. The fact that Dickens is always thought of as a caricaturist, although he was constantly trying to be something else, is perhaps the surest mark of his genius. The monstrosities that he created are still remembered as monstrosities, in spite of getting mixed up in would-be probable melodramas. Their first impact is so vivid that nothing that comes afterwards effaces it. As with the people one knew in childhood, one seems always to remember them in one particular attitude, doing one particular thing. Mrs. Squeers is always ladling out brimstone and treacle, Mrs. Gummidge is always weeping, Mrs. Gargery is always banging her husband's head against the wall, Mrs. Jellyby is always scribbling tracts while her children fall into the area—and there they all are, fixed for ever like little twinkling miniatures painted on snuffbox lids, completely fantastic and incredible, and yet somehow more solid and infinitely more memorable than the efforts of serious novelists. Even by the standards of his time Dickens was an exceptionally artificial writer. As Ruskin said, he "chose to work in a circle of stage fire." His characters are even more distorted and simplified than Smollett's. But there are no rules in novel-writing, and for any work of art there is only one test worth bothering about—survival. By this test Dickens's characters have succeeded, even if the people who remember them hardly think of them as human beings. They are monsters, but at any rate they *exist.*

But all the same there is a disadvantage in writing about monsters. It amounts to this, that it is only certain moods that Dickens can speak to. There are large areas of the human mind that he never touches. There is no poetic feeling anywhere in his books, and no genuine tragedy, and even sexual love is almost outside his scope. Actually his books are not so sexless as they are sometimes declared to be, and considering the time in which he was writing, he is reasonably frank. But there is not a trace in him of the feeling that one finds in *Manon Lescaut, Salammbô, Carmen, Wuthering Heights.* According to Aldous Huxley, D. H. Lawrence once said that Balzac was "a gigantic dwarf," and in a sense the same is true of Dickens. There are whole worlds which he either knows nothing about or does not wish to mention. Except in a rather roundabout way, one cannot *learn* very much from Dickens. And to say this is to think almost immediately of the great Russian novelists of the nineteenth century. Why is it that Tolstoy's grasp seems to be so much larger than Dickens's—why is it that he seems able to tell you so much more *about yourself*? It is not that he is more gifted, or even, in the last analysis, more intelligent. It is because he is writing about people who are growing. His characters are struggling to make their souls, whereas Dickens's are already finished and perfect. In my own mind Dickens's people are present far more often and far more vividly than Tolstoy's, but always in a single unchangeable attitude, like pictures or pieces of furniture. You cannot hold an imaginary conversation with a Dickens character as you can with, say, Peter Bezukhov. And this is not merely because of Tolstoy's greater seriousness, for there are also comic characters that you can imagine yourself talking to—Bloom, for instance, or Pécuchet, or even Wells's Mr. Polly. It is because Dickens's characters have no mental life. They say perfectly the thing that they have to say, but they cannot be conceived as talking about anything else. They never learn, never speculate. Perhaps the most meditative of his characters is Paul Dombey, and his thoughts are mush. Does this mean that Tolstoy's novels are "better" than Dickens's? The truth is that it is absurd to make such comparisons in terms of "better" and "worse." If I were forced to compare Tolstoy with Dickens, I should say that Tolstoy's appeal will probably be wider in the long run, because Dickens is scarcely intelligible outside the English-speaking culture; on the other hand, Dickens is able to reach simple people, which Tolstoy is not. Tolstoy's characters can cross a frontier, Dickens's can be portrayed on a cigarette-card. But one is no more obliged to choose between them than between a sausage and a rose. Their purposes barely intersect.

6

If Dickens had been *merely* a comic writer, the chances are that no one would now remember his name. Or at best a few of his books would survive in rather the same way as books like *Frank Fairleigh, Mr Verdant Green* and *Mrs Caudle's Curtain Lectures,*[10] as a sort of hangover of the Victorian atmosphere, a pleasant little whiff of oysters and brown stout. Who has not felt sometimes that it was "a pity" that Dickens ever deserted the vein of *Pickwick* for things like *Little Dorrit* and *Hard Times*? What people always demand of a popular novelist is that he shall write the same book over and over again, forgetting that a man who would write the same book twice could not even write it once. Any writer who is not utterly lifeless moves upon a kind of parabola, and the downward curve is implied in the upward one. Joyce has to start with the frigid competence of *Dubliners* and end with the dream-language of *Finnegans Wake,* but *Ulysses* and *Portrait of the Artist* are part of the trajectory. The thing that drove Dickens forward into a form of art for which he was not really suited, and at the same time caused us to remember him, was simply the fact that he was a moralist, the consciousness of "having something to say." He is always preaching a sermon, and that is the final secret of his inventiveness. For you can only create if you can *care.* Types like Squeers and Micawber could not have been produced by a hack writer looking for something to be funny about. A joke worth laughing at always has an idea behind it, and usually a subversive idea. Dickens is able to go on being funny because he is in revolt against authority, and authority is always there to be laughed at. There is always room for one more custard pie.

His radicalism is of the vaguest kind, and yet one always knows that it is there. That is the difference between being a moralist and a politician. He has no constructive suggestions, not even a clear grasp of the nature of the society he is attacking, only an emotional perception that something is wrong. All he can finally say is, "Behave decently," which, as I suggested earlier, is not necessarily so shallow as it sounds. Most revolutionaries are potential Tories, because they imagine that everything can be put right by altering the *shape* of society; once that change is effected, as it sometimes is, they see no need for any other. Dickens has not this kind of mental coarseness. The vagueness of his discontent is the mark of its permanence. What he is out against is not this or that institution, but, as Chesterton put it, "an expression on the human face." Roughly speaking, his morality is the Christian morality, but in spite of his Anglican upbringing he was essentially a Bible-Christian, as he took care to make plain when writing his will. In any case he cannot properly be described as a religious man. He "believed," undoubtedly, but religion in the devotional sense does not seem to have entered much into his thoughts.* Where he is Christian is in his quasi-instinctive siding with the oppressed against the oppressors. As a matter of course he is on the side of the underdog, always and everywhere. To carry this to its

*From a letter to his youngest son (in 1868): "You will remember that you have never at home been harassed about religious observances, or mere formalities. I have always been anxious not to weary my children with such things, before they are old enough to form opinions respecting them. You will therefore understand the better that I now most solemnly impress upon you the truth and beauty of the Christian Religion, as it came from Christ Himself, and the impossibility of your going far wrong if you humbly but heartily respect it . . . Never abandon the wholesome practice of saying your own private prayers, night and morning. I have never abandoned it myself, and I know the comfort of it" [Orwell's footnote].

logical conclusion one has got to change sides when the underdog becomes an upperdog, and in fact Dickens does tend to do so. He loathes the Catholic Church, for instance, but as soon as the Catholics are persecuted (*Barnaby Rudge*) he is on their side. He loathes the aristocratic class even more, but as soon as they are really overthrown (the revolutionary chapters in *A Tale of Two Cities*) his sympathies swing round. Whenever he departs from this emotional attitude he goes astray. A well-known example is at the ending of *David Copperfield,* in which everyone who reads it feels that something has gone wrong. What is wrong is that the closing chapters are pervaded, faintly but noticeably, by the cult of success. It is the gospel according to Smiles, instead of the gospel according to Dickens. The attractive, out-at-elbow characters are got rid of, Micawber makes a fortune, Heep gets into prison—both of these events are flagrantly impossible—and even Dora is killed off to make way for Agnes. If you like, you can read Dora as Dickens's wife and Agnes as his sister-in-law, but the essential point is that Dickens has "turned respectable" and done violence to his own nature. Perhaps that is why Agnes is the most disagreeable of his heroines, the real legless angel of Victorian romance, almost as bad as Thackeray's Laura.

No grown-up person can read Dickens without feeling his limitations, and yet there does remain his native generosity of mind, which acts as a kind of anchor and nearly always keeps him where he belongs. It is probably the central secret of his popularity. A good-tempered antinomianism rather of Dickens's type is one of the marks of Western popular culture. One sees it in folk-stories and comic songs, in dream-figures like Mickey Mouse and Popeye the Sailor (both of them variants of Jack the Giant-killer), in the history of working-class Socialism, in the popular protests (always ineffective but not always a sham) against imperialism, in the impulse that makes a jury award excessive damages when a rich man's car runs over a poor man; it is the feeling that one is always on the side of the underdog, on the side of the weak against the strong. In one sense it is a feeling that is fifty years out of date. The common man is still living in the mental world of Dickens, but nearly every modern intellectual has gone over to some or other form of totalitarianism. From the Marxist or Fascist point of view, nearly all that Dickens stands for can be written off as "bourgeois morality." But in moral outlook no one could be more "bourgeois" than the English working classes. The ordinary people in the Western countries have never entered, mentally, into the world of "realism" and power-politics. They may do so before long, in which case Dickens will be as out of date as the cab-horse. But in his own age and ours he has been popular chiefly because he was able to express in a comic, simplified and therefore memorable form the native decency of the common man. And it is important that from this point of view people of very different types can be described as "common." In a country like England, in spite of its class-structure, there does exist a certain cultural unity. All through the Christian ages, and especially since the French Revolution, the Western world has been haunted by the idea of freedom and equality; it is only an *idea,* but it has penetrated to all ranks of society. The most atrocious injustices, cruelties, lies, snobberies exist everywhere, but there are not many people who can regard these things with the same indifference as, say, a Roman slave-owner. Even the millionaire suffers from a vague sense of guilt, like a dog eating a stolen leg of mutton. Nearly everyone, whatever his actual conduct may be, responds emotionally to the idea of human brotherhood. Dickens voiced a code which was and on the whole still is believed in, even by people who violate it. It is difficult otherwise to explain why he could be both read by working people (a thing that has happened to no other novelist of his stature) and buried in Westminster Abbey.

When one reads any strongly individual piece of writing, one has the impression of seeing a face somewhere behind the page. It is not necessarily the actual face of the writer. I feel this very strongly with Swift, with Defoe, with Fielding, Stendhal, Thackeray, Flaubert, though in several cases I do not know what these people looked like and do not want to know. What one sees is the face that the writer *ought* to have. Well, in the case of Dickens I see a face that is not quite the face of Dickens's photographs, though it resembles it. It is the face of a man of about forty, with a small beard and a high colour. He is laughing, with a touch of anger in his laughter, but no triumph, no malignity. It is the face of a man who is always fighting against something, but who fights in the open and is not frightened, the face of a man who is *generously angry*—in other words, of a nineteenth-century liberal, a free intelligence, a type hated with equal hatred by all the smelly little orthodoxies which are now contending for our souls.

Boys' Weeklies

Inside the Whale, March 11, 1940

You never walk far through any poor quarter in any big town without coming upon a small newsagent's shop. The general appearance of these shops is always very much the same: a few posters for the *Daily Mail* and the *News of the World* outside, a poky little window with sweet-bottles and packets of Players, and a dark interior smelling of liquorice allsorts and festooned from floor to ceiling with vilely printed twopenny papers, most of them with lurid cover-illustrations in three colours.

Except for the daily and evening papers, the stock of these shops hardly overlaps at all with that of the big newsagents. Their main selling line is the twopenny weekly, and the number and variety of these are almost unbelievable. Every hobby and pastime—cage-birds, fretwork, carpentering, bees, carrier-pigeons, home conjuring, philately, chess—has at least one paper devoted to it, and generally several. Gardening and livestock-keeping must have at least a score between them. Then there are the sporting papers, the radio papers, the children's comics, the various snippet papers such as *Tit-bits,* the large range of papers devoted to the movies and all more or less exploiting women's legs, the various trade papers, the women's story-papers (the *Oracle, Secrets, Peg's Paper,* etc. etc.), the needlework papers—these so numerous that a display of them alone will often fill an entire window—and in addition the long series of "Yank Mags" (*Fight Stories, Action Stories, Western Short Stories,* etc.), which are imported shop-soiled from

America and sold at twopence halfpenny or threepence. And the periodical proper shades off into the fourpenny novelette, the *Aldine Boxing Novels,* the *Boys' Friend Library,* the *Schoolgirls' Own Library* and many others.

Probably the contents of these shops is the best available indication of what the mass of the English people really feels and thinks. Certainly nothing half so revealing exists in documentary form. Best-seller novels, for instance, tell one a great deal, but the novel is aimed almost exclusively at people above the £4-a-week level. The movies are probably a very unsafe guide to popular taste, because the film industry is virtually a monopoly, which means that it is not obliged to study its public at all closely. The same applies to some extent to the daily papers, and most of all to the radio. But it does not apply to the weekly paper with a smallish circulation and specialised subject-matter. Papers like the *Exchange and Mart,* for instance, or *Cage-Birds,* or the *Oracle,* or *Prediction,* or the *Matrimonial Times,* only exist because there is a definite demand for them, and they reflect the minds of their readers as a great national daily with a circulation of millions cannot possibly do.

Here I am only dealing with a single series of papers, the boys' twopenny weeklies, often inaccurately described as "penny dreadfuls." Falling strictly within this class there are at present ten papers, the *Gem, Magnet, Modern Boy, Triumph* and *Champion,* all owned by the Amalgamated Press, and the *Wizard, Rover, Skipper, Hotspur* and *Adventure,* all owned by D. C. Thomson & Co. What the circulations of these papers are, I do not know. The editors and proprietors refuse to name any figures, and in any case the circulation of a paper carrying serial stories is bound to fluctuate widely. But there is no question that the combined public of the ten papers is a very large one. They are on sale in every town in England, and nearly every boy who reads at all goes through a phase of reading one or more of them. The *Gem* and *Magnet,* which are much the oldest of these papers, are of rather different type from the rest, and they have evidently lost some of their popularity during the past few years. A good many boys now regard them as old fashioned and "slow." Nevertheless I want to discuss them first, because they are more interesting psychologically than the others, and also because the mere survival of such papers into the nineteen-thirties is a rather startling phenomenon.

The *Gem* and *Magnet* are sister-papers (characters out of one paper frequently appear in the other), and were both started more than thirty years ago. At that time, together with *Chums* and the old *B.O.P.,*[1] they were the leading papers for boys, and they remained dominant till quite recently. Each of them carries every week a fifteen-or twenty-thousand-word school story, complete in itself, but usually more or less connected with the story of the week before. The *Gem* in addition to its school story carries one or more adventure serials. Otherwise the two papers are so much alike that they can be treated as one, though the *Magnet* has always been the better known of the two, probably because it possesses a really first-rate character in the fat boy, Billy Bunter.

The stories are stories of what purports to be public-school life, and the schools (Greyfriars in the *Magnet* and St. Jim's in the *Gem*) are represented as ancient and fashionable foundations of the type of Eton or Winchester. All the leading characters are fourth-form boys aged fourteen or fifteen, older or younger boys only appearing in very minor parts. Like Sexton Blake and Nelson Lee, these boys continue week after week and year after year, never growing any older. Very occasionally a new boy arrives or a minor character drops out, but in at any rate the last twenty-five years the personnel has barely altered. All the principal characters in both papers—Bob Cherry, Tom Merry, Harry Wharton, Johnny Bull, Billy Bunter and the rest of them—were at Greyfriars or St. Jim's long before the Great War, exactly the same age as at present, having much the same kind of adventures and talking almost exactly the same dialect. And not only the characters but the whole atmosphere of both *Gem* and *Magnet* has been preserved unchanged, partly by means of very elaborate stylisation. The stories in the *Magnet* are signed "Frank Richards" and those in the *Gem,* "Martin Clifford" but a series lasting thirty years could hardly be the work of the same person every week.[2] Consequently they have to be written in a style that is easily imitated—an extraordinary, artificial, repetitive style, quite different from anything else now existing in English literature. A couple of extracts will do as illustrations. Here is one from the *Magnet*:

> Groan!
>
> "Shut up, Bunter!"
>
> Groan!
>
> Shutting up was not really in Billy Bunter's line. He seldom shut up, though often requested to do so. On the present awful occasion the fat Owl of Greyfriars was less inclined than ever to shut up. And he did not shut up! He groaned, and groaned, and went on groaning.
>
> Even groaning did not fully express Bunter's feelings. His feelings, in fact, were inexpressible.
>
> There were six of them in the soup! Only one of the six uttered sounds of woe and lamentation. But that one, William George Bunter, uttered enough for the whole party and a little over.
>
> Harry Wharton & Co. stood in a wrathy and worried group. They were landed and stranded, diddled, dished and done! etc. etc. etc.

Here is one from the *Gem*:

> "Oh cwumbs!"
> "Oh gum!"
> "Oooogh!"
> "Urrggh!"
> Arthur Augustus sat up dizzily. He grabbed his handkerchief and pressed it to his damaged nose. Tom Merry sat up, gasping for breath. They looked at one another.
> "Bai Jove! This is a go, deah boy!" gurgled Arthur Augustus. "I have been thwown into quite a fluttah! Oogh! The wottahs! The wuffians! The feahful outsidahs! Wow!" etc. etc. etc.

Both of these extracts are entirely typical; you would find something like them in almost every chapter of every number, to-day or twenty-five years ago. The first thing that anyone would notice is the extraordinary amount of tautology (the first of these two passages contains a hundred and twenty-five words and could be compressed into about thirty), seemingly designed to spin out the story, but actually playing its part in creating the atmosphere. For the same reason various facetious expressions are repeated over and over again; "wrathy," for instance, is a great favourite, and so is "diddled, dished and done." "Oooogh!," "Grooo!" and "Yaroo!" (stylised cries of pain) recur constantly, and so does "Ha! ha! ha!," always given a line to itself, so that sometimes a quarter of a column or thereabouts consists of "Ha! ha! ha!" The slang ("Go and eat coke!," "What the thump!," "You frabjous ass!," etc. etc.) has never been altered, so that the boys are now using slang which is at least thirty years out of date. In addition, the various nicknames are rubbed in on every possible occasion. Every few lines we are reminded that Harry Wharton & Co. are "the Famous

Five," Bunter is always "the fat Owl" or "the Owl of the Remove," Vernon-Smith is always "the Bounder of Greyfriars," Gussy (the Honourable Arthur Augustus D'Arcy) is always "the swell of St. Jim's," and so on and so forth. There is a constant, untiring effort to keep the atmosphere intact and to make sure that every new reader learns immediately who is who. The result has been to make Greyfriars and St. Jim's into an extraordinary little world of their own, a world which cannot be taken seriously by anyone over fifteen, but which at any rate is not easily forgotten. By a debasement of the Dickens technique a series of stereotyped "characters" has been built up, in several cases very successfully. Billy Bunter, for instance, must be one of the best-known figures in English fiction; for the mere number of people who know him he ranks with Sexton Blake, Tarzan, Sherlock Holmes and a handful of characters in Dickens.

Needless to say, these stories are fantastically unlike life at a real public school. They run in cycles of rather differing types, but in general they are the clean-fun, knockabout type of story, with interest centring round horseplay, practical jokes, ragging masters, fights, canings, football, cricket and food. A constantly recurring story is one in which a boy is accused of some misdeed committed by another and is too much of a sportsman to reveal the truth. The "good" boys are "good" in the clean-living Englishman tradition—they keep in hard training, wash behind their ears, never hit below the belt, etc. etc.—and by way of contrast there is a series of "bad" boys, Racke, Crooke, Loder and others, whose badness consists in betting, smoking cigarettes and frequenting public-houses. All these boys are constantly on the verge of expulsion, but as it would mean a change of personnel if any boy were actually expelled, no one is ever caught out in any really serious offence. Stealing, for instance, barely enters as a motif. Sex is completely taboo, especially in the form in which it actually arises at public schools. Occasionally girls enter into the stories, and very rarely there is something approaching a mild flirtation, but it is always entirely in the spirit of clean fun. A boy and a girl enjoy going for bicycle rides together—that is all it ever amounts to. Kissing, for instance, would be regarded as "soppy." Even the bad boys are presumed to be completely sexless. When the *Gem* and *Magnet* were started, it is probable that there was a deliberate intention to get away from the guilty sex-ridden atmosphere that pervaded so much of the earlier literature for boys. In the 'nineties the *Boy's Own Paper,* for instance, used to have its correspondence columns full of terrifying warnings against masturbation, and books like *St. Winifred's* and *Tom Brown's Schooldays* were heavy with homosexual feeling, though no doubt the authors were not fully aware of it. In the *Gem* and *Magnet* sex simply does not exist as a problem. Religion is also taboo; in the whole thirty years' issue of the two papers the word "God" probably does not occur, except in "God save the King." On the other hand, there has always been a very strong "temperance" strain. Drinking and, by association, smoking are regarded as rather disgraceful even in an adult ("shady" is the usual word), but at the same time as something irresistibly fascinating, a sort of substitute for sex. In their moral atmosphere the *Gem* and *Magnet* have a great deal in common with the Boy Scout movement, which started at about the same time.

All literature of this kind is partly plagiarism. Sexton Blake, for instance, started off quite frankly as an imitation of Sherlock Holmes, and still resembles him fairly strongly; he has hawklike features, lives in Baker Street, smokes enormously and puts on a dressing-gown when he wants to think. The *Gem* and *Magnet* probably owe something to the school story writers who were flourishing when they began, Gunby Hadath,[3] Desmond Coke[4] and the rest, but they owe more to nineteenth-century models. In so far as Greyfriars and St. Jim's are like real schools at all, they are much more like Tom Brown's Rugby than a modern public school. Neither school has an O.T.C.,[5] for instance, games are not compulsory, and the boys are even allowed to wear what clothes they like. But without doubt the main origin of these papers is *Stalky & Co.* This book has had an immense influence on boys' literature, and it is one of those books which have a sort of traditional reputation among people who have never even seen a copy of it. More than once in boys' weekly papers I have come across a reference to *Stalky & Co.* in which the word was spelt "Storky." Even the name of the chief comic among the Greyfriars masters, Mr. Prout, is taken from *Stalky & Co.,* and so is much of the slang; "jape," "merry," "giddy," "bizney" (business), "frabjous," "don't" for "doesn't"—all of them out of date even when *Gem* and *Magnet* started. There are also traces of earlier origins. The name "Greyfriars" is probably taken from Thackeray, and Gosling, the school porter in the *Magnet,* talks in an imitation of Dickens's dialect.

With all this, the supposed "glamour" of public-school life is played for all it is worth. There is all the usual paraphernalia—lock-up, roll-call, house matches, fagging, prefects, cosy teas round the study fire, etc. etc.—and constant reference to the "old school," the "old grey stones" (both schools were founded in the early sixteenth century), the "team spirit" of the "Greyfriars men." As for the snob-appeal, it is completely shameless. Each school has a titled boy or two whose titles are constantly thrust in the reader's face; other boys have the names of well-known aristocratic families, Talbot, Manners, Lowther. We are for ever being reminded that Gussy is the Honourable Arthur A. D'Arcy, son of Lord Eastwood, that Jack Blake is heir to "broad acres," that Hurree Jamset Ram Singh (nicknamed Inky) is the Nabob of

Bhanipur, that Vernon-Smith's father is a millionaire. Till recently the illustrations in both papers always depicted the boys in clothes imitated from those of Eton; in the last few years Greyfriars has changed over to blazers and flannel trousers, but St. Jim's still sticks to the Eton jacket, and Gussy sticks to his top-hat. In the school magazine which appears every week as part of the *Magnet,* Harry Wharton writes an article discussing the pocket-money received by the "fellows in the Remove," and reveals that some of them get as much as five pounds a week! This kind of thing is a perfectly deliberate incitement to wealth-fantasy. And here it is worth noticing a rather curious fact, and that is that the school story is a thing peculiar to England. So far as I know, there are extremely few school stories in foreign languages. The reason, obviously, is that in England education is mainly a matter of status. The most definite dividing-line between the petite-bourgeoisie and the working class is that the former pay for their education, and within the bourgeoisie there is another unbridgeable gulf between the "public" school and the "private" school. It is quite clear that there are tens and scores of thousands of people to whom every detail of life at a "posh" public school is wildly thrilling and romantic. They happen to be outside that mystic world of quadrangles and house-colours, but they yearn after it, day-dream about it, live mentally in it for hours at a stretch. The question is, Who are these people? Who reads the *Gem* and *Magnet*?

Obviously one can never be quite certain about this kind of thing. All I can say from my own observation is this. Boys who are likely to go to public schools themselves generally read the *Gem* and *Magnet,* but they nearly always stop reading them when they are about twelve; they may continue for another year from force of habit, but by that time they have ceased to take them seriously. On the other hand, the boys at very cheap private schools, the schools that are designed for people who can't afford a public school but consider the Council schools "common," continue reading the *Gem* and *Magnet* for several years longer. A few years ago I was a teacher at two of these schools myself. I found that not only did virtually all the boys read the *Gem* and *Magnet,* but that they were still taking them fairly seriously when they were fifteen or even sixteen. These boys were the sons of shopkeepers, office employees and small business and professional men, and obviously it is this class that the *Gem* and *Magnet* are aimed at. But they are certainly read by working-class boys as well. They are generally on sale in the poorest quarters of big towns, and I have known them to be read by boys whom one might expect to be completely immune from public-school "glamour." I have seen a young coal-miner, for instance, a lad who had already worked a year or two underground, eagerly reading the *Gem.* Recently I offered a batch of English papers to some British legionaries of the French Foreign Legion in North Africa; they picked out the *Gem* and *Magnet* first. Both papers are much read by girls,* and the Pen Pals department of the *Gem* shows that it is read in every corner of the British Empire, by Australians, Canadians, Palestine Jews, Malays, Arabs, Straits Chinese, etc. etc. The editors evidently expect their readers to be aged round about fourteen, and the advertisements (milk chocolate, postage stamps, water pistols, blushing cured, home conjuring tricks, itching powder, the Phine Phun Ring which runs a needle into your friend's hand, etc. etc.) indicate roughly the same age; there are also the Admiralty advertisements, however, which call for youths between seventeen and twenty-two. And there is no question that these papers are also read by adults. It is quite common for people to write to the editor and say that

*There are several corresponding girls' papers. The *Schoolgirl* is a companion-paper to the *Magnet* and has stories by "Hilda Richards." The characters are interchangeable to some extent. Bessie Bunter, Billy Bunter's sister, figures in the *Schoolgirl* [Orwell's footnote].[6]

they have read every number of the *Gem* or *Magnet* for the past thirty years. Here, for instance, is a letter from a lady in Salisbury:

> I can say of your splendid yarns of Harry Wharton & Co., of Greyfriars, that they never fail to reach a high standard. Without doubt they are the finest stories of their type on the market to-day, which is saying a good deal. They seem to bring you face to face with Nature. I have taken the *Magnet* from the start, and have followed the adventures of Harry Wharton & Co. with rapt interest. I have no sons, but two daughters, and there's always a rush to be the first to read the grand old paper. My husband, too, was a staunch reader of the *Magnet* until he was suddenly taken away from us.

It is well worth getting hold of some copies of the *Gem* and *Magnet,* especially the *Gem,* simply to have a look at the correspondence columns. What is truly startling is the intense interest with which the pettiest details of life at Greyfriars and St. Jim's are followed up. Here, for instance, are a few of the questions sent in by readers:

> "What age is Dick Roylance?" "How old is St. Jim's?" "Can you give me a list of the Shell and their studies?" "How much did D'Arcy's monocle cost?" "How is it fellows like Crooke are in the Shell and decent fellows like yourself are only in the Fourth?" "What are the Form captain's three chief duties?" "Who is the chemistry master at St. Jim's?" (From a girl) "Where is St. Jim's situated? *Could* you tell me how to get there, as I would love to see the building? Are you boys just 'phoneys,' as I think you are?"

It is clear that many of the boys and girls who write these letters are living a complete fantasy-life. Sometimes a boy will write, for instance, giving his age, height, weight, chest and bicep measurements and asking which member of the Shell or Fourth Form he most exactly resembles. The demand for a list of the studies on the Shell passage, with an exact account of who lives in each, is a very common one. The editors, of course, do everything in their power to keep up the illusion. In the *Gem* Jack Blake is supposed to write the answers to correspondents, and in the *Magnet* a couple of pages is always given up to the school magazine (the *Greyfriars Herald,* edited by Harry Wharton), and there is another page in which one or other character is written up each week. The stories run in cycles, two or three characters being kept in the foreground for several weeks at a time. First there will be a series of rollicking adventure stories, featuring the Famous Five and Billy Bunter; then a run of stories turning on mistaken identity, with Wibley (the make-up wizard) in the star part; then a run of more serious stories in which Vernon-Smith is trembling on the verge of expulsion. And here one comes upon the real secret of the *Gem* and *Magnet* and the probable reason why they continue to be read in spite of their obvious out-of-dateness.

It is that the characters are so carefully graded as to give almost every type of reader a character he can identify himself with. Most boys' papers aim at doing this, hence the boy-assistant (Sexton Blake's Tinker, Nelson Lee's Nipper, etc.) who usually accompanies the explorer, detective or what-not on his adventures. But in these cases there is only one boy, and usually it is much the same type of boy. In the *Gem* and *Magnet* there is a model for very nearly everybody. There is the normal, athletic, high-spirited boy (Tom Merry, Jack Blake, Frank Nugent), a slightly rowdier version of this type (Bob Cherry), a more aristocratic version (Talbot, Manners), a quieter, more serious version (Harry Wharton), and a stolid, "bulldog" version (Johnny Bull). Then there is the reckless, dare-devil type of boy (Vernon-Smith), the definitely "clever," studious boy (Mark Linley, Dick Penfold), and the eccentric boy who is not good at games but possesses some special talent (Skinner, Wibley). And there is the scholarship-boy (Tom Redwing), an important figure in this class of story because he makes it possible for boys from very poor homes to project themselves into the public-school atmosphere. In addition there are Australian, Irish, Welsh, Manx, Yorkshire and Lancashire boys to play upon local patriotism. But the subtlety of characterisation goes deeper than this. If one studies the correspondence columns one sees that there is probably *no* character in the *Gem* and *Magnet* whom some or other reader does not identify with, except the out-and-out comics, Coker, Billy Bunter, Fisher T. Fish (the money-grubbing American boy) and, of course, the masters. Bunter, though in his origin he probably owed something to the fat boy in *Pickwick,* is a real creation. His tight trousers against which boots and canes are constantly thudding, his astuteness in search of food, his postal order which never turns up, have made him famous wherever the Union Jack waves. But he is not a subject for daydreams. On the other hand, another seeming figure of fun, Gussy (the Honourable Arthur A. D'Arcy, "the swell of St. Jim's"), is evidently much admired. Like everything else in the *Gem* and *Magnet,* Gussy is at least thirty years out of date. He is the "knut" of the early twentieth century or even the "masher" of the 'nineties ("Bai Jove, deah boy!" and "Weally, I shall be obliged to give you a feahful thwashin'!"), the monocled idiot who made good on the fields of Mons and Le Cateau.[7] And his evident popularity goes to show how deep the snob-appeal of this type is. English people are extremely fond of the titled ass (cf. Lord Peter Wimsey) who always turns up trumps in the moment of emergency. Here is a letter from one of Gussy's girl admirers:

I think you're too hard on Gussy. I wonder he's still in existence, the way you treat him. He's my hero. Did you know I write lyrics? How's this—to the tune of "Goody Goody"?

Gonna get my gas-mask, join the A. R. P.
'Cos I'm wise to all those bombs you drop on me.
        Gonna dig myself a trench
        Inside the garden fence;
    Gonna seal my windows up with tin
    So that the tear gas can't get in;
Gonna park my cannon right outside the kerb
With a note to Adolf Hitler: "Don't disturb!"
        And if I never fall in Nazi hands
        That's soon enough for me
        Gonna get my gas-mask, join the A. R. P.[8]

P.S.—Do you get on well with girls?

I quote this in full because (dated April 1939) it is interesting as being probably the earliest mention of Hitler in the *Gem.* In the *Gem* there is also a heroic fat boy, Fatty Wynn, as a set-off against Bunter. Vernon-Smith, "the Bounder of the Remove," a Byronic character, always on the verge of the sack, is another great favourite. And even some of the cads probably have their following. Loder, for instance, "the rotter of the Sixth," is a cad, but he is also a highbrow and given to saying sarcastic things about football and the team spirit. The boys of the Remove only think him all the more of a cad for this, but a certain type of boy would probably identify with him. Even Racke, Crooke and Co. are probably admired by small boys who think it diabolically wicked to smoke cigarettes. (A frequent question in the correspondence column: "What brand of cigarettes does Racke smoke?")

Naturally the politics of the *Gem* and *Magnet* are Conservative, but in a completely pre-1914 style, with no Fascist tinge. In reality their basic political assumptions are two: nothing ever changes, and foreigners are funny. In the *Gem* of 1939 Frenchmen are still Froggies and Italians are still Dagoes. Mossoo, the French master at Greyfriars, is the usual comic-paper Frog, with pointed beard, peg-top trousers, etc. Inky, the Indian boy, though a rajah, and therefore possessing snob-appeal, is also the comic babu of the *Punch* tradition. ("'The rowfulness is not the proper caper, my esteemed Bob,' said Inky. 'Let dogs delight in the barkfulness and bitefulness, but the soft answer is the cracked pitcher that goes longest to a bird in the bush, as the English proverb remarks.'") Fisher T. Fish is the old-style stage Yankee ("'Waal, I guess,'" etc.) dating from a period of Anglo-American jealousy. Wun Lung, the Chinese boy (he has rather faded out of late, no doubt because some of the *Magnet*'s readers are Straits Chinese), is the nineteenth-century pantomime Chinaman, with saucer-shaped hat, pigtail and pidgin-English. The assumption all along is not only that foreigners are comics who are put there for us to laugh at, but that they can be classified in much the same way as insects. That is why in all boys' papers, not only the *Gem* and *Magnet,* a Chinese is invariably portrayed with a pigtail. It is the thing you recognise him by, like the Frenchman's beard or the Italian's barrel-organ. In papers of this kind it occasionally happens that when the setting of a story is in a foreign country some attempt is made to describe the natives as individual human beings, but as a rule it is assumed that foreigners of any one race are all alike and will conform more or less exactly to the following patterns:

FRENCHMAN: Excitable. Wears beard, gesticulates wildly.
SPANIARD, MEXICAN, etc.: Sinister, treacherous.
ARAB, AFGHAN, etc.: Sinister, treacherous.
CHINESE: Sinister, treacherous. Wears pigtail.

ITALIAN: Excitable. Grinds barrel-organ or carries stiletto.
SWEDE, DANE, etc.: Kind hearted, stupid.
NEGRO: Comic, very faithful.

The working classes only enter into the *Gem* and *Magnet* as comics or semi-villains (race-course touts, etc.). As for class-friction, trade unionism, strikes, slumps, unemployment, Fascism and civil war—not a mention. Somewhere or other in the thirty years' issue of the two papers you might perhaps find the word "Socialism," but you would have to look a long time for it. If the Russian Revolution is anywhere referred to, it will be indirectly, in the word "Bolshy" (meaning a person of violent disagreeable habits). Hitler and the Nazis are just beginning to make their appearance, in the sort of reference I quoted above. The war-crisis of September 1938 made just enough impression to produce a story in which Mr. Vernon-Smith, the Bounder's millionaire father, cashed in on the general panic by buying up country houses in order to sell them to "crisis scuttlers." But that is probably as near to noticing the European situation as the *Gem* and *Magnet* will come, until the war actually starts.* That does not mean that these papers are unpatriotic—quite the contrary! Throughout the Great War the *Gem* and *Magnet* were perhaps the most consistently and cheerfully patriotic papers in England. Almost every week the boys caught a spy or pushed a conchy into the army, and during the rationing period "EAT LESS BREAD" was printed in large type on every page. But their patriotism has nothing whatever to do with power-politics or "ideological" warfare. It is more akin to family loyalty, and actually it gives one a valuable clue to the attitude of ordinary people, especially the huge untouched block of

*This was written some months before the outbreak of war. Up to the end of September 1939 no mention of the war has appeared in either paper [Orwell's footnote].

the middle class and the better-off working class. These people are patriotic to the middle of their bones, but they do not feel that what happens in foreign countries is any of their business. When England is in danger they rally to its defence as a matter of course, but in between-times they are not interested. After all, England is always in the right and England always wins, so why worry? It is an attitude that has been shaken during the past twenty years, but not so deeply as is sometimes supposed. Failure to understand it is one of the reasons why left-wing political parties are seldom able to produce an acceptable foreign policy.

The mental world of the *Gem* and *Magnet,* therefore, is something like this:

The year is 1910—or 1940, but it is all the same. You are at Greyfriars, a rosy-cheeked boy of fourteen in posh tailor-made clothes, sitting down to tea in your study on the Remove passage after an exciting game of football which was won by an odd goal in the last half-minute. There is a cosy fire in the study, and outside the wind is whistling. The ivy clusters thickly round the old grey stones. The King is on his throne and the pound is worth a pound. Over in Europe the comic foreigners are jabbering and gesticulating, but the grim grey battleships of the British Fleet are steaming up the Channel and at the outposts of Empire the monocled Englishmen are holding the niggers at bay. Lord Mauleverer has just got another fiver and we are all settling down to a tremendous tea of sausages, sardines, crumpets, potted meat, jam and doughnuts. After tea we shall sit round the study fire having a good laugh at Billy Bunter and discussing the team for next week's match against Rookwood. Everything is safe, solid and unquestionable. Everything will be the same for ever and ever. That approximately is the atmosphere.

But now turn from the *Gem* and *Magnet* to the more up-to-date papers which have appeared since the Great War. The truly significant thing is that they have more points of resemblance to the *Gem* and *Magnet* than points of difference. But it is better to consider the differences first.

There are eight of these newer papers, the *Modern Boy, Triumph, Champion, Wizard, Rover, Skipper, Hotspur* and *Adventure.* All of these have appeared since the Great War, but except for the *Modern Boy* none of them is less than five years old. Two papers which ought also to be mentioned briefly here, though they are not strictly in the same class as the rest, are the *Detective Weekly* and the *Thriller,* both owned by the Amalgamated Press. The *Detective Weekly* has taken over Sexton Blake. Both of these papers admit a certain amount of sex-interest into their stories, and though certainly read by boys, they are not aimed at them exclusively. All the others are boys' papers pure and simple, and they are sufficiently alike to be considered together. There does not seem to be any notable difference between Thomson's publications and those of the Amalgamated Press.

As soon as one looks at these papers one sees their technical superiority to the *Gem* and *Magnet.* To begin with, they have the great advantage of not being written entirely by one person. Instead of one long complete story, a number of the *Wizard* or *Hotspur* consists of half a dozen or more serials, none of which goes on for ever. Consequently there is far more variety and far less padding, and none of the tiresome stylisation and facetiousness of the *Gem* and *Magnet.* Look at these two extracts, for example:

> Billy Bunter groaned.
>
> A quarter of an hour had elapsed out of the two hours that Bunter was booked for extra French.
>
> In a quarter of an hour there were only fifteen minutes! But every one of those minutes seemed inordinately long to Bunter. They seemed to crawl by like tired snails.

Looking at the clock in Class-room No. 10 the fat Owl could hardly believe that only fifteen minutes had passed. It seemed more like fifteen hours, if not fifteen days!

Other fellows were in extra French as well as Bunter. They did not matter. Bunter did! (*Magnet*).

After a terrible climb, hacking out handholds in the smooth ice every step of the way up, Sergeant Lionheart Logan of the Mounties was now clinging like a human fly to the face of an icy cliff, as smooth and treacherous as a giant pane of glass.

An Arctic blizzard, in all its fury, was buffeting his body, driving the blinding snow into his face, seeking to tear his fingers loose from their handholds and dash him to death on the jagged boulders which lay at the foot of the cliff a hundred feet below.

Crouching among those boulders were eleven villainous trappers who had done their best to shoot down Lionheart and his companion, Constable Jim Rogers—until the blizzard had blotted the two Mounties out of sight from below. (*Wizard*).

The second extract gets you some distance with the story, the first takes a hundred words to tell you that Bunter is in the detention class. Moreover, by not concentrating on school stories (in point of numbers the school story slightly predominates in all these papers, except the *Thriller* and *Detective Weekly*), the *Wizard, Hotspur,* etc., have far greater opportunities for sensationalism. Merely looking at the cover illustrations of the papers which I have on the table in front of me, here are some of the things I see. On one a cowboy is clinging by his toes to the wing of an aeroplane in mid-air and shooting down another aeroplane with his revolver.

On another a Chinese is swimming for his life down a sewer with a swarm of ravenous-looking rats swimming after him. On another an engineer is lighting a stick of dynamite while a steel robot feels for him with its claws. On another a man in airman's costume is fighting barehanded against a rat somewhat larger than a donkey. On another a nearly naked man of terrific muscular development had just seized a lion by the tail and flung it thirty yards over the wall of an arena, with the words, "Take back your blooming lion!" Clearly no school story can compete with this kind of thing. From time to time the school buildings may catch fire or the French master may turn out to be the head of an international anarchist gang, but in a general way the interest must centre round cricket, school rivalries, practical jokes, etc. There is not much room for bombs, death-rays, sub-machine guns, aeroplanes, mustangs, octopuses, grizzly bears or gangsters.

Examination of a large number of these papers shows that, putting aside school stories, the favourite subjects are Wild West, Frozen North, Foreign Legion, crime (always from the detective's angle), the Great War (Air Force or Secret Service, not the infantry), the Tarzan motif in varying forms, professional football, tropical exploration, historical romance (Robin Hood, Cavaliers and Roundheads, etc.) and scientific invention. The Wild West still leads, at any rate as a setting, though the Red Indian seems to be fading out. The one theme that is really new is the scientific one. Death-rays, Martians, invisible men, robots, helicopters and interplanetary rockets figure largely; here and there there are even far-off rumours of psychotherapy and ductless-glands. Whereas the *Gem* and *Magnet* derive from Dickens and Kipling, the *Wizard, Champion, Modern Boy,* etc., owe a great deal to H. G. Wells, who, rather than Jules Verne, is the father of "Scientifiction." Naturally it is the magical, Martian aspect of science that is most exploited, but one or two papers include serious articles on scientific subjects, besides quantities of informative snippets. (Examples: "A Kauri tree in Queensland, Australia, is over 12,000 years old"; "Nearly 50,000 thunderstorms occur every day"; "Helium gas costs £1 per 1000 cubic feet"; "There are over 500 varieties of spiders in Great Britain"; "London firemen use 14,000,000 gallons of water annually," etc. etc.). There is a marked advance in intellectual curiosity and, on the whole, in the demand made on the reader's attention. In practice the *Gem* and *Magnet* and the post-war papers are read by much the same public, but the mental age aimed at seems to have risen by a year or two years—an improvement probably corresponding to the improvement in elementary education since 1909.

The other thing that has emerged in the post-war boys' papers, though not to anything like the extent one would expect, is bully-worship and the cult of violence.

If one compares the *Gem* and *Magnet* with a genuinely modern paper, the thing that immediately strikes one is the absence of the leader-principle. There is no central dominating character; instead there are fifteen or twenty characters, all more or less on an equality, with whom readers of different types can identify. In the more modern papers this is not usually the case. Instead of identifying with a schoolboy of more or less his own age, the reader of the *Skipper, Hotspur,* etc., is led to identify with a G-man, with a Foreign Legionary, with some variant of Tarzan, with an air ace, a master spy, an explorer, a pugilist—at any rate with some single all-powerful character who dominates everyone about him and whose usual method of solving any problem is a sock on the jaw. This character is intended as a superman, and as physical strength is the form of power that boys can best understand, he is usually a sort of human gorilla; in the Tarzan type of story he is sometimes actually a giant, eight or ten feet high. At the same time the scenes of violence in nearly all these stories are remarkably harmless and unconvincing. There is a great difference in tone between even the most bloodthirsty English paper and the threepenny Yank Mags, *Fight Stories, Action Stories,* etc. (not strictly boys' papers, but largely read by boys). In the Yank Mags you get real blood-lust, really gory descriptions of the all-in, jump-on-his-testicles style of fighting, written in a jargon that has been perfected by people who brood endlessly on violence. A paper like *Fight Stories,* for instance, would have very little appeal except to sadists and masochists. You can see the comparative gentleness of the English civilisation by the amateurish way in which prize-fighting is always described in the boys' weeklies. There is no specialised vocabulary. Look at these four extracts, two English, two American:

> When the gong sounded, both men were breathing heavily, and each had great red marks on his chest. Bill's chin was bleeding, and Ben had a cut over his right eye.
>
> Into their corners they sank, but when the gong clanged again they were up swiftly, and they went like tigers at each other (*Rover*).

> He walked in stolidly and smashed a clublike right to my face. Blood spattered and I went back on my heels, but surged in and ripped my right under the heart. Another right smashed full on Sven's already battered mouth, and, spitting out the fragments of a tooth, he crashed a flailing left to my body (*Fight Stories*).

> It was amazing to watch the Black Panther at work. His muscles rippled and slid under his dark skin. There was all the power and grace of a giant cat in his swift and terrible onslaught.

> He volleyed blows with a bewildering speed for so huge a fellow. In a moment Ben was simply blocking with his gloves as well as he could. Ben was really a past-master of defence. He had many fine victories behind him. But the Negro's rights and lefts crashed through openings that hardly any other fighter could have found (*Wizard*).

> Haymakers which packed the bludgeoning weight of forest monarchs crashing down under the ax hurled into the bodies of the two heavies as they swapped punches (*Fight Stories*).

Notice how much more knowledgeable the American extracts sound. They are written for devotees of the prize-ring, the others are not. Also, it ought to be emphasised that on its level the moral code of the English boys' papers is a decent one. Crime and dishonesty are never held up to admiration, there is none of the cynicism and corruption of the American gangster story. The huge sale of the Yank Mags in England shows that there is a demand for that kind of thing, but very few English writers seem able to produce it. When hatred of Hitler became a major emotion in America, it was interesting to see how promptly "anti-Fascism" was adapted to pornographic purposes by the editors of the Yank Mags. One magazine which I have in front of me is given up to a long, complete story, "When Hell Came to America," in which the agents of a "blood-maddened European dictator" are trying to conquer the U.S.A. with death-rays and invisible aeroplanes. There is the frankest appeal to sadism, scenes in which the Nazis tie bombs to women's backs and fling them off heights to watch them blown to pieces in mid-air, others in which they tie naked girls together by their hair and prod them with knives to make them dance, etc. etc. The editor comments solemnly on all this, and uses it as a plea for tightening up restrictions against immigrants. On another page of the same paper: "LIVES OF THE HOTCHA CHORUS GIRLS. Reveals all the intimate secrets and fascinating pastimes of the famous Broadway Hotcha girls. NOTHING IS OMITTED. Price 10c." "HOW TO LOVE. 10c." "FRENCH PHOTO RING. 25c." "NAUGHTY NUDIES TRANSFERS. From the outside of the glass you see a beautiful girl, innocently dressed. Turn it around and look through the glass and oh! what a difference! Set of 3 transfers 25c.," etc. etc. etc. There is nothing at all like this in any English paper likely to be read by boys. But the process of Americanisation is going on all the same. The American ideal, the "he-man," the "tough guy," the gorilla who puts everything right by socking everybody else on the jaw, now figures in probably a majority of boys' papers. In one serial now running in the *Skipper* he is always portrayed, ominously enough, swinging a rubber truncheon.

The development of the *Wizard, Hotspur,* etc., as against the earlier boys' papers, boils down to this: better technique, more scientific interest, more bloodshed, more leader-worship. But, after all, it is the *lack* of development that is the really striking thing.

To begin with, there is no political development whatever. The world of the *Skipper* and the *Champion* is still the pre-1914 world of the *Magnet* and the *Gem.* The Wild West story, for instance, with its cattle-rustlers, lynch-law and other paraphernalia belonging to the 'eighties, is a curiously archaic thing. It is worth noticing that in papers of this type it is always taken for granted that adventures only happen at the ends of the earth, in tropical forests, in Arctic wastes, in African deserts, on Western prairies, in Chinese opium dens—everywhere, in fact, except the places where things really *do* happen. That is a belief dating from thirty or forty years ago, when the new continents were in process of being opened up. Nowadays, of course, if you really want adventure, the place to look for it is in Europe. But apart from the picturesque side of the

Great War, contemporary history is carefully excluded. And except that Americans are now admired instead of being laughed at, foreigners are exactly the same figures of fun that they always were. If a Chinese character appears, he is still the sinister pig-tailed opium-smuggler of Sax Rohmer; no indication that things have been happening in China since 1912—no indication that a war is going on there, for instance. If a Spaniard appears, he is still a "dago" or "greaser" who rolls cigarettes and stabs people in the back; no indication that things have been happening in Spain. Hitler and the Nazis have not yet appeared, or are barely making their appearance. There will be plenty about them in a little while, but it will be from a strictly patriotic angle (Britain *versus* Germany), with the real meaning of the struggle kept out of sight as much as possible. As for the Russian Revolution, it is extremely difficult to find any reference to it in any of these papers. When Russia is mentioned at all it is usually in an information snippet (example: "There are 29,000 centenarians in the U.S.S.R."), and any reference to the Revolution is indirect and twenty years out of date. In one story in the *Rover,* for instance, somebody has a tame bear, and as it is a Russian bear, it is nicknamed Trotsky—obviously an echo of the 1917–23 period and not of recent controversies. The clock has stopped at 1910. Britannia rules the waves, and no one has heard of slumps, booms, unemployment, dictatorships, purges or concentration camps.

And in social outlook there is hardly any advance. The snobbishness is somewhat less open than in the *Gem* and *Magnet*—that is the most one can possibly say. To begin with, the school story, always partly dependent on snob-appeal, is by no means eliminated. Every number of a boys' paper includes at least one school story, these stories slightly outnumbering the Wild Westerns. The very elaborate fantasy-life of the *Gem* and *Magnet* is not imitated and there is more emphasis on extraneous adventure, but the social atmosphere (old grey stones) is much the same. When a new school is introduced at the beginning of a story we are often told in just those words that "it was a very posh school." From time to time a story appears which is ostensibly directed *against* snobbery. The scholarship-boy (cf. Tom Redwing in the *Magnet*) makes fairly frequent appearances, and what is essentially the same theme is sometimes presented in this form: there is great rivalry between two schools, one of which considers itself more "posh" than the other, and there are fights, practical jokes, football matches, etc., always ending in the discomfiture of the snobs. If one glances very superficially at some of these stories it is possible to imagine that a democratic spirit has crept into the boys' weeklies, but when one looks more closely one sees that they merely reflect the bitter jealousies that exist within the white-collar class. Their real function is to allow the boy who goes to a cheap private school (*not* a Council school) to feel that his school is just as "posh" in the sight of God as Winchester or Eton. The sentiment of school loyalty ("We're better than the fellows down the road"), a thing almost unknown to the real working class, is still kept up. As these stories are written by many different hands, they do, of course, vary a good deal in tone. Some are reasonably free from snobbishness, in others money and pedigree are exploited even more shamelessly than in the *Gem* and *Magnet*. In one that I came cross an actual *majority* of the boys mentioned were titled.

Where working-class characters appear, it is usually either as comics (jokes about tramps, convicts, etc.), or as prize-fighters, acrobats, cowboys, professional footballers and Foreign Legionaries—in other words, as adventurers. There is no facing of the facts about working-class life, or, indeed, about *working* life of any description. Very occasionally one may come across a realistic description of, say, work in a coal-mine, but in all probability it will only be there as the background of some lurid adventure. In any case the central character is not likely to be a coal-miner. Nearly all the time the boy who reads these papers—in nine cases out of ten a boy who is going to spend his life working in a shop, in a factory or in some subordinate job in an office—is led to identify with people in positions of command, above all with people who are never troubled by shortage of money. The Lord Peter Wimsey figure, the seeming idiot who drawls and wears a monocle but is always to the fore in moments of danger, turns up over and over again. (This character is a great favourite in Secret Service stories.) And, as usual, the heroic characters all have to talk B.B.C.; they may talk Scottish or Irish or American, but no one in a star part is ever permitted to drop an aitch. Here it is worth comparing the social atmosphere of the boys' weeklies with that of the women's weeklies, the *Oracle,* the *Family Star, Peg's Paper,* etc.

The women's papers are aimed at an older public and are read for the most part by girls who are working for a living. Consequently they are on the surface much more realistic. It is taken for granted, for example, that nearly everyone has to live in a big town and work at a more or less dull job. Sex, so far from being taboo, is *the* subject. The short, complete stories, the special feature of these papers, are generally of the "came the dawn" type: the heroine narrowly escapes losing her "boy" to a designing rival, or the "boy" loses his job and has to postpone marriage, but presently gets a better job. The changeling-fantasy (a girl brought up in a poor home is "really" the child of rich parents) is another favourite. Where sensationalism comes in, usually in the serials, it arises out of the more domestic type of crime, such as bigamy, forgery or sometimes murder; no Martians, death-rays or international anarchist gangs. These papers are at any rate aiming at credibility, and they have a link with real life in their correspondence columns, where genuine problems are being discussed. Ruby M. Ayres's[9] column of advice in the *Oracle,* for instance, is extremely sensible and well written. And yet the world of the *Oracle* and *Peg's Paper* is a pure fantasy-world. It is the same fantasy all the time: pretending to be richer than you are. The chief impression that one carries away from almost every story in these papers is of a frightful, overwhelming "refinement." Ostensibly the characters are working-class people, but their habits, the interiors of their houses, their clothes, their outlook and, above all, their speech are entirely middle class. They are all living at several pounds a week above their income. And needless to say, that is just the impression that is intended. The idea is to give the bored factory-girl or worn-out mother of five a dream-life in which she pictures herself—not actually as a duchess (that convention has gone out) but as, say, the wife of a bank-manager. Not only is a five-to-six-pound-a-week standard of life set up as the ideal, but it is tacitly assumed that that is how working-class people really *do* live. The major facts are simply not faced. It is admitted, for instance, that people sometimes lose their jobs; but then the dark clouds roll away and they get better jobs instead. No mention of unemployment as something permanent and inevitable, no mention of the dole, no mention of trade unionism. No suggestion anywhere that there can be anything wrong with the system *as a system*; there are only individual misfortunes, which are generally due to somebody's wickedness and can in any case be put right in the last chapter. Always the dark clouds roll away, the kind employer raises Alfred's wages, and there are jobs for everybody except the drunks. It is still the world of the *Wizard* and the *Gem,* except that there are orange-blossoms instead of machine-guns.

The outlook inculcated by all these papers is that of a rather exceptionally stupid member of the Navy League[10] in the year 1910. Yes, it may be said, but what does it matter? And in any case, what else do you expect?

Of course no one in his senses would want to turn the so-called penny dreadful into a realistic novel or a Socialist tract. An adventure story must of its nature be more or less remote from real life. But, as I have tried to make clear, the unreality of the *Wizard* and the *Gem* is not so artless as it looks. These papers exist because of a specialised demand, because boys at certain ages find it necessary to read about Martians, death-rays, grizzly bears and gangsters. They get what they are looking for, but they get it wrapped up in the illusions which their future employers think suitable for them. To what extent people draw their ideas from fiction is disputable. Personally I believe that most people are influenced far more than they would care to admit by novels, serial stories, films and so forth, and that from this point of view the worst books are often the most important, because they are usually the ones that are read earliest in life. It is probable that many people who would consider themselves extremely sophisticated and "advanced" are actually carrying through life an imaginative background which they acquired in childhood from (for instance) Sapper and Ian Hay.[11] If that is so, the boys' twopenny weeklies are of the deepest importance. Here is the stuff that is read somewhere between the ages of twelve and eighteen by a very large proportion, perhaps an actual majority, of English boys, including many who will never read anything else except newspapers; and along with it they are absorbing a set of beliefs which would be regarded as hopelessly out of date in the Central Office of the Conservative Party. All the better because it is done indirectly, there is being pumped into them the conviction that the major problems of our time do not exist, that there is nothing wrong with *laissez-faire* capitalism, that foreigners are unimportant comics and that the British Empire is a sort of charity-concern which will last for ever. Considering who owns these papers, it is difficult to believe that this is unintentional. Of the twelve papers I have been discussing (*i.e.* twelve including the *Thriller* and *Detective Weekly*) seven are the property of the Amalgamated Press, which is one of the biggest press-combines in the world and controls more than a hundred different papers. The *Gem* and *Magnet,* therefore, are closely linked up with the *Daily Telegraph* and the *Financial Times.* This in itself would be enough to rouse certain suspicions, even if it were not obvious that the stories in the boys' weeklies are politically vetted. So it appears that if you feel the need of a fantasy-life in which you travel to Mars and fight lions bare-handed (and what boy doesn't?), you can only have it by delivering yourself over, mentally, to people like Lord Camrose. For there is no competition.[12] Throughout the whole of this run of papers the differences are negligible, and on this level no others exist. This raises the question, why is there no such thing as a left-wing boys' paper?

At first glance such an idea merely makes one slightly sick. It is so horribly easy to imagine what a left-wing boys' paper would be like, if it existed. I remember in 1920 or 1921 some optimistic person handing round Communist tracts among a crowd of public-school boys. The tract I received was of the question-and-answer kind:

> *Q.* "Can a Boy Communist be a Boy Scout, Comrade?"
> *A.* "No, Comrade."
> *Q.* "Why, Comrade?"
> *A.* "Because, Comrade, a Boy Scout must salute the Union Jack, which is the symbol of tyranny and oppression."
> Etc. etc.

Now, suppose that at this moment somebody started a left-wing paper deliberately aimed at boys of twelve or fourteen. I do not suggest that the whole of its contents would be exactly like the tract I have quoted above, but does anyone doubt that they would be *something* like it? Inevitably such a paper would either consist of dreary uplift or it would be under Communist influence and given over to adulation of Soviet Russia; in either case no normal boy would ever look at it. Highbrow literature apart, the whole of the existing left-wing Press, in so far as it is at all vigorously "left," is one long tract. The one Socialist paper in England which could live a week on its merits *as a paper* is the *Daily Herald*: and how much Socialism is there in the *Daily Herald*? At this moment, therefore, a paper with a "left" slant and at the same time likely to have an appeal to ordinary boys in their teens is something almost beyond hoping for.

But it does not follow that it is impossible. There is no clear reason why every adventure story should necessarily be mixed up with snobbishness and gutter patriotism. For, after all, the stories in the *Hotspur* and the *Modern Boy* are not Conservative tracts; they are merely adventure stories with a Conservative bias. It is fairly easy to imagine the process being reversed. It is possible, for instance, to imagine a paper as thrilling and lively as the *Hotspur*, but with subject-matter and "ideology" a little more up to date. It is even possible (though this raises other difficulties) to imagine a women's paper at the same literary level as the *Oracle*, dealing in approximately the same kind of story, but taking rather more account of the realities of working-class life. Such things have been done before, though not in England. In the last years of the Spanish monarchy there was a large output in Spain of left-wing novelettes, some of them evidently of Anarchist origin. Unfortunately at the time when they were appearing I did not see their social significance, and I lost the collection of them that I had, but no doubt copies would still be procurable. In get-up and style of story they were very similar to the English fourpenny novelette, except that their inspiration was "left." If, for instance, a story described police pursuing Anarchists through the mountains, it would be from the point of view of the Anarchists and not of the police. An example nearer to hand is the Soviet film *Chapaiev,*[13] which has been shown a number of times in London. Technically, by the standards of the time when it was made, *Chapaiev* is a first-rate film, but mentally, in spite of the unfamiliar Russian background, it is not so very remote from Hollywood. The one thing that lifts it out of the ordinary is the remarkable performance by the actor who takes the part of the White officer (the fat one)—a performance which looks very like an inspired piece of gagging. Otherwise the atmosphere is familiar. All the usual paraphernalia is there—heroic fight against odds, escape at the last moment, shots of galloping horses, love interest, comic relief. The film is in fact a fairly ordinary one, except that its tendency is "left." In a Hollywood film of the Russian Civil War the Whites would probably be angels and the Reds demons. In the Russian version the Reds are angels and the Whites demons. That also is a lie, but, taking the long view, it is a less pernicious lie than the other.

Here several difficult problems present themselves. Their general nature is obvious enough, and I do not want to discuss them. I am merely pointing to the fact that, in England, popular imaginative literature is a field that left-wing thought has never begun to enter. *All* fiction from the novels in the mushroom libraries downwards is censored in the interests of the ruling class. And boys' fiction above all, the blood-and-thunder stuff which nearly every boy devours at some time or other, is sodden in the worst illusions of 1910. The fact is only unimportant if one believes that what is read in childhood leaves no impression behind. Lord Camrose and his colleagues evidently believe nothing of the kind, and, after all, Lord Camrose ought to know.

Inside the Whale

Inside the Whale, March 11, 1940

I

When Henry Miller's novel, *Tropic of Cancer,* appeared in 1935, it was greeted with rather cautious praise, obviously conditioned in some cases by a fear of seeming to enjoy pornography. Among the people who praised it were T. S. Eliot, Herbert Read, Aldous Huxley, John dos Passos, Ezra Pound—on the whole, not the writers who are in fashion at this moment. And in fact the subject-matter of the book, and to a certain extent its mental atmosphere, belong to the 'twenties rather than to the 'thirties.

Tropic of Cancer is a novel in the first person, or autobiography in the form of a novel, whichever way you like to look at it. Miller himself insists that it is straight autobiography, but the tempo and method of telling the story are those of a novel. It is a story of the American Paris, but not along quite the usual lines, because the Americans who figure in it happen to be people without money. During the boom years, when dollars were plentiful and the exchange-value of the franc was low, Paris was invaded by such a swarm of artists, writers, students, dilettanti, sight-seers, debauchees and plain idlers as the world has probably never seen. In some quarters of the town the so-called artists must actually have outnumbered the working population—indeed, it has been reckoned that in the late 'twenties there were as many as 30,000 painters in Paris, most of them impostors. The populace had grown so hardened to artists that gruff-voiced Lesbians in corduroy breeches and young men in Grecian or medieval costume could walk the streets without attracting a glance, and along the Seine banks by Notre Dame it was almost impossible to pick one's way between the sketching-stools. It was the age of dark horses and neglected genii; the phrase on everybody's lips was "*Quand je serai lancé.*" As it turned out, nobody was "lancé," the slump descended like another Ice Age, the cosmopolitan mob of artists vanished, and the huge Montparnasse cafés which only ten years ago were filled till the small hours by hordes of shrieking poseurs have turned into darkened tombs in which there are not even any ghosts. It is this world—described in, among other novels, Wyndham Lewis's *Tarr*[1]—that Miller is writing about, but he is dealing only with the under side of it, the lumpenproletarian fringe which has been able to survive the slump because it is composed partly of genuine artists and partly of genuine scoundrels. The neglected genii, the paranoiacs who are always "going to" write the novel that will knock Proust into a cocked hat, are there, but they are only genii in the rather rare moments when they are not scouting about for the next meal. For the most part it is a story of bug-ridden rooms in workingmen's hotels, of fights, drinking bouts, cheap brothels, Russian refugees, cadging, swindling and temporary jobs. And the whole atmosphere of the poor quarters of Paris as a foreigner sees them—the cobbled alleys, the sour reek of refuse, the bistros with their greasy zinc counters and worn brick floors, the green waters of the Seine, the blue cloaks of the Republican Guard, the crumbling iron urinals, the peculiar sweetish smell of the Metro stations, the cigarettes that come to pieces, the pigeons in the Luxembourg Gardens—it is all there, or at any rate the feeling of it is there.

On the face of it no material could be less promising. When *Tropic of Cancer* was published the Italians were marching into Abyssinia and Hitler's concentration-camps were already bulging.

The intellectual foci of the world were Rome, Moscow and Berlin. It did not seem to be a moment at which a novel of outstanding value was likely to be written about American dead-beats cadging drinks in the Latin Quarter. Of course a novelist is not obliged to write directly about contemporary history, but a novelist who simply disregards the major public events of the moment is generally either a footler or a plain idiot. From a mere account of the subject-matter of *Tropic of Cancer* most people would probably assume it to be no more than a bit of naughty-naughty left over from the 'twenties. Actually, nearly everyone who read it saw at once that it was nothing of the kind, but a very remarkable book. How or why remarkable? That question is never easy to answer. It is better to begin by describing the impression that *Tropic of Cancer* has left on my own mind.

When I first opened *Tropic of Cancer* and saw that it was full of unprintable words, my immediate reaction was a refusal to be impressed. Most people's would be the same, I believe. Nevertheless, after a lapse of time the atmosphere of the book, besides innumerable details, seemed to linger in my memory in a peculiar way. A year later Miller's second book, *Black Spring,* was published. By this time *Tropic of Cancer* was much more vividly present in my mind than it had been when I first read it. My first feeling about *Black Spring* was that it showed a falling-off, and it is a fact that it has not the same unity as the other book. Yet after another year there were many passages in *Black Spring* that had also rooted themselves in my memory. Evidently these books are of the sort to leave a flavour behind them—books that "create a world of their own," as the saying goes. The books that do this are not necessarily good books, they may be good bad books like *Raffles*[2] or the *Sherlock Holmes* stories, or perverse and morbid books like *Wuthering Heights* or *The House with the Green Shutters.*[3] But now and again there appears a novel which opens up a new world not by revealing what is strange, but by revealing what is familiar. The truly remarkable thing about *Ulysses,* for instance, is the commonplaceness of its material. Of course there is much more in *Ulysses* than this, because Joyce is a kind of poet and also an elephantine pedant, but his real achievement has been to get the familiar onto paper. He dared—for it is a matter of *daring* just as much as of technique—to expose the imbecilities of the inner mind, and in doing so he discovered an America which was under everybody's nose. Here is a whole world of stuff which you have lived with since childhood, stuff which you supposed to be of its nature incommunicable, and somebody has managed to communicate it. The effect is to break down, at any rate momentarily, the solitude in which the human being lives. When you read certain passages in *Ulysses* you feel that Joyce's mind and your mind are one, that he knows all about you though he has never heard your name, that there exists some world outside time and space in which you and he are together. And though he does not resemble Joyce in other ways, there is a touch of this quality in Henry Miller. Not everywhere, because his work is very uneven, and sometimes, especially in *Black Spring,* tends to slide away into mere verbiage or into the squashy universe of the surrealists. But read him for five pages, ten pages, and you feel the peculiar relief that comes not so much from understanding as from *being understood.* "He knows all about me," you feel; "he wrote this specially for me." It is as though you could hear a voice speaking to you, a friendly American voice, with no humbug in it, no moral purpose, merely an implicit assumption that we are all alike. For the moment you have got away from the lies and simplifications, the stylised, marionnette-like quality of ordinary fiction, even quite good fiction, and are dealing with the recognisable experiences of human beings.

But what kind of experience? What kind of human beings? Miller is writing about the man in the street, and it is incidentally rather a pity that it should be a street full of brothels. That is the penalty of leaving your native land. It means transferring your roots into shallower soil. Exile is probably more damaging to a novelist than to a painter or even a poet, because its effect is to take him out of contact with working life and narrow down his range to the street, the café, the church, the brothel and the studio. On the whole, in Miller's books you are reading about people living the expatriate life, people drinking, talking, meditating and fornicating, not about people working, marrying and bringing up children; a pity, because he would have described the one set of activities as well as the other. In *Black Spring* there is a wonderful flashback of New York, the swarming Irish-infested New York of the O. Henry period, but the Paris scenes are the best, and, granted their utter worthlessness as social types, the drunks and dead-beats of the cafés are handled with a feeling for character and a mastery of technique that are unapproached in any at all recent novel. All of them are not only credible but completely familiar; you have the feeling that all their adventures have happened to yourself. Not that they are anything very startling in the way of adventures. Henry gets a job with a melancholy Indian student, gets another job at a dreadful French school during a cold snap when the lavatories are frozen solid, goes on drinking bouts in Le Havre with his friend Collins, the sea captain, goes to brothels where there are wonderful negresses, talks with his friend Van Norden, the novelist, who has got the great novel of the world in his head but can never bring himself to begin writing it. His friend Karl, on the verge of starvation, is picked up by a wealthy widow who wishes to marry him. There are interminable, Hamlet-like conversations in which Karl tries to decide which is worse, being hungry or sleeping with an old woman. In great detail he describes his visits to the widow, how he went to the hotel dressed in his best, how before going in he neglected to urinate, so that the whole evening was one long crescendo of torment, etc., etc. And after all, none of it is true, the widow doesn't even exist—Karl has simply invented her in order to make himself seem important. The whole book is in this vein, more or less. Why is it that these monstrous trivialities are so engrossing? Simply because the whole atmosphere is deeply familiar, because you have all the while the feeling that these things are happening to *you*. And you have this feeling because somebody has chosen to drop the Geneva language of the ordinary novel and drag the *real-politik* of the inner mind into the open. In Miller's case it is not so much a question of exploring the mechanisms of the mind as of owning up to everyday facts and everyday emotions. For the truth is that many ordinary people, perhaps an actual majority, do speak and behave in just the way that is recorded here. The callous coarseness with which the characters in *Tropic of Cancer* talk is very rare in fiction, but it is extremely common in real life; again and again I have heard just such conversations from people who were not even aware that they were talking coarsely. It is worth noticing that *Tropic of Cancer* is not a young man's book. Miller was in his forties when it was published, and though since then he has produced three or four others, it is obvious that this first book had been lived with for years. It is one of those books that are slowly matured in poverty and obscurity, by people who know what they have got to do and therefore are able to wait. The prose is astonishing, and in parts of *Black Spring* it is even better. Unfortunately I cannot quote; unprintable words occur almost everywhere. But get hold of *Tropic of Cancer*, get hold of *Black Spring* and read especially the first hundred pages. They give you an idea of what can still be done, even at this late date, with English prose. In them, English is treated as a spoken language, but spoken *without fear*, i.e., without fear of rhetoric or of the unusual or poetical word. The adjective has come back, after its ten years' exile. It is a flowing, swelling prose, a prose with rhythms in it, something quite different from the flat cautious statements and snackbar dialects that are now in fashion.

When a book like *Tropic of Cancer* appears, it is only natural that the first thing people notice should be its obscenity. Given our current notions of literary decency, it is not at all easy to approach an unprintable book with detachment. Either one is shocked and disgusted, or one is morbidly thrilled, or one is determined above all else not to be impressed. The last is probably the commonest reaction, with the result that unprintable books often get less attention than they deserve. It is rather the fashion to say that nothing is easier than to write an obscene book, that people only do it in order to get themselves talked about and make money, etc., etc. What makes it obvious that this is *not* the case is that books which are obscene in the police-court sense are distinctly uncommon. If there were easy money to be made out of dirty words, a lot more people would be making it. But, because "obscene" books do not appear very frequently, there is a tendency to lump them together, as a rule quite unjustifiably. *Tropic of Cancer* has been vaguely associated with two other books, *Ulysses* and *Voyage au Bout de la Nuit,*[4] but in neither case is there much resemblance. What Miller has in common with Joyce is a willingness to mention the inane squalid facts of everyday life. Putting aside differences of technique, the funeral scene in *Ulysses,* for instance, would fit into *Tropic of Cancer*; the whole chapter is a sort of confession, an *exposé* of the frightful inner callousness of the human being. But there the resemblance ends. As a novel, *Tropic of Cancer* is far inferior to *Ulysses.* Joyce is an artist, in a sense in which Miller is not and probably would not wish to be, and in any case he is attempting much more. He is exploring different states of consciousness, dream, reverie (the "bronze-by-gold" chapter), drunkenness, etc., and dovetailing them all into a huge complex pattern, almost like a Victorian "plot." Miller is simply a hard-boiled person talking about life, an ordinary American businessman with intellectual courage and a gift for words. It is perhaps significant that he *looks* exactly like everyone's idea of an American businessman. As for the comparison with *Voyage au Bout de la Nuit,* it is even further from the point. Both books use unprintable words, both are in some sense autobiographical, but that is all. *Voyage au Bout de la Nuit* is a book-with-a-purpose, and its purpose is to protest against the horror and meaninglessness of modern life—actually, indeed, of *life.* It is a cry of unbearable disgust, a voice from the cesspool. *Tropic of Cancer* is almost exactly the opposite. The thing has become so unusual as to seem almost anomalous, but it is the book of a man who is happy. So is *Black Spring,* though slightly less so, because tinged in places with nostalgia. With years of lumpenproletarian life behind him, hunger, vagabondage, dirt, failure, nights in the open, battles with immigration officers, endless struggles for a bit of cash, Miller finds that he is enjoying himself. Exactly the aspects of life that fill Céline with horror are the ones that appeal to him. So far from protesting, he is *accepting.* And the very word "acceptance" calls up his real affinity, another American, Walt Whitman.

But there is something rather curious in being Whitman in the nineteen-thirties. It is not certain that if Whitman himself were alive at this moment he would write anything in the least degree resembling *Leaves of Grass.* For what he is saying, after all, is "I accept," and there is a radical difference between acceptance now and acceptance then. Whitman was writing in a time of unexampled prosperity, but more than that, he was writing in a country where freedom was something more than a word. The democracy, equality and comradeship that he is always talking about are not remote ideals, but something that existed in front of his eyes.

In mid-nineteenth-century America men felt themselves free and equal, *were* free and equal, so far as that is possible outside a society of pure communism. There was poverty and there were even class-distinctions, but except for the Negroes there was no permanently submerged class. Everyone had inside him, like a kind of core, the knowledge that he could earn a decent living, and earn it without bootlicking. When you read about Mark Twain's Mississippi raftsmen and pilots, or Bret Harte's Western gold-miners, they seem more remote than the cannibals of the Stone Age. The reason is simply that they are free human beings. But it is the same even with the peaceful domesticated America of the Eastern states, the America of *Little Women, Helen's Babies* and "Riding Down from Bangor."[5] Life has a buoyant, carefree quality that you can feel as you read, like a physical sensation in your belly. It is this that Whitman is celebrating, though actually he does it very badly, because he is one of those writers who tell you what you ought to feel instead of making you feel it. Luckily for his beliefs, perhaps, he died too early to see the deterioration in American life that came with the rise of large-scale industry and the exploiting of cheap immigrant labour.

Miller's outlook is deeply akin to that of Whitman, and nearly everyone who has read him has remarked on this. *Tropic of Cancer* ends with an especially Whitmanesque passage, in which, after the lecheries, the swindles, the fights, the drinking bouts and the imbecilities, he simply sits down and watches the Seine flowing past, in a sort of mystical acceptance of the thing-as-it-is. Only, what is he accepting? In the first place, not America, but the ancient bone-heap of Europe, where every grain of soil has passed through innumerable human bodies. Secondly, not an epoch of expansion and liberty, but an epoch of fear, tyranny and regimentation. To say "I accept" in an age like our own is to say that you accept concentration-camps, rubber truncheons, Hitler, Stalin, bombs, aeroplanes, tinned food, machine-guns, putsches, purges, slogans, Bedaux belts,[6] gas-masks, submarines, spies, provocateurs, press-censorship, secret prisons, aspirins, Hollywood films and political murders. Not *only* those things, of course, but those things among others. And on the whole this is Henry Miller's attitude. Not quite always, because at moments he shows signs of a fairly ordinary kind of literary nostalgia. There is a long passage in the earlier part of *Black Spring,* in praise of the Middle Ages, which as prose must be one of the most remarkable pieces of writing in recent years, but which displays an attitude not very different from that of Chesterton. In *Max and the White Phagocytes*[7] there is an attack on modern American civilisation (breakfast cereals, cellophane, etc.) from the usual angle of the literary man who hates industrialism. But in general the attitude is "Let's swallow it whole." And hence the seeming preoccupation with indecency and with the dirty-handkerchief side of life. It is only seeming, for the truth is that life, ordinary everyday life, consists far more largely of horrors than writers of fiction usually care to admit. Whitman himself "accepted" a great deal that his contemporaries found unmentionable. For he is not only writing of the prairie, he also wanders through the city and notes the shattered skull of the suicide, the "grey sick faces of onanists," etc., etc. But unquestionably our own age, at any rate in Western Europe, is less healthy and less hopeful than the age in which Whitman was writing. Unlike Whitman, we live in a *shrinking* world. The "democratic vistas" have ended in barbed wire. There is less feeling of creation and growth, less and less emphasis on the cradle, endlessly rocking, more and more emphasis on the teapot, endlessly stewing. To accept civilisation *as it is* practically means accepting decay. It has ceased to be a strenuous attitude and become a passive attitude — even "decadent," if that word means anything.

But precisely because, in one sense, he is passive to experience, Miller is able to get nearer to the ordinary man than is possible to more purposive writers. For the ordinary man is also passive. Within a narrow circle (home life, and perhaps the trade union or local politics) he feels himself master of his fate, but against major events he is as helpless as against the elements. So far from endeavouring to influence the future, he simply lies down and lets things happen to him. During the past ten years literature has involved itself more and more deeply in politics, with the result that there is now less room in it for the ordinary man than at any time during the past two centuries. One can see the change in the prevailing literary attitude by comparing the books written about the Spanish Civil War with those written about the war of 1914–18. The immediately striking thing about the Spanish war books, at any rate those written in English, is their shocking dullness and badness. But what is more significant is that almost all of them, right-wing or left-wing, are written from a political angle, by cocksure partisans telling you what to think, whereas the books about the Great War were written by common soldiers or junior officers who did not even pretend to understand what the whole thing was about. Books like *All Quiet on the Western Front, Le Feu, A Farewell to Arms, Death of a Hero, Good-bye to All That, Memoirs of an Infantry Officer* and *A Subaltern on the Somme*[8] were written not by propagandists but by *victims.* They are saying in effect, "What the hell is all this about? God knows. All we can do is to endure." And though he is not writing about war, nor, on the whole, about unhappiness, this is nearer to Miller's attitude than the omniscience which is now fashionable. *The Booster,*[9] a short-lived periodical of which he was part-editor, used to describe itself in its advertisements as "non-political, non-educational, non-progressive, non-cooperative, non-ethical, non-literary, non-consistent, non-contemporary," and Miller's own work could be described in nearly the same terms. It is a voice from the crowd, from the underling, from the third-class carriage, from the ordinary, non-political, non-moral, passive man.

I have been using the phrase "ordinary man" rather loosely, and I have taken it for granted that the "ordinary man" exists, a thing now denied by some people. I do not mean that the people Miller is writing about constitute a majority, still less that he is writing about proletarians. No English or American novelist has as yet seriously attempted that. And again, the people in *Tropic of Cancer* fall short of being ordinary to the extent that they are idle, disreputable and more or less "artistic." As I have said already, this is a pity, but it is the necessary result of expatriation. Miller's "ordinary man" is neither the manual worker nor the suburban householder, but the derelict, the declassé, the adventurer, the American intellectual without roots and without money. Still, the experiences even of this type overlap fairly widely with those of more normal people. Miller has been able to get the most out of his rather limited material because he has had the courage to identify with it. The ordinary man, the "average sensual man," has been given the power of speech, like Balaam's ass.

It will be seen that this is something out of date, or at any rate out of fashion. The average sensual man is out of fashion. The passive, non-political attitude is out of fashion. Preoccupation with sex and truthfulness about the inner life are out of fashion. American Paris is out of fashion. A book like *Tropic of Cancer*, published at such a time, must be either a tedious preciosity or something unusual, and I think a majority of the people who have read it would agree that it is not the first. It is worth trying to discover just what this escape from the current literary fashion means. But to do that one has got to see it against its background—that is, against the general development of English literature in the twenty years since the Great War.

2

When one says that a writer is fashionable one practically always means that he is admired by people under thirty. At the beginning of the period I am speaking of, the years during and immediately after the war, the writer who had the deepest hold upon the thinking young was almost certainly Housman.[10] Among people who were adolescent in the years 1910–25, Housman had an influence which was enormous and is now not at all easy to understand. In 1920, when I was about seventeen, I probably knew the whole of *A Shropshire Lad* by heart. I wonder how much impression *A Shropshire Lad* makes at this moment on a boy of the same age and more or less the same cast of mind? No doubt he has heard of it and even glanced into it; it might strike him as rather cheaply clever—probably that would be about all. Yet these are the poems that I and my contemporaries used to recite to ourselves, over and over, in a kind of ecstasy, just as earlier generations had recited Meredith's "Love in a Valley," Swinburne's "Garden of Proserpine," etc., etc.

> With rue my heart is laden
> For golden friends I had,
> For many a rose-lipt maiden
> And many a lightfoot lad.
>
> By brooks too broad for leaping
> The lightfoot boys are laid;
> The rose-lipt girls are sleeping
> In fields where roses fade.

It just tinkles. But it did not seem to tinkle in 1920. Why does the bubble always burst? To answer that question one has to take account of the *external* conditions that make certain writers popular at certain times. Housman's poems had not attracted much notice when they were first published. What was there in them that appealed so deeply to a single generation, the generation born round about 1900?

In the first place, Housman is a "country" poet. His poems are full of the charm of buried villages, the nostalgia of place-names, Clunton and Clunbury, Knighton, Ludlow, "on Wenlock Edge," "in summer time on Bredon," thatched roofs and the jingle of smithies, the wild jonquils in the pastures, the "blue, remembered hills." War poems apart, English verse of the 1910–25 period is mostly "country." The reason no doubt was that the rentier-professional class was ceasing once and for all to have any real relationship with the soil; but at any rate there prevailed then, far more than now, a kind of snobbism of belonging to the country and despising the town. England at that time was hardly more an agricultural country than it is now, but before the light industries began to spread themselves it was easier to think of it as one. Most middle-class boys grew up within sight of a farm, and naturally it was the picturesque side of farm life that appealed to them—the ploughing, harvesting, stack-thrashing and so forth. Unless he has to do it himself a boy is not likely to notice the horrible drudgery of hoeing turnips, milking cows with chapped teats at four o'clock in the morning, etc., etc. Just before, just after and, for that matter, during the war was the great age of the "Nature poet," the heyday of Richard Jefferies and W. H. Hudson.[11] Rupert Brooke's "Grantchester," the star poem of 1913,[12] is nothing but an enormous gush of "country" sentiment, a sort of accumulated vomit from a stomach stuffed with place-names. Considered as a poem "Grantchester" is something worse than worthless, but as an illustration of what the thinking middle-class young of that period *felt* it is a valuable document.

Housman, however, did not enthuse over the rambler roses in

the week-ending spirit of Brooke and the others. The "country" motif is there all the time, but mainly as a background. Most of the poems have a quasi-human subject, a kind of idealised rustic, in reality Strephon or Corydon brought up to date. This in itself had a deep appeal. Experience shows that over-civilised people enjoy reading about rustics (key-phrase, "close to the soil") because they imagine them to be more primitive and passionate than themselves. Hence the "dark earth" novels of Sheila Kaye-Smith,[13] etc. And at that time a middle-class boy, with his "country" bias, would identify with an agricultural worker as he would never have thought of doing with a town worker. Most boys had in their minds a vision of an idealised ploughman, gypsy, poacher, or gamekeeper, always pictured as a wild, free, roving blade, living a life of rabbit-snaring, cockfighting, horses, beer and women. Masefield's *Everlasting Mercy*,[14] another valuable period-piece, immensely popular with boys round about the war years, gives you this vision in a very crude form. But Housman's Maurices and Terences could be taken seriously where Masefield's Saul Kane could not; on this side of him, Housman was Masefield with a dash of Theocritus. Moreover all his themes are adolescent—murder, suicide, unhappy love, early death. They deal with the simple, intelligible disasters that give you the feeling of being up against the "bedrock facts" of life:

The sun burns on the half-mown hill,
By now the blood has dried;
And Maurice amongst the hay lies still
And my knife is in his side.

And again:

They hang us now in Shrewsbury jail:
And whistles blow forlorn,

And trains all night groan on the rail
To men that die at morn.

It is all more or less in the same tune. Everything comes unstuck. "Dick lies long in the churchyard and Ned lies long in jail." And notice also the exquisite self-pity—the "nobody loves me" feeling:

The diamond drops adorning
The low mound on the lea,
Those are the tears of morning,
That weeps, but not for thee.[15]

Hard cheese, old chap! Such poems might have been written expressly for adolescents. And the unvarying sexual pessimism (the girl always dies or marries somebody else) seemed like wisdom to boys who were herded together in public schools and were half-inclined to think of women as something unattainable. Whether Housman ever had the same appeal for girls I doubt. In his poems the woman's point of view is not considered, she is merely the nymph, the siren, the treacherous half-human creature who leads you a little distance and then gives you the slip.

But Housman would not have appealed so deeply to the people who were young in 1920 if it had not been for another strain in him, and that was his blasphemous, antinomian, "cynical" strain. The fight that always occurs between the generations was exceptionally bitter at the end of the Great War; this was partly due to the war itself, and partly it was an indirect result of the Russian Revolution, but an intellectual struggle was in any case due at about that date. Owing probably to the ease and security of life in England, which even the war hardly disturbed, many people whose ideas were formed in the 'eighties or earlier had carried them quite unmodified into the nineteen-twenties. Meanwhile, so far as the younger generation was concerned, the official beliefs were dissolving like sand-castles. The slump in religious belief, for instance, was spectacular. For several years the old–young antagonism took on a quality of real hatred. What was left of the war generation had crept out of the massacre to find their elders still bellowing the slogans of 1914, and a slightly younger generation of boys were writhing under dirty-minded celibate schoolmasters. It was to these that Housman appealed, with his implied sexual revolt and his personal grievance against God. He was patriotic, it was true, but in a harmless old-fashioned way, to the tune of red coats and "God save the Queen" rather than steel helmets and "Hang the Kaiser." And he was satisfyingly anti-Christian—he stood for a kind of bitter, defiant paganism, a conviction that life is short and the gods are against you, which exactly fitted the prevailing mood of the young; and all in charming fragile verse that was composed almost entirely of words of one syllable.

It will be seen that I have discussed Housman as though he were merely a propagandist, an utterer of maxims and quotable "bits." Obviously he was more than that. There is no need to under-rate him now because he was overrated a few years ago. Although one gets into trouble nowadays for saying so, there is a number of poems ("Into my heart an air that kills," for instance, and "Is my team ploughing?") that are not likely to remain long out of favour. But at bottom it is always a writer's tendency, his "purpose," his "message," that makes him liked or disliked. The proof of this is the extreme difficulty of seeing any literary merit in a book that seriously damages your deepest beliefs. And no book is ever truly neutral. Some or other tendency is always discernible, in verse as much as in prose, even if it does no more than determine the form and the choice of imagery. But poets who attain wide popularity, like Housman, are as a rule definitely gnomic writers.

After the war, after Housman and the Nature-poets, there appears a group of writers of completely different tendency—Joyce, Eliot, Pound, Lawrence, Wyndham Lewis, Aldous Huxley, Lytton Strachey. So far as the middle and late 'twenties go, these are "the movement," as surely as the Auden–Spender group have been "the movement" during the past few years. It is true that not all of the gifted writers of the period can be fitted into the pattern. E. M. Forster, for instance, though he wrote his best book in 1923 or thereabouts, was essentially pre-war, and Yeats does not seem in either of his phases to belong to the 'twenties. Others who were still living, Moore, Conrad, Bennett, Wells, Norman Douglas,[16] had shot their bolt before the war ever happened. On the other hand, a writer who should be added to the group, though in the narrowly literary sense he hardly "belongs," is Somerset Maugham. Of course the dates do not fit exactly; most of these writers had already published books before the war, but they can be classified as post-war in the same sense that the younger men now writing are post-slump. Equally of course, you could read through most of the literary papers of the time without grasping that these people *are* "the movement." Even more then than at most times the big shots of literary journalism were busy pretending that the age-before-last had not come to an end. Squire ruled the *London Mercury,* Gibbs and Walpole[17] were the gods of the lending libraries, there was a cult of cheeriness and manliness, beer and cricket, briar pipes and monogamy, and it was at all times possible to earn a few guineas by writing an article denouncing "highbrows." But all the same it was the despised highbrows who had captured the young. The wind was blowing from Europe, and long before 1930 it had blown the beer-and-cricket school naked, except for their knighthoods.

But the first thing one would notice about the group of writers I have named above is that they do not look like a group. Moreover several of them would strongly object to being coupled with several of the others. Lawrence and Eliot were in reality antipathetic, Huxley worshipped Lawrence but was repelled by Joyce, most of the others would have looked down on Huxley, Strachey and Maugham, and Lewis attacked everyone in turn; indeed, his reputation as a writer rests largely on these attacks. And yet there is a certain temperamental similarity, evident enough now, though it would not have been so a dozen years ago. What it amounts to is *pessimism of outlook*. But it is necessary to make clear what is meant by pessimism.

If the keynote of the Georgian poets was "beauty of Nature," the keynote of the post-war writers would be "tragic sense of life." The spirit behind Housman's poems, for instance, is not tragic, merely querulous; it is hedonism disappointed. The same is true of Hardy, though one ought to make an exception of *The Dynasts*. But the Joyce–Eliot group come later in time, puritanism is not their main adversary, they are able from the start to "see through" most of the things that their predecessors had fought for. All of them are temperamentally hostile to the notion of "progress"; it is felt that progress not only doesn't happen, but *ought not* to happen. Given this general similarity, there are, of course, differences of approach between the writers I have named as well as very different degrees of talent. Eliot's pessimism is partly the Christian pessimism, which implies a certain indifference to human misery, partly a lament over the decadence of Western civilisation ("We are the hollow men, we are the stuffed men," etc., etc.), a sort of twilight-of-the-gods feeling, which finally leads him, in "Sweeney

Agonistes," for instance, to achieve the difficult feat of making modern life out to be worse than it is. With Strachey it is merely a polite eighteenth-century scepticism mixed up with a taste for debunking. With Maugham it is a kind of stoical resignation, the stiff upper lip of the pukka sahib somewhere East of Suez, carrying on with his job without believing in it, like an Antonine Emperor. Lawrence at first sight does not seem to be a pessimistic writer, because, like Dickens, he is a "change-of-heart" man and constantly insisting that life here and now would be all right if only you looked at it a little differently. But what he is demanding is a movement away from our mechanised civilisation, which is not going to happen, and which he knows is not going to happen. Therefore his exasperation with the present turns once more into idealisation of the past, this time a safely mythical past, the Bronze Age. When Lawrence prefers the Etruscans (*his* Etruscans) to ourselves it is difficult not to agree with him, and yet, after all, it is a species of defeatism, because that is not the direction in which the world is moving. The kind of life that he is always pointing to, a life centring round the simple mysteries—sex, earth, fire, water, blood—is merely a lost cause. All he has been able to produce, therefore, is a wish that things would happen in a way in which they are manifestly not going to happen. "A wave of generosity or a wave of death," he says, but it is obvious that there are no waves of generosity this side of the horizon. So he flees to Mexico, and then dies at forty-five, a few years before the wave of death gets going. It will be seen that once again I am speaking of these people as though they were not artists, as though they were merely propagandists putting a "message" across. And once again it is obvious that all of them are more than that. It would be absurd, for instance, to look on *Ulysses* as *merely* a show-up of the horror of modern life, the "dirty *Daily Mail* era," as Pound put it. Joyce actually is more of a "pure artist" than most writers. But

Ulysses could not have been written by someone who was merely dabbling with word-patterns; it is the product of a special vision of life, the vision of a Catholic who has lost his faith. What Joyce is saying is "Here is life without God. Just look at it!" and his technical innovations, important though they are, are there primarily to serve this purpose.

But what is noticeable about all these writers is that what "purpose" they have is very much up in the air. There is no attention to the urgent problems of the moment, above all no politics in the narrower sense. Our eyes are directed to Rome, to Byzantium, to Montparnasse, to Mexico, to the Etruscans, to the Subconscious, to the solar plexus—to everywhere except the places where things are actually happening. When one looks back at the 'twenties, nothing is queerer than the way in which every important event in Europe escaped the notice of the English intelligentsia. The Russian Revolution, for instance, all but vanishes from the English consciousness between the death of Lenin and the Ukraine famine—about ten years. Throughout those years Russia means Tolstoy, Dostoievski and exiled counts driving taxi-cabs. Italy means picture-galleries, ruins, churches and museums—but not Blackshirts. Germany means films, nudism and psychoanalysis—but not Hitler, of whom hardly anyone had heard till 1931. In "cultured" circles art-for-art's-saking extended practically to a worship of the meaningless. Literature was supposed to consist solely in the manipulation of words. To judge a book by its subject-matter was the unforgivable sin, and even to be aware of its subject-matter was looked on as a lapse of taste. About 1928, in one of the three genuinely funny jokes that *Punch* has produced since the Great War, an intolerable youth is pictured informing his aunt that he intends to "write." "And what are you going to write about, dear?" asks the aunt. "My dear aunt," says the youth crushingly, "one doesn't write *about* anything, one just *writes*." The best writers of the 'twenties did not subscribe to this doctrine, their "purpose" is in most cases fairly overt, but it is usually a "purpose" along moral-religious-cultural lines. Also, when translatable into political terms, it is in no case "left." In one way or another the tendency of all the writers in this group is conservative. Lewis, for instance, spent years in frenzied witch-smellings after "Bolshevism," which he was able to detect in very unlikely places. Recently he has changed some of his views, perhaps influenced by Hitler's treatment of artists, but it is safe to bet that he will not go very far leftward. Pound seems to have plumped definitely for Fascism, at any rate the Italian variety. Eliot has remained aloof, but if forced at the pistol's point to choose between Fascism and some more democratic form of Socialism, would probably choose Fascism. Huxley starts off with the usual despair-of-life, then, under the influence of Lawrence's "dark abdomen," tries something called Life-Worship, and finally arrives at pacifism—a tenable position, and at this moment an honourable one, but probably in the long run involving rejection of Socialism. It is also noticeable that most of the writers in this group have a certain tenderness for the Catholic Church, though not usually of a kind that an orthodox Catholic would accept.

The mental connexion between pessimism and a reactionary outlook is no doubt obvious enough. What is perhaps less obvious is just *why* the leading writers of the 'twenties were predominantly pessimistic. Why always the sense of decadence, the skulls and cactuses, the yearning after lost faith and impossible civilisations? Was it not, after all, *because* these people were writing in an exceptionally comfortable epoch? It is just in such times that "cosmic despair" can flourish. People with empty bellies never despair of the universe, nor even think about the universe, for that matter. The whole period 1910–30 was a prosperous one, and even the war years were physically tolerable if one happened to be a noncombatant in one of the Allied countries. As for the 'twenties, they were the golden age of the rentier-intellectual, a period of irresponsibility such as the world had never before seen. The war was over, the new totalitarian states had not arisen, moral and religious tabus of all descriptions had vanished, and the cash was rolling in. "Disillusionment" was all the fashion. Everyone with a safe £500 a year turned highbrow and began training himself in *taedium vitae.* It was an age of eagles and of crumpets,[18] facile despairs, backyard Hamlets, cheap return tickets to the end of the night. In some of the minor characteristic novels of the period, books like *Told by an Idiot,*[19] the despair-of-life reaches a Turkish-bath atmosphere of self-pity. And even the best writers of the time can be convicted of a too Olympian attitude, a too great readiness to wash their hands of the immediate practical problem. They see life very comprehensively, much more so than those who come immediately before or after them, but they see it through the wrong end of the telescope. Not that that invalidates their books, as books. The first test of any work of art is survival, and it is a fact that a great deal that was written in the period 1910–30 has survived and looks like continuing to survive. One has only to think of *Ulysses, Of Human Bondage,*[20] most of Lawrence's early work, especially his short stories, and virtually the whole of Eliot's poems up to about 1930, to wonder what is now being written that will wear so well.

But quite suddenly, in the years 1930–35, something happens. The literary climate changes. A new group of writers, Auden and Spender and the rest of them, has made its appearance, and although technically these writers owe something to their predecessors, their "tendency" is entirely different. Suddenly we have got out of the twilight of the gods into a sort of Boy Scout atmosphere of bare knees and community singing. The typical literary man ceases to be a cultured expatriate with a leaning towards the Church, and becomes an eager-minded schoolboy with a leaning towards Communism. If the keynote of the writers of the 'twenties is "tragic sense of life," the keynote of the new writers is "serious purpose."

The differences between the two schools are discussed at some length in Mr. Louis MacNeice's book *Modern Poetry.*[21] This book is, of course, written entirely from the angle of the younger group and takes the superiority of their standards for granted. According to Mr. MacNeice:

> The poets of *New Signatures,** unlike Yeats and Eliot, are emotionally partisan. Yeats proposed to turn his back on desire and hatred; Eliot sat back and watched other people's emotions with ennui and an ironical self-pity . . . The whole poetry, on the other hand, of Auden, Spender and Day-Lewis implies that they have desires and hatreds of their own and, further, that they think some things *ought* to be desired and others hated.

And again:

> The poets of *New Signatures* have swung back . . . to the Greek preference for information or statement. The first requirement is to have something to say, and after that you must say it as well as you can.

In other words, "purpose" has come back, the younger writers have "gone into politics." As I have pointed out already, Eliot & Co. are not really so non-partisan as Mr. MacNeice seems to suggest. Still, it is broadly true that in the 'twenties the literary em-

*Published in 1932 [Orwell's footnote]. Edited by Michael (William Edward) Roberts (1902–1948).

phasis was more on technique and less on subject-matter than it is now.

The leading figures in this group are Auden, Spender, Day-Lewis, MacNeice, and there is a long string of writers of more or less the same tendency, Isherwood, John Lehmann, Arthur Calder-Marshall, Edward Upward, Alec Brown, Philip Henderson, and many others. As before, I am lumping them together simply according to tendency. Obviously there are very great variations in talent. But when one compares these writers with the Joyce–Eliot generation, the immediately striking thing is how much easier it is to form them into a group. Technically they are closer together, politically they are almost indistinguishable, and their criticisms of one another's work have always been (to put it mildly) good natured. The outstanding writers of the 'twenties were of very varied origins, few of them had passed through the ordinary English educational mill (incidentally, the best of them, barring Lawrence, were not Englishmen), and most of them had had at some time to struggle against poverty, neglect, and even downright persecution. On the other hand, nearly all the younger writers fit easily into the public-school–university–Bloomsbury pattern. The few who are of proletarian origin are of the kind that is declassed early in life, first by means of scholarships and then by the bleaching-tub of London "culture." It is significant that several of the writers in this group have been not only boys but, subsequently, masters at public schools. Some years ago I described Auden as "a sort of gutless Kipling."[22] As criticism this was quite unworthy, indeed it was merely a spiteful remark, but it is a fact that in Auden's work, especially his earlier work, an atmosphere of uplift—something rather like Kipling's "If" or Newbolt's "Play up, Play up, and Play the Game!"—never seems to be very far away. Take, for instance, a poem like "You're leaving now, and it's up to you boys."[23] It is pure scoutmaster, the exact note of the ten-minutes' straight talk on the dangers of self-abuse. No doubt there is an element of parody that he intends, but there is also a deeper resemblance that he does not intend. And of course the rather priggish note that is common to most of these writers is a symptom of release. By throwing "pure art" overboard they have freed themselves from the fear of being laughed at and vastly enlarged their scope. The prophetic side of Marxism, for example, is new material for poetry and has great possibilities:

> We are nothing.
> We have fallen
> Into the dark and shall be destroyed.
> Think though, that in this darkness
> We hold the secret hub of an idea
> Whose living sunlit wheel revolves in future years outside.
>
> (Spender, *Trial of a Judge*)[24]

But at the same time, by being Marxised literature has moved no nearer to the masses. Even allowing for the time-lag, Auden and Spender are somewhat farther from being popular writers than Joyce and Eliot, let alone Lawrence. As before, there are many contemporary writers who are outside the current, but there is not much doubt about what *is* the current. For the middle and late 'thirties, Auden, Spender & Co. *are* "the movement," just as Joyce, Eliot & Co. were for the 'twenties. And the movement is in the direction of some rather ill-defined thing called Communism. As early as 1934 or 1935 it was considered eccentric in literary circles not to be more or less "left," and in another year or two there had grown up a left-wing orthodoxy that made a certain set of opinions absolutely *de rigueur* on certain subjects. The idea had begun to gain ground (vide Edward Upward[25] and others) that a writer must either be actively "left" or write badly. Between 1935 and 1939 the Communist Party had an almost irresistible fascination for any writer under forty. It became as normal to hear that so-and-so had "joined" as it had been a few years earlier, when Roman Catholicism was fashionable, to hear that so-and-so had "been received." For about three years, in fact, the central stream of English literature was more or less directly under Communist control. How was it possible for such a thing to happen? And at the same time, what is meant by "Communism"? It is better to answer the second question first.

The Communist movement in Western Europe began as a movement for the violent overthrow of capitalism, and degenerated within a few years into an instrument of Russian foreign policy. This was probably inevitable when the revolutionary ferment that followed the Great War had died down. So far as I know, the only comprehensive history of this subject in English is Franz Borkenau's book, *The Communist International.* What Borkenau's facts even more than his deductions make clear is that Communism could never have developed along its present lines if any real revolutionary feeling had existed in the industrialised countries. In England, for instance, it is obvious that no such feeling has existed for years past. The pathetic membership-figures of all extremist parties show this clearly. It is only natural, therefore, that the English Communist movement should be controlled by people who are mentally subservient to Russia and have no real aim except to manipulate British foreign policy in the Russian interest. Of course such an aim cannot be openly admitted, and it is this fact that gives the Communist Party its very peculiar character. The more vocal kind of Communist is in effect a Russian publicity agent posing as an international Socialist. It is a pose that is easily kept up at normal times, but becomes difficult in moments of crisis, because of the fact that the U.S.S.R. is no more scrupulous in its foreign policy than the rest of the Great Powers.

Alliances, changes of front, etc., which only make sense as part of the game of power politics have to be explained and justified in terms of international Socialism. Every time Stalin swaps partners, "Marxism" has to be hammered into a new shape. This entails sudden and violent changes of "line," purges, denunciations, systematic destruction of party literature, etc., etc. Every Communist is in fact liable at any moment to have to alter his most fundamental convictions, or leave the party. The unquestionable dogma of Monday may become the damnable heresy of Tuesday, and so on. This has happened at least three times during the past ten years. It follows that in any Western country a Communist Party is always unstable and usually very small. Its long-term membership really consists of an inner ring of intellectuals who have identified with the Russian bureaucracy, and a slightly larger body of working-class people who feel a loyalty towards Soviet Russia without necessarily understanding its policies. Otherwise there is only a shifting membership, one lot coming and another going with each change of "line."

In 1930 the English Communist Party was a tiny, barely legal organisation whose main activity was libelling the Labour Party. But by 1935 the face of Europe had changed, and left-wing politics changed with it. Hitler had risen to power and begun to rearm, the Russian five-year plans had succeeded, Russia had reappeared as a great military Power. As Hitler's three targets of attack were, to all appearances, Great Britain, France and the U.S.S.R., the three countries were forced into a sort of uneasy *rapprochement.* This meant that the English or French Communist was obliged to become a good patriot and imperialist—that is, to defend the very things he had been attacking for the past fifteen years. The Comintern slogans suddenly faded from red to pink. "World revolution" and "Social-fascism" gave way to "Defence of democracy" and "Stop Hitler!" The years 1935–39 were the period of anti-

Fascism and the Popular Front, the heyday of the Left Book Club, when red duchesses and "broad-minded" deans toured the battlefields of the Spanish war and Winston Churchill was the blue-eyed boy of the *Daily Worker*. Since then, of course, there has been yet another change of "line." But what is important for my purpose is that it was during the "anti-Fascist" phase that the younger English writers gravitated towards Communism.

The Fascism-democracy dogfight was no doubt an attraction in itself, but in any case their conversion was due at about that date. It was obvious that laissez-faire capitalism was finished and that there had got to be some kind of reconstruction; in the world of 1935 it was hardly possible to remain politically indifferent. But why did these young men turn towards anything so alien as Russian Communism? Why should *writers* be attracted by a form of Socialism that makes mental honesty impossible? The explanation really lies in something that had already made itself felt before the slump and before Hitler: middle-class unemployment.

Unemployment is not merely a matter of not having a job. Most people can *get* a job of sorts, even at the worst of times. The trouble was that by about 1930 there was no activity, except perhaps scientific research, the arts and left-wing politics, that a thinking person could believe in. The debunking of Western civilisation had reached its climax and "disillusionment" was immensely widespread. Who now could take it for granted to go through life in the ordinary middle-class way, as a soldier, a clergyman, a stockbroker, an Indian Civil Servant or what-not? And how many of the values by which our grandfathers lived could now be taken seriously? Patriotism, religion, the Empire, the family, the sanctity of marriage, the Old School Tie, birth, breeding, honour, discipline—anyone of ordinary education could turn the whole lot of them inside out in three minutes. But what do you achieve, after all, by getting rid of such primal things as patriotism and religion? You have not necessarily got rid of the need for *something to believe in.* There had been a sort of false dawn a few years earlier when numbers of young intellectuals, including several quite gifted writers (Evelyn Waugh, Christopher Hollis and others), had fled into the Catholic Church. It is significant that these people went almost invariably to the Roman Church and not, for instance, to the C. of E., the Greek Church or the Protestant sects. They went, that is, to the Church with a world-wide organisation, the one with a rigid discipline, the one with power and prestige behind it. Perhaps it is even worth noticing that the only latter-day convert of really first-rate gifts, Eliot, has embraced not Romanism but Anglo-Catholicism, the ecclesiastical equivalent of Trotskyism. But I do not think one need look farther than this for the reason why the young writers of the 'thirties flocked into or towards the Communist Party. It was simply something to believe in. Here was a church, an army, an orthodoxy, a discipline. Here was a Fatherland and—at any rate since 1935 or thereabouts—a Führer. All the loyalties and superstitions that the intellect had seemingly banished could come rushing back under the thinnest of disguises. Patriotism, religion, empire, military glory—all in one word, Russia. Father, king, leader, hero, saviour—all in one word, Stalin. God—Stalin. The devil—Hitler. Heaven—Moscow. Hell—Berlin. All the gaps were filled up. So, after all, the "Communism" of the English intellectual is something explicable enough. It is the patriotism of the deracinated.

But there is one other thing that undoubtedly contributed to the cult of Russia among the English intelligentsia during these years, and that is the softness and security of life in England itself. With all its injustices, England is still the land of habeas corpus, and the overwhelming majority of English people have no experience of violence or illegality. If you have grown up in that sort of atmosphere it is not at all easy to imagine what a despotic régime is like. Nearly all the dominant writers of the 'thirties belonged to the soft-boiled emancipated middle class and were too young to have effective memories of the Great War. To people of that kind such things as purges, secret police, summary executions, imprisonment without trial, etc., etc., are too remote to be terrifying. They can swallow totalitarianism *because* they have no experience of anything except liberalism. Look, for instance, at this extract from Mr. Auden's poem *Spain* (incidentally this poem is one of the few decent things that have been written about the Spanish war):

To-morrow for the young the poets exploding like bombs,
The walks by the lake, the weeks of perfect communion;
    To-morrow the bicycle races
Through the suburbs on summer evenings. But to-day the struggle.

To-day the deliberate increase in the chances of death,
The conscious acceptance of guilt in the necessary murder;
    To-day the expending of powers
On the flat ephemeral pamphlet and the boring meeting.

The second stanza is intended as a sort of tabloid picture of a day in the life of a "good party man." In the morning a couple of political murders, a ten-minutes' interlude to stifle "bourgeois" remorse, and then a hurried luncheon and a busy afternoon and evening chalking walls and distributing leaflets. All very edifying. But notice the phrase "necessary murder." It could only be written by a person to whom murder is at most a *word*. Personally I would not speak so lightly of murder. It so happens that I have seen the bodies of numbers of murdered men—I don't mean killed in battle, I mean murdered. Therefore I have some conception of what murder means—the terror, the hatred, the howling relatives, the post-mortems, the blood, the smells. To me, murder is something to be avoided. So it is to any ordinary person. The Hitlers and Stalins find murder necessary, but they don't advertise their callousness, and they don't speak of it as murder; it is "liquidation," "elimination" or some other soothing phrase. Mr. Auden's brand of amoralism is only possible if you are the kind of person who is always somewhere else when the trigger is pulled. So much of left-wing thought is a kind of playing with fire by people who don't even know that fire is hot. The war-mongering to which the English intelligentsia gave themselves up in the period 1935–39 was largely based on a sense of personal immunity. The attitude was very different in France, where the military service is hard to dodge and even literary men know the weight of a pack.

Towards the end of Mr. Cyril Connolly's recent book, *Enemies of Promise,*[26] there occurs an interesting and revealing passage. The first part of the book is, more or less, an evaluation of present-day literature. Mr. Connolly belongs exactly to the generation of the writers of "the movement," and with not many reservations their values are his values. It is interesting to notice that among prose-writers he admires chiefly those specialising in violence—the would-be tough American school, Hemingway, etc. The latter part of the book, however, is autobiographical and consists of an account, fascinatingly accurate, of life at a preparatory school and Eton in the years 1910–20. Mr. Connolly ends by remarking:

> Were I to deduce anything from my feelings on leaving Eton, it might be called *The Theory of Permanent Adolescence.* It is the theory that the experiences undergone by boys at the great public schools are so intense as to dominate their lives and to arrest their development.

When you read the second sentence in this passage, your natural impulse is to look for the misprint. Presumably there is a "not" left out, or something. But no, not a bit of it! He means it! And what is more, he is merely speaking the truth, in an inverted fashion. "Cultured" middle-class life has reached a depth of softness at which a public-school education—five years in a lukewarm bath of snobbery—can actually be looked back upon as an eventful period. To nearly all the writers who have counted during the 'thirties, what more has ever happened than Mr. Connolly records in *Enemies of Promise*? It is the same pattern all the time; public school, university, a few trips abroad, then London. Hunger, hardship, solitude, exile, war, prison, persecution, manual labour—hardly even words. No wonder that the huge tribe known as "the right left people" found it so easy to condone the purge-and-Ogpu side of the Russian régime and the horrors of the first Five-Year Plan. They were so gloriously incapable of understanding what it all meant.

By 1937 the whole of the intelligentsia was mentally at war. Left-wing thought had narrowed down to "anti-Fascism," i.e., to a negative, and a torrent of hate-literature directed against Germany and the politicians supposedly friendly to Germany was pouring from the Press. The thing that, to me, was truly frightening about the war in Spain was not such violence as I witnessed, nor even the party feuds behind the lines, but the immediate reappearance in left-wing circles of the mental atmosphere of the Great War. The very people who for twenty years had sniggered over their own superiority to war hysteria were the ones who rushed straight back into the mental slum of 1915. All the familiar war-time idiocies, spy-hunting, orthodoxy-sniffing (Sniff, sniff. Are you a good anti-Fascist?), the retailing of incredible atrocity-stories, came back into vogue as though the intervening years had never happened. Before the end of the Spanish war, and even before Munich, some of the better of the left-wing writers were beginning to squirm. Neither Auden nor, on the whole, Spender wrote about the Spanish war in quite the vein that was expected of them. Since then there has been a change of feeling and much dismay and confusion, because the actual course of events has made nonsense of the left-wing orthodoxy of the last few years. But then it did not need very great acuteness to see that much of it was nonsense from the start. There is no certainty, therefore, that the next orthodoxy to emerge will be any better than the last.

On the whole the literary history of the 'thirties seems to justify the opinion that a writer does well to keep out of politics. For any writer who accepts or partially accepts the discipline of a political party is sooner or later faced with the alternative: toe the line, or shut up. It is, of course, possible to toe the line and go on writing—after a fashion. Any Marxist can demonstrate with the greatest of ease that "bourgeois" liberty of thought is an illusion. But when he has finished his demonstration there remains the psychological *fact* that without this "bourgeois" liberty the creative powers wither away. In the future a totalitarian literature may arise, but it will be quite different from anything we can now imagine. Literature as we know it is an individual thing, demanding mental honesty and a minimum of censorship. And this is even truer of prose than of verse. It is probably not a coincidence that the best writers of the 'thirties have been poets. The atmosphere of orthodoxy is always damaging to prose, and above all it is completely ruinous to the novel, the most anarchical of all forms of literature. How many Roman Catholics have been good novelists? Even the handful one could name have usually been bad Catholics. The novel is practically a Protestant form of art; it is a product of the free mind, of the autonomous individual. No decade in the past hundred and fifty years has been so barren of imaginative prose as the nineteen-thirties. There have been good poems, good sociological works, brilliant pamphlets, but practically no fiction of any value at all. From 1933 onwards the mental climate was increasingly against it. Anyone sensitive enough to be touched by the *zeitgeist* was also involved in politics. Not everyone, of course, was definitely *in* the political racket, but practically everyone was on its periphery and more or less mixed up in propaganda-campaigns and squalid controversies. Communists and near-Communists had a disproportionately large influence in the literary reviews. It was a time of labels, slogans and evasions. At the worst moments you were expected to lock yourself up in a constipating little cage of lies; at the best a sort of voluntary censorship ("Ought I to say this? is it pro-Fascist?") was at work in nearly everyone's mind. It is almost inconceivable that good novels should be written in such an atmosphere. Good novels are not written by orthodoxy-sniffers, nor by people who are conscience-stricken about their own unorthodoxy. Good novels are written by people who are *not frightened.* This brings me back to Henry Miller.

3

If this were a likely moment for the launching of "schools" of literature, Henry Miller might be the starting-point of a new "school." He does at any rate mark an unexpected swing of the pendulum. In his books one gets right away from the "political animal" and back to a viewpoint not only individualistic but completely passive—the viewpoint of a man who believes the world-process to be outside his control and who in any case hardly wishes to control it.

I first met Miller at the end of 1936, when I was passing through Paris on my way to Spain. What most intrigued me about him was to find that he felt no interest in the Spanish war whatever. He merely told me in forcible terms that to go to Spain at that moment was the act of an idiot. He could understand anyone going there from purely selfish motives, out of curiosity, for instance, but to mix oneself up in such things *from a sense of obligation* was sheer stupidity. In any case my ideas about combating Fascism, defending democracy, etc., etc., were all boloney. Our civilisation was destined to be swept away and replaced by something so different that we should scarcely regard it as human—a prospect that did not bother him, he said. And some such outlook is implicit throughout his work. Everywhere there is the sense of the approaching cataclysm, and almost everywhere the implied belief that it doesn't matter. The only political declaration which, so far as I know, he has ever made in print is a purely negative one. A year or so ago an American magazine, the *Marxist Quarterly,* sent out a questionnaire to various American writers asking them to define their attitude on the subject of war. Miller replied in terms of extreme pacifism, but a merely personal pacifism, an individual refusal to fight, with no apparent wish to convert others to the same opinion—practically, in fact, a declaration of irresponsibility.

However, there is more than one kind of irresponsibility. As a rule, writers who do not wish to identify themselves with the historical process of the moment either ignore it or fight against it. If they can ignore it, they are probably fools. If they can understand it well enough to want to fight against it, they probably have enough vision to realise that they cannot win. Look, for instance, at a poem like "The Scholar Gypsy,"[27] with its railing against the "strange disease of modern life" and its magnificent defeatist simile in the final stanza. It expresses one of the normal literary attitudes, perhaps actually the prevailing attitude during the last hundred years. And on the other hand there are the "progressives," the yea-sayers, the Shaw–Wells type, always leaping forward to embrace the ego-projections which they mistake for the future. On the whole the writers of the 'twenties took the first line and the writers of the 'thirties the second. And at any given moment, of course, there is a huge tribe of Barries and Deepings and

Dells[28] who simply don't notice what is happening. Where Miller's work is symptomatically important is in its avoidance of any of these attitudes. He is neither pushing the world-process forward nor trying to drag it back, but on the other hand he is by no means ignoring it. I should say that he believes in the impending ruin of Western civilisation much more firmly than the majority of "revolutionary" writers; only he does not feel called upon to do anything about it. He is fiddling while Rome is burning, and, unlike the enormous majority of people who do this, fiddling with his face towards the flames.

In *Max and the White Phagocytes* there is one of those revealing passages in which a writer tells you a great deal about himself while talking about somebody else. The book includes a long essay on the diaries of Anaïs Nin, which I have never read, except for a few fragments, and which I believe have not been published.[29] Miller claims that they are the only truly feminine writing that has ever appeared, whatever that may mean. But the interesting passage is one in which he compares Anaïs Nin—evidently a completely subjective, introverted writer—to Jonah in the whale's belly. In passing he refers to an essay that Aldous Huxley wrote some years ago about El Greco's picture, "The Dream of Philip the Second."[30] Huxley remarks that the people in El Greco's pictures always look as though they were in the bellies of whales, and professes to find something peculiarly horrible in the idea of being in a "visceral prison." Miller retorts that, on the contrary, there are many worse things than being swallowed by whales, and the passage makes it clear that he himself finds the idea rather attractive. Here he is touching upon what is probably a very widespread fantasy. It is perhaps worth noticing that everyone, at least every English-speaking person, invariably speaks of Jonah and the *whale*. Of course the creature that swallowed Jonah was a fish, and is so described in the Bible (*Jonah* i. 17), but children naturally confuse it with a whale, and this fragment of baby-talk is habitually carried into later life—a sign, perhaps, of the hold that the Jonah myth has upon our imaginations. For the fact is that being inside a whale is a very comfortable, cosy, homelike thought. The historical Jonah, if he can be so called, was glad enough to escape, but in imagination, in day-dream, countless people have envied him. It is, of course, quite obvious why. The whale's belly is simply a womb big enough for an adult. There you are, in the dark, cushioned space that exactly fits you, with yards of blubber between yourself and reality, able to keep up an attitude of the completest indifference, no matter *what* happens. A storm that would sink all the battleships in the world would hardly reach you as an echo. Even the whale's own movements would probably be imperceptible to you. He might be wallowing among the surface waves or shooting down into the blackness of the middle seas (a mile deep, according to Herman Melville), but you would never notice the difference. Short of being dead, it is the final, unsurpassable stage of irresponsibility. And however it may be with Anaïs Nin, there is no question that Miller himself is inside the whale. All his best and most characteristic passages are written from the angle of Jonah, a willing Jonah. Not that he is especially introverted—quite the contrary. In his case the whale happens to be transparent. Only he feels no impulse to alter or control the process that he is undergoing. He has performed the essential Jonah act of allowing himself to be swallowed, remaining passive, *accepting*.

It will be seen what this amounts to. It is a species of quietism, implying either complete unbelief or else a degree of belief amounting to mysticism. The attitude is "*Je m'en fous*" or "Though He slay me, yet will I trust in Him,"[31] whichever way you like to look at it; for practical purposes both are identical, the moral in either case being "Sit on your bum." But in a time like ours, is this a defensible attitude? Notice that it is almost impossible to refrain from asking this question. At the moment of writing we are still in a period in which it is taken for granted that books ought always to be positive, serious and "constructive." A dozen years ago this idea would have been greeted with titters. ("My dear aunt, one doesn't write *about* anything, one just *writes.*") Then the pendulum swung away from the frivolous notion that art is merely technique, but it swung a very long distance, to the point of asserting that a book can only be "good" if it is founded on a "true" vision of life. Naturally the people who believe this also believe that they are in possession of the truth themselves. Catholic critics, for instance, tend to claim that books are only "good" when they are of Catholic tendency. Marxist critics make the same claim more boldly for Marxist books. For instance, Mr. Edward Upward ("A Marxist Interpretation of Literature," in *The Mind in Chains*[32]):

> Literary criticism which aims at being Marxist must . . . proclaim that no book written *at the present time* can be "good" unless it is written from a Marxist or near-Marxist viewpoint.

Various other writers have made similar or comparable statements. Mr. Upward italicises "at the present time" because he realises that you cannot, for instance, dismiss *Hamlet* on the ground that Shakespeare was not a Marxist. Nevertheless his interesting essay only glances very shortly at this difficulty. Much of the literature that comes to us out of the past is permeated by and in fact founded on beliefs (the belief in the immortality of the soul, for example) which now seem to us false and in some cases contemptibly silly. Yet it is "good" literature, if survival is any test. Mr. Upward would no doubt answer that a belief which was appropriate several centuries ago might be inappropriate and therefore stultifying now. But this does not get one much farther, because it assumes that in any age there will be *one* body of belief which is the current approximation to truth, and that the best literature of the time will be more or less in harmony with it. Actually no such uniformity has ever existed. In seventeenth-century England, for instance, there was a religious and political cleavage which distinctly resembled the left-right antagonism of today. Looking back, most modern people would feel that the bourgeois-Puritan viewpoint was a better approximation to truth than the Catholic-feudal one. But it is certainly not the case that all or even a majority of the best writers of the time were Puritans. And more than this, there exist "good" writers whose world-view would in *any* age be recognised as false and silly. Edgar Allan Poe is an example. Poe's outlook is at best a wild romanticism and at worst is not far from being insane in the literal clinical sense. Why is it, then, that stories like "The Black Cat," "The Tell-tale Heart," "The Fall of the House of Usher" and so forth, which might very nearly have been written by a lunatic, do not convey a feeling of falsity? Because they are true within a certain framework, they keep the rules of their own peculiar world, like a Japanese picture. But it appears that to write successfully about such a world you have got to believe in it. One sees the difference immediately if one compares Poe's *Tales* with what is, in my opinion, an insincere attempt to work up a similar atmosphere, Julian Green's *Minuit.*[33] The thing that immediately strikes one about *Minuit* is that there is no reason why any of the events in it should happen. Everything is completely arbitrary; there is no emotional sequence. But this is exactly what one does *not* feel with Poe's stories. Their maniacal logic, in its own setting, is quite convincing. When, for instance, the drunkard seizes the black cat and cuts its eye out with his penknife, one knows exactly *why* he did it, even to the point of feeling that one would have done the same oneself. It seems therefore that for a creative writer possession of the "truth" is less important than emotional sincerity. Even Mr. Upward would not claim that a writer needs nothing beyond a Marxist training. He also needs talent. But talent, apparently, is a matter of being able to *care,* of really *believing* in your beliefs, whether they are true or false. The difference between, for instance, Céline and Evelyn Waugh is a difference of emotional intensity. It is the difference between a genuine despair and a despair that is at least partly a pretence. And with this there goes another consideration which is perhaps less obvious: that there are occasions when an "untrue" belief is more likely to be sincerely held than a "true" one.

If one looks at the books of personal reminiscence written about the war of 1914–18, one notices that nearly all that have remained readable after a lapse of time are written from a passive, negative angle. They are the records of something completely meaningless, a nightmare happening in a void. That was not actually the truth about the war, but it was the truth about the individual reaction. The soldier advancing into a machine-gun barrage or standing waist-deep in a flooded trench knew only that here was an appalling experience in which he was all but helpless. He was likelier to make a good book out of his helplessness and his ignorance than out of a pretended power to see the whole thing in perspective. As for the books that were written during the war itself, the best of them were nearly all the work of people who simply turned their backs and tried not to notice that the war was happening. Mr. E. M. Forster[34] has described how in 1917 he read "Prufrock" and others of Eliot's early poems, and how it heartened him at such a time to get hold of poems that were "innocent of public-spiritedness":

> They sang of private disgust and diffidence, and of people who seemed genuine because they were unattractive or weak . . . Here was a protest, and a feeble one, and the more congenial for being feeble . . . He who could turn aside to

> complain of ladies and drawing-rooms preserved a tiny drop of our self-respect, he carried on the human heritage.

That is very well said. Mr. MacNeice, in the book I have referred to already, quotes this passage and somewhat smugly adds:

> Ten years later less feeble protests were to be made by poets and the human heritage carried on rather differently . . . The contemplation of a world of fragments becomes boring and Eliot's successors are more interested in tidying it up.

Similar remarks are scattered throughout Mr. MacNeice's book. What he wishes us to believe is that Eliot's "successors" (meaning Mr. MacNeice and his friends) have in some way "protested" more effectively than Eliot did by publishing "Prufrock" at the moment when the Allied armies were assaulting the Hindenburg Line. Just where these "protests" are to be found I do not know. But in the contrast between Mr. Forster's comment and Mr. MacNeice's lies all the difference between a man who knows what the 1914–18 war was like and a man who barely remembers it. The truth is that in 1917 there was nothing that a thinking and sensitive person could do, except to remain human, if possible. And a gesture of helplessness, even of frivolity, might be the best way of doing that. If I had been a soldier fighting in the Great War, I would sooner have got hold of "Prufrock" than *The First Hundred Thousand* or Horatio Bottomley's *Letters to the Boys in the Trenches.*[35] I should have felt, like Mr. Forster, that by simply standing aloof and keeping touch with pre-war emotions, Eliot was carrying on the human heritage. What a relief it would have been at such a time, to read about the hesitations of a middle-aged highbrow with a bald spot! So different from bayonet-drill! After the bombs and the food-queues and the recruiting-posters, a human voice! What a relief!

But, after all, the war of 1914–18 was only a heightened moment in an almost continuous crisis. At this date it hardly even needs a war to bring home to us the disintegration of our society and the increasing helplessness of all decent people. It is for this reason that I think that the passive, non-cooperative attitude implied in Henry Miller's work is justified. Whether or not it is an expression of what people *ought* to feel, it probably comes somewhere near to expressing what they *do* feel. Once again it is the human voice among the bomb-explosions, a friendly American voice, "innocent of public-spiritedness." No sermons, merely the subjective truth. And along those lines, apparently, it is still possible for a good novel to be written. Not necessarily an edifying novel, but a novel worth reading and likely to be remembered after it is read.

While I have been writing this book another European war has broken out. It will either last several years and tear Western civilisation to pieces, or it will end inconclusively and prepare the way for yet another war which will do the job once and for all. But war is only "peace intensified." What is quite obviously happening, war or no war, is the break-up of laissez-faire capitalism and of the liberal-Christian culture. Until recently the full implications of this were not foreseen, because it was generally imagined that Socialism could preserve and even enlarge the atmosphere of liberalism. It is now beginning to be realised how false this idea was. Almost certainly we are moving into an age of totalitarian dictatorships—an age in which freedom of thought will be at first a deadly sin and later on a meaningless abstraction. The autonomous individual is going to be stamped out of existence. But this means that literature, in the form in which we know it, must suffer at least a temporary death. The literature of liberalism is coming to an end and the literature of totalitarianism has not yet appeared and is barely imaginable. As for the writer, he is sitting on a melting iceberg; he is merely an anachronism, a hangover from the bourgeois age, as surely doomed as the hippopotamus. Miller seems to me a man out of the common because he saw and proclaimed this fact a long while before most of his contemporaries—at a time, indeed, when many of them were actually burbling about a renaissance of literature. Wyndham Lewis had said years earlier that the major history of the English language was finished, but he was basing this on different and rather trivial reasons. But from now onwards the all-important fact for the creative writer is going to be that this is not a writer's world. That does not mean that he cannot help to bring the new society into being, but he can take no part in the process *as a writer.* For *as a writer* he is a liberal, and what is happening is the destruction of liberalism. It seems likely, therefore, that in the remaining years of free speech any novel worth reading will follow more or less along the lines that Miller has followed—I do not mean in technique or subject-matter, but in implied outlook. The passive attitude will come back, and it will be more consciously passive than before. Progress and reaction have both turned out to be swindles. Seemingly there is nothing left but quietism—robbing reality of its terrors by simply submitting to it. Get inside the whale—or rather, admit that you are inside the whale (for you *are,* of course). Give yourself over to the world-process, stop fighting against it or pretending that you control it; simply accept it, endure it, record it. That seems to be the formula that any sensitive novelist is now likely to adopt. A novel on more positive, "constructive" lines, and not emotionally spurious, is at present very difficult to imagine.

But do I mean by this that Miller is a "great author," a new hope for English prose? Nothing of the kind. Miller himself would be the last to claim or want any such thing. No doubt he will go on writing—anybody who has once started always goes on writing—and associated with him there is a number of writers of approximately the same tendency, Lawrence Durrell, Michael Fraenkel[36] and others, almost amounting to a "school." But he himself seems to me essentially a man of one book. Sooner or later I should expect him to descend into unintelligibility, or into charlatanism; there are signs of both in his later work. His last book, *Tropic of Capricorn,* I have not even read. This was not because I did not want to read it, but because the police and customs authorities have so far managed to prevent me from getting hold of it. But it would surprise me if it came anywhere near *Tropic of Cancer* or the opening chapters of *Black Spring.* Like certain other autobiographical novelists, he had it in him to do just one thing perfectly, and he did it. Considering what the fiction of the nineteen-thirties has been like, that is something.

Miller's books are published by the Obelisk Press in Paris. What will happen to the Obelisk Press, now that war has broken out and Jack Kahane,[37] the publisher, is dead, I do not know, but at any rate the books are still procurable. I earnestly counsel anyone who has not done so to read at least *Tropic of Cancer.* With a little ingenuity, or by paying a little over the published price, you can get hold of it, and even if parts of it disgust you, it will stick in your memory. It is also an "important" book, in a sense different from the sense in which that word is generally used. As a rule novels are spoken of as "important" when they are either a "terrible indictment" of something or other or when they introduce some technical innovation. Neither of these applies to *Tropic of Cancer.* Its importance is merely symptomatic. Here in my opinion is the only imaginative prose-writer of the slightest value who has appeared among the English-speaking races for some years past. Even if that is objected to as an overstatement, it will probably be admitted that

Miller is a writer out of the ordinary, worth more than a single glance; and, after all, he is a completely negative, unconstructive, amoral writer, a mere Jonah, a passive accepter of evil, a sort of Whitman among the corpses. Symptomatically, that is more significant than the mere fact that five thousand novels are published in England every year and four thousand nine hundred of them are tripe. It is a demonstration of the *impossibility* of any major literature until the world has shaken itself into its new shape.

Drama Reviews

Time and Tide, June 8, 1940

The Tempest by William Shakespeare; The Old Vic

If there is really such a thing as turning in one's grave, Shakespeare must get a lot of exercise. The production of *The Tempest* at the Old Vic has no doubt given him another nasty jolt, though one must admire the enterprise of the managers in putting it on at such a moment.

Why is it that Shakespeare is nearly always acted in a way that makes anyone who cares for him squirm? The real fault lies not with the actors but with the audiences. These plays have to be performed in front of people who for the most part have no acquaintance with Elizabethan English and are therefore incapable of following any but the simplest passages. The tragedies, which are better-known than the others and in any case are chock-full of murders, often succeed reasonably well, but the comedies and the best of the histories (*Henry IV* and *Henry V*), especially their prose interludes, are hopeless, because nine-tenths of the people watching don't know the text and can be counted on to miss the point of any joke that is not followed up by a kick on the buttocks. All that the actors can do is to gabble their lines at top speed and throw in as much horseplay as possible, well knowing that if the audience ever laughs it will be at a gag and not at anything that Shakespeare wrote. *The Tempest* at the Old Vic was no exception. All the Stephano and Trinculo scenes were ruined by the usual clowning and roaring on the stage, not to mention the noise and fidgeting which seem to be a cherished tradition with Old Vic audiences. As for Ariel and Caliban, they looked like something that had escaped from a circus. Admittedly these are difficult parts to cast, but there was no need to make them quite so grotesque as was done on this occasion. Caliban was got up definitely as a monkey, complete with tail and, apparently, with some disgusting disease of the face. This would have ruined the effect of his lines even if he had spoken them more musically. Ariel, although for some reason he was painted bright blue, was horribly whimsical and indulged in exaggeratedly homosexual mannerisms, a sort of Peter Pansy.

John Gielgud, as a middle-aged rather than elderly Prospero, with the minimum of abracadabra, gave a performance that was a long way ahead of the rest of the company. Miss Jessica Tandy, as Miranda, spoke her lines well, but was wrongly cast for the part. No Miranda ought to have blue eyes and fair hair, any more than Cordelia ought to have dark hair. The best feature of the evening was the incidental music, which fitted the romantic setting of the play a great deal better than did the scenery. All in all, a well-intentioned performance, but demonstrating once again that Shakespeare, except for about half a dozen well-known plays, will remain unactable until the general public takes to reading him.

The Peaceful Inn by Denis Ogden; Duke of York's

An uncanny play possibly owing something to *Outward Bound.* Six travellers find themselves stranded by chance at a country inn which in fact does not exist, and a murder which happened there exactly a year earlier is re-enacted in front of them. As a result the various personal problems which brought them there are solved. The dialogue is convincing and the mysterious atmosphere is well worked up, but the play's weakness is that the problems of the six main personages are of such a nature that it is impossible to take them seriously. The clergyman has lost his faith because his brother died of pneumonia, the young society beauty finds her life hollow, etc., etc. Although cast in 1940, the play makes no reference to the war, direct or indirect; bourgeois peacetime life, with all interest centring round financial success, motor-cars, divorce, etc., is apparently looked upon as something eternal. Miss Louise Hampton gave a very fine performance as Joanna Spring, successful journalist and editor of the Women's Page ("Write to Auntie Madge about it"), and the acting as a whole was worthy of better material.

Film Review

Time and Tide, December 21, 1940

The Great Dictator; Prince of Wales,
Gaumont Haymarket, Marble Arch Pavilion

France, 1918, Charlie Chaplin, in field grey and German steel helmet, is pulling the string of Big Bertha, falling down every time she fires. A little later, losing his way in the smoke screen, he finds himself attacking in the middle of the American infantry. Later he is in flight with a wounded staff officer, in an aeroplane which flies upside down for such lengths of time that Charlie is puzzled to know why his watch persists in standing up on the end of its chain. Finally, falling out of the aeroplane into a mud-hole, he loses his memory and is shut up in a mental home for twenty years, completely ignorant of what is happening in the world outside.

At this point the film really begins. Hynkel, Dictator of Tomania, who happens to be Charlie's double (Chaplin plays both parts) is directing an extra-special purge against the Jews at the moment when Charlie, his mind restored, escapes from the asylum and goes back to his little barber's shop in the Ghetto. There are some glorious scenes of fights against Storm Troopers which are not less, perhaps actually *more* moving because the tragedy of wrecked Jewish households is mixed up with the kind of humour that depends on mishaps with pails of whitewash and blows on the head with a frying-pan. But the best farcical interludes are those that take place in the Dictator's palace, especially in his scenes with his hated rival, Napaloni, Dictator of Bacteria. (Jack

Oakie, in this part, has an even closer physical resemblance to Mussolini than Chaplin has to Hitler.) There is a lovely moment at the supper table when Hynkel is so intent on outwitting Napaloni that he does not notice that he is ladling mustard on to his strawberries by mistake for cream. The invasion of Osterlich (Austria) is about to take place, and Charlie, who has been incarcerated for resisting the Storm Troopers, escapes from the concentration camp in a stolen uniform just at the moment when Hynkel is due to cross the frontier. He is mistaken for the Dictator and carried into the capital of the conquered country amid cheering crowds. The little Jewish barber finds himself raised upon an enormous rostrum, with serried ranks of Nazi dignitaries behind him and thousands of troops below, all waiting to hear his triumphal speech.

And here occurs the big moment of the film. Instead of making the speech that is expected of him, Charlie makes a powerful fighting speech in favour of democracy, tolerance, and common decency. It is really a tremendous speech, a sort of version of Lincoln's Gettysburg address done into Hollywood English, one of the strongest pieces of propaganda I have heard for a long time. It is, of course, understating the matter to say that it is out of tune with the rest of the film. It has no connection with it whatever, except the sort of connection that exists in a dream—the kind of dream, for instance, in which you are Emperor of China at one moment and a dormouse the next. So completely is the thread broken that after that the story can go no further, and the film simply fades out, leaving it uncertain whether the speech takes effect or whether the Nazis on the platform detect the impostor and shoot him dead on the spot.

How good a film is this, simply as a film? I should be falsifying my own opinion if I did not admit that it has very great faults. Although it is good at almost every level it exists at so many levels that it has no more unity than one finds, for instance, in a pantomime. Some of the early scenes are simply the old Chaplin of the two-reelers of thirty years ago, bowler hat, shuffling walk and all. The Ghetto scenes are sentimental comedy with a tendency to break into farce, the scenes between Hynkel and Napaloni are the lowest kind of slapstick, and mixed up with all this is a quite serious political "message." Chaplin never seems to have profited by certain modern advances of technique, so that all his films have a kind of jerkiness, an impression of being tied together with bits of string. Yet this film gets away with it. The hard-boiled audience of the press show to which I went laughed almost continuously and were visibly moved by the great speech at the end. What is Chaplin's peculiar gift? It is his power to stand for a sort of concentrated essence of the common man, for the ineradicable belief in decency that exists in the hearts of ordinary people, at any rate in the West. We live in a period in which democracy is almost everywhere in retreat, supermen in control of three-quarters of the world, liberty explained away by sleek professors, Jew-baiting defended by pacifists. And yet everywhere, under the surface, the common man sticks obstinately to the beliefs that he derives from the Christian culture. The common man is wiser than the intellectuals, just as animals are wiser than men. Any intellectual can make you out a splendid "case" for smashing the German Trade Unions and torturing the Jews. But the common man, who has no intellect, only instinct and tradition, knows that "it isn't right." Anyone who has not lost his moral sense—and an education in Marxism and similar creeds consists largely in destroying your moral sense—knows that "it isn't right" to march into the houses of harmless little Jewish shopkeepers and set fire to their furniture. More than in any humorous trick, I believe, Chaplin's appeal lies in his power to reassert the fact, overlaid by Fascism and, ironically enough, by Socialism, that *vox populi is vox Dei*[1] and giants are vermin.

No wonder that Hitler, from the moment he came to power, has banned Chaplin's films in Germany! The resemblance between the two men (almost twins, it is interesting to remember) is ludicrous, especially in the wooden movements of their arms. And no wonder that pro-Fascist writers of the type of Wyndham Lewis and Roy Campbell have always pursued Chaplin with such a peculiar venomous hatred! From the point of view of anyone who believes in supermen, it is a most disastrous accident that the greatest of all the supermen should be almost the double of an absurd little Jewish foundling with a tendency to fall into pails of whitewash. It is the sort of fact that ought to be kept dark. However, luckily, it can't be kept dark, and the allure of power politics will be a fraction weaker for every human being who sees this film.

If our Government had a little more imagination they would subsidize *The Great Dictator* heavily and would make every effort to get a few copies into Germany—a thing that ought not to be beyond human ingenuity. At present it is opening at three West End picture houses whose seats the majority of people cannot afford. But though it will probably get a mixed reception from the critics, I think it is safe to prophesy for it the nationwide success it deserves. Apart from Chaplin himself, Jack Oakie, Henry Daniell (as Goebbels), Maurice Moscovitch and the exceptionally attractive Paulette Goddard supply the best of the acting.

Wells, Hitler and the World State

Horizon, August 1941

"In March or April, say the wiseacres, there is to be a stupendous knockout blow at Britain. . . . What Hitler has to do it with, I cannot imagine. His ebbing and dispersed military resources are now probably not so very much greater than the Italians' before they were put to the test in Greece and Africa."

"The German air power has been largely spent. It is behind the times and its first-rate men are mostly dead or disheartened or worn out."

"In 1914 the Hohenzollern army was the best in the world. Behind that screaming little defective in Berlin there is nothing of the sort. . . . Yet our military 'experts' discuss the waiting phantom. In their imaginations it is perfect in its equipment and invincible in discipline. Sometimes it is to strike a decisive 'blow' through Spain and North Africa and on, or march through the Balkans, march from the Danube to Ankara, to Persia, to India, or 'crush Russia,' or 'pour' over the Brenner into Italy. The weeks pass and the phantom does none of these things—for one excellent reason. It does not exist to that extent. Most of such inadequate guns and munitions as it possessed must have been taken away from it and fooled away in Hitler's silly feints to invade Britain.

> And its raw jerry-built discipline is wilting under the creeping realisation that the Blitzkrieg is spent, and the war is coming home to roost."

These quotations are not taken from the *Cavalry Quarterly* but from a series of newspaper articles by Mr. H. G. Wells, written at the beginning of this year and now reprinted in a book entitled *Guide to the New World.* Since they were written, the German Army has overrun the Balkans and reconquered Cyrenaica, it can march through Turkey or Spain at such time as may suit it, and it has undertaken the invasion of Russia. How that campaign will turn out I do not know, but it is worth noticing that the German general staff, whose opinion is probably worth something, would not have begun it if they had not felt fairly certain of finishing it within three months. So much for the idea that the German Army is a bogey, its equipment inadequate, its morale breaking down, etc. etc.

What has Wells to set against the "screaming little defective in Berlin"? The usual rigmarole about a World State, plus the Sankey Declaration,[1] which is an attempted definition of fundamental human rights, of anti-totalitarian tendency. Except that he is now especially concerned with federal world control of air power, it is the same gospel as he has been preaching almost without interruption for the past forty years, always with an air of angry surprise at the human beings who can fail to grasp anything so obvious.

What is the use of saying that we need federal world control of the air? The whole question is how we are to get it. What is the use of pointing out that a World State is desirable? What matters is that not one of the five great military powers would think of submitting to such a thing. All sensible men for decades past have been substantially in agreement with what Mr. Wells says; but the sensible men have no power and, in too many cases, no disposition to sacrifice themselves. Hitler is a criminal lunatic, and Hitler has an army of millions of men, aeroplanes in thousands, tanks in tens of thousands. For his sake a great nation has been willing to overwork itself for six years and then to fight for two years more, whereas for the common-sense, essentially hedonistic world-view which Mr. Wells puts forward, hardly a human creature is willing to shed a pint of blood. Before you can even talk of world reconstruction, or even of peace, you have got to eliminate Hitler, which means bringing into being a dynamic not necessarily the same as that of the Nazis, but probably quite as unacceptable to "enlightened" and hedonistic people. What has kept England on its feet during the past year? In part, no doubt, some vague idea about a better future, but chiefly the atavistic emotion of patriotism, the ingrained feeling of the English-speaking peoples that they are superior to foreigners. For the last twenty years the main object of English left-wing intellectuals has been to break this feeling down, and if they had succeeded, we might be watching the S.S. men patrolling the London streets at this moment. Similarly, why are the Russians fighting like tigers against the German invasion? In part, perhaps, for some half-remembered ideal of Utopian Socialism, but chiefly in defence of Holy Russia (the "sacred soil of the Fatherland," etc. etc.), which Stalin has revived in an only slightly altered form. The energy that actually shapes the world springs from emotions—racial pride, leader-worship, religious belief, love of war—which liberal intellectuals mechanically write off as anachronisms, and which they have usually destroyed so completely in themselves as to have lost all power of action.

The people who say that Hitler is Antichrist, or alternatively, the Holy Ghost, are nearer an understanding of the truth than the intellectuals who for ten dreadful years have kept it up that he is merely a figure out of comic opera, not worth taking seriously. All that this idea really reflects is the sheltered conditions of English life. The Left Book Club was at bottom a product of Scotland

Yard, just as the Peace Pledge Union is a product of the Navy. One development of the last ten years has been the appearance of the "political book," a sort of enlarged pamphlet combining history with political criticism, as an important literary form. But the best writers in this line—Trotsky, Rauschning, Rosenberg, Silone, Borkenau, Koestler[2] and others—have none of them been Englishmen, and nearly all of them have been renegades from one or other extremist party, who have seen totalitarianism at close quarters and known the meaning of exile and persecution. Only in the English-speaking countries was it fashionable to believe, right up to the outbreak of war, that Hitler was an unimportant lunatic and the German tanks made of cardboard. Mr. Wells, it will be seen from the quotations I have given above, believes something of the kind still. I do not suppose that either the bombs or the German campaign in Greece have altered his opinion. A lifelong habit of thought stands between him and an understanding of Hitler's power.

Mr. Wells, like Dickens, belongs to the non-military middle class. The thunder of guns, the jingle of spurs, the catch in the throat when the old flag goes by, leave him manifestly cold. He has an invincible hatred of the fighting, hunting, swashbuckling side of life, symbolised in all his early books by a violent propaganda against horses. The principal villain of his *Outline of History* is the military adventurer, Napoleon. If one looks through nearly any book that he has written in the last forty years one finds the same idea constantly recurring: the supposed antithesis between the man of science who is working towards a planned World State and the reactionary who is trying to restore a disorderly past. In novels, Utopias, essays, films, pamphlets, the antithesis crops up, always more or less the same. On the one side science, order, progress, internationalism, aeroplanes, steel, concrete, hygiene: on the other side war, nationalism, religion, monarchy, peasants,

Greek professors, poets, horses. History as he sees it is a series of victories won by the scientific man over the romantic man. Now, he is probably right in assuming that a "reasonable," planned form of society, with scientists rather than witch-doctors in control, will prevail sooner or later, but that is a different matter from assuming that it is just round the corner. There survives somewhere or other an interesting controversy which took place between Wells and Churchill at the time of the Russian Revolution. Wells accuses Churchill of not really believing his own propaganda about the Bolsheviks being monsters dripping with blood, etc., but of merely fearing that they were going to introduce an era of common sense and scientific control, in which flag-wavers like Churchill himself would have no place. Churchill's estimate of the Bolsheviks, however, was nearer the mark than Wells's. The early Bolsheviks may have been angels or demons, according as one chooses to regard them, but at any rate they were not sensible men. They were not introducing a Wellsian Utopia but a Rule of the Saints, which, like the English Rule of the Saints, was a military despotism enlivened by witchcraft trials. The same misconception reappears in an inverted form in Wells's attitude to the Nazis. Hitler is all the warlords and witch-doctors in history rolled into one. Therefore, argues Wells, he is an absurdity, a ghost from the past, a creature doomed to disappear almost immediately. But unfortunately the equation of science with common sense does not really hold good. The aeroplane, which was looked forward to as a civilising influence but in practice has hardly been used except for dropping bombs, is the symbol of that fact. Modern Germany is far more scientific than England, and far more barbarous. Much of what Wells has imagined and worked for is physically there in Nazi Germany. The order, the planning, the State encouragement of science, the steel, the concrete, the aeroplanes, are all there, but all in the service of ideas appropriate to the Stone Age. Science is fighting on the side of superstition. But obviously it is impossible for Wells to accept this. It would contradict the world-view on which his own works are based. The war-lords and the witch-doctors *must* fail, the common-sense World State, as seen by a nineteenth-century Liberal whose heart does not leap at the sound of bugles, *must* triumph. Treachery and defeatism apart, Hitler *cannot* be a danger. That he should finally win would be an impossible reversal of history, like a Jacobite restoration.

But is it not a sort of parricide for a person of my age (thirty-eight) to find fault with H. G. Wells? Thinking people who were born about the beginning of this century are in some sense Wells's own creation. How much influence any mere writer has, and especially a "popular" writer whose work takes effect quickly, is questionable, but I doubt whether anyone who was writing books between 1900 and 1920, at any rate in the English language, influenced the young so much. The minds of all of us, and therefore the physical world, would be perceptibly different if Wells had never existed. Only, just the singleness of mind, the one-sided imagination that made him seem like an inspired prophet in the Edwardian age, make him a shallow, inadequate thinker now. When Wells was young, the antithesis between science and reaction was not false. Society was ruled by narrow-minded, profoundly incurious people, predatory business men, dull squires, bishops, politicians who could quote Horace but had never heard of algebra. Science was faintly disreputable and religious belief obligatory. Traditionalism, stupidity, snobbishness, patriotism, superstition and love of war seemed to be all on the same side; there was need of someone who could state the opposite point of view. Back in the nineteen-hundreds it was a wonderful experience for a boy to discover H. G. Wells. There you were, in a world of pedants, clergymen and golfers, with your future employers exhorting you to "get on or get out," your parents systematically warping your sexual life, and your dull-witted schoolmasters sniggering over their Latin tags; and here was this wonderful man who could tell you about the inhabitants of the planets and the bottom of the sea, and who *knew* that the future was not going to be what respectable people imagined. A decade or so before aeroplanes were technically feasible Wells knew that within a little while men would be able to fly. He knew that because he himself *wanted* to be able to fly, and therefore felt sure that research in that direction would continue. On the other hand, even when I was a little boy, at a time when the Wright brothers had actually lifted their machine off the ground for fifty-nine seconds, the generally accepted opinion was that if God had meant us to fly He would have given us wings. Up to 1914 Wells was in the main a true prophet. In physical details his vision of the new world has been fulfilled to a surprising extent.

But because he belonged to the nineteenth century and to a non-military nation and class, he could not grasp the tremendous strength of the old world which was symbolised in his mind by fox-hunting Tories. He was, and still is, quite incapable of understanding that nationalism, religious bigotry and feudal loyalty are far more powerful forces than what he himself would describe as sanity. Creatures out of the Dark Ages have come marching into the present, and if they are ghosts they are at any rate ghosts which need a strong magic to lay them. The people who have shown the best understanding of Fascism are either those who have suffered under it or those who have a Fascist streak in themselves. A crude book like *The Iron Heel,* written nearly thirty years ago, is a truer prophecy of the future than either *Brave New World* or *The Shape of Things to Come.* If one had to choose among Wells's own contemporaries a writer who could stand towards him as a corrective, one might choose Kipling, who was not deaf to the evil voices of power and military "glory." Kipling would have understood the appeal of Hitler, or for that matter of Stalin, whatever his attitude towards them might be. Wells is too sane to understand the modern world. The succession of lower-middle-class novels which are his greatest achievement stopped short at the other war and never really began again, and since 1920 he has squandered his talents in slaying paper dragons. But how much it is, after all, to have any talents to squander.

The Art of Donald McGill

Horizon, September 1941[1]

Who does not know the "comics" of the cheap stationers' windows, the penny or twopenny coloured post cards with their endless succession of fat women in tight bathing-dresses and their crude drawing and unbearable colours, chiefly hedge-sparrow's egg tint and Post Office red?

This question ought to be rhetorical, but it is a curious fact that many people seem to be unaware of the existence of these things, or else to have a vague notion that they are something to be found only at the seaside, like nigger minstrels or peppermint rock. Actually they are on sale everywhere—they can be bought at nearly any Woolworth's, for example—and they are evidently produced in enormous numbers, new series constantly appearing. They are not to be confused with the various other types of comic illustrated post card, such as the sentimental ones dealing with puppies and kittens or the Wendyish, sub-pornographic ones which exploit the love-affairs of children. They are a *genre* of their own, specialising in very "low" humour, the mother-in-law, baby's nappy, policemen's boots type of joke, and distinguishable from all the other kinds by having no artistic pretensions. Some half-dozen publishing houses issue them, though the people who draw them seem not to be numerous at any one time.

I have associated them especially with the name of Donald McGill because he is not only the most prolific and by far the best of contemporary post card artists, but also the most representative, the most perfect in the tradition. Who Donald McGill is, I do not know.[2] He is apparently a trade name, for at least one series of post cards is issued simply as "The Donald McGill Comics," but he is also unquestionably a real person with a style of drawing which is recognisable at a glance. Anyone who examines his post cards in bulk will notice that many of them are not despicable even as drawings, but it would be mere dilettantism to pretend that they have any direct æsthetic value. A comic post card is simply an illustration to a joke, invariably a "low" joke, and it stands or falls by its ability to raise a laugh. Beyond that it has only "ideological" interest. McGill is a clever draughtsman with a real caricaturist's touch in the drawing of faces, but the special value of his post cards is that they are so completely typical. They represent, as it were, the norm of the comic post card. Without being in the least imitative, they are exactly what comic post cards have been any time these last forty years, and from them the meaning and purpose of the whole *genre* can be inferred.

Get hold of a dozen of these things, preferably McGill's—if you pick out from a pile the ones that seem to you funniest, you will probably find that most of them are McGill's—and spread them out on a table. What do you see?

Your first impression is of overpowering vulgarity. This is quite apart from the ever-present obscenity, and apart also from the hideousness of the colours. They have an utter lowness of mental atmosphere which comes out not only in the nature of the jokes but, even more, in the grotesque, staring, blatant quality of the drawings. The designs, like those of a child, are full of heavy lines and empty spaces, and all the figures in them, every gesture and attitude, are deliberately ugly, the faces grinning and vacuous, the women monstrously parodied, with bottoms like Hottentots. Your second impression, however, is of indefinable familiarity. What do these things remind you of? What are they so like? In the first place, of course, they remind you of the barely different post cards which you probably gazed at in your childhood. But more than this, what you are really looking at is something as traditional as Greek tragedy, a sort of sub-world of smacked bottoms and scrawny mothers-in-law which is a part of Western European consciousness. Not that the jokes, taken one by one, are necessarily stale. Not being debarred from smuttiness, comic post cards repeat themselves less often than the joke columns in reputable magazines, but their basic subject-matter, the *kind* of joke they are aiming at, never varies. A few are genuinely witty, in a Max Millerish style. Examples:

> "I like seeing experienced girls home."
> "But I'm not experienced!"
> "You're not home yet!"

> "I've been struggling for years to get a fur coat. How did you get yours?"
> "I left off struggling."

> JUDGE: "You are prevaricating, sir. Did you or did you not sleep with this woman?"
> CO-RESPONDENT: "Not a wink, my lord!"

In general, however, they are not witty but humorous, and it must be said for McGill's post cards, in particular, that the drawing is often a good deal funnier than the joke beneath it. Obviously the outstanding characteristic of comic post cards is their obscenity, and I must discuss that more fully later. But I give here a rough analysis of their habitual subject-matter, with such explanatory remarks as seem to be needed:

Sex.—More than half, perhaps three-quarters, of the jokes are sex jokes, ranging from the harmless to the all but unprintable. First favourite is probably the illegitimate baby. Typical captions: "Could you exchange this lucky charm for a baby's feeding-bottle?" "She didn't ask me to the christening, so I'm not going to the wedding." Also newlyweds, old maids, nude statues and women in bathing-dresses. All of these are *ipso facto* funny, mere mention of them being enough to raise a laugh. The cuckoldry joke is very seldom exploited, and there are no references to homosexuality.

Conventions of the sex joke:

(i) Marriage only benefits the women. Every man is plotting seduction and every woman is plotting marriage. No woman ever remains unmarried voluntarily.

(ii) Sex-appeal vanishes at about the age of twenty-five. Well-preserved and good-looking people beyond their first youth are never represented. The amorous honeymooning couple reappear as the grim-visaged wife and shapeless, moustachioed, red-nosed husband, no intermediate stage being allowed for.

Home life.—Next to sex, the henpecked husband is the favourite joke. Typical caption: "Did they get an X-ray of your wife's jaw at the hospital?"—"No, they got a moving picture instead."

Conventions:

(i) There is no such thing as a happy marriage.

(ii) No man ever gets the better of a woman in argument.

Drunkenness.—Both drunkenness and teetotalism are *ipso facto* funny.

Conventions:
(i) All drunken men have optical illusions.
(ii) Drunkenness is something peculiar to middle-aged men. Drunken youths or women are never represented.

W.C. jokes.—There is not a large number of these. Chamberpots are *ipso facto* funny, and so are public lavatories. A typical post card, captioned "A Friend in Need," shows a man's hat blown off his head and disappearing down the steps of a ladies' lavatory.

Inter-working-class snobbery.—Much in these post cards suggests that they are aimed at the better-off working class and poorer middle class. There are many jokes turning on malapropisms, illiteracy, dropped aitches and the rough manners of slum-dwellers. Countless post cards show draggled hags of the stage-charwoman type exchanging "unladylike" abuse. Typical repartee: "I wish you were a statue and I was a pigeon!" A certain number produced since the war treat evacuation from the anti-evacuee angle. There are the usual jokes about tramps, beggars and criminals, and the comic maidservant appears fairly frequently. Also the comic navvy, bargee, etc.; but there are no anti Trade-Union jokes. Broadly speaking, everyone with much over or much under £5 a week is regarded as laughable. The "swell" is almost as automatically a figure of fun as the slum-dweller.

Stock figures.—Foreigners seldom or never appear. The chief locality joke is the Scotsman, who is almost inexhaustible. The lawyer is always a swindler, the clergyman always a nervous idiot who says the wrong thing. The "knut" or "masher" still appears, almost as in Edwardian days, in out-of-date-looking evening-clothes and an opera hat, or even with spats and a knobby cane. Another survival is the Suffragette, one of the big jokes of the pre-

1914 period and too valuable to be relinquished. She has reappeared, unchanged in physical appearance, as the Feminist lecturer or Temperance fanatic. A feature of the last few years is the complete absence of anti-Jew post cards. The "Jew joke," always somewhat more ill-natured than the "Scotch joke," disappeared abruptly soon after the rise of Hitler.

Politics.—Any contemporary event, cult or activity which has comic possibilities (for example, "free love," feminism, A.R.P.,[3] nudism) rapidly finds its way into the picture post cards, but their general atmosphere is extremely old-fashioned. The implied political outlook is a Radicalism appropriate to about the year 1900. At normal times they are not only not patriotic, but go in for a mild guying of patriotism, with jokes about "God save the King," the Union Jack, etc. The European situation only began to reflect itself in them at some time in 1939, and first did so through the comic aspects of A.R.P. Even at this date few post cards mention the war except in A.R.P. jokes (fat woman stuck in the mouth of Anderson shelter,[4] Wardens neglecting their duty while young woman undresses at window she has forgotten to black out, etc. etc.). A few express anti-Hitler sentiments of a not very vindictive kind. One, not McGill's, shows Hitler, with the usual hypertrophied backside, bending down to pick a flower. Caption: "What would *you* do, chums?" This is about as high a flight of patriotism as any post card is likely to attain. Unlike the twopenny weekly papers, comic post cards are not the product of any great monopoly company, and eventually they are not regarded as having any importance in forming public opinion. There is no sign in them of any attempt to induce an outlook acceptable to the ruling class.

Here one comes back to the outstanding, all-important feature of comic post cards—their obscenity. It is by this that everyone remembers them, and it is also central to their purpose, though not in a way that is immediately obvious.

A recurrent, almost dominant motif in comic post cards is the woman with the stuck-out behind. In perhaps half of them, or more than half, even when the point of the joke has nothing to do with sex, the same female figure appears, a plump "voluptuous" figure with the dress clinging to it as tightly as another skin and with breasts or buttocks grossly over-emphasised, according to which way it is turned. There can be no doubt that these pictures lift the lid off a very widespread repression, natural enough in a country whose women when young tend to be slim to the point of skimpiness. But at the same time the McGill post card—and this applies to all other post cards in this *genre*—is not intended as pornography but, a subtler thing, as a skit on pornography. The Hottentot figures of the women are caricatures of the Englishman's secret ideal, not portraits of it. When one examines McGill's post cards more closely, one notices that his brand of humour only has meaning in relation to a fairly strict moral code. Whereas in papers like *Esquire,* for instance, or *La Vie Parisienne,* the imaginary background of the jokes is always promiscuity, the utter breakdown of all standards, the background of the McGill post card is marriage. The four leading jokes are nakedness, illegitimate babies, old maids and newly married couples, none of which would seem funny in a really dissolute or even "sophisticated" society. The post cards dealing with honeymoon couples always have the enthusiastic indecency of those village weddings where it is still considered screamingly funny to sew bells to the bridal bed. In one, for example, a young bridegroom is shown getting out of bed the morning after his wedding night. "The first morning in our own little home, darling!" he is saying; "I'll go and get the milk and paper and bring you up a cup of tea." Inset is a picture of the front doorstep; on it are four newspapers and four bottles of milk.

This is obscene, if you like, but it is not immoral. Its implication—and this is just the implication [that] *Esquire* or the *New Yorker* would avoid at all costs—is that marriage is something profoundly exciting and important, the biggest event in the average human being's life. So also with jokes about nagging wives and tyrannous mothers-in-law. They do at least imply a stable society in which marriage is indissoluble and family loyalty taken for granted. And bound up with this is something I noted earlier, the fact that there are no pictures, or hardly any, of good-looking people beyond their first youth. There is the "spooning" couple and the middle-aged, cat-and-dog couple, but nothing in between. The liaison, the illicit but more or less decorous love-affair which used to be the stock joke of French comic papers, is not a post card subject. And this reflects, on a comic level, the working-class outlook which takes it as a matter of course that youth and adventure—almost, indeed, individual life—end with marriage. One of the few authentic class-differences, as opposed to class-distinctions, still existing in England is that the working classes age very much earlier. They do not live less long, provided that they survive their childhood, nor do they lose their physical activity earlier, but they do lose very early their youthful appearance. This fact is observable everywhere, but can be most easily verified by watching one of the higher age groups registering for military service; the middle- and upper-class members look, on average, ten years younger than the others. It is usual to attribute this to the harder lives that the working classes have to live, but it is doubtful whether any such difference now exists as would account for it. More probably the truth is that the working classes reach middle age earlier because they accept it earlier. For to look young after, say, thirty is largely a matter of wanting to do so. This generalisation is less true of the better-paid workers, especially those who live in council houses and labour-saving flats, but it is true enough even of them to point to a difference of outlook. And in this, as usual, they are more traditional, more in accord with the Christian past than the well-to-do women who try to stay young at forty by means of physical jerks, cosmetics and avoidance of child-bearing. The impulse to cling to youth at all costs, to attempt to preserve your sexual attraction, to see even in middle age a future for yourself and not merely for your children, is a thing of recent growth and has only precariously established itself. It will probably disappear again when our standard of living drops and our birth-rate rises. "Youth's a stuff will not endure" expresses the normal, traditional attitude. It is this ancient wisdom that McGill and his colleagues are reflecting, no doubt unconsciously, when they allow for no transition stage between the honeymoon couple and those glamourless figures, Mum and Dad.

I have said that at least half McGill's post cards are sex jokes, and a proportion, perhaps ten per cent, are far more obscene than anything else that is now printed in England. Newsagents are occasionally prosecuted for selling them, and there would be many more prosecutions if the broadest jokes were not invariably protected by double meanings. A single example will be enough to show how this is done. In one post card, captioned "They didn't believe her," a young woman is demonstrating, with her hands held apart, something about two feet long to a couple of open-mouthed acquaintances. Behind her on the wall is a stuffed fish in a glass case, and beside that is a photograph of a nearly naked athlete. Obviously it is not the fish that she is referring to, but this could never be proved. Now, it is doubtful whether there is any paper in England that would print a joke of this kind, and certainly there is no paper that does so habitually. There is an immense amount of pornography of a mild sort, countless illustrated papers cashing in on women's legs, but there is no popular literature specialising in the "vulgar," farcical aspect of sex. On the other hand, jokes exactly like McGill's are the ordinary small change of the revue and music-hall stage, and are also to be heard on the radio, at moments when the censor happens to be nodding. In England the gap between what can be said and what can be printed is rather exceptionally wide. Remarks and gestures which hardly anyone objects to on the stage would raise a public outcry if any attempt were made to reproduce them on paper. (Compare Max Miller's stage patter with his weekly column in the *Sunday Dispatch.*) The comic post cards are the only existing exception to this rule, the only medium in which really "low" humour is considered to be printable. Only in post cards and on the variety stage can the stuck-out behind, dog and lamp-post, baby's nappy type of joke be freely exploited. Remembering that, one sees what function these post cards, in their humble way, are performing.

What they are doing is to give expression to the Sancho Panza view of life, the attitude to life that Miss Rebecca West once summed up as "extracting as much fun as possible from smacking behinds in basement kitchens." The Don Quixote–Sancho Panza combination, which of course is simply the ancient dualism of body and soul in fiction form, recurs more frequently in the literature of the last four hundred years than can be explained by mere imitation. It comes up again and again, in endless variations, Bouvard and Pécuchet, Jeeves and Wooster, Bloom and Dedalus, Holmes and Watson (the Holmes-Watson variant is an exceptionally subtle one, because the usual physical characteristics of two partners have been transposed). Evidently it corresponds to something enduring in our civilisation, not in the sense that either character is to be found in a "pure" state in real life, but in the sense that the two principles, noble folly and base wisdom, exist side by side in nearly every human being. If you look into your own mind, which are you, Don Quixote or Sancho Panza? Almost certainly you are both. There is one part of you that wishes to be a hero or a saint, but another part of you is a little fat man who sees very clearly the advantages of staying alive with a whole skin. He is your unofficial self, the voice of the belly protesting against the soul. His tastes lie towards safety, soft beds, no work, pots of beer and women with "voluptuous" figures. He it is who punctures your fine attitudes and urges you to look after Number One, to be unfaithful to your wife, to bilk your debts, and so on and so forth. Whether you allow yourself to be influenced by him is a different question. But it is simply a lie to say that he is not part of you, just as it is a lie to say that Don Quixote is not part of you either, though most of what is said and written consists of one lie or the other, usually the first.

But though in varying forms he is one of the stock figures of literature, in real life, especially in the way society is ordered, his point of view never gets a fair hearing. There is a constant world-wide conspiracy to pretend that he is not there, or at least that he doesn't matter. Codes of law and morals, or religious systems, never have much room in them for a humorous view of life. Whatever is funny is subversive, every joke is ultimately a custard pie, and the reason why so large a proportion of jokes centre round obscenity is simply that all societies, as the price of survival, have to insist on a fairly high standard of sexual morality. A dirty joke is not, of course, a serious attack upon morality, but it is a sort of mental rebellion, a momentary wish that things were otherwise. So also with all other jokes, which always centre round cowardice, laziness, dishonesty or some other quality which society cannot afford to encourage. Society has always to demand a little more from human beings than it will get in practice. It has to demand faultless discipline and self-sacrifice, it must expect its subjects to work hard, pay their taxes, and be faithful to their wives, it must assume that men think it glorious to die on the battlefield and women want to wear themselves out with child-bearing. The whole of what one may call official literature is founded on such assumptions. I never read the proclamations of generals before battle, the speeches of führers and prime ministers, the solidarity songs of public schools and Left Wing political parties, national anthems, Temperance tracts, papal encyclicals and sermons against gambling and contraception, without seeming to hear in the background a chorus of raspberries from all the millions of common men to whom these high sentiments make no appeal. Nevertheless the high sentiments always win in the end, leaders who offer blood, toil, tears and sweat[5] always get more out of their followers than those who offer safety and a good time. When it comes to the pinch, human beings are heroic. Women face childbed and the scrubbing brush, revolutionaries keep their mouths shut in the torture chamber, battleships go down with their guns still firing when their decks are awash. It is only that the other element in man, the lazy, cowardly, debt-bilking adulterer who is inside all of us, can never be suppressed altogether and needs a hearing occasionally.

The comic post cards are one expression of his point of view, a humble one, less important than the music halls, but still worthy of attention. In a society which is still basically Christian they naturally concentrate on sex jokes; in a totalitarian society, if they had any freedom of expression at all, they would probably concentrate on laziness or cowardice, but at any rate on the unheroic in one form or another. It will not do to condemn them on the ground that they are vulgar and ugly. That is exactly what they are meant to be. Their whole meaning and virtue is in their unredeemed lowness, not only in the sense of obscenity, but lowness of outlook in every direction whatever. The slightest hint of "higher" influences would ruin them utterly. They stand for the worm's-eye view of life, for the music-hall world where marriage is a dirty joke or a comic disaster, where the rent is always behind and the clothes are always up the spout, where the lawyer is always a crook and the Scotsman always a miser, where the newlyweds make fools of themselves on the hideous beds of seaside lodging-houses and the drunken, red-nosed husbands roll home at four in the morning to meet the linen-nightgowned wives who wait for them behind the front door, poker in hand. Their existence, the fact that people want them, is symptomatically important. Like the music halls, they are a sort of saturnalia, a harmless rebellion against virtue. They express only one tendency in the human mind, but a tendency which is always there and will find its own outlet, like water. On the whole, human beings want to be good, but not too good, and not quite all the time. For:

> "there is a just man that perishes in his righteousness, and there is a wicked man that prolongeth his life in his wickedness. Be not righteous over much; neither make thyself over wise; why shouldst thou destroy thyself? Be not overmuch wicked, neither be thou foolish: why shouldst thou die before thy time?"[6]

In the past the mood of the comic post card could enter into the central stream of literature, and jokes barely different from McGill's could casually be uttered between the murders in Shakespeare's tragedies. That is no longer possible, and a whole category of humour, integral to our literature till 1800 or thereabouts, has dwindled down to these ill-drawn post cards, leading a barely legal existence in cheap stationers' windows. The corner of the human heart that they speak for might easily manifest itself in worse forms, and I for one should be sorry to see them vanish.

No, Not One

Review of *No Such Liberty* by Alex Comfort,
The Adelphi, October 1941

Mr. Murry said years ago that the works of the best modern writers, Joyce, Eliot and the like, simply demonstrated the *impossibility* of great art in a time like the present, and since then we have moved onwards into a period in which any sort of *joy* in writing, any such notion as telling a story for the purpose of pure entertainment, has also become impossible. All writing nowadays is propaganda. If, therefore, I treat Mr. Comfort's novel as a tract, I am only doing what he himself has done already. It is a good novel as novels go at this moment, but the motive for writing it was not what Trollope or Balzac, or even Tolstoy, would have recognised as a novelist's impulse. It was written in order to put forward the "message" of pacifism, and it was to fit that "message" that the main incidents in it were devised. I think I am also justified in assuming that it is autobiographical, not in the sense that the events described in it have actually happened, but in the sense that the author identifies himself with the hero, thinks him worthy of sympathy and agrees with the sentiments that he expresses.

Here is the outline of the story. A young German doctor who has been convalescent for two years in Switzerland returns to Cologne a little before Munich to find that his wife has been helping war-resisters to escape from the country and is in imminent danger of arrest. He and she flee to Holland just in time to escape the massacre which followed on vom Rath's assassination.[1] Partly by accident they reach England, he having been seriously wounded on the way. After his recovery he manages to get a hospital appointment, but at the outbreak of war he is brought before a tribunal and put in the B class of aliens. The reason for this is that he has declared that he will not fight against the Nazis, thinking it better to "overcome Hitler by love." Asked why he did not stay in Germany and overcome Hitler by love there, he admits that there is no answer. In the panic following on the invasion of the Low Countries he is arrested a few minutes after his wife has given birth to a baby and kept for a long time in a concentration camp where he cannot communicate with her and where the conditions of dirt, overcrowding, etc., are as bad as anything in Germany. Finally he is packed on to the "Arandora Star" (it is given another name, of course),[2] sunk at sea, rescued, and put in another somewhat better camp. When he is at last released and makes contact with his wife, it is to find that she has been confined in another camp in which the baby has died of neglect and underfeeding. The book ends with the couple looking forward to sailing for America and hoping that the war fever will not by this time have spread there as well.

Now, before considering the implications of this story, just consider one or two facts which underlie the structure of modern society and which it is necessary to ignore if the pacifist "message" is to be accepted uncritically.

(i) Civilisation rests ultimately on coercion. What holds society together is not the policeman but the good will of common men, and yet that good will is powerless unless the policeman is there to back it up. Any government which refused to use violence in its own defence would cease almost immediately to exist, because it could be overthrown by any body of men, or even any individual, that was less scrupulous. Objectively, whoever is not on the side of the policeman is on the side of the criminal, and vice versa. In so far as it hampers the British war effort, British pacifism is on the side of the Nazis, and German pacifism, if it exists, is on the side of Britain and the U.S.S.R. Since pacifists have more freedom of action in countries where traces of democracy survive, pacifism can act more effectively against democracy than for it. Objectively the pacifist is pro-Nazi.

(ii) Since coercion can never be altogether dispensed with, the only difference is between degrees of violence. During the last twenty years there has been less violence and less militarism inside the English-speaking world than outside it, because there has been more money and more security. The hatred of war which undoubtedly characterises the English-speaking peoples is a reflection of their favoured position. Pacifism is only a considerable force in places where people feel themselves very safe, chiefly maritime states. Even in such places, turn-the-other-cheek pacifism only flourishes among the more prosperous classes, or among workers who have in some way escaped from their own class. The real working class, though they hate war and are immune to jingoism, are never really pacifist, because their life teaches them something different. To abjure violence it is necessary to have no experience of it.

If one keeps the above facts in mind one can, I think, see the events, in Mr. Comfort's novel in truer perspective. It is a question of putting aside subjective feelings and trying to see whither one's actions will lead in practice and where one's motives ultimately spring from. The hero is a research worker—a pathologist. He has not been especially fortunate, he has a defective lung, thanks to the carrying-on of the British blockade into 1919, but in so far as he is a member of the middle class, doing work which he has chosen for himself, he is one of a few million favoured human beings who live ultimately on the degradation of the rest. He wants to get on with his work, wants to be out of reach of Nazi tyranny and regimentation, but he will not *act* against the Nazis in any other way than by running away from them. Arrived in England, he is in terror of being sent back to Germany, but refuses to take part in any physical effort to keep the Nazis out of England. His greatest hope is to get to America, with another three thousand miles of water between himself and the Nazis. He will only get there, you note, if British ships and planes protect him on the way, and having got there he will simply be living under the protection of American ships and planes instead of British ones. If he is lucky he will be able to continue with his work as a pathologist, at the same time keeping up his attitude of moral superiority towards the men who make his work possible. And underlying everything there will still be his position as a research-worker, a favoured person living ultimately on dividends which would cease forthwith if not extorted by the threat of violence.

I do not think this is an unfair summary of Mr. Comfort's book. And I think the relevant fact is that this story of a German doctor is written by an Englishman. The argument which is implied all the way through, and sometimes explicitly stated, that there is next to no difference between Britain and Germany, political persecution is as bad in one as in the other, those who fight against the Nazis always go Nazi themselves, would be more convincing if it came from a German. There are probably sixty thousand German refugees in this country, and there would be hundreds of thousands more if we had not meanly kept them out. Why did they come here if there is virtually no difference between the social atmosphere of the two countries? And how many of them have asked to go back? They have "voted with their feet," as Lenin put it. As I pointed out above, the comparative gentleness of the English-speaking civilisation is due to money and security, but that is not to say that no difference exists. Once let it be admitted, however, that there *is* a certain difference, that it matters quite a lot who wins, and the usual short-term case for pacifism falls to the ground. You can be explicitly pro-Nazi without claiming to be a pacifist—and there is a very strong case for the Nazis, though not many people in this country have the courage to utter it—but you can only pretend that Nazism and capitalist democracy are Tweedledum and Tweedledee if you also pretend that every horror from the June purge onwards has been cancelled by an exactly similar horror in England. In practice this has to be done by means of selection and exaggeration. Mr. Comfort is in effect claiming that a "hard case" is typical. The sufferings of this German doctor in a so-called democratic country are so terrible, he implies, as to wipe out every shred of moral justification for the struggle against Fascism. One must, however, keep a sense of proportion. Before raising a squeal because two thousand internees have only eighteen latrine buckets between them, one might as well remember what has happened these last few years in Poland, in Spain, in Czechoslovakia, etc., etc. If one clings too closely to the "those who fight against Fascism become Fascist themselves" formula, one is simply led into falsification. It is not true, for instance, as Mr. Comfort implies, that there is widespread spy-mania and that the prejudice against foreigners increases as the war gathers in momentum. The feeling against foreigners, which was one of the factors that made the internment of the refugees possible, has greatly died away, and Germans and Italians are now allowed into jobs that they would have been debarred from in peace time. It is not true, as he explicitly says, that the only difference between political persecution in England and in Germany is that in England nobody hears about it. Nor is it true that all the evil in our life is traceable to war or war-preparation. "I knew," he says, "that the English people, like the Germans, had never been happy since they put their trust in rearmament." Were they so conspicuously happy before? Is it not the truth, on the contrary, that rearmament, by reducing unemployment, made the English people somewhat happier, if anything? From my own observation I should say that, by and large, the war itself has made England happier; and this is not an argument in favour of war, but simply tells one something about the nature of so-called peace.

The fact is that the ordinary short-term case for pacifism, the claim that you can best frustrate the Nazis by not resisting them, cannot be sustained. If you don't resist the Nazis you are helping them, and ought to admit it. For then the long-term case for pacifism can be made out. You can say: "Yes, I know I am helping Hitler, and I want to help him. Let him conquer Britain, the U.S.S.R. and America. Let the Nazis rule the world; in the end they will grow into something different." That is at any rate a tenable position. It looks forward into human history, beyond the term of our own lives. What is not tenable is the idea that everything in the garden would be lovely *now* if only we stopped the wicked fighting, and that to fight back is exactly what the Nazis want us to do. Which does Hitler fear more, the P.P.U. or the R.A.F.? Which has he made greater efforts to sabotage? Is he trying to bring America into the war or to keep America out of it? Would he be deeply distressed if the Russians stopped fighting tomorrow? And after all, the history of the last ten years suggests that Hitler has a pretty shrewd idea of his own interests.

The notion that you can somehow defeat violence by submitting to it is simply a flight from fact. As I have said, it is only possible to people who have money and guns between themselves and reality. But why should they want to make this flight, in any case? Because, rightly hating violence, they do not wish to recognise that it is integral to modern society and that their own fine feelings and noble attitudes are all the fruit of injustice backed up by force. They do not want to learn where their incomes come from. Underneath this lies the hard fact, so difficult for many people to face, that individual salvation is not possible, that the choice before human beings is not, as a rule, between good and evil but between two evils. You can let the Nazis rule the world; that is evil; or you can overthrow them by war, which is also evil. There is no other choice before you, and whichever you choose you will not come out with clean hands. It seems to me that the text for our time is not "Woe to him through whom the evil cometh" but the one from which I took the title of this article, "There is not one that is righteous, no, not one."[3] We have all touched pitch, we are all perishing by the sword. We do not have the chance, in a time like this, to say "Tomorrow we can all start being good." That is moonshine. We only have the chance of choosing the lesser evil and of working for the establishment of a new kind of society in which common decency will again be possible. There is no such thing as neutrality in this war. The whole population of the world is involved in it, from the Esquimos to the Andamanese, and since one must inevitably help one side or the other, it is better to know what one is doing and count the cost. Men like Darlan and Laval have at any rate had the courage to make their choice and proclaim it openly. The New Order, they say, must be established at all costs, and "il faut érabouiller l'Angleterre." Mr. Murry appears, at any rate at moments, to think likewise. The Nazis, he says, are "doing the dirty work of the Lord" (they certainly did an exceptionally dirty job when they attacked Russia), and we must be careful "lest in fighting against Hitler we are fighting against God." Those are not pacifist sentiments, since if carried to their logical conclusion they involve not only surrendering to Hitler but helping him in his various forthcoming wars, but they are at least straightforward and courageous. I do not myself see Hitler as the saviour, even the unconscious saviour, of humanity, but there is a strong case for thinking him so, far stronger than most people in England imagine. What there is no case for is to denounce Hitler and at the same time look down your nose at the people who actually keep you out of his clutches. That is simply a highbrow variant of British hypocrisy, a product of capitalism in decay, and the sort of thing for which Europeans, who at any rate understand the nature of a policeman and a dividend, justifiably despise us.

Rudyard Kipling[1]

Horizon, February 1942

It was a pity that Mr. Eliot should be so much on the defensive in the long essay with which he prefaces this selection of Kipling's poetry, but it was not to be avoided, because before one can even speak about Kipling one has to clear away a legend that has been created by two sets of people who have not read his works. Kipling is in the peculiar position of having been a by-word for fifty years. During five literary generations every enlightened person has despised him, and at the end of that time nine-tenths of those enlightened persons are forgotten and Kipling is in some sense still there. Mr. Eliot never satisfactorily explains this fact, because in answering the shallow and familiar charge that Kipling is a "Fascist," he falls into the opposite error of defending him where he is not defensible. It is no use pretending that Kipling's view of life, as a whole, can be accepted or even forgiven by any civilised person. It is no use claiming, for instance, that when Kipling describes a British soldier beating a "nigger" with a cleaning rod in order to get money out of him, he is acting merely as a reporter and does not necessarily approve what he describes. There is not the slightest sign anywhere in Kipling's work that he disapproves of that kind of conduct—on the contrary, there is a definite strain of sadism in him, over and above the brutality which a writer of that type has to have. Kipling *is* a jingo imperialist, he *is* morally insensitive and æsthetically disgusting. It is better to start by admitting that, and then to try to find out why it is that he survives while the refined people who have sniggered at him seem to wear so badly.

And yet the "Fascist" charge has to be answered, because the first clue to any understanding of Kipling, morally or politically, is the fact that he was *not* a Fascist. He was further from being one than the most humane or the most "progressive" person is able to be nowadays. An interesting instance of the way in which quotations are parroted to and fro without any attempt to look up their context or discover their meaning is the line from "Recessional," "Lesser breeds without the Law."[2] This line is always good for a snigger in pansy-left circles. It is assumed as a matter of course that the "lesser breeds" are "natives," and a mental picture is called up of some pukka sahib in a pith helmet kicking a coolie. In its context the sense of the line is almost the exact opposite of this. The phrase "lesser breeds" refers almost certainly to the Germans, and especially the pan-German writers, who are "without the Law" in the sense of being lawless, not in the sense of being powerless. The whole poem, conventionally thought of as an orgy of boasting, is a denunciation of power politics, British as well as German. Two stanzas are worth quoting (I am quoting this as politics, not as poetry):

> "If, drunk with sight of power, we loose
> Wild tongues that have not Thee in awe,
> Such boastings as the Gentiles use,
> Or lesser breeds without the Law—
> Lord God of Hosts, be with us yet,
> Lest we forget—lest we forget!
>
> "For heathen heart that puts her trust
> In reeking tube and iron shard,
> All valiant dust that builds on dust,

And guarding, calls not Thee to guard,
For frantic boast and foolish word—
Thy mercy on Thy People, Lord!"

Much of Kipling's phraseology is taken from the Bible, and no doubt in the second stanza he had in mind the text from Psalm cxxvii: "Except the Lord build the house, they labour in vain that build it; except the Lord keep the city, the watchman waketh but in vain." It is not a text that makes much impression on the post-Hitler mind. No one, in our time, believes in any sanction greater than military power; no one believes that it is possible to overcome force except by greater force. There is no "law," there is only power. I am not saying that that is a true belief, merely that it is the belief which all modern men do actually hold. Those who pretend otherwise are either intellectual cowards, or power-worshippers under a thin disguise, or have simply not caught up with the age they are living in. Kipling's outlook is pre-Fascist. He still believes that pride comes before a fall and that the gods punish *hubris.* He does not foresee the tank, the bombing plane, the radio and the secret police, or their psychological results.

But in saying this, does not one unsay what I said above about Kipling's jingoism and brutality? No, one is merely saying that the nineteenth-century imperialist outlook and the modern gangster outlook are two different things. Kipling belongs very definitely to the period 1885–1902. The Great War and its aftermath embittered him, but he shows little sign of having learned anything from any event later than the Boer War. He was the prophet of British Imperialism in its expansionist phase (even more than his poems, his solitary novel, *The Light that Failed,*[3] gives you the atmosphere of that time) and also the unofficial historian of the British Army, the old mercenary army which began to change its shape in 1914.

All his confidence, his bouncing vulgar vitality, sprang out of limitations which no Fascist or near-Fascist shares.

Kipling spent the later part of his life in sulking, and no doubt it was political disappointment rather than literary vanity that accounted for this. Somehow history had not gone according to plan. After the greatest victory she had ever known, Britain was a lesser world power than before, and Kipling was quite acute enough to see this. The virtue had gone out of the classes he idealised, the young were hedonistic or disaffected, the desire to paint the map red had evaporated. He could not understand what was happening, because he had never had any grasp of the economic forces underlying imperial expansion. It is notable that Kipling does not seem to realise, any more than the average soldier or colonial administrator, that an empire is primarily a money-making concern. Imperialism as he sees it is a sort of forcible evangelising. You turn a Gatling gun on a mob of unarmed "natives," and then you establish "the Law," which includes roads, railways and a court-house. He could not foresee, therefore, that the same motives which brought the Empire into existence would end by destroying it. It was the same motive, for example, that caused the Malayan jungles to be cleared for rubber estates, and which now causes those estates to be handed over intact to the Japanese.[4] The modern totalitarians know what they are doing, and the nineteenth-century English did not know what they were doing. Both attitudes have their advantages, but Kipling was never able to move forward from one into the other. His outlook, allowing for the fact that after all he was an artist, was that of the salaried bureaucrat who despises the "box-wallah"[5] and often lives a lifetime without realising that the "box-wallah" calls the tune.

But because he identifies himself with the official class, he does possess one thing which "enlightened" people seldom or never possess, and that is a sense of responsibility. The middle-class Left hate him for this quite as much as for his cruelty and vulgarity. All left-wing parties in the highly industrialised countries are at bottom a sham, because they make it their business to fight against something which they do not really wish to destroy. They have internationalist aims, and at the same time they struggle to keep up a standard of life with which those aims are incompatible. We all live by robbing Asiatic coolies, and those of us who are "enlightened" all maintain that those coolies ought to be set free; but our standard of living, and hence our "enlightenment," demands that the robbery shall continue. A humanitarian is always a hypocrite, and Kipling's understanding of this is perhaps the central secret of his power to create telling phrases. It would be difficult to hit off the one-eyed pacifism of the English in fewer words than in the phrase, "making mock of uniforms that guard you while you sleep."[6] It is true that Kipling does not understand the economic aspect of the relationship between the highbrow and the blimp. He does not see that the map is painted red chiefly in order that the coolie may be exploited. Instead of the coolie he sees the Indian Civil Servant; but even on that plane his grasp of function, of who protects whom, is very sound. He sees clearly that men can only be highly civilised while other men, inevitably less civilised, are there to guard and feed them.

How far does Kipling really identify himself with the administrators, soldiers and engineers whose praises he sings? Not so completely as is sometimes assumed. He had travelled very widely while he was still a young man, he had grown up with a brilliant mind in mainly philistine surroundings, and some streak in him that may have been partly neurotic led him to prefer the active man to the sensitive man. The nineteenth-century Anglo-Indians, to name the least sympathetic of his idols, were at any rate people who did things. It may be that all that they did was evil, but they changed the face of the earth (it is instructive to look at a map of

Asia and compare the railway system of India with that of the surrounding countries), whereas they could have achieved nothing, could not have maintained themselves in power for a single week, if the normal Anglo-Indian outlook had been that of, say, E. M. Forster. Tawdry and shallow though it is, Kipling's is the only literary picture that we possess of nineteenth-century Anglo-India, and he could only make it because he was just coarse enough to be able to exist and keep his mouth shut in clubs and regimental messes. But he did not greatly resemble the people he admired. I know from several private sources that many of the Anglo-Indians who were Kipling's contemporaries did not like or approve of him. They said, no doubt truly, that he knew nothing about India, and on the other hand, he was from their point of view too much of a highbrow. While in India he tended to mix with "the wrong" people, and because of his dark complexion he was wrongly suspected of having a streak of Asiatic blood. Much in his development is traceable to his having been born in India and having left school early. With a slightly different background he might have been a good novelist or a superlative writer of music-hall songs. But how true is it that he was a vulgar flag-waver, a sort of publicity agent for Cecil Rhodes? It is true, but it is not true that he was a yes-man or a time-server. After his early days, if then, he never courted public opinion. Mr. Eliot says that what is held against him is that he expressed unpopular views in a popular style. This narrows the issue by assuming that "unpopular" means unpopular with the intelligentsia, but it is a fact that Kipling's "message" was one that the big public did not want, and, indeed, has never accepted. The mass of the people, in the 'nineties as now, were anti-militarist, bored by the Empire, and only unconsciously patriotic. Kipling's official admirers are and were the "service" middle class, the people who read *Blackwood's*. In the stupid early years of this century, the blimps, having at last discovered someone who could be called a poet and who was on their side, set Kipling on a pedestal, and some of his more sententious poems, such as "If," were given almost Biblical status. But it is doubtful whether the blimps have ever read him with attention, any more than they have read the Bible. Much of what he says they could not possibly approve. Few people who have criticised England from the inside have said bitterer things about her than this gutter patriot. As a rule it is the British working class that he is attacking, but not always. That phrase about "the flannelled fools at the wicket or the muddied oafs at the goals"[7] sticks like an arrow to this day, and it is aimed at the Eton and Harrow match as well as the Cup-Tie Final. Some of the verses he wrote about the Boer War have a curiously modern ring, so far as their subject-matter goes. "Stellenbosch,"[8] which must have been written about 1902, sums up what every intelligent infantry officer was saying in 1918, or is saying now, for that matter.

Kipling's romantic ideas about England and the Empire might not have mattered if he could have held them without having the class-prejudices which at that time went with them. If one examines his best and most representative work, his soldier poems, especially *Barrack-Room Ballads,* one notices that what more than anything else spoils them is an underlying air of patronage. Kipling idealises the army officer, especially the junior officer, and that to an idiotic extent, but the private soldier, though lovable and romantic, has to be a comic. He is always made to speak in a sort of stylised Cockney, not very broad but with all the aitches and final "g's" carefully omitted. Very often the result is as embarrassing as the humorous recitation at a church social. And this accounts for the curious fact that one can often improve Kipling's poems, make them less facetious and less blatant, by simply going through them and translating them from Cockney into standard speech. This is especially true of his refrains, which often have a truly lyrical quality. Two examples will do (one is about a funeral and the other about a wedding):

> "So it's knock out your pipes and follow me!
> And it's finish up your swipes and follow me!
> Oh, hark to the big drum calling,
> Follow me—follow me home!"[9]

and again:

> "Cheer for the Sergeant's wedding—
> Give them one cheer more!
> Grey gun-horses in the lando,
> And a rogue is married to a whore!"[10]

Here I have restored the aitches, etc. Kipling ought to have known better. He ought to have seen that the two closing lines of the first of these stanzas are very beautiful lines, and that ought to have overriden his impulse to make fun of a working-man's accent. In the ancient ballads the lord and the peasant speak the same language. This is impossible to Kipling, who is looking down a distorting class-perspective, and by a piece of poetic justice one of his best lines is spoiled—for "follow me 'ome" is much uglier than "follow me home." But even where it makes no difference musically the facetiousness of his stage Cockney dialect is irritating. However, he is more often quoted aloud than read on the printed page, and most people instinctively make the necessary alterations when they quote him.

Can one imagine any private soldier, in the 'nineties or now, reading *Barrack-Room Ballads* and feeling that here was a writer who spoke for him? It is very hard to do so. Any soldier capable of reading a book of verse would notice at once that Kipling is almost unconscious of the class war that goes on in an army as much as elsewhere. It is not only that he thinks the soldier comic, but that he thinks him patriotic, feudal, a ready admirer of his officers and proud to be a soldier of the Queen. Of course that is partly true, or battles could not be fought, but "What have I done for thee, England, my England?" is essentially a middle-class query.[11] Almost any working-man would follow it up immediately with "What has England done for me?" In so far as Kipling grasps this, he simply sets it down to "the intense selfishness of the lower classes" (his own phrase).[12] When he is writing not of British but of "loyal" Indians he carries the "Salaam, sahib" motif to sometimes disgusting lengths. Yet it remains true that he has far more interest in the common soldier, far more anxiety that he shall get a fair deal, than most of the "liberals" of his day or our own. He sees that the soldier is neglected, meanly underpaid and hypocritically despised by the people whose incomes he safeguards. "I came to realise," he says in his posthumous memoirs, "the bare horrors of the private's life, and the unnecessary torments he endured."[13] He is accused of glorifying war, and perhaps he does so, but not in the usual manner, by pretending that war is a sort of football match. Like most people capable of writing battle poetry, Kipling had never been in battle,[14] but his vision of war is realistic. He knows that bullets hurt, that under fire everyone is terrified, that the ordinary soldier never knows what the war is about or what is happening except in his own corner of the battlefield, and that British troops, like other troops, frequently run away:

"I 'eard the knives be'ind me, but I dursn't face my man,
Nor I don't know where I went to, 'cause I didn't stop to see,
Till I 'eard a beggar squealin' out for quarter as 'e ran,
An' I thought I knew the voice an'—it was me!"[15]

Modernize the style of this, and it might have come out of one of the debunking war books of the nineteen-twenties. Or again:

"An' now the hugly bullets come peckin' through the dust,
An' no one wants to face 'em, but every beggar must;
So, like a man in irons, which isn't glad to go,
They moves 'em off by companies uncommon stiff an' slow."[16]

Compare this with:

"Forward the Light Brigade!
Was there a man dismayed?
No! though the soldier knew
Someone had blundered."[17]

If anything, Kipling overdoes the horrors, for the wars of his youth were hardly wars at all by our standards. Perhaps that is due to the neurotic strain in him, the hunger for cruelty. But at least he knows that men ordered to attack impossible objectives *are* dismayed, and also that fourpence a day is not a generous pension.

How complete or truthful a picture has Kipling left us of the long-service, mercenary army of the late nineteenth century? One must say of this, as of what Kipling wrote about nineteenth-century Anglo-India, that it is not only the best but almost the only literary picture we have. He has put on record an immense amount of stuff that one could otherwise only gather from verbal tradition or from unreadable regimental histories. Perhaps his picture of army life seems fuller and more accurate than it is because any middle-class English person is likely to know enough to fill up the gaps. At any rate, reading the essay on Kipling that Mr. Edmund Wilson has just published or is just about to publish, I was struck by the number of things that are boringly familiar to us and seem to be barely intelligible to an American. But from the body of Kipling's early work there does seem to emerge a vivid and not seriously misleading picture of the old pre-machine-gun army—the sweltering barracks in Gibraltar or Lucknow, the red coats, the pipeclayed belts and the pillbox hats, the beer, the fights, the floggings, hangings and crucifixions, the bugle-calls, the smell of oats and horse-piss, the bellowing sergeants with foot-long moustaches, the bloody skirmishes, invariably mismanaged, the crowded troopships, the cholera-stricken camps, the "native" concubines, the ultimate death in the workhouse. It is a crude, vulgar picture, in which a patriotic music-hall turn seems to have got mixed up with one of Zola's gorier passages, but from it future generations will be able to gather some idea of what a long-term volunteer army was like. On about the same level they will be able to learn something of British India in the days when motorcars and refrigerators were unheard of. It is an error to imagine that we might have had better books on these subjects if, for example, George Moore, or Gissing, or Thomas Hardy, had had Kipling's opportunities. That is the kind of accident that cannot happen. It was not possible that nineteenth-century England should produce a book like *War and Peace,* or like Tolstoy's minor stories of army life, such as *Sebastopol* or *The Cossacks,* not because the talent was necessarily lacking but because no one with sufficient sensitiveness to write such books would ever have made the appropriate contacts. Tolstoy lived in a great military empire in which it seemed natural for almost any young man of family to spend a few years in the army, whereas the British Empire was and still is demilitarised to a degree which continental observers find almost incredible. Civilised men do not readily move away from the centres of civilisation, and in most languages there is a great dearth of what one might call colonial literature. It took a very improbable combination of circumstances to produce Kipling's gaudy tableau, in which Private Ortheris and Mrs. Hauksbee pose against a background of palm trees to the sound of temple bells, and one necessary circumstance was that Kipling himself was only half civilised.

Kipling is the only English writer of our time who has added phrases to the language. The phrases and neologisms which we take over and use without remembering their origin do not always come from writers we admire. It is strange, for instance, to hear the Nazi broadcasters referring to the Russian soldiers as "robots," thus unconsciously borrowing a word from a Czech democrat whom they would have killed if they could have laid hands on him.[18] Here are half a dozen phrases coined by Kipling which one sees quoted in leaderettes in the gutter press or overhears in saloon bars from people who have barely heard his name. It will be seen that they all have a certain characteristic in common:

"East is East, and West is West.
The white man's burden.
What do they know of England who only England know?
The female of the species is more deadly than the male.
Somewhere East of Suez.
Paying the Dane-geld."[19]

There are various others, including some that have outlived their context by many years. The phrase "killing Kruger with your mouth,"[20] for instance, was current till very recently. It is also possible that it was Kipling who first let loose the use of the word "Huns" for Germans; at any rate he began using it as soon as the guns opened fire in 1914. But what the phrases I have listed above have in common is that they are all of them phrases which one utters semi-derisively (as it might be "For I'm to be Queen o' the May, mother, I'm to be Queen o' the May"[21]), but which one is bound to make use of sooner or later. Nothing could exceed the contempt of the *New Statesman,* for instance, for Kipling, but how many times during the Munich period did the *New Statesman* find itself quoting that phrase about paying the Dane-geld? The fact is that Kipling, apart from his snack-bar wisdom and his gift for packing much cheap picturesqueness into a few words ("Palm and Pine"—"East of Suez"—"The Road to Mandalay"), is generally talking about things that are of urgent interest. It does not matter, from this point of view, that thinking and decent people generally find themselves on the other side of the fence from him. "White man's burden" instantly conjures up a real problem, even if one feels that it ought to be altered to "black man's burden." One may disagree to the middle of one's bones with the political attitude implied in "The Islanders,"[22] but one cannot say that it is a frivolous attitude. Kipling deals in thoughts which are both vulgar and permanent. This raises the question of his special status as a poet, or verse-writer.

Mr. Eliot describes Kipling's metrical work as "verse" and not "poetry," but adds that it is "*great* verse," and further qualifies this by saying that a writer can only be described as a "great verse-writer" if there is some of his work "of which we cannot say whether it is verse or poetry." Apparently Kipling was a versifier who occasionally wrote poems, in which case it was a pity that Mr. Eliot did not specify these poems by name. The trouble is that whenever an æsthetic judgment on Kipling's work seems to be called for, Mr. Eliot is too much on the defensive to be able to speak plainly. What he does not say, and what I think one ought to start by saying in any discussion of Kipling, is that most of Kipling's verse is so horribly vulgar that it gives one the same sensation as one gets from watching a third-rate music-hall performer recite "The Pigtail of Wu Fang Fu" with the purple limelight on his face, *and yet* there is much of it that is capable of giving pleasure to people who know what poetry means. At his worst, and also his most vital, in poems like "Gunga Din" or "Danny Deever,"[23] Kipling is almost a shameful pleasure, like the taste for cheap sweets that some people secretly carry into middle life. But even with his best passages one has the same sense of being seduced by something spurious, and yet unquestionably seduced. Unless one is merely a snob and a liar it is impossible to say that no one who cares for poetry could get any pleasure out of such lines as:

> "For the wind is in the palm-trees, and the temple-bells they say,
> 'Come you back, you British soldier; come you back to
> Mandalay!' "[24]

and yet those lines are not poetry in the same sense as "Felix Randal" or "When icicles hang by the wall" are poetry. One can, perhaps, place Kipling more satisfactorily than by juggling with the words "verse" and "poetry," if one describes him simply as a good bad poet. He is as a poet what Harriet Beecher Stowe was as a novelist.[25] And the mere existence of work of this kind, which is perceived by generation after generation to be vulgar and yet goes on being read, tells one something about the age we live in.

There is a great deal of good bad poetry in English, all of it, I should say, subsequent to 1790. Examples of good bad poems—I am deliberately choosing diverse ones—are "The Bridge of Sighs," "When all the World is Young, Lad," "The Charge of the Light Brigade," Bret Harte's "Dickens in Camp," "The Burial of Sir John Moore," "Jenny Kissed Me," "Keith of Ravelston," "Casablanca."[26] All of these reek of sentimentality, and yet—not these particular poems, perhaps, but poems of this kind, are capable of giving true pleasure to people who can see clearly what is wrong with them. One could fill a fair-sized anthology with good bad poems, if it were not for the significant fact that good bad poetry is usually too well known to be worth reprinting. It is no use pretending that in an age like our own, "good" poetry can have any genuine popularity. It is, and must be, the cult of a very few people, the least tolerated of the arts. Perhaps that statement needs a certain amount of qualification. True poetry can sometimes be acceptable to the mass of the people when it disguises itself as something else. One can see an example of this in the folk-poetry that England still possesses, certain nursery rhymes and mnemonic rhymes, for instance, and the songs that soldiers make up, including the words that go to some of the bugle-calls. But in general ours is a civilisation in which the very word "poetry" evokes a hostile snigger or, at best, the sort of frozen disgust that most people feel when they hear the word "God." If you are good at playing the concertina you could probably go into the nearest public bar and get yourself an appreciative audience within five minutes. But what would be the attitude of that same audience if you suggested reading them Shakespeare's sonnets, for instance? Good bad poetry, however, can get across to the most unpromising audiences if the right atmosphere has been worked up beforehand. Some months back Churchill produced a great effect by quoting Clough's "Endeavour"[27] in one of his broadcast speeches. I listened to this speech among people who could certainly not be accused of caring for poetry, and I am convinced that the lapse into verse impressed them and did not embarrass them. But not even Churchill could have got away with it if he had quoted anything much better than this.

In so far as a writer of verse can be popular, Kipling has been and probably still is popular. In his own lifetime some of his poems travelled far beyond the bounds of the reading public, beyond the world of school prize-days, Boy Scout singsongs, limp-leather editions, pokerwork and calendars, and out into the yet vaster world of the music halls. Nevertheless, Mr. Eliot thinks it worth while to edit him, thus confessing to a taste which others share but are not always honest enough to mention. The fact that such a thing as good bad poetry can exist is a sign of the emotional overlap between the intellectual and the ordinary man. The intellectual *is* different from the ordinary man, but only in certain sections of his personality, and even then not all the time. But what is the peculiarity of a good bad poem? A good bad poem is a graceful monument to the obvious. It records in memorable form—for verse is a mnemonic device, among other things—some emotion which very nearly every human being can share. The merit of a poem like "When all the world is young, lad" is that, however sentimental it may be, its sentiment is "true" sentiment in the sense that you are bound to find yourself thinking the thought it expresses sooner or later; and then, if you happen to know the poem, it will come back into your mind and seem better than it did before. Such poems are a kind of rhyming proverb, and it is a fact that definitely popular poetry is usually gnomic or sententious. One example from Kipling will do:

> "White hands cling to the tightened rein,
> Slipping the spur from the booted heel,
> Tenderest voices cry 'Turn again,'
> Red lips tarnish the scabbarded steel,
> High hopes faint on a warm hearth-stone—
> He travels the fastest who travels alone."

There is a vulgar thought vigorously expressed. It may not be true, but at any rate it is a thought that everyone thinks. Sooner or later you will have occasion to feel that he travels the fastest who travels alone, and there the thought is, ready made and, as it were, waiting for you. So the chances are that, having once heard this line, you will remember it.

One reason for Kipling's power as a good bad poet I have already suggested—his sense of responsibility, which made it possible for him to have a world-view, even though it happened to be a false one. Although he had no direct connection with any political party, Kipling was a Conservative, a thing that does not exist nowadays. Those who now call themselves Conservatives are either Liberals, Fascists or the accomplices of Fascists. He identified himself with the ruling power and not with the opposition. In a gifted writer this seems to us strange and even disgusting, but it did have the advantage of giving Kipling a certain grip on reality. The ruling power is always faced with the question, "In such and such circumstances, what would you *do*?," whereas the opposition is not obliged to take responsibility or make any real decisions. Where it is a permanent and pensioned opposition, as in England, the quality of its thought deteriorates accordingly. Moreover, anyone who starts out with a pessimistic, reactionary view of life tends to be justified by events, for Utopia never arrives and "the gods of the copybook headings," as Kipling himself put it, always return.[28] Kipling sold out to the British governing class, not financially but emotionally. This warped his political judgment, for the British ruling class were not what he imagined, and it led him into abysses of folly and snobbery, but he gained a corresponding advantage from having at least tried to imagine what action and responsibility are like. It is a great thing in his favour that he is not witty, not "daring," has no wish to *épater les bourgeois*. He dealt largely in platitudes, and since we live in a world of platitudes, much of what he said sticks. Even his worst follies seem less shallow and less irritating than the "enlightened" utterances of the same period, such as Wilde's epigrams or the collection of cracker-mottoes at the end of *Man and Superman*.

T. S. Eliot

Poetry (London), October–November 1942

This review article discusses Eliot's *Burnt Norton, East Coker,* and *The Dry Salvages,* each of which was published separately.

There is very little in Eliot's later work that makes any deep impression on me. That is a confession of something lacking in myself, but it is not, as it may appear at first sight, a reason for simply shutting up and saying no more, since the change in my own reaction probably points to some external change which is worth investigating.

I know a respectable quantity of Eliot's earlier work by heart. I did not sit down and learn it, it simply stuck in my mind as any passage of verse is liable to do when it has really rung the bell. Sometimes after only one reading it is possible to remember the whole of a poem of, say, twenty or thirty lines, the act of memory being partly an act of reconstruction. But as for these three latest poems, I suppose I have read each of them two or three times since they were published, and how much do I verbally remember? "Time and the bell have buried the day," "At the still point of the turning world," "The vast waters of the petrel and the porpoise," and bits of the passage beginning "O dark dark dark. They all go into the dark." (I don't count "In my end is my beginning," which is a quotation.) That is about all that sticks in my head of its own accord. Now one cannot take this as proving that *Burnt Norton* and the rest are worse than the more memorable early poems, and one might even take it as proving the contrary, since it is arguable that that which lodges itself most easily in the mind is the obvious and even the vulgar. But it is clear that something has departed, some kind of current has been switched off, the later verse does not *contain* the earlier, even if it is claimed as an improvement upon it. I think one is justified in explaining this by a deterioration in Mr. Eliot's subject-matter. Before going any further, here are a couple of extracts, just near enough to one another in meaning to be comparable. The first is the concluding passage of *The Dry Salvages:*

> And right action is freedom
> From past and future also.
> For most of us, this is the aim
> Never here to be realised;
> Who are only undefeated
> Because we have gone on trying;
> We, content at the last
> If our temporal reversion nourish
> (Not too far from the yew-tree)
> The life of significant soil.

Here is an extract from a much earlier poem:

> Daffodil bulbs instead of balls
> Stared from the sockets of the eyes!
> He knew that thought clings round dead limbs
> Tightening its lusts and luxuries.
> . . .
> He knew the anguish of the marrow
> The ague of the skeleton;
> No contact possible to flesh
> Allayed the fever of the bone.[1]

The two passages will bear comparison since they both deal with the same subject, namely death. The first of them follows upon a longer passage in which it is explained, first of all, that scientific research is all nonsense, a childish superstition on the same level as fortune-telling, and then that the only people ever likely to reach an understanding of the universe are saints, the rest of us being reduced to "hints and guesses." The keynote of the closing passage is, "resignation." There is a "meaning" in life and also in death; unfortunately we don't know what it is, but the fact that it exists should be a comfort to us as we push up the crocuses, or whatever it is that grows under the yew trees in country churchyards. But now look at the other two stanzas I have quoted. Though fathered on to somebody else, they probably express what Mr. Eliot himself felt about death at that time, at least in certain moods. They are not voicing resignation. On the contrary, they are voicing the pagan attitude towards death, the belief in the next world as a shadowy place full of thin, squeaking ghosts, envious of the living, the belief that however bad life may be, death is worse. This conception of death seems to have been general in antiquity, and in a sense it is general now. "The anguish of the marrow, the ague of the skeleton," Horace's famous ode *Eheu fugaces,* and Bloom's unuttered thoughts during Paddy Dignam's funeral, are all very much of a muchness. So long as man regards himself as an individual, his attitude towards death must be one of simple resentment. And however unsatisfactory this may be, if it is intensely felt it is more likely to produce good literature than a religious faith which is not really *felt* at all, but merely accepted against the emotional grain. So far as they can be compared, the two passages I have quoted seem to me to bear this out. I do not think it is questionable that the second of them is superior as verse, and also more intense in feeling, in spite of a tinge of burlesque.

What are these three poems, *Burnt Norton* and the rest, "about"? It is not so easy to say what they are about, but what they appear on the surface to be about is certain localities in England and America with which Mr. Eliot has ancestral connections. Mixed up with this is a rather gloomy musing upon the nature and purpose of life, with the rather indefinite conclusion I have mentioned above. Life has a "meaning," but it is not a meaning one feels inclined to grow lyrical about; there is faith, but not much hope, and certainly no enthusiasm. Now the subject-matter of Mr. Eliot's early poems was very different from this. They were not hopeful, but neither were they depressed or depressing. If one wants to deal in antitheses, one might say that the later poems express a melancholy faith and the earlier ones a glowing despair. They were based on the dilemma of modern man, who despairs of life and does not want to be dead, and on top of this they expressed the horror of an over-civilised intellectual confronted with the ugliness and spiritual emptiness of the machine age. Instead of "not too far from the yew-tree" the keynote was "weeping, weeping multitudes," or perhaps "the broken fingernails of dirty hands." Naturally these poems were denounced as "decadent" when they first appeared, the attacks only being called off when it was perceived that Eliot's political and social tendencies were reactionary. There was, however, a sense in which the charge of "decadence" could be justified. Clearly these poems were an end-product, the last gasp of a cultural tradition, poems which spoke only for the cultivated third-generation rentier, for people able to feel and criticise but no longer able to act. E. M. Forster praised *Prufrock* on its first appearance because "it sang of people who were ineffectual and weak" and because it was "innocent of public spirit" (this was during the other war, when public spirit was a good deal more rampant than it is now). The qualities by which any society which is to last longer than a generation actually has to be sustained—industry, courage, patriotism, frugality, philoprogenitiveness—obviously could not find any place in Eliot's early poems. There was only room for rentier values, the values of people too civilised to work, fight or even reproduce themselves. But that was the price that had to be paid, at any rate at that time, for writing a poem worth reading. The mood of lassitude, irony, disbelief, disgust, and not the sort of beefy enthusiasm demanded by the Squires[2] and Herberts,[3] was what sensitive people actually felt. It is fashionable to say that in verse only the words count and the "meaning" is irrelevant, but in fact every poem contains a prose-meaning, and when the poem is any good it is a meaning which the poet urgently wishes to express. All art is to some extent propaganda. *Prufrock* is an expression of futility, but it is also a poem of wonderful vitality and power, culminating in a sort of rocket-burst in the closing stanzas:

> I have seen them riding seaward on the waves
> Combing the white hair of the waves blown back
> When the wind blows the water white and black.
>
> We have lingered in the chambers of the sea
> By sea-girls wreathed with seaweed red and brown
> Till human voices wake us, and we drown.[4]

There is nothing like that in the later poems, although the rentier despair on which these lines are founded has been consciously dropped.

But the trouble is that conscious futility is something only for the young. One cannot go on "despairing of life" into a ripe old age. One cannot go on and on being "decadent," since decadence means falling and one can only be said to be falling if one is going to reach the bottom reasonably soon. Sooner or later one is obliged to adopt a positive attitude towards life and society. It would be putting it too crudely to say that every poet in our time must either die young, enter the Catholic Church, or join the Communist Party, but in fact the escape from the consciousness of futility is along those general lines. There are other deaths besides physical deaths, and there are other sects and creeds besides the Catholic Church and the Communist Party, but it remains true that after a certain age one must either stop writing or dedicate oneself to some purpose not wholly aesthetic. Such a dedication necessarily means a break with the past:

> . . . every attempt
> Is a wholly new start, and a different kind of failure
> Because one has only learnt to get the better of words
> For the thing one no longer has to say, or the way in which
> One is no longer disposed to say it. And so each venture
> Is a new beginning, a raid on the inarticulate
> With shabby equipment always deteriorating
> In the general mess of imprecision of feeling,
> Undisciplined squads of emotion.

Eliot's escape from individualism was into the Church, the Anglican Church as it happened. One ought not to assume that the gloomy Pétainism to which he now appears to have given himself over was the unavoidable result of his conversion. The Anglo-Catholic movement does not impose any political "line" on its followers, and a reactionary or Austrofascist tendency had always been apparent in his work, especially his prose writings. In theory it is still possible to be an orthodox religious believer without being intellectually crippled in the process; but it is far from easy, and in practice books by orthodox believers usually show the same cramped, blinkered outlook as books by orthodox Stalinists or others who are mentally unfree. The reason is that the Christian churches still demand assent to doctrines which no one seriously believes in. The most obvious case is the immortality of the soul.

The various "proofs" of personal immortality which can be advanced by Christian apologists are psychologically of no importance; what matters, psychologically, is that hardly anyone nowadays *feels* himself to be immortal. The next world may be in some sense "believed in" but it has not anywhere near the same actuality in people's minds as it had a few centuries ago. Compare for instance the gloomy mumblings of these three poems with *Jerusalem my happy home*; the comparison is not altogether pointless. In the second case you have a man to whom the next world is as real as this one. It is true that his vision of it is incredibly vulgar—a choir practice in a jeweller's shop—but he believes in what he is saying and his belief gives vitality to his words. In the other case you have a man who does not really *feel* his faith, but merely assents to it for complex reasons. It does not in itself give him any fresh literary impulse. At a certain stage he feels the need for a "purpose," and he wants a "purpose" which is reactionary and not progressive; the immediately available refuge is the Church, which demands intellectual absurdities of its members; so his work becomes a continuous nibbling round those absurdities, an attempt to make them acceptable to himself. The Church has not now any living imagery, any new vocabulary to offer:

The rest
Is prayer, observance, discipline, thought and action.

Perhaps what we need is prayer, observance, etc., but you do not make a line of poetry by stringing those words together. Mr. Eliot speaks also of

the intolerable wrestle
With words and meanings. The poetry does not matter.

I do not know, but I should imagine that the struggle with meanings would have loomed smaller, and the poetry would have seemed to matter more, if he could have found his way to some creed which did not start off by forcing one to believe the incredible.

There is no saying whether Mr. Eliot's development could have been much other than it has been. All writers who are any good develop throughout life, and the general direction of their development is determined. It is absurd to attack Eliot, as some left-wing critics have done, for being a "reactionary" and to imagine that he might have used his gifts in the cause of democracy and Socialism. Obviously a scepticism about democracy and a disbelief in "progress" are an integral part of him; without them he could not have written a line of his works. But it is arguable that he would have done better to go much further in the direction implied in his famous "Anglo-Catholic and Royalist" declaration. He could not have developed into a Socialist, but he might have developed into the last apologist of aristocracy.

Neither feudalism nor indeed Fascism is necessarily deadly to poets, though both are to prose-writers. The thing that is really deadly to both is Conservatism of the half-hearted modern kind.

It is at least imaginable that if Eliot had followed wholeheartedly the anti-democratic, anti-perfectionist strain in himself he might have struck a new vein comparable to his earlier one. But the negative, Pétainism, which turns its eyes to the past, accepts defeat, writes off earthly happiness as impossible, mumbles about prayer and repentance and thinks it a spiritual advance to see life as "a pattern of living worms in the guts of the women of Canterbury"—that, surely, is the least hopeful road a poet could take.

Can Socialists Be Happy?[1]

Tribune, December 24, 1943

The thought of Christmas raises almost automatically the thought of Charles Dickens, and for two very good reasons. To begin with, Dickens is one of the few English writers who have actually written about Christmas. Christmas is the most popular of English festivals, and yet it has produced astonishingly little literature. There are the carols, mostly medieval in origin; there is a tiny handful of poems by Robert Bridges, T. S. Eliot, and some others, and there is Dickens; but there is very little else. Secondly, Dickens is remarkable, indeed almost unique, among modern writers in being able to give a convincing picture of *happiness.*

Dickens dealt successfully with Christmas twice—in a well-known chapter of *The Pickwick Papers* and in *The Christmas Carol.* The latter story was read to Lenin on his deathbed and, according to his wife, he found its "bourgeois sentimentality" completely intolerable. Now in a sense Lenin was right; but if he had been in better health he would perhaps have noticed that the story has some interesting sociological implications. To begin with, however thick Dickens may lay on the paint, however disgusting the "pathos" of Tiny Tim may be, the Cratchit family do give the impression of enjoying themselves. They sound happy as, for instance, the citizens of William Morris's *News From Nowhere* don't sound happy. Moreover—and Dickens's understanding of this is one of the secrets of his power—their happiness derives mainly from contrast. They are in high spirits because for once in a way they have enough to eat. The wolf is at the door, but he is wagging his tail. The steam of the Christmas pudding drifts across a background of pawnshops and sweated labour, and in a double sense the ghost of Scrooge stands beside the dinner table. Bob Cratchit even wants to drink Scrooge's health, which Mrs. Cratchit rightly refuses. The Cratchits are able to enjoy their Christmas precisely because Christmas only comes once a year. Their happiness is convincing just because it is described as incomplete.

All efforts to describe *permanent* happiness, on the other hand, have been failures, from earliest history onwards. Utopias (incidentally the coined word Utopia doesn't mean "a good place," it means merely "a non-existent place") have been common in the literature of the past three or four hundred years, but the "favourable" ones are invariably unappetising, and usually lacking in vitality as well.

By far the best known modern Utopias are those of H. G. Wells. Wells's vision of the future, implicit all through his early work and partly set forth in *Anticipations* and *A Modern Utopia,* is most fully expressed in two books written in the early 'twenties, *The Dream* and *Men Like Gods.* Here you have a picture of the world as Wells would like to see it—or thinks he would like to see it. It is a world whose keynotes are enlightened hedonism and scientific curiosity. All the evils and miseries that we now suffer from have vanished. Ignorance, war, poverty, dirt, disease, frustration, hunger, fear, overwork, superstition—all vanished. So expressed, it is impossible to deny that that is the kind of world we all hope for. We all want to abolish the things that Wells wants to abolish. But is there anyone who actually wants to live in a Wellsian Utopia? On the contrary, *not* to live in a world like that, *not* to wake up in a hygienic garden suburb infested by naked schoolmarms, has actually become a conscious political motive. A book like *Brave New World* is an expression of the actual fear that modern man feels of the rationalised hedonistic society which it is within his power to create. A Catholic writer said recently that Utopias are now technically feasible and that in consequence *how to avoid Utopia* had become a serious problem. With the Fascist movement in front of our eyes we cannot write this off as a merely silly remark. For one of the sources of the Fascist movement is the desire to avoid a too-rational and too-comfortable world.

All "favourable" Utopias seem to be alike in postulating perfection while being unable to suggest happiness. *News From Nowhere* is a sort of goody-goody version of the Wellsian Utopia. Everyone is kindly and reasonable, all the upholstery comes from Liberty's, but the impression left behind is of a sort of watery melancholy. Lord Samuel's recent effort in the same direction, *An Unknown Country,* is even more dismal. The inhabitants of Bensalem (the word is borrowed from Francis Bacon) give the impression of looking on life as simply an evil to be got through with as little fuss as possible. All that their wisdom has brought them is permanent low spirits. But it is more impressive that Jonathan Swift, one of the greatest imaginative writers who have ever lived, is no more successful in constructing a "favourable" Utopia than the others.

The earlier parts of *Gulliver's Travels* are probably the most devastating attack on human society that has ever been written. Every word of them is relevant to-day; in places they contain quite detailed prophecies of the political horrors of our own time. Where Swift fails, however, is in trying to describe a race of beings whom he *does* admire. In the last part, in contrast with the disgusting Yahoos, we are shown the noble Houyhnhnms, a race of intelligent horses who are free from human failings. Now these horses, for all their high character and unfailing common sense, are remarkably dreary creatures. Like the inhabitants of various other Utopias, they are chiefly concerned with avoiding fuss. They live uneventful, subdued, "reasonable" lives, free not only from quarrels, disorder or insecurity of any kind, but also from "passion," including physical love. They choose their mates on eugenic principles, avoid excesses of affection, and appear somewhat glad to die when their time comes. In the earlier parts of the book Swift has shown where man's folly and scoundrelism lead him: but take away the folly and the scoundrelism, and all you are left with, apparently, is a tepid sort of existence, hardly worth leading.

Attempts at describing a definitely other-worldly happiness have been no more successful. Heaven is as great a flop as Utopia—though Hell, it is worth noting, occupies a respectable place in literature, and has often been described most minutely and convincingly.

It is a commonplace that the Christian Heaven, as usually portrayed, would attract nobody. Almost all Christian writers dealing with Heaven either say frankly that it is indescribable or conjure up a vague picture of gold, precious stones, and the endless singing of hymns. This has, it is true, inspired some of the best poems in the world:

> Thy walls are of chalcedony,
> Thy bulwarks diamonds square,
> Thy gates are of right orient pearl
> Exceeding rich and rare!

Or:

> Holy, holy, holy, all the saints adore Thee,
> Casting down their golden crowns about the glassy sea,
> Cherubim and seraphim falling down before Thee,
> That wast, and art, and evermore shalt be!

But what it could not do was to describe a place or condition in which the ordinary human being actively wanted to be. Many a revivalist minister, many a Jesuit priest (see, for instance, the terrific sermon in James Joyce's *Portrait of the Artist*) has frightened his congregation almost out of their skins with his word-pictures of Hell. But as soon as it comes to Heaven, there is a prompt falling-back on words like "ecstasy" and "bliss," with little attempt to say what they consist in. Perhaps the most vital bit of writing on this subject is the famous passage in which Tertullian explains that one of the chief joys of Heaven is watching the tortures of the damned.

The various pagan versions of Paradise are little better, if at all. One has the feeling that it is always twilight in the Elysian fields. Olympus, where the gods lived, with their nectar and ambrosia, and their nymphs and Hebes, the "immortal tarts" as D. H. Lawrence called them, might be a bit more homelike than the Christian Heaven, but you would not want to spend a long time there. As for the Moslem Paradise, with its seventy-seven houris per man, all presumably clamouring for attention at the same moment, it is just a nightmare. Nor are the Spiritualists, though constantly assuring us that "all is bright and beautiful," able to describe any next-world activity which a thinking person would find endurable, let alone attractive.

It is the same with attempted descriptions of perfect happiness which are neither Utopian nor other-worldly, but merely sensual. They always give an impression of emptiness or vulgarity, or both. At the beginning of *La Pucelle* Voltaire describes the life of Charles IX with his mistress, Agnes Sorel. They were "always happy," he says. And what did their happiness consist in? Apparently in an endless round of feasting, drinking, hunting and love-making. Who would not sicken of such an existence after a few weeks? Rabelais describes the fortunate spirits who have a good time in the next world to console them for having had a bad time in this one. They sing a song which can be roughly translated: "To leap, to dance, to play tricks, to drink the wine both white and red, and to do nothing all day long except count gold crowns"—how boring it sounds, after all! The emptiness of the whole notion of an everlasting "good time" is shown up in Breughel's picture "The Land of the Sluggard," where the three great lumps of fat lie asleep, head to head, with the boiled eggs and roast legs of pork coming up to be eaten of their own accord.

It would seem that human beings are not able to describe, nor perhaps to imagine, happiness except in terms of contrast. That is why the conception of Heaven or Utopia varies from age to age. In pre-industrial society Heaven was described as a place of endless rest, and as being paved with gold, because the experience of the average human being was overwork and poverty. The houris of the Moslem Paradise reflected a polygamous society where most of the women disappeared into the harems of the rich. But these pictures of "eternal bliss" always failed because as soon as the bliss became eternal (eternity being thought of as endless time), the contrast ceased to operate. Some of the conventions which have become embedded in our literature first arose from physical conditions which have now ceased to exist. The cult of spring is an example. In the Middle Ages spring did not primarily mean swallows and wild flowers. It meant green vegetables, milk and fresh meat after several months of living on salt pork in smoky windowless huts. The spring songs were gay—

> Do nothing but eat and make good cheer,
> And thank Heaven for the merry year
> When flesh is cheap and females dear,
> And lusty lads roam here and there,
> So merrily,
> And ever among so merrily!

because there was something to be gay about. The winter was over, that was the great thing. Christmas itself, a pre-Christian festival, probably started because there had to be an occasional outburst of overeating and drinking to make a break in the unbearable northern winter.

The inability of mankind to imagine happiness except in the form of *relief,* either from effort or pain, presents Socialists with a serious problem. Dickens can describe a poverty-stricken family tucking into a roast goose, and can make them appear happy; on the other hand, the inhabitants of perfect universes seem to have no spontaneous gaiety and are usually somewhat repulsive into the bargain. But clearly we are not aiming at the kind of world Dickens described, nor, probably, at any world he was capable of imagining. The Socialist objective is not a society where everything comes right in the end, because kind old gentlemen give away turkeys. What are we aiming at, if not a society in which "charity" would be unnecessary? We want a world where Scrooge, with his dividends, and Tiny Tim, with his tuberculous leg, would both be unthinkable. But does that mean that we are aiming at some painless, effortless Utopia?

At the risk of saying something which the editors of *Tribune* may not endorse, I suggest that the real objective of Socialism is not happiness. Happiness hitherto has been a by-product, and for all we know it may always remain so. The real objective of Socialism is human brotherhood. This is widely felt to be the case, though it is not usually said, or not said loudly enough. Men use up their lives in heart-breaking political struggles, or get themselves killed in civil wars, or tortured in the secret prisons of the Gestapo, not in order to establish some central-heated, air-conditioned, strip-lighted Paradise, but because they want a world in which human beings love one another instead of swindling and murdering one another. And they want that world as a first step. Where they go from there is not so certain, and the attempt to foresee it in detail merely confuses the issue.

Socialist thought has to deal in prediction, but only in broad terms. One often has to aim at objectives which one can only very dimly see. At this moment, for instance, the world is at war and wants peace. Yet the world has no experience of peace, and never has had, unless the Noble Savage once existed. The world wants something which it is dimly aware could exist, but which it cannot accurately define. This Christmas day, thousands of men will be bleeding to death in the Russian snows, or drowning in icy waters, or blowing one another to pieces with hand grenades on swampy islands of the Pacific; homeless children will be scrabbling for food among the wreckage of German cities. To make that kind of thing impossible is a good objective. But to say in detail what a peaceful world would be like is a different matter, and to attempt to do so is apt to lead to the horrors so enthusiastically presented by Gerald Heard.[2]

Nearly all creators of Utopia have resembled the man who has toothache, and therefore thinks that happiness consists in not having toothache. They wanted to produce a perfect society by an endless continuation of something that had only been valuable because it was temporary. The wiser course would be to say that there are certain lines along which humanity must move, the grand strategy is mapped out, but detailed prophecy is not our business. Whoever tries to imagine perfection simply reveals his own emptiness. This is the case even with a great writer like Swift, who can flay a bishop or a politician so neatly, but who, when he tries to create a superman, merely leaves one with the impression—the very last he can have intended—that the stinking Yahoos had in them more possibility of development than the enlightened Houyhnhnms.

Benefit of Clergy: Some Notes on Salvador Dali

Intended for *Saturday Book*, 4, 1944

"Benefit of Clergy" is entered in Orwell's Payments Book against June 1, 1944. He was paid £25 for the essay, although, as he explained in a note when it was published, in 1946, in *Critical Essays* (and the U.S. edition, *Dickens, Dali & Others*, 1946), it did not appear in copies of the *Saturday Book* that were intended for distribution to the public. "'Benefit of Clergy' made a sort of phantom appearance in the *Saturday Book* for 1944. The book was in print when its publishers, Messrs Hutchinson, decided that this essay must be suppressed on grounds of obscenity. It was accordingly cut out of each copy, though for technical reasons it was impossible to remove its title from the table of contents."

Orwell's own copy of the *Saturday Book* (and a few others that eluded Hutchinson's censors) included the essay, and it is from that copy that this essay is reproduced here.

Autobiography is only to be trusted when it reveals something disgraceful. A man who gives a good account of himself is probably lying, since any life when viewed from the inside is simply a series of defeats. However, even the most flagrantly dishonest book (Frank Harris's autobiographical writings are an example) can without intending it give a true picture of its author. Dali's recently-published *Life** comes under this heading. Some of the incidents in it are flatly incredible, others have been re-arranged and romanticised, and not merely the humiliation but the persistent *ordinariness* of everyday life has been cut out. Dali is even by his own diagnosis narcissistic, and his autobiography is simply a strip-tease act conducted in pink limelight. But as a record of fantasy, of

**The Secret Life of Salvador Dali* (the Dial Press, New York) [Orwell's footnote].

the perversion of instinct that has been made possible by the machine age, it has great value.

Here then are some of the episodes in Dali's life, from his earliest years onward. Which of them are true and which are imaginary hardly matters: the point is that this is the kind of thing that Dali would have *liked* to do.

When he is six years old there is some excitement over the appearance of Halley's comet:

> "Suddenly one of my father's office clerks appeared in the drawing-room doorway and announced that the comet could be seen from the terrace. . . . While crossing the hall I caught sight of my little three-year-old sister crawling unobtrusively through a doorway. I stopped, hesitated a second, then gave her a terrible kick in the head as though it had been a ball, and continued running carried away with a 'delirious joy' induced by this savage act. But my father, who was behind me, caught me and led me down into his office, where I remained as a punishment till dinner time."

A year earlier than this Dali had "suddenly, as most of my ideas occur" flung another little boy off a suspension bridge. Several other incidents of the same kind are recorded, including (this was when he was twenty-nine years old) knocking down and trampling on a girl "until they had to tear her, bleeding, out of my reach."

When he is about five he gets hold of a wounded bat which he puts into a tin pail. Next morning he finds that the bat is almost dead and is covered with ants which are devouring it. He puts it in his mouth, ants and all, and bites it almost in half.

When he is adolescent a girl falls desperately in love with him. He kisses and caresses her so as to excite her as much as possible, but refuses to go further. He resolves to keep this up for five years (he calls it his "five year plan"), enjoying her humiliation and the sense of power it gives him. He frequently tells her that at the end of five years he will desert her, and when the time comes he does so.

Till well into adult life he keeps up the practice of masturbation, and likes to do this, apparently, in front of a looking-glass. For ordinary purposes he is impotent, it appears, till the age of thirty or so. When he first meets his future wife, Gala, he is greatly tempted to push her off a precipice. He is aware that there is something that she wants him to do to her, and after their first kiss the confession is made:

> "I threw back Gala's head, pulling it by the hair, and, trembling with complete hysteria, I commanded,
>
> " 'Now tell me what you want me to do with you! But tell me slowly, looking me in the eye, with the crudest, the most ferociously erotic words that can make both of us feel the greatest shame!'
>
> ". . . Then, Gala, transforming the last glimmer of her expression of pleasure into the hard light of her own tyranny, answered,
>
> " 'I want you to kill me!' "

He is somewhat disappointed by this demand, since it is merely what he wanted to do already. He contemplates throwing her off the bell-tower of the Cathedral of Toledo, but refrains from doing so.

During the Spanish civil war he astutely avoids taking sides and makes a trip to Italy. He feels himself more and more drawn towards the aristocracy, frequents smart salons, finds himself wealthy patrons, and is photographed with the plump Vicomte de

Noailles, whom he describes as his "Maecenas." When the European war approaches he has one preoccupation only: how to find a place which has good cookery and from which he can make a quick bolt if danger comes too near. He fixes on Bordeaux, and duly flees to Spain during the Battle of France. He stays in Spain long enough to pick up a few anti-red atrocity stories, then makes for America. The story ends in a blaze of respectability. Dali, at thirty-seven, has become a devoted husband, is cured of his aberrations, or some of them, and is completely reconciled to the Catholic Church. He is also, one gathers, making a good deal of money.

However, he has by no means ceased to take pride in the pictures of his Surrealist period, with titles like *The Great Masturbator, Sodomy of a Skull with a Grand Piano,* etc. There are reproductions of these all the way through the book. Many of Dali's drawings are simply representational and have a characteristic to be noted later. But from his Surrealist paintings and photographs the two things that stand out are sexual perversity and necrophilia. Sexual objects and symbols—some of them well-known, like our old friend the high-heeled slipper, others, like the crutch and the cup of warm milk, patented by Dali himself—recur over and over again, and there is a fairly well-marked excretory motif as well. In his painting *Le Jeu Lugubre,* he says, "the drawers bespattered with excrement were painted with such minute and realistic complacency that the whole little surrealist group was anguished by the question: Is he coprophagic or not?" Dali adds firmly that he is *not,* and that he regards this aberration as "repulsive," but it seems to be only at that point that his interest in excrement stops. Even when he recounts the experience of watching a woman urinate standing up, he has to add the detail that she misses her aim and dirties her shoes. It is not given to any one person to have all the vices, and Dali also boasts that he is not homosexual, but otherwise he seems to have as good an outfit of perversions as anyone could wish for.

However, his most notable characteristic is his necrophilia. He himself freely admits to this, and claims to have been cured of it. Dead faces, skulls, corpses of animals occur fairly frequently in his pictures, and the ants which devoured the dying bat make countless reappearances. One photograph shows an exhumed corpse, far gone in decomposition. Another shows the dead donkeys putrefying on top of grand pianos which formed part of the Surrealist film *Le Chien Andalou.* Dali still looks back on these donkeys with great enthusiasm:

> "I 'made up' the putrefaction of the donkeys with great pots of sticky glue which I poured over them. Also I emptied their eye sockets and made them larger by hacking them out with scissors. In the same way I furiously cut their mouths open to make the white rows of their teeth show to better advantage, and I added several jaws to each mouth so that it would appear that although the donkeys were already rotting they were vomiting up a little more of their own death, above those other rows of teeth formed by the keys of the black pianos."

And finally there is the picture—apparently some kind of faked photograph—of "Mannequin rotting in a taxicab." Over the already somewhat bloated face and breast of the apparently dead girl, huge snails are crawling. In the caption below the picture Dali notes that these are Burgundy snails—that is, the edible kind.

Of course, in this long book of 400 quarto pages there is more than I have indicated, but I do not think that I have given an unfair account of its moral atmosphere and mental scenery. It is a book that stinks. If it were possible for a book to give a physical stink off its pages, this one would—a thought that might please Dali, who before wooing his future wife for the first time rubbed himself all over with an ointment made of goat's dung boiled up in fish glue. But against this has to be set the fact that Dali is a draughtsman of very exceptional gifts. He is also, to judge by the minuteness and the sureness of his drawings, a very hard worker. He is an exhibitionist and a careerist, but he is not a fraud. He has fifty times more talent than most of the people who would denounce his morals and jeer at his paintings. And these two sets of facts, taken together, raise a question which for lack of any basis of agreement seldom gets a real discussion.

The point is that you have here a direct, unmistakable assault on sanity and decency: and even—since some of Dali's pictures would tend to poison the imagination like a pornographic postcard—on life itself. What Dali has done and what he has imagined is debatable, but in his outlook, his character, the bedrock decency of a human being does not exist. He is as anti-social as a flea. Clearly, such people are undesirable, and a society in which they can flourish has something wrong with it.

Now, if you showed this book, with its illustrations, to Lord Elton, to Mr. Alfred Noyes, to *The Times* leader-writers who exult over the "eclipse of the highbrow," in fact to any "sensible" art-hating English person, it is easy to imagine what kind of response you would get. They would flatly refuse to see any merit in Dali whatever. Such people are not only unable to admit that what is morally degraded can be aesthetically right, but their real demand of every artist is that he shall pat them on the back and tell them that thought is unneccessary. And they can be especially dangerous at a time like the present, when the Ministry of Information and the British Council put power into their hands. For their impulse is not only to crush every new talent as it appears, but to castrate the past as well. Witness the renewed highbrow-baiting that is now going on in this country and America, with its outcry not only against Joyce, Proust, and Lawrence, but even against T. S. Eliot.

But if you talk to the kind of person who *can* see Dali's merits, the response that you get is not as a rule very much better. If you say that Dali, though a brilliant draughtsman, is a dirty little scoundrel, you are looked upon as a savage. If you say that you don't like rotting corpses, and that people who do like rotting corpses are mentally diseased, it is assumed that you lack the aesthetic sense. Since "Mannequin rotting in a taxicab" is a good composition (as it undoubtedly is), it cannot be a disgusting, degrading picture: whereas Noyes, Elton, etc., would tell you that because it is disgusting it cannot be a good composition. And between these two fallacies there is no middle position: or rather, there is a middle position, but we seldom hear much about it. On the one side, *Kulturbolschevismus*: on the other (though the phrase itself is out of fashion) "Art for Art's sake." Obscenity is a very difficult question to discuss honestly. People are too frightened either of seeming to be shocked, or of seeming not to be shocked, to be able to define the relationship between art and morals.

It will be seen that what the defenders of Dali are claiming is a kind of *benefit of clergy*. The artist is to be exempt from the moral laws that are binding on ordinary people. Just pronounce the magic word "Art," and everything is O.K. Rotting corpses with snails crawling over them are O.K.; kicking little girls on the head is O.K.; even a film like *L'Age d'Or* is O.K.* It is also O.K. that Dali should batten on France for years and then scuttle off like a rat as

*Dali mentions *L'Age d'Or* and adds that its first public showing was broken up by hooligans, but he does not say in detail what it was about. According to Henry Miller's account of it, it showed among other things some fairly detailed shots of a woman defaecating [Orwell's footnote].

soon as France is in danger. So long as you can paint well enough to pass the test, all shall be forgiven you.

One can see how false this is if one extends it to cover ordinary crime. In an age like our own, when the artist is an altogether exceptional person, he must be allowed a certain amount of irresponsibility, just as a pregnant woman is. Still, no one would say that a pregnant woman should be allowed to commit murder, nor would anyone make such a claim for the artist, however gifted. If Shakespeare returned to the earth to-morrow, and if it were found that his favourite recreation was raping little girls in railway carriages, we should not tell him to go ahead with it on the ground that he might write another *King Lear.* And after all, the worst crimes are not always the punishable ones. By encouraging necrophilic reveries one probably does quite as much harm as by, say, picking pockets at the races. One ought to be able to hold in one's head simultaneously the two facts that Dali is a good draughtsman and a disgusting human being. The one does not invalidate or, in a sense, affect the other. The first thing that we demand of a wall is that it shall stand up. If it stands up it is a good wall, and the question of what purpose it serves is separable from that. And yet even the best wall in the world deserves to be pulled down if it surrounds a concentration camp. In the same way it should be possible to say, "This is a good book or a good picture, and it ought to be burned by the public hangman." Unless one can say that, at least in imagination, one is shirking the implications of the fact that an artist is also a citizen and a human being.

Not, of course, that Dali's autobiography, or his pictures, ought to be suppressed. Short of the dirty postcards that used to be sold in Mediterranean seaport towns, it is doubtful policy to suppress anything, and Dali's fantasies probably cast useful light on the decay of capitalist civilisation. But what he clearly needs is diagnosis. The question is not so much *what* he is as *why* he is like that. It ought not to be in doubt that he is a diseased intelligence, probably not much altered by his alleged conversion, since genuine penitents, or people who have returned to sanity, do not flaunt their past vices in that complacent way. He is a symptom of the world's illness. The important thing is not to denounce him as a cad who ought to be horsewhipped, or to defend him as a genius who ought not to be questioned, but to find out *why* he exhibits that particular set of aberrations.

The answer is probably discoverable in his pictures, and those I myself am not competent to examine. But I can point to one clue which perhaps takes one part of the distance. This is the old-fashioned, over-ornate, Edwardian style of drawing to which Dali tends to return when he is not being Surrealist. Some of Dali's drawings are reminiscent of Dürer, one (p. 113) seems to show the influence of Beardsley, another (p. 269) seems to borrow something from Blake. But the most persistent strain is the Edwardian one. When I opened this book for the first time and looked at its innumerable marginal illustrations, I was haunted by a resemblance which I could not immediately pin down. I fetched up at the ornamental candlestick at the beginning of Part I (p. 7). What did this thing remind me of? Finally I tracked it down. It reminded me of a large, vulgar, expensively got-up edition of Anatole France (in translation) which must have been published about 1913. That had ornamental chapter headings and tailpieces after this style. Dali's candlestick displays at one end a curly fish-like creature that looks curiously familiar (it seems to be based on the conventional dolphin), and at the other is the burning candle. This candle, which recurs in one picture after another, is a very old friend. You will find it, with the same picturesque gouts of wax arranged on its sides, in those phoney electric lights done up as candlesticks which are popular in sham-Tudor country hotels. This candle, and the design beneath it, convey at once an intense feeling of sentimentality. As though to counteract this Dali has spattered a quill-ful of ink all over the page, but without avail. The same impression keeps popping up on page after page. The design at the bottom of page 62, for instance, would nearly go into *Peter Pan.* The figure on page 224, in spite of having her cranium elongated into an immense sausage-like shape, is the witch of the fairy-tale books. The horse on page 234 and the unicorn on page 218 might be illustrations to James Branch Cabell. The rather pansified drawings of youths on pages 97, 100, and elsewhere convey the same impression. Picturesqueness keeps breaking in. Take away the skulls, ants, lobsters, telephones, and other paraphernalia, and every now and again you are back in the world of Barrie, Rackham, Dunsany and *Where the Rainbow Ends.*

Curiously enough, some of the naughty-naughty touches in Dali's autobiography tie up with the same period. When I read the passage I quoted at the beginning, about the kicking of the little sister's head, I was aware of another phantom resemblance. What was it? Of course! *Ruthless Rhymes for Heartless Homes* by Harry Graham. Such rhymes were very popular round about 1912, and one that ran:

Poor little Willy is crying so sore,
A sad little boy is he,
For he's broken his little sister's neck
And he'll have no jam for tea.

might almost have been founded on Dali's anecdote. Dali, of course, is aware of his Edwardian leanings, and makes capital out of them, more or less in a spirit of pastiche. He professes an especial affection for the year 1900, and claims that every ornamental object of 1900 is full of mystery, poetry, eroticism, madness, perversity, etc. Pastiche, however, usually implies a real affection for the thing parodied. It seems to be, if not the rule, at any rate distinctly common for an intellectual bent to be accompanied by a non-rational, even childish urge in the same direction. A sculptor, for instance, is interested in planes and curves, but he is also a person who enjoys the physical act of mucking about with clay or stone. An engineer is a person who enjoys the feel of tools, the noise of dynamos and the smell of oil. A psychiatrist usually has a leaning towards some sexual aberration himself. Darwin became a biologist partly because he was a country gentleman and fond of animals. It may be, therefore, that Dali's seemingly perverse cult of Edwardian things (for example his "discovery of the 1900 subway entrances") is merely the symptom of a much deeper, less conscious affection. The innumerable, beautifully executed copies of textbook illustrations, solemnly labelled "le rossignol," "une montre" and so on, which he scatters all over his margins, may be meant partly as a joke. The little boy in knickerbockers playing with a diabolo on page 103 is a perfect period piece. But perhaps these things are also there because Dali can't help drawing that kind of thing, because it is to that period and that style of drawing that he really belongs.

If so, his aberrations are partly explicable. Perhaps they are a way of assuring himself that he is not commonplace. The two qualities that Dali unquestionably possesses are a gift for drawing and an atrocious egoism. "At seven," he says in the first paragraph of his book, "I wanted to be Napoleon. And my ambition has been growing steadily ever since." This is worded in a deliberately startling way, but no doubt it is substantially true. Such feelings are common enough. "I knew I was a genius," somebody once said to me, "long before I knew what I was going to be a genius *about*." And suppose that you have nothing in you except your egoism and a dexterity that goes no higher than the elbow: suppose that your real gift is for a detailed, academic, representational style of drawing, your real *métier* to be an illustrator of scientific text-books. How then do you become Napoleon?

There is always one escape: *into wickedness.* Always do the thing that will shock and wound people. At five, throw a little boy off a bridge, strike an old doctor across the face with a whip and break his spectacles—or, at any rate, dream about doing such things. Twenty years later, gouge the eyes out of dead donkeys with a pair of scissors. Along those lines you can always feel yourself original. And after all, it pays! It is much less dangerous than crime. Making all allowance for the probable suppressions in Dali's autobiography, it is clear that he has not had to suffer for his eccentricities as he would have done in an earlier age. He grew up into the corrupt world of the nineteen-twenties, when sophistication was immensely widespread and every European capital swarmed with aristocrats and rentiers who had given up sport and politics and taken to patronising the arts. If you threw dead donkeys at people they threw money back. A phobia for grasshoppers—which a few decades back would merely have provoked a snigger—was now an interesting "complex" which could be profitably exploited. And when that particular world collapsed before the German Army, America was waiting. You could even top it all up with religious conversion, moving at one hop and without a shadow of repentance from the fashionable salons of Paris to Abraham's bosom.

That, perhaps, is the essential outline of Dali's history. But why his aberrations should be the particular ones they were, and why it should be so easy to "sell" such horrors as rotting corpses to a sophisticated public—those are questions for the psychologist and the sociological critic. Marxist criticism has a short way with such phenomena as Surrealism. They are "bourgeois decadence" (much play is made with the phrases "corpse poisons" and "decaying rentier class"), and that is that. But though this probably states a fact, it does not establish a connection. One would still like to know *why* Dali's leaning was towards necrophilia (and not, say, homosexuality), and *why* the rentiers and the aristocrats should buy his pictures instead of hunting and making love like their grandfathers. Mere moral disapproval does not get one any further. But neither ought one to pretend, in the name of "detachment," that such pictures as "Mannequin rotting in a taxicab" are morally neutral. They are diseased and disgusting, and any investigation ought to start out from that fact.

Propaganda and Demotic Speech

Persuasion, Summer Quarter, 1944, 2, No. 2

When I was leaving England for Morocco at the end of 1938, some of the people in my village (less than fifty miles from London)[1] wanted to know whether it would be necessary to cross the sea to get there. In 1940, during General Wavell's African campaign, I discovered that the woman from whom I bought my rations thought Cyrenaica was in Italy. A year or two ago a friend of mine, who had been giving an A.B.C.A. lecture to some A.T.s,[2] tried the experiment of asking them a few general knowledge questions: among the answers he got were, (*a*) that there are only six Members of Parliament, and (*b*) that Singapore is the capital of India. If there were any point in doing so I could give many more instances of this kind of thing. I mention these three, simply as a preliminary reminder of the ignorance which any speech or piece of writing aimed at a large public has to take into account.

However, when you examine Government leaflets and White Papers, or leading articles in the newspapers, or the speeches and broadcasts of politicians, or the pamphlets and manifestos of any political party whatever, the thing that nearly always strikes you is their remoteness from the average man. It is not merely that they assume non-existent knowledge: often it is right and necessary to do that. It is also that clear, popular, everyday language seems to be instinctively avoided. The bloodless dialect of Government spokesmen (characteristic phrases are: in due course, no stone unturned, take the earliest opportunity, the answer is in the affirmative) is too well known to be worth dwelling on. Newspaper leaders are written either in this same dialect or in an inflated bombastic style with a tendency to fall back on archaic words (peril, valour, might, foe, succour, vengeance, dastardly, rampart, bulwark, bastion) which no normal person would ever think of using. Left-wing political parties specialise in a bastard vocabulary made up of Russian and German phrases translated with the maximum of clumsiness. And even posters, leaflets and broadcasts which are intended to give instructions, to tell people what to do in certain circumstances, often fail in their effect. For example, during the first air raids on London, it was found that innumerable people did not know which siren meant the Alert and which the All Clear. This was after months or years of gazing at A.R.P. posters. These posters had described the Alert as a "warbling note": a phrase which made no impression, since air-raid sirens don't warble, and few people attach any definite meaning to the word.

When Sir Richard Acland, in the early months of the war, was drawing up a Manifesto to be presented to the Government, he engaged a squad of Mass Observers to find out what meaning, if any, the ordinary man attaches to the high-sounding abstract words which are flung to and fro in politics. The most fantastic misunderstandings came to light. It was found, for instance, that most people don't know that "immorality" means anything besides sexual immorality.* One man thought that "movement" had something to do with constipation. And it is a nightly experience in any pub to see broadcast speeches and news bulletins make no impression on the average listener, because they are uttered in stilted bookish language and, incidentally, in an upper-class accent. At the time of Dunkirk I watched a gang of navvies eating their

*In spite of this, Common Wealth has adopted the astonishingly feeble slogan: "What is morally wrong cannot be politically right" [Orwell's footnote].

bread and cheese in a pub while the one o'clock news came over. Nothing registered: they just went on stolidly eating. Then, just for an instant, reporting the words of some soldier who had been hauled aboard a boat, the announcer dropped into spoken English, with the phrase, "Well, I've learned to swim this trip, anyway!" Promptly you could see ears being pricked up: it was ordinary language, and so it got across. A few weeks later, the day after Italy entered the war, Duff-Cooper announced that Mussolini's rash act would "add to the ruins for which Italy has been famous." It was neat enough, and a true prophecy, but how much impression does that kind of language make on nine people out of ten? The colloquial version of it would have been: "Italy has always been famous for ruins. Well, there are going to be a damn' sight more of them now." But that is not how Cabinet Ministers speak, at any rate in public.

Examples of futile slogans, obviously incapable of stirring strong feelings or being circulated by word of mouth, are: "Deserve Victory," "Freedom is in Peril. Defend it with all your Might," "Socialism the only Solution," "Expropriate the Expropriators," "Austerity," "Evolution not Revolution," "Peace is Indivisible." Examples of slogans phrased in spoken English are: "Hands off Russia," "Make Germany Pay," "Stop Hitler," "No Stomach Taxes," "Buy a Spitfire," "Votes for Women." Examples about mid-way between these two classes are: "Go To It," "Dig for Victory," "It all depends on ME," and some of Churchill's phrases, such as "the end of the beginning," "soft underbelly," "blood, toil, tears and sweat," and "never was so much owed by so many to so few." (Significantly, in so far as this last saying has been repeated by word of mouth, the bookish phrase *in the field of human conflict* has dropped out of it.) One has to take into account the fact that nearly all English people dislike anything that sounds high-flown and boastful. Slogans like "They shall not pass," or "Better to die on your feet than live on your knees," which have thrilled continental nations, seem slightly embarrassing to an Englishman, especially a working man. But the main weakness of propagandists and popularisers is their failure to notice that spoken and written English are two different things.

When recently I protested in print against the Marxist dialect which makes use of phrases like "objectively counter-revolutionary left-deviationism" or "drastic liquidation of petty-bourgeois elements," I received indignant letters from lifelong Socialists who told me that I was "insulting the language of the proletariat." In rather the same spirit, Professor Harold Laski devotes a long passage in his last book, *Faith, Reason and Civilisation,* to an attack on Mr. T. S. Eliot, whom he accuses of "writing only for a few." Now Eliot, as it happens, is one of the few writers of our time who have tried seriously to write English as it is spoken. Lines like—

> "And nobody came, and nobody went,
> But he took in the milk and he paid the rent"[3]

are about as near to spoken English as print can come. On the other hand, here is an entirely typical sentence from Laski's own writing:

> "As a whole, our system was a compromise between democracy in the political realm—itself a very recent development in our history—and an economic power oligarchically organised which was in its turn related to a certain aristocratic vestigia still able to influence profoundly the habits of our society."

This sentence, incidentally, comes from a reprinted lecture; so one must assume that Professor Laski actually stood up on a platform and spouted it forth, parenthesis and all. It is clear that people capable of speaking or writing in such a way have simply forgotten what everyday language is like. But this is nothing to some of the other passages I could dig out of Professor Laski's writings, or better still, from Communist literature, or best of all, from Trotskyist pamphlets. Indeed, from reading the Left-wing press you get the impression that the louder people yap about the proletariat, the more they despise its language.

I have said already that spoken English and written English are two different things. This variation exists in all languages, but is probably greater in English than in most. Spoken English is full of slang, it is abbreviated wherever possible, and people of all social classes treat its grammar and syntax in a slovenly way. Extremely few English people ever button up a sentence if they are speaking extempore. Above all, the vast English vocabulary contains thousands of words which everyone uses when writing, but which have no real currency in speech: and it also contains thousands more which are really obsolete but which are dragged forth by anyone who wants to sound clever or uplifting. If one keeps this in mind, one can think of ways of ensuring that propaganda, spoken or written, shall reach the audience it is aimed at.

So far as writing goes, all one can attempt is a process of simplification. The first step—and any social survey organisation could do this for a few hundreds or thousands of pounds—is to find out which of the abstract words habitually used by politicians are really understood by large numbers of people. If phrases like "unprincipled violation of declared pledges" or "insidious threat to the basic principles of democracy" don't mean anything to the average man, then it is stupid to use them. Secondly, in writing one can keep the spoken word constantly in mind. To get genuine spoken English on to paper is a complicated matter, as I shall show in a moment. But if you habitually say to yourself, "Could I simplify this? Could I make it more like speech?," you are not likely to produce sentences like the one quoted from Professor Laski above: nor are you likely to say "eliminate" when you mean kill, or "static water" when you mean fire tank.

Spoken propaganda, however, offers greater possibilities of improvement. It is here that the problem of writing in spoken English really arises.

Speeches, broadcasts, lectures and even sermons are normally written down beforehand. The most effective orators, like Hitler or Lloyd George, usually speak extempore, but they are very great rarities. As a rule—you can test this by listening at Hyde Park Corner—the so-called extempore speaker only keeps going by endlessly tacking one cliché on to another. In any case, he is probably delivering a speech which he has delivered dozens of times before. Only a few exceptionally gifted speakers can achieve the simplicity and intelligibility which even the most tongue-tied person achieves in ordinary conversation. On the air extempore speaking is seldom even attempted. Except for a few programmes, like the Brains Trust, which in any case are carefully rehearsed beforehand, every word that comes from the B.B.C. has been written down, and is delivered exactly as written. This is not only for censorship reasons: it is also because many speakers are liable to dry up at the microphone if they have no script to follow. The result is the heavy, dull, bookish lingo which causes most radio-users to switch off as soon as a talk is announced. It might be thought that one could get nearer to colloquial speech by dictating than by writing; but actually, it is the other way about. Dictating, at any rate to a human being, is always slightly embarrassing. One's impulse is to avoid long pauses, and one necessarily does so by clutching at the ready-made phrases and the dead and stinking metaphors (ring the changes on, ride rough-shod over, cross swords with, take up the cudgels for) with which the English language is littered. A dictated script is usually less life-like than a written one. What is wanted, evidently, is some way of getting ordinary, slipshod, colloquial English on to paper.

But is this possible? I think it is, and by a quite simple method which so far as I know has never been tried. It is this: Set a fairly ready speaker down at the microphone and let him just talk, either continuously or intermittently, on any subject he chooses. Do this with a dozen different speakers, recording it every time. Vary it with a few dialogues or conversations between three or four people. Then play your recordings back and let a stenographer reduce them to writing: not in the shortened, rationalised version that stenographers usually produce, but word for word, with such punctuation as seems appropriate. You would then—for the first time, I believe—have on paper some authentic specimens of spoken English. Probably they would not be readable as a book or a newspaper article is readable, but then spoken English is not meant to be read, it is meant to be listened to. From these specimens you could, I believe, formulate the rules of spoken English and find out how it differs from the written language. And when writing in spoken English had become practicable, the average speaker or lecturer who has to write his material down beforehand could bring it far closer to his natural diction, make it more essentially speakable, than he can at present.

Of course, demotic speech is not solely a matter of being colloquial and avoiding ill-understood words. There is also the question of accent. It seems certain that in modern England the "educated" upper-class accent is deadly to any speaker who is aiming at a large audience. All effective speakers in recent times have had either cockney or provincial accents. The success of Priestley's broadcasts in 1940 was largely due to his Yorkshire accent, which he probably broadened a little for the occasion. Churchill is only a seeming exception to this rule. Too old to have acquired the modern "educated" accent, he speaks with the Edwardian upper-class twang which to the average man's ear sounds like cockney. The "educated" accent, of which the accent of the B.B.C. announcers is a sort of parody, has no asset except its intelligibility to English-speaking foreigners. In England the minority to whom it is natural don't particularly like it, while in the other three-quarters of the population it arouses an immediate class antagonism. It is also noticeable that where there is doubt about the pronunciation of a name, successful speakers will stick to the working-class pronunciation even if they know it to be wrong. Churchill, for instance, mispronounced "Nazi" and "Gestapo" as long as the common people continued to do so. Lloyd George during the last war rendered "Kaiser" as "Kayser," which was the popular version of the word.

In the early days of the war the Government had the greatest difficulty in inducing people to bother to collect their ration books. At parliamentary elections, even when there is an up-to-date register, it often happens that less than half of the electorate use their votes. Things like these are symptoms of the intellectual gulf between the rulers and the ruled. But the same gulf lies always between the intelligentsia and the common man. Journalists, as we can see by their election forecasts, never know what the public is thinking. Revolutionary propaganda is incredibly ineffective. Churches are empty all over the country. The whole idea of trying to find out what the average man thinks, instead of assuming that he thinks what he ought to think, is novel and unwelcome. Social surveys are viciously attacked from Left and Right alike. Yet some mechanism for testing public opinion is an obvious necessity of modern government, and more so in a democratic country than in a totalitarian one. Its complement is the ability to speak to the ordinary man in words that he will understand and respond to.

At present propaganda only seems to succeed when it coincides with what people are inclined to do in any case. During the present war, for instance, the Government has done extraordinarily little to preserve morale: it has merely drawn on the existing reserves of good-will. And all political parties alike have failed to interest the public in vitally important questions—in the problem of India, to name only one. But some day we may have a genuinely democratic government, a government which will want to tell people what is happening, and what must be done next, and what sacrifices are necessary, and why. It will need the mechanisms for doing so, of which the first are the right words, the right tone of voice. The fact that when you suggest finding out what the common man is like, and approaching him accordingly, you are either accused of being an intellectual snob who wants to "talk down to" the masses, or else suspected of plotting to establish an English Gestapo, shows how sluggishly nineteenth-century our notion of democracy has remained.

Raffles and Miss Blandish

August 28, 1944; *Horizon,* October 1944; *Politics,* November 1944

Nearly half a century after his first appearance, Raffles, "the amateur cracksman," is still one of the best-known characters in English fiction. Very few people would need telling that he played cricket for England, had bachelor chambers in the Albany and burgled the Mayfair houses which he also entered as a guest. Just for that reason he and his exploits make a suitable background against which to examine a more modern crime story such as *No Orchids for Miss Blandish.*[1] Any such choice is necessarily arbitrary—I might equally well have chosen *Arsène Lupin,* for instance—but at any rate *No Orchids* and the Raffles books* have the common quality of being crime stories which play the limelight on the criminal rather than the policeman. For sociological purposes they can be compared. *No Orchids* is the 1939 version of glamourised crime, *Raffles* the 1900 version. What I am concerned with here is the immense difference in moral atmosphere between the two books, and the change in the popular attitude that this probably implies.

At this date, the charm of *Raffles* is partly in the period atmosphere, and partly in the technical excellence of the stories. Hornung was a very conscientious and, on his level, a very able writer. Anyone who cares for sheer efficiency must admire his work.

**Raffles, A Thief in the Night* and *Mr. Justice Raffles,* by E. W. Hornung. The third of these is definitely a failure, and only the first has the true Raffles atmosphere. Hornung wrote a number of crime stories, usually with a tendency to take the side of the criminal. A successful book in rather the same vein as *Raffles* is *Stingaree* [Orwell's footnote].

However, the truly dramatic thing about Raffles, the thing that makes him a sort of by-word even to this day (only a few weeks ago, in a burglary case, a magistrate referred to the prisoner as "a Raffles in real life"), is the fact that he is *a gentleman.* Raffles is presented to us—and this is rubbed home in countless scraps of dialogue and casual remarks—not as an honest man who has gone astray, but as a public-school man who has gone astray. His remorse, when he feels any, is almost purely social: he has disgraced "the old school," he has lost his right to enter "decent society," he has forfeited his amateur status and become a cad. Neither Raffles nor Bunny appears to feel at all strongly that stealing is wrong in itself, though Raffles does once justify himself by the casual remark that "the distribution of property is all wrong anyway." They think of themselves not as sinners but as renegades, or simply as outcasts. And the moral code of most of us is still so close to Raffles's own that we do feel his situation to be an especially ironical one. A West End clubman who is really a burglar! That is almost a story in itself, is it not? But how if it were a plumber or a greengrocer who was really a burglar? Would there be anything inherently dramatic in that? No—although the theme of the "double life," of respectability covering crime, is still there. Even Charles Peace[2] in his clergyman's dog-collar seems somewhat less of a hypocrite than Raffles in his Zingari[3] blazer.

Raffles, of course, is good at all games, but it is peculiarly fitting that his chosen game should be cricket. This allows not only of endless analogies between his cunning as a slow bowler and his cunning as a burglar, but also helps to define the exact nature of his crime. Cricket is not in reality a very popular game in England—it is nowhere near so popular as football, for instance—but it gives expression to a well-marked trait in the English character, the tendency to value "form" or "style" more highly than success. In the eyes of any true cricket-lover it is possible for an innings of ten runs to be "better" (i.e. more elegant) than an innings of a hundred runs: cricket is also one of the very few games in which the amateur can excel the professional. It is a game full of forlorn hopes and sudden dramatic changes of fortune, and its rules are so ill-defined that their interpretation is partly an ethical business. When Larwood, for instance, practised body-line bowling in Australia he was not actually breaking any rule: he was merely doing something that was "not cricket." Since cricket takes up a lot of time and is rather expensive to play, it is predominantly an upper-class game, but for the whole nation it is bound up with such concepts as "good form," "playing the game," etc., and it has declined in popularity just as the tradition of "don't hit a man when he's down" has declined. It is not a twentieth-century game, and nearly all modern-minded people dislike it. The Nazis, for instance, were at pains to discourage cricket, which had gained a certain footing in Germany before and after the last war. In making Raffles a cricketer as well as a burglar Hornung was not merely providing him with a plausible disguise; he was also drawing the sharpest moral contrast that he was able to imagine.

Raffles, no less than *Great Expectations* or *Le Rouge et le Noir,* is a story of snobbery, and it gains a great deal from the precariousness of Raffles's social position. A cruder writer would have made the "gentleman burglar" a member of the peerage, or at least a baronet. Raffles, however, is of upper-middle-class origin and is only accepted by the aristocracy because of his personal charm. "We were in Society but not of it," he says to Bunny towards the end of the book; and "I was asked about for my cricket." Both he and Bunny accept the values of "Society" unquestioningly, and would settle down in it for good if only they could get away with a big enough haul. The ruin that constantly threatens them is all the blacker because they only doubtfully "belong." A duke who has served a prison sentence is still a duke, whereas a mere man-about town if once disgraced, ceases to be "about town" for evermore. The closing chapters of the book, when Raffles has been exposed and is living under an assumed name, have a twilight-of-the-gods feeling, a mental atmosphere rather similar to that of Kipling's poem, *Gentleman Rankers*:

> A trooper of the forces—
> I, who kept my own six horses! etc.

Raffles now belongs irrevocably to the "cohorts of the damned."[4] He can still commit successful burglaries, but there is no way back into Paradise, which means Piccadilly and the M.C.C.[5] According to the public-school code there is only one means of rehabilitation: death in battle. Raffles dies fighting against the Boers (a practiced reader would foresee this from the start), and in the eyes of both Bunny and his creator this cancels his crimes.

Both Raffles and Bunny, of course, are devoid of religious belief, and they have no real ethical code, merely certain rules of behaviour which they observe semi-instinctively. But it is just here that the deep moral difference between *Raffles* and *No Orchids* becomes apparent. Raffles and Bunny, after all, are gentlemen, and such standards as they do have are not to be violated. Certain things are "not done," and the idea of doing them hardly arises. Raffles will not, for example, abuse hospitality. He will commit a burglary in a house where he is staying as a guest, but the victim must be a fellow-guest and not the host. He will not commit murder,* and he avoids violence wherever possible and prefers to

*1945. Actually Raffles does kill one man and is more or less consciously responsible for the death of two others. But all three of them are foreigners and have behaved in a very reprehensible manner. He also, on one occasion, contemplates murdering a blackmailer. It is, however, a fairly well-established convention in crime stories that murdering a blackmailer "doesn't count" [Orwell's footnote].

carry out his robberies unarmed. He regards friendship as sacred, and is chivalrous though not moral in his relations with women. He will take extra risks in the name of "sportsmanship," and sometimes even for aesthetic reasons. And above all he is intensely patriotic. He celebrates the Diamond Jubilee ("For sixty years, Bunny, we've been ruled over by absolutely the finest sovereign the world has ever seen") by despatching to the Queen, through the post, an antique gold cup which he has stolen from the British Museum. He steals, from partly political motives, a pearl which the German Emperor is sending to one of the enemies of Britain, and when the Boer War begins to go badly his one thought is to find his way into the fighting line. At the front he unmasks a spy at the cost of revealing his own identity, and then dies gloriously by a Boer bullet. In this combination of crime and patriotism he resembles his near-contemporary Arsène Lupin, who also scores off the German Emperor and wipes out his very dirty past by enlisting in the Foreign Legion.

It is important to note that by modern standards Raffles's crimes are very petty ones. Four hundred pounds' worth of jewelry seems to him an excellent haul. And though the stories are convincing in their physical detail, they contain very little sensationalism—very few corpses, hardly any blood, no sex crimes, no sadism, no perversions of any kind. It seems to be the case that the crime story, at any rate on its higher levels, has greatly increased in bloodthirstiness during the past twenty years. Some of the early detective stories do not even contain a murder. The Sherlock Holmes stories, for instance, are not all murders, and some of them do not even deal with an indictable crime. So also with the John Thorndyke stories, while of the Max Carrados stories only a minority are murders. Since 1918, however, a detective story not containing a murder has been a great rarity, and the most disgusting details of dismemberment and exhumation are commonly exploited. Some of the Peter Wimsey stories, for instance, seem to point to definite necrophilia. The Raffles stories, written from the angle of the criminal, are much less anti-social than many modern stories written from the angle of the detective. The main impression that they leave behind is of boyishness. They belong to a time when people had standards, though they happened to be foolish standards. Their key phrase is "not done." The line that they draw between good and evil is as senseless as a Polynesian taboo, but at least, like the taboo, it has the advantage that everyone accepts it.

So much for *Raffles*. Now for a header into the cesspool. *No Orchids for Miss Blandish,* by James Hadley Chase, was published in 1939 but seems to have enjoyed its greatest popularity in 1940, during the Battle of Britain and the blitz. In its main outlines its story is this:

Miss Blandish, the daughter of a millionaire, is kidnapped by some gangsters who are almost immediately surprised and killed off by a larger and better organised gang. They hold her to ransom and extract half a million dollars from her father. Their original plan had been to kill her as soon as the ransom-money was received, but a chance keeps her alive. One of the gang is a young man named Slim whose sole pleasure in life consists in driving knives into other people's bellies. In childhood he has graduated by cutting up living animals with a pair of rusty scissors. Slim is sexually impotent, but takes a kind of fancy to Miss Blandish. Slim's mother, who is the real brains of the gang, sees in this the chance of curing Slim's impotence, and decides to keep Miss Blandish in custody till Slim shall have succeeded in raping her. After many efforts and much persuasion, including the flogging of Miss Blandish with a length of rubber hosepipe, the rape is achieved. Meanwhile Miss Blandish's father has hired a private detective, and by means of bribery and torture the detective and the police manage to round up and exterminate the whole gang. Slim escapes with Miss Blandish and is killed after a final rape, and the detective prepares to restore Miss Blandish to her family. By this time, however, she has developed such a taste for Slim's caresses* that she feels unable to live without him, and she jumps out of the window of a skyscraper.

Several other points need noticing before one can grasp the full implications of this book. To begin with its central story is an impudent plagiarism of William Faulkner's novel, *Sanctuary*. Secondly it is not, as one might expect, the product of an illiterate hack, but a brilliant piece of writing, with hardly a wasted word or a jarring note anywhere. Thirdly, the whole book, récit as well as dialogue, is written in the American language: the author, an Englishman who has (I believe) never been in the United States, seems to have made a complete mental transference to the American underworld. Fourthly, the book sold, according to its publishers, no less than half a million copies.

I have already outlined the plot, but the subject-matter is much more sordid and brutal than this suggests. The book contains eight full-dress murders, an unassessable number of casual killings and woundings, an exhumation (with a careful reminder of the stench), the flogging of Miss Blandish, the torture of another woman with redhot cigarette ends, a strip-tease act, a third-degree scene of unheard-of cruelty, and much else of the same kind. It assumes great sexual sophistication in its readers (there is a scene, for instance, in which a gangster, presumably of masochistic tendency, has an orgasm in the moment of being knifed), and it takes for granted the most complete corruption and self-seeking as the norm of human behaviour. The detective, for instance, is almost as great a rogue as the gangsters, and actuated by nearly the same motives.

*1945. Another reading of the final episode is possible. It may mean merely that Miss Blandish is pregnant. But the interpretation I have given above seems more in keeping with the general brutality of the book [Orwell's footnote].

Like them, he is in pursuit of "five hundred grand." It is necessary to the machinery of the story that Mr. Blandish should be anxious to get his daughter back, but apart from this such things as affection, friendship, good-nature or even ordinary politeness simply do not enter. Nor, to any great extent, does normal sexuality. Ultimately only one motive is at work throughout the whole story: the pursuit of power.

It should be noticed that the book is not in the ordinary sense pornography. Unlike most books that deal in sexual sadism, it lays the emphasis on the cruelty and not on the pleasure. Slim, the ravisher of Miss Blandish, has "wet, slobbering lips": this is disgusting, and it is meant to be disgusting. But the scenes describing cruelty to women are comparatively perfunctory. The real high-spots of the book are cruelties committed by men upon other men: above all the third-degreeing of the gangster, Eddie Schultz, who is lashed into a chair and flogged on the windpipe with truncheons, his arms broken by fresh blows as he breaks loose. In another of Mr. Chase's books, *He Won't Need It Now,* the hero, who is intended to be a sympathetic and perhaps even noble character, is described as stamping on somebody's face, and then, having crushed the man's mouth in, grinding his heel round and round in it. Even when physical incidents of this kind are not occurring, the mental atmosphere of these books is always the same. Their whole theme is the struggle for power and the triumph of the strong over the weak. The big gangsters wipe out the little ones as mercilessly as a pike gobbling up the little fish in a pond; the police kill off the criminals as cruelly as the angler kills the pike. If ultimately one sides with the police against the gangsters it is merely because they are better organised and more powerful, because, in fact, the law is a bigger racket than crime. Might is right: vae victis.

As I have mentioned already, *No Orchids* enjoyed its greatest vogue in 1940, though it was successfully running as a play till some time later. It was, in fact, one of the things that helped to console people for the boredom of being bombed. Early in the war the *New Yorker* had a picture of a little man approaching a news-stall littered with papers with such headlines as GREAT TANK BATTLES IN NORTHERN FRANCE, BIG NAVAL BATTLE IN THE NORTH SEA, HUGE AIR BATTLES OVER THE CHANNEL, etc. etc. The little man is saying, "*Action Stories,* please." That little man stood for all the drugged millions to whom the world of the gangsters and the prize-ring is more "real," more "tough" than such things as wars, revolutions, earthquakes, famines and pestilences. From the point of view of a reader of *Action Stories,* a description of the London blitz, or of the struggles of the European underground parties, would be "sissy stuff." On the other hand some puny gun-battle in Chicago, resulting in perhaps half a dozen deaths, would seem genuinely "tough." This habit of mind is now extremely widespread. A soldier sprawls in a muddy trench, with the machine-gun bullets crackling a foot or two overhead and whiles away his intolerable boredom by reading an American gangster story. And what is it that makes that story so exciting? Precisely the fact that people are shooting at each other with machine-guns! Neither the soldier nor anyone else sees anything curious in this. It is taken for granted that an imaginary bullet is more thrilling than a real one.

The obvious explanation is that in real life one is usually a passive victim, whereas in the adventure story one can think of oneself as being at the centre of events. But there is more to it than that. Here it is necessary to refer again to the curious fact of *No Orchids* being written—with technical errors, perhaps, but certainly with considerable skill—in the American language.

There exists in America an enormous literature of more or less the same stamp as *No Orchids.* Quite apart from books, there is the huge array of "pulp magazines," graded so as to cater for different kinds of fantasy but nearly all having much the same mental atmosphere. A few of them go in for straight pornography but the great majority are quite plainly aimed at sadists and masochists. Sold at threepence a copy under the title of Yank Mags,* these things used to enjoy considerable popularity in England, but when the supply dried up owing to the war, no satisfactory substitute was forthcoming. English imitations of the "pulp magazine" do now exist, but they are poor things compared with the original. English crook films, again, never approach the American crook film in brutality. And yet the career of Mr. Chase shows how deep the American influence has already gone. Not only is he himself living a continuous fantasy-life in the Chicago underworld, but he can count on hundreds of thousands of readers who know what is meant by a "clipshop" or the "hotsquat," do not have to do mental arithmetic when confronted by "fifty grand," and understand at sight a sentence like "Johnnie was a rummy and only two jumps ahead of the nut-factory." Evidently there are great numbers of English people who are partly Americanised in language and, one ought to add, in moral outlook. For there was no popular protest against *No Orchids*. In the end it was withdrawn, but only retrospectively, when a later work, *Miss Callaghan comes to Grief* brought Mr. Chase's books to the attention of the authorities. Judging by casual conversations at the time, ordinary readers got a mild thrill out of the obscenities in *No Orchids,* but saw nothing undesirable in the book as a whole. Many people, incidentally, were under the impression that it was an American book re-issued in England.

The thing that the ordinary reader *ought* to have objected to—almost certainly would have objected to, a few decades earlier—was the equivocal attitude towards crime. It is implied throughout

*They are said to have been imported into this country as ballast, which accounted for their low price and crumpled appearance. Since the war the ships have been ballasted with something more useful, probably gravel [Orwell's footnote].

No Orchids that being a criminal is only reprehensible in the sense that it does not pay. Being a policeman pays better, but there is no moral difference, since the police use essentially criminal methods. In a book like *He Won't Need It Now* the distinction between crime and crime-prevention practically disappears. This is a new departure for English sensational fiction, in which till recently there has always been a sharp distinction between right and wrong and a general agreement that virtue must triumph in the last chapter. English books glorifying crime (modern crime, that is—pirates and highwaymen are different) are very rare. Even a book like *Raffles,* as I have pointed out, is governed by powerful taboos, and it is clearly understood that Raffles's crimes must be expiated sooner or later. In America, both in life and fiction, the tendency to tolerate crime, even to admire the criminal so long as he is successful, is very much more marked. It is, indeed, ultimately this attitude that has made it possible for crime to flourish upon so huge a scale. Books have been written about Al Capone that are hardly different in tone from the books written about Henry Ford, Stalin, Lord Northcliffe and all the rest of the "log cabin to White House" brigade. And switching back eighty years, one finds Mark Twain adopting much the same attitude towards the disgusting bandit Slade, hero of twenty-eight murders, and towards the Western desperadoes generally. They were successful, they "made good," therefore he admired them.

In a book like *No Orchids* one is not, as in the old-style crime story, simply escaping from dull reality into an imaginary world of action. One's escape is essentially into cruelty and sexual perversion. *No Orchids* is aimed at the power-instinct which *Raffles* or the Sherlock Holmes stories are not. At the same time the English attitude towards crime is not so superior to the American as I may have seemed to imply. It too is mixed up with power-worship, and has become more noticeably so in the last twenty years. A writer who is worth examining is Edgar Wallace, especially in such typical books as *The Orator* and the Mr. J. G. Reeder stories. Wallace was one of the first crime-story writers to break away from the old tradition of the private detective and make his central figure a Scotland Yard official. Sherlock Holmes is an amateur, solving his problems without the help and even, in the earlier stories, against the opposition of the police. Moreover, like Dupin, he is essentially an intellectual, even a scientist. He reasons logically from observed fact, and his intellectuality is constantly contrasted with the routine methods of the police. Wallace objected strongly to this slur, as he considered it, on Scotland Yard, and in several newspaper articles he went out of his way to denounce Holmes by name. His own ideal was the detective-inspector who catches criminals not because he is intellectually brilliant but because he is part of an all-powerful organisation. Hence the curious fact that in Wallace's most characteristic stories the "clue" and the "deduction" play no part. The criminal is always defeated either by an incredible coincidence, or because in some unexplained manner the police know all about the crime beforehand. The tone of the stories makes it quite clear that Wallace's admiration for the police is pure bully-worship. A Scotland Yard detective is the most powerful kind of being that he can imagine, while the criminal figures in his mind as an outlaw against whom anything is permissible, like the condemned slaves in the Roman arena. His policemen behave much more brutally than British policemen do in real life—they hit people without provocation, fire revolvers past their ears to terrify them, and so on—and some of the stories exhibit a fearful intellectual sadism. (For instance, Wallace likes to arrange things so that the villain is hanged on the same day as the heroine is married.) But it is sadism after the English fashion: that is to say it is unconscious, there is not overtly any sex in it, and it keeps within the bounds of the law. The British public tolerates a harsh criminal law and gets a kick out of monstrously unfair murder trials: but still that is better, on any count, than tolerating or admiring crime. If one must worship a bully, it is better that he should be a policeman than a gangster. Wallace is still governed to some extent by the concept of "not done." In *No Orchids* anything is "done" so long as it leads on to power. All the barriers are down, all the motives are out in the open. Chase is a worse symptom than Wallace, to the extent that all-in wrestling is worse than boxing, or Fascism is worse than capitalist democracy.

In borrowing from William Faulkner's *Sanctuary,* Chase only took the plot; the mental atmosphere of the two books is not similar. Chase really derives from other sources, and this particular bit of borrowing is only symbolic. What it symbolises is the vulgarisation of ideas which is constantly happening, and which probably happens faster in an age of print. Chase has been described as "Faulkner for the masses," but it would be more accurate to describe him as Carlyle for the masses. He is a popular writer—there are many such in America, but they are still rarities in England—who has caught up with what it is now fashionable to call "realism," meaning the doctrine that might is right. The growth of "realism" has been the great feature of the intellectual history of our own age. Why this should be so is a complicated question. The interconnection between sadism, masochism, success-worship, power-worship, nationalism and totalitarianism is a huge subject whose edges have barely been scratched, and even to mention it is considered somewhat indelicate. To take merely the first example that comes to mind, I believe no one has ever pointed out the sadistic and masochistic element in Bernard Shaw's work, still less suggested that this probably has some connection with Shaw's admiration for dictators.

Fascism is often loosely equated with sadism, but nearly always by people who see nothing wrong in the most slavish worship of Stalin. The truth is, of course, that the countless English intellectuals who kiss the arse of Stalin are not different from the minority who give their allegiance to Hitler or Mussolini, nor from the efficiency experts who preached "punch," "drive," "personality" and "learn to be a Tiger Man" in the nineteen-twenties, nor from the older generation of intellectuals, Carlyle, Creasey and the rest of them, who bowed down before German militarism. All of them are worshipping power and successful cruelty. It is important to notice that the cult of power tends to be mixed up with a love of cruelty and wickedness *for their own sakes.* A tyrant is all the more admired if he happens to be a bloodstained crook as well, and "the end justifies the means" often becomes, in effect, "the means justify themselves provided they are dirty enough." This idea colours the outlook of all sympathisers with totalitarianism, and accounts, for instance, for the positive delight with which many English intellectuals greeted the Nazi-Soviet pact. It was a step only doubtfully useful to the USSR, but it was entirely unmoral, and for that reason to be admired: the explanations of it, which were numerous and self-contradictory, could come afterwards.

Until recently the characteristic adventure stories of the English-speaking peoples have been stories in which the hero fights *against odds.* This is true all the way from Robin Hood to Popeye the Sailor. Perhaps the basic myth of the Western world is Jack the Giant Killer. But to be brought up to date this should be renamed Jack the Dwarf Killer, and there already exists a considerable literature which teaches, either overtly or implicitly, that one should side with the big man against the little man. Most of what is now written about foreign policy is simply an embroidery on this theme, and for several decades such phrases as "play the game," "don't hit a man when he's down" and "it's not cricket" have never failed to draw a snigger from anyone of intellectual pretensions. What is comparatively new is to find the accepted pattern according to which (a) right is right and wrong is wrong, whoever wins, and (b) weakness must be respected, disappearing from popular literature as well. When I first read D. H. Lawrence's novels, at the age of about twenty, I was puzzled by the fact that there did not seem to be any classification of the characters into "good" and "bad." Lawrence seemed to sympathise with all of them about equally, and this was so unusual as to give me the feeling of having lost my bearings. Today no one would think of looking for heroes and villains in a serious novel, but in lowbrow fiction one still expects to find a sharp distinction between right and wrong and between legality and illegality. The common people, on the whole, are still living in the world of absolute good and evil from which the intellectuals have long since escaped. But the popularity of *No Orchids* and the American books and magazines to which it is akin shows how rapidly the doctrine of "realism" is gaining ground.

Several people, after reading *No Orchids,* have remarked to me, "It's pure Fascism." This is a correct description, although the book has not the smallest connection with politics and very little with social or economic problems. It has merely the same relation to Fascism as, say, Trollope's novels have to nineteenth-century capitalism. It is a daydream appropriate to a totalitarian age. In his imagined world of gangsters Chase is presenting, as it were, a distilled version of the modern political scene, in which such things as mass bombing of civilians, the use of hostages, torture to obtain confessions, secret prisons, execution without trial, floggings with rubber truncheons, drownings in cesspools, systematic falsification of records and statistics, treachery, bribery and quislingism are normal and morally neutral, even admirable when they are done in a large and bold way. The average man is not directly interested in politics, and when he reads he wants the current struggles of the world to be translated into a simple story about individuals. He can take an interest in Slim and Fenner as he could not in the GPU and the Gestapo. People worship power in the form in which they are able to understand it. A twelve-year-old boy worships Jack Dempsey. An adolescent in a Glasgow slum worships Al Capone. An aspiring pupil at a business college worships Lord Nuffield. A *New Statesman* reader worships Stalin. There is a difference in intellectual maturity, but none in moral outlook. Thirty years ago the heroes of popular fiction had nothing in common with Mr. Chase's gangsters and detectives, and the idols of the English liberal intelligentsia were also comparatively sympathetic figures. Between Holmes and Fenner on the one hand, and between Abraham Lincoln and Stalin on the other, there is a similar gulf.

One ought not to infer too much from the success of Mr. Chase's books. It is possible that it is an isolated phenomenon, brought about by the mingled boredom and brutality of war. But if such books should definitely acclimatise themselves in England, instead of being merely a half-understood import from America, there would be good grounds for dismay. In choosing *Raffles* as a background for *No Orchids,* I deliberately chose a book which by the standards of its time was morally equivocal. Raffles, as I have pointed out, has no real moral code, no religion, certainly no social consciousness. All he has is a set of reflexes—the nervous system, as it were, of a gentleman. Give him a sharp tap on this reflex or that (they are called "sport," "pal," "woman," "king and country" and so forth), and you get a predictable reaction. In Mr. Chase's book there are no gentlemen, and no taboos. Emancipation is complete, Freud and Macchiavelli have reached the outer suburbs. Comparing the schoolboy atmosphere of the one book with the cruelty and corruption of the other, one is driven to feel that snobbishness, like hypocrisy, is a check upon behaviour whose value from a social point of view has been underrated.

Good Bad Books

Tribune, November 2, 1945

Not long ago a publisher commissioned me to write an introduction for a reprint of a novel by Leonard Merrick. This publishing house, it appears, is going to re-issue a long series of minor and partly-forgotten novels of the twentieth century. It is a valuable service in these bookless days, and I rather envy the person whose job it will be to scout round the threepenny boxes, hunting down copies of his boyhood favourites.

A type of book which we hardly seem to produce in these days, but which flowered with great richness in the late nineteenth and early twentieth centuries, is what Chesterton called the "good bad book": that is, the kind of book that has no literary pretentions but which remains readable when more serious productions have perished. Obviously outstanding books in this line are *Raffles* and the Sherlock Holmes stories, which have kept their place when innumerable "problem novels," "human documents" and "terrible indictments" of this or that have fallen into deserved oblivion. (Who has worn better, Conan Doyle or Meredith?) Almost in the same class as these I put R. Austin Freeman's earlier stories—*The Singing Bone, The Eye of Osiris* and others—Ernest Bramah's *Max Carrados,* and, dropping the standard a bit, Guy Boothby's Tibetan thriller, *Dr. Nikola,* a sort of schoolboy version of Huc's *Travels in Tartary,* which would probably make a real visit to Central Asia seem a dismal anti-climax.

But apart from thrillers, there were the minor humorous writers of the period. For example, Pett Ridge—but I admit his full-length books no longer seem readable—E. Nesbit (*The Treasure Seekers*), George Birmingham, who was good so long as he kept off politics, the pornographic Binstead ("Pitcher" of the *Pink 'Un*), and, if American books can be included, Booth Tarkington's Penrod stories. A cut above most of these was Barry Pain. Some of Pain's humorous writings are, I suppose, still in print, but to anyone who comes across it I recommend what must now be a very rare book—*The Octave of Claudius,* a brilliant exercise in the macabre. Somewhat later in time there was Peter Blundell, who wrote in the W. W. Jacobs vein about Far Eastern seaport towns, and who seems to be rather unaccountably forgotten, in spite of having been praised in print by H. G. Wells.

However, all the books I have been speaking of are frankly "escape" literature. They form pleasant patches in one's memory, quiet corners where the mind can browse at odd moments, but they hardly pretend to have anything to do with real life. There is another kind of good bad book which is more seriously intended, and which tells us, I think, something about the nature of the novel and the reasons for its present decadence. During the last fifty years there has been a whole series of writers—some of them are still writing—whom it is quite impossible to call "good" by any strictly literary standard, but who are natural novelists and who seem to attain sincerity partly because they are not inhibited by good taste. In this class I put Leonard Merrick himself, W. L. George, J. D. Beresford, Ernest Raymond, May Sinclair, and—at a lower level than the others but still essentially similar—A. S. M. Hutchinson.

Most of these have been prolific writers, and their output has naturally varied in quality. I am thinking in each case of one or two outstanding books: for example, Merrick's *Cynthia,* J. D. Beresford's *A Candidate for Truth,* W. L. George's *Caliban,* May Sinclair's *The Combined Maze,* and Ernest Raymond's *We, the Accused.* In each of these books the author has been able to identify himself with his imagined characters, to feel with them and invite sympathy on their behalf, with a kind of abandonment that cleverer people would find it difficult to achieve. They bring out the fact that intellectual refinement can be a disadvantage to a story-teller, as it would be to a music-hall comedian.

Take, for example, Ernest Raymond's *We, the Accused*—a peculiarly sordid and convincing murder story, probably based on the Crippen case. I think it gains a great deal from the fact that the author only partly grasps the pathetic vulgarity of the people he is writing about, and therefore does not despise them. Perhaps it even—like Theodore Dreiser's *An American Tragedy*—gains something from the clumsy, long-winded manner in which it is written; detail is piled on detail, with almost no attempt at selection, and in the process an effect of terrible, grinding cruelty is slowly built up. So also with *A Candidate for Truth.* Here there is not the same clumsiness, but there is the same ability to take seriously the problems of commonplace people. So also with *Cynthia* and at any rate the earlier part of *Caliban.* The greater part of what W. L. George wrote was shoddy rubbish, but in this particular book, based on the career of Northcliffe, he achieved some memorable and truthful pictures of lower-middle class London life. Parts of this book are probably autobiographical, and one of the advantages of good bad writers is their lack of shame in writing autobiography. Exhibition and self-pity are the bane of the novelist, and yet if he is too frightened of them his creative gift may suffer.

The existence of good bad literature—the fact that one can be amused or excited or even moved by a book that one's intellect simply refuses to take seriously—is a reminder that art is not the same thing as cerebration. I imagine that by any test that could be devised, Carlyle would be found to be a more intelligent man than Trollope. Yet Trollope has remained readable and Carlyle has not: with all his cleverness he had not even the wit to write in plain straightforward English. In novelists, almost as much as in poets, the connection between intelligence and creative power is hard to establish. A good novelist may be a prodigy of self-discipline like Flaubert, or he may be an intellectual sprawl like Dickens. Enough talent to set up dozens of ordinary writers has been poured into Wyndham Lewis's so-called novels, such as *Tarr* or *Snooty Baronet.* Yet it would be a very heavy labour to read one of these books right through. Some indefinable quality, a sort of literary vitamin, which exists even in a book like *If Winter Comes,* is absent from them.

Perhaps the supreme example of the "good bad" book is *Uncle Tom's Cabin.* It is an unintentionally ludicrous book, full of preposterous melodramatic incidents; it is also deeply moving and essentially true; it is hard to say which quality outweighs the other. But *Uncle Tom's Cabin,* after all, is trying to be serious and to deal with the real world. How about the frankly escapist writers, the purveyors of thrills and "light" humour? How about *Sherlock Holmes, Vice Versa, Dracula, Helen's Babies* or *King Solomon's Mines*? All of these are definitely absurd books, books which one is more inclined to laugh *at* than *with,* and which were hardly taken seriously even by their authors; yet they have survived, and will probably continue to do so. All one can say is that, while civilisation remains such that one needs distraction from time to time, "light" literature has its appointed place; also that there is such a thing as sheer skill, or native grace, which may have more survival value than erudition or intellectual power. There are music-hall songs which are better poems than three-quarters of the stuff that gets into the anthologies:

Come where the booze is cheaper,
Come where the pots hold more,
Come where the boss is a bit of a sport,
Come to the pub next door!

Or again:

Two lovely black eyes—
Oh, what a surprise!
Only for calling another man wrong,
Two lovely black eyes!

I would far rather have written either of those than, say, *The Blessed Damozel* or *Love in a Valley*. And by the same token I would back *Uncle Tom's Cabin* to outlive the complete works of Virginia Woolf or George Moore, though I know of no strictly literary test which would show where the superiority lies.

The Prevention of Literature

Polemic, January 1946

About a year ago I attended a meeting of the P.E.N. Club, the occasion being the tercentenary of Milton's *Areopagitica*—a pamphlet, it may be remembered, in defence of freedom of the Press. Milton's famous phrase about the sin of "killing" a book was printed on the leaflets advertising the meeting which had been circulated beforehand.

There were four speakers on the platform. One of them delivered a speech which did deal with the freedom of the Press, but only in relation to India; another said, hesitantly, and in very general terms, that liberty was a good thing; a third delivered an attack on the laws relating to obscenity in literature. The fourth devoted most of his speech to a defence of the Russian purges. Of the speeches from the body of the hall, some reverted to the question of obscenity and the laws that deal with it, others were simply eulogies of Soviet Russia. Moral liberty—the liberty to discuss sex questions frankly in print—seemed to be generally approved, but political liberty was not mentioned. Out of this concourse of several hundred people, perhaps half of whom were directly connected with the writing trade, there was not a single one who could point out that freedom of the Press, if it means anything at all, means the freedom to criticise and oppose. Significantly, no speaker quoted from the pamphlet which was ostensibly being commemorated. Nor was there any mention of the various books that have been "killed" in this country and the United States during the war. In its net effect the meeting was a demonstration in favour of censorship.*

There was nothing particularly surprising in this. In our age, the idea of intellectual liberty is under attack from two directions. On the one side are its theoretical enemies, the apologists of totalitarianism, and on the other its immediate, practical enemies, monopoly and bureaucracy. Any writer or journalist who wants to retain his integrity finds himself thwarted by the general drift of society rather than by active persecution. The sort of things that are working against him are the concentration of the Press in the hands of a few rich men, the grip of monopoly on radio and the films, the unwillingness of the public to spend money on books, making it necessary for nearly every writer to earn part of his living by hackwork, the encroachment of official bodies like the M.O.I. and the British Council, which help the writer to keep alive but also waste his time and dictate his opinions, and the continuous war atmosphere of the past ten years, whose distorting effects no one has been able to escape. Everything in our age conspires to turn the writer, and every other kind of artist as well, into a minor official, working on themes handed to [him] from above and never telling what seems to him the whole of the truth. But in struggling against this fate he gets no help from his own side: that is, there is no large body of opinion which will assure him that he is in the right. In the past, at any rate throughout the Protestant centuries, the idea of rebellion and the idea of intellectual integrity were mixed up. A heretic—political, moral, religious, or æs-

*It is fair to say that the P.E.N. Club celebrations, which lasted a week or more, did not always stick at quite the same level. I happened to strike a bad day. But an examination of the speeches (printed under the title *Freedom of Expression*) shows that almost nobody in our own day is able to speak out as roundly in favour of intellectual liberty as Milton could do 300 years ago—and this in spite of the fact Milton was writing in a period of civil war [Orwell's footnote].

thetic—was one who refused to outrage his own conscience. His outlook was summed up in the words of the Revivalist hymn:

Dare to be a Daniel,
Dare to stand alone;
Dare to have a purpose firm,
Dare to make it known.

To bring this hymn up to date one would have to add a "Don't" at the beginning of each line. For it is the peculiarity of our age that the rebels against the existing order, at any rate the most numerous and characteristic of them, are also rebelling against the idea of individual integrity. "Daring to stand alone" is ideologically criminal as well as practically dangerous. The independence of the writer and the artist is eaten away by vague economic forces, and at the same time it is undermined by those who should be its defenders. It is with the second process that I am concerned here.

Freedom of speech and of the Press are usually attacked by arguments which are not worth bothering about. Anyone who has experience in lecturing and debating knows them backwards. Here I am not trying to deal with the familiar claim that freedom is an illusion, or with the claim that there is more freedom in totalitarian countries than in democratic ones, but with the much more tenable and dangerous proposition that freedom is undesirable and that intellectual honesty is a form of anti-social selfishness. Although other aspects of the question are usually in the foreground, the controversy over freedom of speech and of the Press is at bottom a controversy over the desirability, or otherwise, of telling lies. What is really at issue is the right to report contemporary events truthfully, or as truthfully as is consistent with the ignorance, bias and self-deception from which every observer necessarily suffers. In saying this I may seem to be saying that straightforward "reportage" is the only branch of literature that matters: but I will try to show later that at every literary level, and probably in every one of the arts, the same issue arises in more or less subtilised forms. Meanwhile, it is necessary to strip away the irrelevancies in which this controversy is usually wrapped up.

The enemies of intellectual liberty always try to present their case as a plea for discipline versus individualism. The issue truth-versus-untruth is as far as possible kept in the background. Although the point of emphasis may vary, the writer who refuses to sell his opinions is always branded as a mere egoist. He is accused, that is, either of wanting to shut himself up in an ivory tower, or of making an exhibitionist display of his own personality, or of resisting the inevitable current of history in an attempt to cling to unjustified privileges. The Catholic and the Communist are alike in assuming that an opponent cannot be both honest and intelligent. Each of them tacitly claims that "the truth" has already been revealed, and that the heretic, if he is not simply a fool, is secretly aware of "the truth" and merely resists it out of selfish motives. In Communist literature the attack on intellectual liberty is usually masked by oratory about "petty-bourgeois individualism," "the illusions of nineteenth-century liberalism," etc., and backed up by words of abuse such as "romantic" and "sentimental," which, since they do not have any agreed meaning, are difficult to answer. In this way the controversy is manœuvred away from its real issue. One can accept, and most enlightened people would accept, the Communist thesis that pure freedom will only exist in a classless society, and that one is most nearly free when one is working to bring about such a society. But slipped in with this is the quite unfounded claim that the Communist party is itself aiming at the establishment of the classless society, and that in the U.S.S.R. this aim is actually on the way to being realised. If the first claim is allowed to entail the second, there is almost no assault on common sense and common decency that cannot be justified. But meanwhile, the real point has been dodged. Freedom of the intellect means the freedom to report what one has seen, heard, and felt, and not to be obliged to fabricate imaginary facts and feelings. The familiar tirades against "escapism," "individualism," "romanticism" and so forth, are merely a forensic device, the aim of which is to make the perversion of history seem respectable.

Fifteen years ago, when one defended the freedom of the intellect, one had to defend it against Conservatives, against Catholics, and to some extent—for in England they were not of great importance—against Fascists. To-day one has to defend it against Communists and "fellow travellers." One ought not to exaggerate the direct influence of the small English Communist party, but there can be no question about the poisonous effect of the Russian *mythos* on English intellectual life. Because of it, known facts are suppressed and distorted to such an extent as to make it doubtful whether a true history of our times can ever be written. Let me give just one instance out of the hundreds that could be cited. When Germany collapsed, it was found that very large numbers of Soviet Russians—mostly, no doubt, from non-political motives—had changed sides and were fighting for the Germans. Also, a small but not negligible proportion of the Russian prisoners and Displaced Persons refused to go back to the U.S.S.R., and some of them, at least, were repatriated against their will. These facts, known to many journalists on the spot, went almost unmentioned in the British Press, while at the same time Russophile publicists in England continued to justify the purges and deportations of 1936–38 by claiming that the U.S.S.R. "had no quislings." The fog of lies and misinformation that surrounds such subjects as the Ukraine famine, the Spanish civil war, Russian policy in Poland, and so forth, is not due entirely to conscious dishonesty, but any writer or journalist who is fully sympathetic to the

U.S.S.R.—sympathetic, that is, in the way the Russians themselves would want him to be—does have to acquiesce in deliberate falsification on important issues. I have before me what must be a very rare pamphlet, written by Maxim Litvinoff in 1918 and outlining the recent events in the Russian Revolution. It makes no mention of Stalin, but gives high praise to Trotsky, and also to Zinoviev, Kamenev, and others. What could be the attitude of even the most intellectually scrupulous Communist towards such a pamphlet? At best, he would take the obscurantist attitude that it is an undesirable document and better suppressed. And if for some reason it should be decided to issue a garbled version of the pamphlet, denigrating Trotsky and inserting references to Stalin, no Communist who remained faithful to his party could protest. Forgeries almost as gross as this have been committed in recent years. But the significant thing is not that they happen, but that even when they are known, they provoke no reaction from the Left-wing intelligentsia as a whole. The argument that to tell the truth would be "inopportune" or would "play into the hands of" somebody or other is felt to be unanswerable, and few people are bothered by the prospect that the lies which they condone will get out of the newspapers and into the history books.

The organised lying practised by totalitarian states is not, as is sometimes claimed, a temporary expedient of the same nature as military deception. It is something integral to totalitarianism, something that would still continue even if concentration camps and secret police forces had ceased to be necessary. Among intelligent Communists there is an underground legend to the effect that although the Russian government is obliged now to deal in lying propaganda, frame-up trials, and so forth, it is secretly recording the facts and will publish them at some future time. We can, I believe, be quite certain that this is not the case, because the mentality implied by such an action is that of a liberal historian who believes that the past cannot be altered and that a correct knowledge of history is valuable as a matter of course. From the totalitarian point of view history is something to be created rather than learned. A totalitarian state is in effect a theocracy, and its ruling caste, in order to keep its position, has to be thought of as infallible. But since, in practice, no one is infallible, it is frequently necessary to rearrange past events in order to show that this or that mistake was not made, or that this or that imaginary triumph actually happened. Then, again, every major change in policy demands a corresponding change of doctrine and a revaluation of prominent historical figures. This kind of thing happens everywhere, but clearly it is likelier to lead to outright falsification in societies where only one opinion is permissible at any given moment. Totalitarianism demands, in fact, the continuous alteration of the past, and in the long run probably demands a disbelief in the very existence of objective truth. The friends of totalitarianism in this country usually tend to argue that since absolute truth is not attainable, a big lie is no worse than a little lie. It is pointed out that all historical records are biased and inaccurate, or, on the other hand, that modern physics has proved that what seems to us the real world is an illusion, so that to believe in the evidence of one's senses is simply vulgar philistinism. A totalitarian society which succeeded in perpetuating itself would probably set up a schizophrenic system of thought, in which the laws of common sense held good in everyday life and in certain exact sciences, but could be disregarded by the politician, the historian, and the sociologist. Already there are countless people who would think it scandalous to falsify a scientific textbook, but would see nothing wrong in falsifying a historical fact. It is at the point where literature and politics cross that totalitarianism exerts its greatest pressure on the intellectual. The exact sciences are not, at this date, menaced to anything like the same extent. This difference partly accounts for the fact that in all countries it is easier for the scientists than for the writers to line up behind their respective governments.

To keep the matter in perspective, let me repeat what I said at the beginning of this essay: that in England the immediate enemies of truthfulness, and hence of freedom of thought, are the Press lords, the film magnates, and the bureaucrats, but that on a long view the weakening of the desire for liberty among the intellectuals themselves is the most serious symptom of all. It may seem that all this time I have been talking about the effects of censorship, not on literature as a whole, but merely on one department of political journalism. Granted that Soviet Russia constitutes a sort of forbidden area in the British Press, granted that issues like Poland, the Spanish civil war, the Russo-German pact, and so forth, are debarred from serious discussion, and that if you possess information that conflicts with the prevailing orthodoxy you are expected either to distort it or to keep quiet about it—granted all this, why should literature in the wider sense be affected? Is every writer a politician, and is every book necessarily a work of straightforward "reportage"? Even under the tightest dictatorship, cannot the individual writer remain free inside his own mind and distil or disguise his unorthodox ideas in such a way that the authorities will be too stupid to recognise them? And if the writer himself is in agreement with the prevailing orthodoxy, why should it have a cramping effect on him? Is not literature, or any of the arts, likeliest to flourish in societies in which there are no major conflicts of opinion and no sharp distinctions between the artist and his audience? Does one have to assume that every writer is a rebel, or even that a writer as such is an exceptional person?

Whenever one attempts to defend intellectual liberty against the claims of totalitarianism, one meets with these arguments in one form or another. They are based on a complete misunderstanding of what literature is, and how—one should perhaps rather say *why*—it comes into being. They assume that a writer is either a mere entertainer or else a venal hack who can switch from one line of propaganda to another as easily as an organ grinder changes tunes. But after all, how is it that books ever come to be written? Above a quite low level, literature is an attempt to influence the views of one's contemporaries by recording experience. And so far as freedom of expression is concerned, there is not much difference between a mere journalist and the most "unpolitical" imaginative writer. The journalist is unfree, and is conscious of unfreedom, when he is forced to write lies or suppress what seems to him important news: the imaginative writer is unfree when he has to falsify his subjective feelings, which from his point of view are facts. He may distort and caricature reality in order to make his meaning clearer, but he cannot misrepresent the scenery of his own mind: he cannot say with any conviction that he likes what he dislikes, or believes what he disbelieves. If he is forced to do so, the only result is that his creative faculties dry up. Nor can the imaginative writer solve the problem by keeping away from controversial topics. There is no such thing as genuinely non-political literature, and least of all in an age like our own, when fears, hatreds, and loyalties of a directly political kind are near to the surface of everyone's consciousness. Even a single tabu can have an all-round crippling effect upon the mind, because there is always the danger that any thought which is freely followed up may lead to the forbidden thought. It follows that the atmosphere of totalitarianism is deadly to any kind of prose writer, though a poet, at any rate a lyric poet, might possibly find it breathable. And in any totalitarian society that survives for more than a couple of generations, it is probable that prose literature, of the kind that has existed during the past four hundred years, must actually *come to an end.*

Literature has sometimes flourished under despotic regimes, but, as has often been pointed out, the despotisms of the past were not totalitarian. Their repressive apparatus was always inefficient, their ruling classes were usually either corrupt or apathetic or half-liberal in outlook, and the prevailing religious doctrines usually worked against perfectionism and the notion of human infallibility. Even so it is broadly true that prose literature has reached its highest levels in periods of democracy and free speculation. What is new in totalitarianism is that its doctrines are not only unchallengeable but also unstable. They have to be accepted on pain of damnation, but on the other hand they are always liable to be altered at a moment's notice. Consider, for example, the various attitudes, completely incompatible with one another, which an English Communist or "fellow traveller" has had to adopt towards the war between Britain and Germany. For years before September 1939 he was expected to be in a continuous stew about "the horrors of Nazism" and to twist everything he wrote into a denunciation of Hitler; after September 1939, for twenty months, he had to believe that Germany was more sinned against than sinning, and the word "Nazi," at least so far as print went, had to drop right out of his vocabulary. Immediately after hearing the 8 o'clock news bulletin on the morning of June 22, 1941, he had to start believing once again that Nazism was the most hideous evil the world had ever seen. Now, it is easy for a politician to make such changes: for a writer the case is somewhat different. If he is to switch his allegiance at exactly the right moment, he must either tell lies about his subjective feelings, or else suppress them altogether. In either case he has destroyed his dynamo. Not only will ideas refuse to come to him, but the very words he uses will seem to stiffen under his touch. Political writing in our time consists almost entirely of prefabricated phrases bolted together like the pieces of a child's Meccano set. It is the unavoidable result of self-censorship. To write in plain, vigorous language one has to think fearlessly, and if one thinks fearlessly one cannot be politically orthodox. It might be otherwise in an "age of faith," when the prevailing orthodoxy has been long established and is not taken too seriously. In that case it would be possible, or might be possible, for large areas of one's mind to remain unaffected by what one officially believed. Even so, it is worth noticing that prose literature almost disappeared during the only age of faith that Europe has ever enjoyed. Throughout the whole of the Middle Ages there was almost no imaginative prose literature and very little in the way of historical writing: and the intellectual leaders of society expressed their most serious thoughts in a dead language which barely altered during a thousand years.

Totalitarianism, however, does not so much promise an age of faith as an age of schizophrenia. A society becomes totalitarian when its structure becomes flagrantly artificial: that is, when its ruling class has lost its function but succeeds in clinging to power by force or fraud. Such a society, no matter how long it persists, can never afford to become either tolerant or intellectually stable. It can never permit either the truthful recording of facts, or the emotional sincerity, that literary creation demands. But to be corrupted by totalitarianism one does not have to live in a totalitarian country. The mere prevalence of certain ideas can spread a poison that makes one subject after another impossible for literary purposes. Wherever there is an enforced orthodoxy—or even two orthodoxies, as often happens—good writing stops. This was well illustrated by the Spanish civil war. To many English intellectuals the war was a deeply moving experience, but not an experience about which they could write sincerely. There were only two things that you were allowed to say, and both of them were palpable lies: as a result, the war produced acres of print but almost nothing worth reading.

It is not certain whether the effects of totalitarianism upon verse need be so deadly as its effects on prose. There is a whole series of converging reasons why it is somewhat easier for a poet than for a prose writer to feel at home in an authoritarian society. To begin with, bureaucrats and other "practical" men usually despise the poet too deeply to be much interested in what he is saying. Secondly, what the poet is saying—that is, what his poem "means" if translated into prose—is relatively unimportant even to himself. The thought contained in a poem is always simple, and is no more the primary purpose of the poem than the anecdote is the primary purpose of a picture. A poem is an arrangement of sounds and associations, as a painting is an arrangement of brushmarks. For short snatches, indeed, as in the refrain of a song, poetry can even dispense with meaning altogether. It is therefore fairly easy for a poet to keep away from dangerous subjects and avoid uttering heresies: and even when he does utter them, they may escape notice. But above all, good verse, unlike good prose, is not necessarily an individual product. Certain kinds of poems, such as ballads, or, on the other hand, very artificial verse forms, can be composed co-operatively by groups of people. Whether the ancient English and Scottish ballads were originally produced by individuals, or by the people at large, is disputed; but at any rate they are non-individual in the sense that they constantly change in passing from mouth to mouth. Even in print no two versions of a ballad are ever quite the same. Many primitive peoples compose verse communally. Someone begins to improvise, probably accompanying himself on a musical instrument, somebody else chips in with a line or a rhyme when the first singer breaks down, and so the process continues until there exists a whole song or ballad which has no identifiable author.

In prose, this kind of intimate collaboration is quite impossible. Serious prose, in any case, has to be composed in solitude, whereas the excitement of being part of a group is actually an aid to certain kinds of versification. Verse—and perhaps good verse of its kind, though it would not be the highest kind—might survive under even the most inquisitorial regime. Even in a society where liberty and individuality had been extinguished, there would still be need either for patriotic songs and heroic ballads celebrating victories, or for elaborate exercises in flattery: and these are the kinds of poetry that can be written to order, or composed communally, without necessarily lacking artistic value. Prose is a different matter, since the prose writer cannot narrow the range of his thoughts without killing his inventiveness. But the history of totalitarian societies, or of groups of people who have adopted the totalitarian outlook, suggests that loss of liberty is inimical to *all* forms of literature. German literature almost disappeared during the Hitler regime, and the case was not much better in Italy. Russian literature, so far as one can judge by translations, has deteriorated markedly since the early days of the Revolution, though some of the verse appears to be better than the prose. Few if any Russian novels that it is possible to take seriously have been translated for about fifteen years. In western Europe and America large sections of the literary intelligentsia have either passed through the Communist party or been warmly sympathetic to it, but this whole leftward movement has produced extraordinarily few books worth reading. Orthodox Catholicism, again, seems to have a crushing effect upon certain literary forms, especially the novel. During a period of three hundred years, how many people have been at once good novelists and good Catholics? The fact is that certain themes cannot be celebrated in words, and tyranny is one of them. No one ever wrote a good book in praise of the Inquisition. Poetry *might* survive in a totalitarian age, and certain arts or half-arts, such as architecture, might even find tyranny beneficial, but the prose writer would have no choice between silence and death. Prose literature as we know it is the product of rationalism, of the Protestant centuries, of the autonomous individual. And the destruction of intellectual liberty cripples the journalist, the sociological writer, the historian, the novelist, the critic, and the poet, in that order. In the future it is possible that a new kind of literature, not involving individual feeling or truthful observation, may arise, but no such thing is at present imaginable. It seems much likelier that if the liberal culture that we have lived in since the Renaissance actually comes to an end, the literary art will perish with it.

Of course, print will continue to be used, and it is interesting to speculate what kinds of reading matter would survive in a rigidly totalitarian society. Newspapers will presumably continue until television technique reaches a higher level, but apart from newspapers it is doubtful even now whether the great mass of people in the industrialised countries feel the need for any kind of literature. They are unwilling, at any rate, to spend anywhere near as much on reading matter as they spend on several other recreations. Probably novels and stories will be completely superseded by film and radio productions. Or perhaps some kind of low-grade sensational fiction will survive, produced by a sort of conveyor-belt process that reduces human initiative to the minimum.

It would probably not be beyond human ingenuity to write books by machinery. But a sort of mechanising process can already be seen at work in the film and radio, in publicity and propaganda, and in the lower reaches of journalism. The Disney films, for instance, are produced by what is essentially a factory process, the work being done partly mechanically and partly by teams of artists who have to subordinate their individual style. Radio features are commonly written by tired hacks to whom the subject and the manner of treatment are dictated beforehand: even so, what they write is merely a kind of raw material to be chopped into shape by producers and censors. So also with the innumerable books and pamphlets commissioned by government departments. Even more machine-like is the production of short stories, serials, and poems for the very cheap magazines. Papers such as the *Writer* abound with advertisements of Literary Schools, all of them offering you readymade plots at a few shillings a time. Some, together with the plot, supply the opening and closing sentences of each chapter. Others furnish you with a sort of algebraical formula by the use of which you can construct your plots for yourself. Others offer packs of cards marked with characters and situations, which have only to be shuffled and dealt in order to produce ingenious stories automatically. It is probably in some such way that the literature of a totalitarian society would be produced, if literature were still felt to be necessary. Imagination—even consciousness, so far as possible—would be eliminated from the process of writing. Books would be planned in their broad lines by bureaucrats, and would pass through so many hands that when finished they would be no more an individual product than a Ford car at the end of the assembly line. It goes without saying that anything so produced would be rubbish; but anything that was not rubbish would endanger the structure of the state. As for the surviving literature of the past, it would have to be suppressed or at least elaborately rewritten.

Meanwhile totalitarianism has not fully triumphed anywhere. Our own society is still, broadly speaking, liberal. To exercise your right of free speech you have to fight against economic pressure and against strong sections of public opinion, but not, as yet, against a secret police force. You can say or print almost anything so long as you are willing to do it in a hole-and-corner way. But what is sinister, as I said at the beginning of this essay, is that the conscious enemies of liberty are those to whom liberty ought to mean most. The public do not care about the matter one way or the other. They are not in favour of persecuting the heretic, and they will not exert themselves to defend him. They are at once too sane and too stupid to acquire the totalitarian outlook. The direct, conscious attack on intellectual decency comes from the intellectuals themselves.

It is possible that the Russophile intelligentsia, if they had not succumbed to that particular myth, would have succumbed to another of much the same kind. But at any rate the Russian myth is there, and the corruption it causes stinks. When one sees highly educated men looking on indifferently at oppression and persecution, one wonders which to despise more, their cynicism or their short-sightedness. Many scientists, for example, are uncritical admirers of the U.S.S.R. They appear to think that the destruction of liberty is of no importance so long as their own line of work is for the moment unaffected. The U.S.S.R. is a large, rapidly developing country which has acute need of scientific workers and, consequently, treats them generously. Provided that they steer clear of dangerous subjects such as psychology, scientists are privileged persons. Writers, on the other hand, are viciously persecuted. It is true that literary prostitutes like Ilya Ehrenburg or Alexei Tolstoy are paid huge sums of money, but the only thing which is of any value to the writer as such—his freedom of expression—is taken away from him. Some, at least, of the English scientists who speak so enthusiastically of the opportunities enjoyed by scientists in Russia are capable of understanding this. But their reflection appears to be: "Writers are persecuted in Russia. So what? I am not a writer." They do not see that *any* attack on intellectual liberty, and on the concept of objective truth, threatens in the long run every department of thought.

For the moment the totalitarian state tolerates the scientist because it needs him. Even in Nazi Germany, scientists, other than Jews, were relatively well treated, and the German scientific community, as a whole, offered no resistance to Hitler. At this stage of history, even the most autocratic ruler is forced to take account of physical reality, partly because of the lingering-on of liberal habits of thought, partly because of the need to prepare for war. So long as physical reality cannot be altogether ignored, so long as two and two have to make four when you are, for example, drawing the blueprint of an aeroplane, the scientist has his function, and can even be allowed a measure of liberty. His awakening will come later, when the totalitarian state is firmly established. Meanwhile, if he wants to safeguard the integrity of science, it is his job to develop some kind of solidarity with his literary colleagues and not regard it as a matter of indifference when writers are silenced or driven to suicide, and newspapers systematically falsified.

But however it may be with the physical sciences, or with music, painting, and architecture, it is—as I have tried to show—certain that literature is doomed if liberty of thought perishes. Not only is it doomed in any country which retains a totalitarian structure; but any writer who adopts the totalitarian outlook, who finds excuses for persecution and the falsification of reality, thereby destroys himself as a writer. There is no way out of this. No tirades against "individualism" and "the ivory tower," no pious platitudes to the effect that "true individuality is only attained through identification with the community," can get over the fact that a bought mind is a spoiled mind. Unless spontaneity enters at some point or another, literary creation is impossible, and language itself becomes ossified. At some time in the future, if the human mind becomes something totally different from what it now is, we may learn to separate literary creation from intellectual honesty. At present we know only that the imagination, like certain wild animals, will not breed in captivity. Any writer or journalist who denies that fact—and nearly all the current praise of the Soviet Union contains or implies such a denial—is, in effect, demanding his own destruction.

Politics and the English Language

1945; *Horizon*, April 1946

Most people who bother with the matter at all would admit that the English language is in a bad way, but it is generally assumed that we cannot by conscious action do anything about it. Our civilization is decadent, and our language—so the argument runs—must inevitably share in the general collapse. It follows that any struggle against the abuse of language is a sentimental archaism, like preferring candles to electric light or hansom cabs to aeroplanes. Underneath this lies the half-conscious belief that language is a natural growth and not an instrument which we shape for our own purposes.

Now, it is clear that the decline of a language must ultimately have political and economic causes: it is not due simply to the bad influence of this or that individual writer. But an effect can become a cause, reinforcing the original cause and producing the same effect in an intensified form, and so on indefinitely. A man may take to drink because he feels himself to be a failure, and then fail all the more completely because he drinks. It is rather the same thing that is happening to the English language. It becomes ugly and inaccurate because our thoughts are foolish, but the slovenliness of our language makes it easier for us to have foolish thoughts. The point is that the process is reversible. Modern English, especially written English, is full of bad habits which spread by imitation and which can be avoided if one is willing to take the necessary trouble. If one gets rid of these habits one can think more clearly, and to think clearly is a necessary first step towards political regeneration: so that the fight against bad English is not frivolous and is not the exclusive concern of professional writers. I will come back to this presently, and I hope that by that time the meaning of what I have said here will have become clearer. Meanwhile, here are five specimens of the English language as it is now habitually written.

These five passages have not been picked out because they are especially bad—I could have quoted far worse if I had chosen—but because they illustrate various of the mental vices from which we now suffer. They are a little below the average, but are fairly representative samples. I number them so that I can refer back to them when necessary:

"(1) I am not, indeed, sure whether it is not true to say that the Milton who once seemed not unlike a seventeenth-century Shelley had not become, out of an experience ever more bitter in each year, more alien (*sic*) to the founder of that Jesuit sect which nothing could induce him to tolerate."

Professor Harold Laski (Essay in *Freedom of Expression*).

"(2) Above all, we cannot play ducks and drakes with a native battery of idioms which prescribes such egregious collocations of vocables as the Basic *put up with* for *tolerate* or *put at a loss* for *bewilder*."

Professor Lancelot Hogben (*Interglossa*).

"(3) On the one side we have the free personality: by definition it is not neurotic, for it has neither conflict nor dream. Its desires, such as they are, are transparent, for they are just what institutional approval keeps in the forefront of consciousness; another institutional pattern would alter their number and intensity; there is little in them that is natural, irreducible, or culturally dangerous. But *on the other side,* the social bond itself is nothing but the mutual reflection of these self-secure integrities. Recall the definition of love. Is not this the very picture of a small academic? Where is there a place in this hall of mirrors for either personality or fraternity?"

Essay on psychology in *Politics* (New York).

"(4) All the 'best people' from the gentlemen's clubs, and all the frantic fascist captains, united in common hatred of Socialism and bestial horror of the rising tide of the mass revolutionary movement, have turned to acts of provocation, to foul incendiarism, to medieval legends of poisoned wells, to legalize their own destruction of proletarian organizations, and rouse the agitated petty-bourgeoisie to chauvinistic fervour on behalf of the fight against the revolutionary way out of the crisis."

Communist pamphlet.

"(5) If a new spirit *is* to be infused into this old country, there is one thorny and contentious reform which must be tackled, and that is the humanization and galvanization of the B.B.C. Timidity here will bespeak canker and atrophy of the soul. The heart of Britain may be sound and of strong beat, for instance, but the British lion's roar at present is like that of Bottom in Shakespeare's *Midsummer Night's Dream*—as gentle as any sucking dove. A virile new Britain cannot continue indefinitely to be traduced in the eyes, or rather ears, of the world by the effete languors of Langham Place, brazenly masquerading as 'standard English.' When the Voice of Britain is heard at nine o'clock, better far and infinitely less ludicrous to hear aitches honestly dropped than the present priggish, inflated, inhibited, school-ma'amish arch braying of blameless bashful mewing maidens!"

Letter in *Tribune.*

Each of these passages has faults of its own, but, quite apart from avoidable ugliness, two qualities are common to all of them. The first is staleness of imagery: the other is lack of precision. The writer either has a meaning and cannot express it, or he inadvertently says something else, or he is almost indifferent as to whether his words mean anything or not. This mixture of vagueness and sheer incompetence is the most marked characteristic of modern English prose, and especially of any kind of political writing. As soon as certain topics are raised, the concrete melts into the abstract and no one seems able to think of turns of speech that are not hackneyed: prose consists less and less of *words* chosen for the sake of their meaning, and more and more of *phrases* tacked together like the sections of a prefabricated hen-house. I list below, with notes and examples, various of the tricks by means of which the work of prose-construction is habitually dodged:

Dying metaphors. A newly invented metaphor assists thought by evoking a visual image, while on the other hand a metaphor which is technically "dead" (e.g. *iron resolution*) has in effect reverted to being an ordinary word and can generally be used without loss of vividness. But in between these two classes there is a huge dump of worn-out metaphors which have lost all evocative power and are merely used because they save people the trouble of inventing phrases for themselves. Examples are: *Ring the changes on, take up the cudgels for, toe the line, ride roughshod over, stand shoulder to shoulder with, play into the hands of, no axe to grind, grist to the mill, fishing in troubled waters,* [*rift within the lute*],[1] *on the order of the day, Achilles' heel, swan song, hotbed.* Many of these are used without knowledge of their meaning (what is a "rift," for instance?), and incompatible metaphors are frequently mixed, a sure sign that the writer is not interested in what he is saying. Some metaphors now current have been twisted out of their original meaning without those who use them even being aware of the fact. For example, *toe the line* is sometimes written *tow the line.* Another example is *the hammer and the anvil,* now always used with the implication that the anvil gets the worst of it. In real life it is always the anvil that breaks the hammer, never the other way about: a writer who stopped to think what he was saying would be aware of this, and would avoid perverting the original phrase.

Operators, or *verbal false limbs.* These save the trouble of picking out appropriate verbs and nouns, and at the same time pad each sentence with extra syllables which give it an appearance of symmetry. Characteristic phrases are: *render inoperative, militate against, prove unacceptable, make contact with, be subjected to, give rise to, give grounds for, have the effect of, play a leading part (role) in, make itself felt, take effect, exhibit a tendency to, serve the purpose of,* etc., etc. The keynote is the elimination of simple verbs. Instead of being a single word, such as *break, stop, spoil, mend, kill,* a verb becomes a *phrase,* made up of a noun or adjective tacked on to some general-purposes verb such as *prove, serve, form, play, render.* In addition, the passive voice is wherever possible used in preference to the active, and noun constructions are used instead of gerunds (*by examination of* instead of *by examining*). The range of verbs is further cut down by means of the *-ize* and *de-* formations, and banal statements are given an appearance of profundity by means of the *not un-*formation. Simple conjunctions and prepositions are replaced by such phrases as *with respect to, having regard to, the fact that, by dint of, in view of, in the interests of, on the hypothesis that*; and the ends of sentences are saved from anticlimax by such resounding commonplaces as *greatly to be desired, cannot be left out of account, a development to be expected in the near future, deserving of serious consideration, brought to a satisfactory conclusion,* and so on and so forth.

Pretentious diction. Words like *phenomenon, element, individual* (as noun), *objective, categorical, effective, virtual, basic, primary, promote, constitute, exhibit, exploit, utilize, eliminate, liquidate,* are used to dress up simple statement[s] and give an air of scientific impartiality to biased judgements. Adjectives like *epoch-making, epic, historic, unforgettable, triumphant, age-old, inevitable, inexorable, veritable,* are used to dignify the sordid processes of international politics, while writing that aims at glorifying war usually takes on an archaic colour, its characteristic words being: *realm, throne, chariot, mailed fist, trident, sword, shield, buckler, banner, jackboot, clarion.* Foreign words and expressions such as *cul de sac, ancien régime, deus ex machina, mutatis mutandis, status quo, gleichschaltung, weltanschauung,* are used to give an air of culture and elegance. Except for the useful abbreviations *i.e., e.g.,* and *etc.,* there is no real need for any of the hundreds of foreign phrases now current in English. Bad writers, and especially scientific, political and sociological writers, are nearly always haunted by the notion that Latin or Greek words are grander than Saxon ones, and unnecessary words like *expedite, ameliorate, predict, extraneous, deracinated, clandestine, subaqueous* and hundreds of others constantly gain ground from their Anglo-Saxon opposite numbers.* The jargon peculiar to Marxist writing (*hyena, hangman, cannibal, petty bourgeois, these gentry, lacquey, flunkey, mad dog, White Guard,* etc.) consists largely of words and phrases translated from Russian, German or French; but the normal way of coining a new word is to use a Latin or Greek root with the appropriate affix and, where necessary, the –ize formation. It is often easier to make up words of this kind (*deregionalize, impermissible, extramarital, nonfragmentary* and so forth) than to think up the English words that will cover one's meaning. The result, in general, is an increase in slovenliness and vagueness.

*An interesting illustration of this is the way in which the English flower names which were in use till very recently are being ousted by Greek ones, *snapdragon* becoming *antirrhinum, forget-me-not* becoming *myosotis,* etc. It is hard to see any practical reason for this change of fashion: it is probably due to an instinctive turning-away from the more homely word and a vague feeling that the Greek word is scientific [Orwell's footnote].

Meaningless words. In certain kinds of writing, particularly in art criticism and literary criticism, it is normal to come across long passages which are almost completely lacking in meaning.* Words like *romantic, plastic, values, human, dead, sentimental, natural, vitality,* as used in art criticism, are strictly meaningless, in the sense that they not only do not point to any discoverable object, but are hardly even expected to do so by the reader. When one critic writes, "The outstanding feature of Mr. X's work is its living quality," while another writes, "The immediately striking thing about Mr. X's work is its peculiar deadness," the reader accepts this as a simple difference of opinion. If words like *black* and *white* were involved, instead of the jargon words *dead* and *living,* he would see at once that language was being used in an improper way. Many political words are similarly abused. The word *Fascism* has now no meaning except in so far as it signifies "something not desirable." The words *democracy, socialism, freedom, patriotic, realistic, justice,* have each of them several different meanings which cannot be reconciled with one another. In the case of a word like *democracy,* not only is there no agreed definition, but the attempt to make one is resisted from all sides. It is almost universally felt that when we call a country democratic we are praising it: consequently the defenders of every kind of régime claim that it is a democracy, and fear that they might have to stop using the word if it were tied down to any one meaning. Words of this kind are often used in a consciously dishonest way. That is, the person who uses them has his own private definition, but allows his hearer to think he means something quite

*Example: "Comfort's catholicity of perception and image, strangely Whitmanesque in range, almost the exact opposite in aesthetic compulsion, continues to evoke that trembling atmospheric accumulative hinting at a cruel, an inexorably serene timelessness. . . . Wrey Gardiner scores by aiming at simple bullseyes with precision. Only they are not so simple, and through this contented sadness runs more than the surface bitter-sweet of resignation" (*Poetry Quarterly*) [Orwell's footnote].

different. Statements like *Marshal Pétain was a true patriot, The Soviet Press is the freest in the world, The Catholic Church is opposed to persecution,* are almost always made with intent to deceive. Other words used in variable meanings, in most cases more or less dishonestly, are: *class, totalitarian, science, progressive, reactionary, bourgeois, equality.*

Now that I have made this catalogue of swindles and perversions, let me give another example of the kind of writing that they lead to. This time it must of its nature be an imaginary one. I am going to translate a passage of good English into modern English of the worst sort. Here is a well-known verse from *Ecclesiastes*:

> "I returned, and saw under the sun, that the race is not to the swift, nor the battle to the strong, neither yet bread to the wise, nor yet riches to men of understanding, nor yet favour to men of skill; but time and chance happeneth to them all."

Here it is in modern English:

> "Objective consideration of contemporary phenomena compels the conclusion that success or failure in competitive activities exhibits no tendency to be commensurate with innate capacity, but that a considerable element of the unpredictable must invariably be taken into account."

This is a parody, but not a very gross one. Exhibit (3), above, for instance, contains several patches of the same kind of English. It will be seen that I have not made a full translation. The beginning and ending of the sentence follow the original meaning fairly closely, but in the middle the concrete illustrations—race, battle, bread—dissolve into the vague phrase "success or failure in competitive activities." This had to be so, because no modern writer of the kind I am discussing—no one capable of using phrases like "objective consideration of contemporary phenomena"—would ever tabulate his thoughts in that precise and detailed way. The whole tendency of modern prose is away from concreteness. Now analyse these two sentences a little more closely. The first contains 49 words but only 60 syllables, and all its words are those of everyday life. The second contains 38 words of 90 syllables: 18 of its words are from Latin roots, and one from Greek. The first sentence contains six vivid images, and only one phrase ("time and chance") that could be called vague. The second contains not a single fresh, arresting phrase, and in spite of its 90 syllables it gives only a shortened version of the meaning contained in the first. Yet without a doubt it is the second kind of sentence that is gaining ground in modern English. I do not want to exaggerate. This kind of writing is not yet universal, and outcrops of simplicity will occur here and there in the worst-written page. Still, if you or I were told to write a few lines on the uncertainty of human fortunes, we should probably come much nearer to my imaginary sentence than to the one from *Ecclesiastes*.

As I have tried to show, modern writing at its worst does not consist in picking out words for the sake of their meaning and inventing images in order to make the meaning clearer. It consists in gumming together long strips of words which have already been set in order by someone else, and making the results presentable by sheer humbug. The attraction of this way of writing is that it is easy. It is easier—even quicker, once you have the habit—to say *In my opinion it is a not unjustifiable assumption that* than to say *I think*. If you use ready-made phrases, you not only don't have to hunt about for words; you also don't have to bother with the rhythms of your sentences, since these phrases are generally so arranged as to be more or less euphonious. When you are composing in a hurry—when you are dictating to a stenographer, for instance, or making a public speech—it is natural to fall into a pretentious, Latinized style. Tags like *a consideration which we should do well to bear in mind* or *a conclusion to which all of us would readily assent* will save many a sentence from coming down with a bump. By using stale metaphors, similes and idioms, you save much mental effort, at the cost of leaving your meaning vague, not only for your reader but for yourself. This is the significance of mixed metaphors. The sole aim of a metaphor is to call up a visual image. When these images clash—as in *The Fascist octopus has sung its swan song, the jack-boot is thrown into the melting pot*—it can be taken as certain that the writer is not seeing a mental image of the objects he is naming; in other words he is not really thinking. Look again at the examples I gave at the beginning of this essay. Professor Laski (1) uses five negatives in 53 words. One of these is superfluous, making nonsense of the whole passage, and in addition there is the slip *alien* for akin, making further nonsense, and several avoidable pieces of clumsiness which increase the general vagueness. Professor Hogben (2) plays ducks and drakes with a battery which is able to write prescriptions, and, while disapproving of the everyday phrase *put up with,* is unwilling to look *egregious* up in the dictionary and see what it means. (3), if one takes an uncharitable attitude towards it, [it] is simply meaningless: probably one could work out its intended meaning by reading the whole of the article in which it occurs. In (4), the writer knows more or less what he wants to say, but an accumulation of stale phrases chokes him like tea leaves blocking a sink. In (5), words and meaning have almost parted company. People who write in this manner usually have a general emotional meaning—they dislike one thing and want to express solidarity with another—but they are not interested in the detail of what they are saying. A scrupulous writer, in every sentence that he writes, will ask himself at least four questions, thus: What am I trying to say? What words will express it? What image or idiom will make it clearer? Is this image fresh enough to have an effect? And he will probably ask himself two more: Could I put it more shortly? Have I said anything that is avoidably ugly? But you are not obliged to go to all this trouble. You can shirk it by simply throwing your mind open and letting the ready-made phrases come crowding in. They will construct your sentences for you—even think your thoughts for you, to a certain extent—and at need they will perform the important service of partially concealing your meaning even from yourself. It is at this point that the special connection between politics and the debasement of language becomes clear.

In our time it is broadly true that political writing is bad writing. Where it is not true, it will generally be found that the writer is some kind of rebel, expressing his private opinions and not a "party line." Orthodoxy, of whatever colour, seems to demand a lifeless, imitative style. The political dialects to be found in pamphlets, leading articles, manifestos, White Papers and the speeches of under-secretaries do, of course, vary from party to party, but they are all alike in that one almost never finds in them a fresh, vivid, home-made turn of speech. When one watches some tired hack on the platform mechanically repeating the familiar phrases—*bestial atrocities, iron heel, bloodstained tyranny, free peoples of the world, stand shoulder to shoulder*—one often has a curious feeling that one is not watching a live human being but some kind of dummy: a feeling which suddenly becomes stronger at moments when the light catches the speaker's spectacles and turns them into blank discs which seem to have no eyes behind them. And this is not altogether fanciful. A speaker who uses that kind of phraseology has gone some distance towards turning himself into a machine. The appropriate noises are coming out of his larynx, but his brain is not involved as it would be if he were choosing his words for himself. If the speech he is making is one that he is accustomed to make over and over again, he may be almost unconscious of what he is saying, as one is when one utters the responses in church. And this reduced state of consciousness, if not indispensable, is at any rate favourable to political conformity.

In our time, political speech and writing are largely the defence of the indefensible. Things like the continuance of British rule in India, the Russian purges and deportations, the dropping of the atom bombs on Japan, can indeed be defended, but only by arguments which are too brutal for most people to face, and which do not square with the professed aims of political parties. Thus political language has to consist largely of euphemism, question-begging and sheer cloudy vagueness. Defenceless villages are bombarded from the air, the inhabitants driven out into the countryside, the cattle machine-gunned, the huts set on fire with incendiary bullets: this is called *pacification.* Millions of peasants are robbed of their farms and sent trudging along the roads with no more than they can carry: this is called *transfer of population* or *rectification of frontiers.* People are imprisoned for years without trial, or shot in the back of the neck or sent to die of scurvy in Arctic lumber camps: this is called *elimination of unreliable elements.* Such phraseology is needed if one wants to name things without calling up mental pictures of them. Consider for instance some comfortable English professor defending Russian totalitarianism. He cannot say outright, "I believe in killing off your opponents when you can get good results by doing so." Probably, therefore, he will say something like this:

"While freely conceding that the Soviet régime exhibits certain features which the humanitarian may be inclined to deplore, we must, I think, agree that a certain curtailment of the right to political opposition is an unavoidable concomitant of transitional periods, and that the rigours which the Russian people have been called upon to undergo have been amply justified in the sphere of concrete achievement."

The inflated style is itself a kind of euphemism. A mass of Latin words falls upon the facts like soft snow, blurring the outlines and covering up all the details. The great enemy of clear language is insincerity. When there is a gap between one's real and one's declared aims, one turns as it were instinctively to long words and exhausted idioms, like a cuttlefish squirting out ink. In our age there is no such thing as "keeping out of politics." All issues are political issues, and politics itself is a mass of lies, evasions, folly, hatred and schizophrenia. When the general atmosphere is bad, language must suffer. I should expect to find—this is a guess which I have not sufficient knowledge to verify—that the German, Russian and Italian languages have all deteriorated in the last ten or fifteen years, as a result of dictatorship.

But if thought corrupts language, language can also corrupt thought. A bad usage can spread by tradition and imitation, even among people who should and do know better. The debased language that I have been discussing is in some ways very convenient. Phrases like *a not unjustifiable assumption, leaves much to be desired, would serve no good purpose, a consideration which we should do well to bear in mind,* are a continuous temptation, a packet of aspirins always at one's elbow. Look back through this essay, and for certain you will find that I have again and again committed the very faults I am protesting against. By this morning's post I have received a pamphlet dealing with conditions in Germany. The author tells me that he "felt impelled" to write it. I open it at random, and here is almost the first sentence that I see: "(The Allies) have an opportunity not only of achieving a radical transformation of Germany's social and political structure in such a way as to avoid a nationalistic reaction in Germany itself, but at the same time of laying the foundations of a co-operative and unified Europe." You see, he "feels impelled" to write—feels, presumably, that he has something new to say—and yet his words, like cavalry horses answering the bugle, group themselves automatically into the familiar dreary pattern. This invasion of one's mind by ready-made phrases (*lay the foundations, achieve a radical transformation*) can only be prevented if one is constantly on guard against them, and every such phrase anaesthetizes a portion of one's brain.

I said earlier that the decadence of our language is probably curable. Those who deny this would argue, if they produced an argument at all, that language merely reflects existing, social conditions, and that we cannot influence its development by any direct tinkering with words and constructions. So far as the general tone or spirit of a language goes, this may be true, but it is not true in detail. Silly words and expressions have often disappeared, not through any evolutionary process but owing to the conscious action of a minority. Two recent examples were *explore every avenue* and *leave no stone unturned,* which were killed by the jeers of a few journalists. There is a long list of flyblown metaphors which could similarly be got rid of if enough people would interest themselves in the job; and it should also be possible to laugh the *not un-* formation out of existence,* to reduce the amount of Latin and Greek in the average sentence, to drive out foreign phrases and strayed scientific words, and, in general, to make pretentiousness unfashionable. But all these are minor points. The defence of the English language implies more than this, and perhaps it is best to start by saying what it does *not* imply.

To begin with, it has nothing to do with archaism, with the salvaging of obsolete words and turns of speech, or with the

*One can cure oneself of the *not un-* formation by memorizing this sentence: *A not unblack dog was chasing a not unsmall rabbit across a not ungreen field* [Orwell's footnote].

setting-up of a "standard English" which must never be departed from. On the contrary, it is especially concerned with the scrapping of every word or idiom which has outworn its usefulness. It has nothing to do with correct grammar and syntax, which are of no importance so long as one makes one's meaning clear, or with the avoidance of Americanisms, or with having what is called a "good prose style." On the other hand it is not concerned with fake simplicity and the attempt to make written English colloquial. Nor does it even imply in every case preferring the Saxon word to the Latin one, though it does imply using the fewest and shortest words that will cover one's meaning. What is above all needed is to let the meaning choose the word, and not the other way about. In prose, the worst thing one can do with words is to surrender to them. When you think of a concrete object, you think wordlessly, and then, if you want to describe the thing you have been visualizing, you probably hunt about till you find the exact words that seem to fit it. When you think of something abstract you are more inclined to use words from the start, and unless you make a conscious effort to prevent it, the existing dialect will come rushing in and do the job for you, at the expense of blurring or even changing your meaning. Probably it is better to put off using words as long as possible and get one's meaning as clear as one can through pictures or sensations. Afterwards one can choose—not simply *accept*—the phrases that will best cover the meaning, and then switch round and decide what impression one's words are likely to make on another person. This last effort of the mind cuts out all stale or mixed images, all prefabricated phrases, needless repetitions, and humbug and vagueness generally. But one can often be in doubt about the effect of a word or a phrase, and one needs rules that one can rely on when instinct fails. I think the following rules will cover most cases:

(i) Never use a metaphor, simile or other figure of speech which you are used to seeing in print.
(ii) Never use a long word where a short one will do.
(iii) If it is possible to cut a word out, always cut it out.
(iv) Never use the passive where you can use the active.
(v) Never use a foreign phrase, a scientific word or a jargon word if you can think of an everyday English equivalent.
(vi) Break any of these rules sooner than say anything outright barbarous. These rules sound elementary, and so they are, but they demand a deep change of attitude in anyone who has grown used to writing in the style now fashionable. One could keep all of them and still write bad English, but one could not write the kind of stuff that I quoted in those five specimens at the beginning of this article.

I have not here been considering the literary use of language, but merely language as an instrument for expressing and not for concealing or preventing thought. Stuart Chase[2] and others have come near to claiming that all abstract words are meaningless, and have used this as a pretext for advocating a kind of political quietism. Since you don't know what Fascism is, how can you struggle against Fascism? One need not swallow such absurdities as this, but one ought to recognize that the present political chaos is connected with the decay of language, and that one can probably bring about some improvement by starting at the verbal end. If you simplify your English, you are freed from the worst follies of orthodoxy. You cannot speak any of the necessary dialects, and when you make a stupid remark its stupidity will be obvious, even to yourself. Political language—and with variations this is true of all political parties, from Conservatives to Anarchists—is designed to make lies sound truthful and murder respectable, and to give an appearance of solidity to pure wind. One cannot change this all in a moment, but one can at least change one's own habits, and from time to time one can even, if one jeers loudly enough, send some worn-out and useless phrase—some *jackboot, Achilles' heel, hotbed, melting pot, acid test, veritable inferno* or other lump of verbal refuse—into the dustbin where it belongs.

Confessions of a Book Reviewer

Tribune, May 3, 1946

In a cold but stuffy bed-sitting room littered with cigarette ends and half-empty cups of tea, a man in a moth-eaten dressing gown sits at a rickety table, trying to find room for his typewriter among the piles of dusty papers that surround it. He cannot throw the papers away because the wastepaper basket is already overflowing, and besides, somewhere among the unanswered letters and unpaid bills it is possible that there is a cheque for two guineas which he is nearly certain he forgot to pay into the bank. There are also letters with addresses which ought to be entered in his address book. He has lost his address book, and the thought of looking for it, or indeed of looking for anything, afflicts him with acute suicidal impulses.

He is a man of 35, but looks 50. He is bald, has varicose veins and wears spectacles, or would wear them if his only pair were not chronically lost. If things are normal with him he will be suffering from malnutrition, but if he has recently had a lucky streak he will be suffering from a hangover. At present it is half past eleven in the morning, and according to his schedule he should have started work two hours ago; but even if he had made any serious effort to start he would have been frustrated by the almost continuous ringing of the telephone bell, the yells of the baby, the rattle of an electric drill out in the street, and the heavy boots of his creditors clumping up and down the stairs. The most recent interruption was the arrival of the second post, which brought him two circulars and an income tax demand printed in red.

Needless to say this person is a writer. He might be a poet, a novelist, or a writer of film scripts or radio features, for all literary people are very much alike, but let us say that he is a book reviewer. Half hidden among the pile of papers is a bulky parcel containing five volumes which his editor has sent with a note suggesting that they "ought to go well together." They arrived four days ago, but for 48 hours the reviewer was prevented by moral paralysis from opening the parcel. Yesterday in a resolute moment he ripped the string off it and found the five volumes to be *Palestine at the Cross Roads, Scientific Dairy Farming, A Short History of European Democracy* (this one is 680 pages and weighs four pounds), *Tribal Customs in Portuguese East Africa,* and a novel, *It's Nicer Lying Down,* probably included by mistake. His review—800 words, say—has got to be "in" by mid-day tomorrow.

Three of these books deal with subjects of which he is so ignorant that he will have to read at least 50 pages if he is to avoid making some howler which will betray him not merely to the author (who of course knows all about the habits of book reviewers), but even to the general reader. By four in the afternoon he will have taken the books out of their wrapping paper but will still be suffering from a nervous inability to open them. The prospect of having to read them, and even the smell of the paper, affects him like the prospect of eating cold ground-rice pudding flavoured with castor oil. And yet curiously enough his copy will get to the office in time. Somehow it always does get there in time. At about nine p.m. his mind will grow relatively clear, and until the small hours he will sit in a room which grows colder and colder, while the cigarette smoke grows thicker and thicker, skipping expertly through one book after another and laying each down with the final comment, "God, what tripe!" In the morning, blear-eyed, surly and unshaven, he will gaze for an hour or two at a blank sheet of paper until the menacing finger of the clock frightens him into action. Then suddenly he will snap into it. All the stale old phrases—"a book that no one should miss," "something memorable on every page," "of special value are the chapters dealing with, etc., etc."—will jump into their places like iron filings obeying the magnet, and the review will end up at exactly the right length and with just about three minutes to go. Meanwhile another wad of ill-assorted, unappetising books will have arrived by post. So it goes on. And yet with what high hopes this down-trodden, nerve-racked creature started his career, only a few years ago.

Do I seem to exaggerate? I ask any regular reviewer—anyone who reviews, say, a minimum of 100 books a year—whether he can deny in honesty that his habits and character are such as I have described. Every writer, in any case, is rather that kind of person, but the prolonged, indiscriminate reviewing of books is a quite exceptionally thankless, irritating and exhausting job. It not only involves praising trash—though it does involve that, as I will show in a moment—but constantly *inventing* reactions towards books about which one has no spontaneous feelings whatever. The reviewer, jaded though he may be, is professionally interested in books, and out of the thousands that appear annually, there are probably fifty or a hundred that he would enjoy writing about. If he is a top-notcher in his profession he may get hold of ten or twenty of them: more probably he gets hold of two or three. The rest of his work, however conscientious he may be in praising or damning, is in essence humbug. He is pouring his immortal spirit down the drain, half a pint at a time.

The great majority of reviewers give an inadequate or misleading account of the book that is dealt with. Since the war publishers have been less able than before to twist the tails of literary editors and evoke a paean of praise for every book that they produce, but on the other hand the standard of reviewing has gone down owing to lack of space and other inconveniences. Seeing the results, people sometimes suggest that the solution lies in getting book-reviewing out of the hands of hacks. Books on specialized subjects ought to be dealt with by experts, and on the other hand a good deal of reviewing, especially of novels, might well be done by amateurs. Nearly every book is capable of arousing passionate feeling, if it is only a passionate dislike, in some or other reader, whose ideas about it would surely be worth more than those of a bored professional. But, unfortunately, as every editor knows, that kind of thing is very difficult to organize. In practice the editor always finds himself reverting to his team of hacks—his "regulars," as he calls them.

None of this is remediable so long as it is taken for granted that every book deserves to be reviewed. It is almost impossible to mention books in bulk without grossly over-praising the great majority of them. Until one has some kind of professional relationship with books one does not discover how bad the majority of them are. In much more than nine cases out of ten the only objectively truthful criticism would be, "This book is worthless," while the truth about the reviewer's own reaction would probably be: "This book does not interest me in any way, and I would not write about it unless I were paid to." But the public will not pay to read that kind of thing. Why should they? They want some kind of guide to the books they are asked to read, and they want some kind of evaluation. But as soon as values are mentioned, standards collapse. For if one says—and nearly every reviewer says this kind of thing at least once a week—that "King Lear" is a good play and *The Four Just Men* is a good thriller, what meaning is there in the word "good"?

The best practice, it has always seemed to me, would be simply to ignore the great majority of books and to give very long reviews—1,000 words is a bare minimum—to the few that seem to matter. Short notes of a line or two on forthcoming books can be useful, but the usual middle-length review of about 600 words is bound to be worthless even if the reviewer genuinely wants to write it. Normally he doesn't want to write it, and the week-in, week-out production of snippets soon reduces him to the crushed figure in a dressing gown whom I described at the beginning of this article. However, everyone in this world has someone else whom he can look down on, and I must say, from experience of both trades, that the book reviewer is better off than the film critic, who cannot even do his work at home, but has to attend trade shows at eleven in the morning and, with one or two notable exceptions, is expected to sell his honour for a glass of inferior sherry.

Politics vs. Literature: An Examination of *Gulliver's Travels*

Polemic, 5, September–October 1946

In *Gulliver's Travels* humanity is attacked, or criticised, from at least three different angles, and the implied character of Gulliver himself necessarily changes somewhat in the process. In Part I he is the typical eighteenth-century voyager, bold, practical and unromantic, his homely outlook skilfully impressed on the reader by the biographical details at the beginning, by his age (he is a man of forty, with two children, when his adventures start), and by the inventory of the things in his pockets, especially his spectacles, which make several appearances. In Part II he has in general the same character, but at moments when the story demands it he has a tendency to develop into an imbecile who is capable of boasting of "our noble Country, the Mistress of Arts and Arms, the Scourge of France," etc., etc., and at the same time of betraying every available scandalous fact about the country which he professes to love. In Part III he is much as he was in Part I, though, as he is consorting chiefly with courtiers and men of learning, one has the impression that he has risen in the social scale. In Part IV he conceives a horror of the human race which is not apparent, or only intermittently apparent, in the earlier books, and changes into a sort of unreligious anchorite whose one desire is to live in some desolate spot where he can devote himself to meditating on the goodness of the Houyhnhnms. However, these inconsistencies are forced upon Swift by the fact that Gulliver is there chiefly to provide a contrast. It is necessary, for instance, that he should appear sensible in Part I and at least intermittently silly in Part II, because in both books the essential manoeuvre is the same, i.e. to make the human being look ridiculous by imagining him as a creature six inches high. Whenever Gulliver is not acting as a stooge there is a sort of continuity in his character, which comes out especially in his resourcefulness and his observation of physical detail. He is much the same kind of person, with the same prose style, when he bears off the warships of Blefuscu, when he rips open the belly of the monstrous rat, and when he sails away upon the ocean in his frail coracle made from the skins of Yahoos. Moreover, it is difficult not to feel that in his shrewder moments Gulliver is simply Swift himself, and there is at least one incident in which Swift seems to be venting his private grievance against contemporary Society. It will be remembered that when the Emperor of Lilliput's palace catches fire, Gulliver puts it out by urinating on it. Instead of being congratulated on his presence of mind, he finds that he has committed a capital offence by making water in the precincts of the palace, and

> I was privately assured, that the Empress, conceiving the greatest Abhorrence of what I had done, removed to the most distant Side of the Court, firmly resolved that those buildings should never be repaired for her Use; and, in the Presence of her chief Confidents, could not forbear vowing Revenge.

According to Professor G. M. Trevelyan (*England under Queen Anne*), part of the reason for Swift's failure to get preferment was that the Queen was scandalised by the *Tale of a Tub*—a pamphlet in which Swift probably felt that he had done a great service to the English Crown, since it scarifies the Dissenters and still more the Catholics while leaving the Established Church alone. In any case no one would deny that *Gulliver's Travels* is a rancorous as well as a pessimistic book, and that especially in Parts I and III it often descends into political partisanship of a narrow kind. Pettiness and magnanimity, republicanism and authoritarianism, love of reason and lack of curiosity, are all mixed up in it. The hatred of the human body with which Swift is especially associated is only dominant in Part IV, but somehow this new preoccupation does not come as a surprise. One feels that all these adventures, and all these changes of mood, could have happened to the same person, and the inter-connection between Swift's political loyalties and his ultimate despair is one of the most interesting features of the book.

Politically, Swift was one of those people who are driven into a sort of perverse Toryism by the follies of the progressive party of the moment. Part I of *Gulliver's Travels,* ostensibly a satire on human greatness, can be seen, if one looks a little deeper, to be simply an attack on England, on the dominant Whig party, and on the war with France, which—however bad the motives of the Allies may have been—did save Europe from being tyrannised over by a single reactionary power. Swift was not a Jacobite nor strictly speaking a Tory, and his declared aim in the war was merely a moderate peace treaty and not the outright defeat of England. Nevertheless there is a tinge of quislingism in his attitude, which comes out in the ending of Part I and slightly interferes with the allegory. When Gulliver flees from Lilliput (England) to Blefuscu (France) the assumption that a human being six inches high is inherently contemptible seems to be dropped. Whereas the people of Lilliput have behaved towards Gulliver with the utmost treachery and meanness, those of Blefuscu behave generously and straightforwardly, and indeed this section of the book ends on a different note from the all-round disillusionment of the earlier chapters. Evidently Swift's animus is, in the first place, against *England.* It is "your Natives" (i.e. Gulliver's fellow-countrymen) whom the King of Brobdingnag considers to be "the most pernicious Race of little odious Vermin that Nature ever suffered to crawl upon the surface of the Earth," and the long passage at the end, denouncing colonisation and foreign conquest, is plainly aimed at England, although the contrary is elaborately stated. The Dutch, England's allies and target of one of Swift's most famous pamphlets, are also more or less wantonly attacked in Part III. There is even what sounds like a personal note in the passage in which Gulliver records his satisfaction that the various countries he has discovered cannot be made colonies of the British Crown:

> The *Houyhnhnms,* indeed, appear not to be so well prepared for War, a Science to which they are perfect Strangers, and especially against missive Weapons. However, supposing myself to be a Minister of State, I could never give my advice for invading them. . . . Imagine twenty thousand of them breaking into the midst of an *European* army, confounding the Ranks, overturning the Carriages, battering the Warriors' Faces into Mummy, by terrible Yerks from their hinder Hoofs . . .

Considering that Swift does not waste words, that phrase, "battering the warriors' faces into mummy," probably indicates a secret wish to see the invincible armies of the Duke of Marlborough treated in a like manner. There are similar touches elsewhere. Even the country mentioned in Part III, where "the Bulk of the People consist, in a Manner, wholly of Discoverers, Witnesses, Informers, Accusers, Prosecutors, Evidences, Swearers, together with their several subservient and subaltern Instruments, all under the Colours, the Conduct, and Pay of Ministers of State," is called Langdon, which is within one letter of being an anagram of England. (As the early editions of the book contain misprints, it may perhaps have been intended as a complete anagram.) Swift's *physical* repulsion from humanity is certainly real enough, but one has the feeling that his debunking of human grandeur, his diatribes against lords, politicians, court favourites, etc., has mainly a local application and springs from the fact that he belonged to the unsuccessful party. He denounces injustice and oppression, but he gives no evidence of liking democracy. In spite of his enormously greater powers, his implied position is very similar to that of the innumerable silly-clever Conservatives of our own day—people like Sir Alan Herbert, Professor G. M. Young, Lord Elton,[1] the Tory Reform Committee or the long line of Catholic apologists from W. H. Mallock[2] onwards: people who specialise in cracking neat jokes at the expense of whatever is "modern" and "progressive," and whose opinions are often all the more extreme because they know that they cannot influence the actual drift of events. After all, such a pamphlet as *An Argument to prove that the Abolishing of Christianity,* etc. is very like "Timothy Shy" having a bit of clean fun with the Brains Trust,[3] or Father Ronald Knox exposing the errors of Bertrand Russell.[4] And the ease with which Swift has been forgiven—and forgiven, sometimes, by devout believers—for the blasphemies of *A Tale of a Tub* demonstrates clearly enough the feebleness of religious sentiments as compared with political ones.

However, the reactionary cast of Swift's mind does not show itself chiefly in his political affiliations. The important thing is his attitude towards Science, and, more broadly, towards intellectual curiosity. The famous Academy of Lagado, described in Part III of *Gulliver's Travels,* is no doubt a justified satire on most of the so-called scientists of Swift's own day. Significantly, the people at work in it are described as "Projectors," that is, people not engaged in disinterested research but merely on the look-out for gadgets which will save labour and bring in money. But there is no sign—indeed, all through the book there are many signs to the contrary—that "pure" science would have struck Swift as a worth-while activity. The more serious kind of scientist has already had a kick in the pants in Part II, when the "Scholars" patronised by the King of Brobdingnag try to account for Gulliver's small stature:

> After much Debate, they concluded unanimously that I was only *Relplum Scalcath,* which is interpreted literally, *Lusus Naturae*; a Determination exactly agreeable to the modern philosophy of *Europe,* whose Professors, disdaining the old Evasion of *occult Causes,* whereby the followers of *Aristotle* endeavoured in vain to disguise their Ignorance, have invented this wonderful Solution of all Difficulties, to the unspeakable Advancement of human Knowledge.

If this stood by itself one might assume that Swift is merely the enemy of *sham* science. In a number of places, however, he goes out of his way to proclaim the uselessness of all learning or speculation not directed towards some practical end:

> The Learning of (the Brobdingnagians) is very defective, consisting only in Morality, History, Poetry, and Mathematics, wherein they must be allowed to excel. But, the last of these is wholly applied to what may be useful in Life, to the Improvement of Agriculture, and all mechanical Arts; so that among us it would be little esteemed. And as to Ideas, Entities, Abstractions, and Transcendentals, I could never drive the least Conception into their Heads.

The Houyhnhnms, Swift's ideal beings, are backward even in a mechanical sense. They are unacquainted with metals, have never heard of boats, do not, properly speaking, practise agriculture (we are told that the oats which they live upon "grow naturally"), and appear not to have invented wheels.* They have no alphabet, and evidently have not much curiosity about the physical world. They do not believe that any inhabited country exists beside their own, and though they understand the motions of the sun and moon, and the nature of eclipses, "this is the utmost Progress of their *Astronomy*." By contrast, the philosophers of the flying island of Laputa are so continuously absorbed in mathematical speculations that before speaking to them one has to attract their attention by flapping them on the ear with a bladder. They have catalogued ten thousand fixed stars, have settled the periods of ninety-three comets, and have discovered, in advance of the astronomers of Europe, that Mars has two moons—all of which information Swift evidently regards as ridiculous, useless and uninteresting. As one might expect, he believes that the scientist's place, if he has a place, is in the laboratory and that scientific knowledge has no bearing on political matters:

> What I . . . thought altogether unaccountable, was the strong Disposition I observed in them towards News and Politics, perpetually enquiring into Public Affairs, giving their judgments in Matters of State, and passionately disputing every Inch of a Party Opinion. I have, indeed, observed the same Disposition among most of the Mathematicians I have known in *Europe*, though I could never discover the least Analogy between the two Sciences; unless those People suppose, that, because the smallest Circle hath as many Degrees as the largest, therefore the Regulation and Management of the World require no more Abilities, than the Handling and Turning of a Globe.

*Houyhnhnms too old to walk are described as being carried in "sledges" or in "a kind of vehicle, drawn like a sledge." Presumably these had no wheels [Orwell's footnote].

Is there not something familiar in that phrase "I could never discover the least analogy between the two sciences"? It has precisely the note of the popular Catholic apologists who profess to be astonished when a scientist utters an opinion on such questions as the existence of God or the immortality of the soul. The scientist, we are told, is an expert only in one restricted field: why should his opinions be of value in any other? The implication is that theology is just as much an exact science as, for instance, chemistry, and that the priest is also an expert whose conclusions on certain subjects must be accepted. Swift in effect makes the same claim for the politician, but he goes one better in that he will not allow the scientist—either the "pure" scientist or the *ad-hoc* investigator—to be a useful person in his own line. Even if he had not written Part III of *Gulliver's Travels,* one could infer from the rest of the book that, like Tolstoy and like Blake, he hates the very idea of studying the processes of Nature. The "Reason" which he so admires in the Houyhnhnms does not primarily mean the power of drawing logical inferences from observed facts. Although he never defines it, it appears in most contexts to mean either common sense—i.e. acceptance of the obvious and contempt for quibbles and abstractions—or absence of passion and superstition. In general he assumes that we know all that we need to know already, and merely use our knowledge incorrectly. Medicine, for instance, is a useless science, because if we lived in a more natural way, there would be no diseases. Swift, however, is not a simple-lifer or an admirer of the Noble Savage. He is in favour of civilisation and the arts of civilisation. Not only does he see the value of good manners, good conversation, and even learning of a literary and historical kind, he also sees that agriculture, navigation and architecture need to be studied and could with advantage be improved. But his implied aim is a static, incurious civilisation—the world of his own day, a little cleaner, a little saner, with no radical change and no poking into the unknowable. More than one would expect in anyone so free from accepted fallacies, he reveres the past, especially classical antiquity, and believes that modern man has degenerated sharply during the past hundred years.* In the island of sorcerers, where the spirits of the dead can be called up at will:

> I desired that the Senate of *Rome* might appear before me in one large Chamber, and a modern Representative in Counterview, in another. The first seemed to be an Assembly of Heroes and Demy-Gods, the other a Knot of Pedlars, Pickpockets, Highwaymen, and Bullies.

Although Swift uses this section of Part III to attack the truthfulness of recorded history, his critical spirit deserts him as soon as he is dealing with Greeks and Romans. He remarks, of course, upon the corruption of imperial Rome, but he has an almost unreasoning admiration for some of the leading figures of the ancient world:

> I was struck with profound Veneration at the Sight of *Brutus,* and could easily discover the most consummate Virtue, the greatest Intrepidity and Firmness of Mind, the truest Love of his Country, and general Benevolence for mankind, in every Lineament of his Countenance. . . . I had the Honour to have much Conversation with *Brutus,* and was told, that his Ancestor *Junius, Socrates, Epaminondas, Cato* the

*The physical decadence which Swift claims to have observed may have been a reality at that date. He attributes it to syphilis, which was a new disease in Europe and may have been more virulent than it is now. Distilled liquors, also, were a novelty in the seventeenth century and must have led at first to a great increase in drunkenness [Orwell's footnote].

> younger, *Sir Thomas More,* and himself, were perpetually together: a *Sextumvirate,* to which all the Ages of the World cannot add a seventh.

It will be noticed that of these six people, only one is a Christian. This is an important point. If one adds together Swift's pessimism, his reverence for the past, his incuriosity and his horror of the human body, one arrives at an attitude common among religious reactionaries—that is, people who defend an unjust order of Society by claiming that this world cannot be substantially improved and only the "next world" matters. However, Swift shows no sign of having any religious beliefs, at least in any ordinary sense of the words. He does not appear to believe seriously in life after death, and his idea of goodness is bound up with republicanism, love of liberty, courage, "benevolence" (meaning in effect public spirit), "reason" and other pagan qualities. This reminds one that there is another strain in Swift, not quite congruous with his disbelief in progress and his general hatred of humanity.

To begin with, he has moments when he is "constructive" and even "advanced." To be occasionally inconsistent is almost a mark of vitality in Utopia books, and Swift sometimes inserts a word of praise into a passage that ought to be purely satirical. Thus, his ideas about the education of the young are fathered on to the Lilliputians, who have much the same views on this subject as the Houyhnhnms. The Lilliputians also have various social and legal institutions (for instance, there are old age pensions, and people are rewarded for keeping the law as well as punished for breaking it) which Swift would have liked to see prevailing in his own country. In the middle of this passage Swift remembers his satirical intention and adds, "In relating these and the following Laws, I would only be understood to mean the original Institutions, and not the most scandalous Corruptions into which these people are fallen by the degenerate Nature of Man": but as Lilliput is supposed to represent England, and the laws he is speaking of have never had their parallel in England, it is clear that the impulse to make constructive suggestions has been too much for him. But Swift's greatest contribution to political thought, in the narrower sense of the words, is his attack, especially in Part III, on what would now be called totalitarianism. He has an extraordinarily clear prevision of the spy-haunted "police State," with its endless heresy-hunts and treason trials, all really designed to neutralise popular discontent by changing it into war hysteria. And one must remember that Swift is here inferring the whole from a quite small part, for the feeble governments of his own day did not give him illustrations ready-made. For example, there is the professor at the School of Political Projectors who "shewed me a large Paper of Instructions for discovering Plots and Conspiracies," and who claimed that one can find people's secret thoughts by examining their excrement:

> Because Men are never so serious, thoughtful, and intent, as when they are at Stool, which he found by frequent Experiment: for in such Conjunctures, when he used meerly as a Trial to consider what was the best Way of murdering the King, his Ordure would have a Tincture of Green; but quite different when he thought only of raising an Insurrection, or burning the Metropolis.

The professor and his theory are said to have been suggested to Swift by the—from our point of view—not particularly astonishing or disgusting fact that in a recent State trial some letters found in somebody's privy had been put in evidence. Later in the same chapter we seem to be positively in the middle of the Russian purges:

> In the Kingdom of Tribnia, by the Natives called Langdon . . . the Bulk of the People consist, in a Manner, wholly of Discoverers, Witnesses, Informers, Accusers, Prosecutors, Evidences, Swearers. . . . It is first agreed, and settled among them, what suspected Persons shall be accused of a Plot: Then, effectual Care is taken to secure all their Letters and Papers, and put the Owners in Chains. These papers are delivered to a Sett of Artists, very dexterous in finding out the mysterious Meanings of Words, Syllables, and Letters. . . . Where this Method fails, they have two others more effectual, which the Learned among them call *Acrostics* and *Anagrams. First,* they can decypher all initial Letters into political Meanings: Thus, N shall signify a Plot, B a Regiment of Horse, L a Fleet at Sea: Or, *Secondly,* by transposing the Letters of the Alphabet in any suspected Paper, they can lay open the deepest Designs of a discontented Party. So, for Example, if I should say in a Letter to a Friend, *Our Brother Tom has just got the Piles,* a skilful Decypherer would discover that the same Letters, which compose that Sentence, may be analysed in the following Words: *Resist—a Plot is brought Home—The Tour.** And this is the anagrammatic Method.

Other professors at the same school invent simplified languages, write books by machinery, educate their pupils by inscribing the lesson on a wafer and causing them to swallow it, or propose to abolish individuality altogether by cutting off part of the brain of

*Tower [Orwell's footnote].

one man and grafting it on to the head of another. There is something queerly familiar in the atmosphere of these chapters, because, mixed up with much fooling, there is a perception that one of the aims of totalitarianism is not merely to make sure that people will think the right thoughts, but actually to make them *less conscious*. Then, again, Swift's account of the Leader who is usually to be found ruling over a tribe of Yahoos, and of the "favourite" who acts first as a dirty-worker and later as a scapegoat, fits remarkably well into the pattern of our own times. But are we to infer from all this that Swift was first and foremost an enemy of tyranny and a champion of the free intelligence? No: his own views, so far as one can discern them, are not markedly liberal. No doubt he hates lords, kings, bishops, generals, ladies of fashion, orders, titles and flummery generally, but he does not seem to think better of the common people than of their rulers, or to be in favour of increased social equality, or to be enthusiastic about representative institutions. The Houyhnhnms are organised upon a sort of caste system which is racial in character, the horses which do the menial work being of different colours from their masters and not interbreeding with them. The educational system which Swift admires in the Lilliputians takes hereditary class distinctions for granted, and the children of the poorest class do not go to school, because "their Business being only to till and cultivate the Earth . . . therefore their Education is of little Consequence to the Public." Nor does he seem to have been strongly in favour of freedom of speech and the Press, in spite of the toleration which his own writings enjoyed. The King of Brobdingnag is astonished at the multiplicity of religious and political sects in England, and considers that those who hold "opinions prejudicial to the public" (in the context this seems to mean simply heretical opinions), though they need not be obliged to change them, ought to be obliged to conceal them: for "as it was Tyranny in any Government to require the first, so it was

Weakness not to enforce the second." There is a subtler indication of Swift's own attitude in the manner in which Gulliver leaves the land of the Houyhnhnms. Intermittently, at least, Swift was a kind of anarchist, and Part IV of *Gulliver's Travels* is a picture of an anarchistic Society, not governed by law in the ordinary sense, but by the dictates of "Reason," which are voluntarily accepted by everyone. The General Assembly of the Houyhnhnms "exhorts" Gulliver's master to get rid of him, and his neighbours put pressure on him to make him comply. Two reasons are given. One is that the presence of this unusual Yahoo may unsettle the rest of the tribe, and the other is that a friendly relationship between a Houyhnhnm and a Yahoo is "not agreeable to Reason or Nature, or a Thing ever heard of before among them." Gulliver's master is somewhat unwilling to obey, but the "exhortation" (a Houyhnhnm, we are told, is never *compelled* to do anything, he is merely "exhorted" or "advised") cannot be disregarded. This illustrates very well the totalitarian tendency which is implicit in the anarchist or pacifist vision of Society. In a Society in which there is no law, and in theory no compulsion, the only arbiter of behaviour is public opinion. But public opinion, because of the tremendous urge to conformity in gregarious animals, is less tolerant than any system of law. When human beings are governed by "thou shalt not," the individual can practise a certain amount of eccentricity: when they are supposedly governed by "love" or "reason," he is under continuous pressure to make him behave and think in exactly the same way as everyone else. The Houyhnhnms, we are told, were unanimous on almost all subjects. The only question they ever *discussed* was how to deal with the Yahoos. Otherwise there was no room for disagreement among them, because the truth is always either self-evident, or else it is undiscoverable and unimportant. They had apparently no word for "opinion" in their language, and in their conversations there was no "difference of sentiments." They had reached, in fact, the highest stage of totalitarian organisation, the stage when conformity has become so general that there is no need for a police force. Swift approves of this kind of thing because among his many gifts neither curiosity nor good-nature was included. Disagreement would always seem to him sheer perversity. "Reason," among the Houyhnhnms, he says, "is not a Point Problematical, as with us, where men can argue with Plausibility on both Sides of a Question; but strikes you with immediate Conviction; as it must needs do, where it is not mingled, obscured, or discoloured by Passion and Interest." In other words, we know everything already, so why should dissident opinions be tolerated? The totalitarian Society of the Houyhnhnms, where there can be no freedom and no development, follows naturally from this.

We are right to think of Swift as a rebel and iconoclast, but except in certain secondary matters, such as his insistence that women should receive the same education as men, he cannot be labelled "Left." He is a Tory anarchist, despising authority while disbelieving in liberty, and preserving the aristocratic outlook while seeing clearly that the existing aristocracy is degenerate and contemptible. When Swift utters one of his characteristic diatribes against the rich and powerful, one must probably, as I said earlier, write off something for the fact that he himself belonged to the less successful party, and was personally disappointed. The "outs," for obvious reasons, are always more radical than the "ins."* But

*At the end of the book, as typical specimens of human folly and viciousness, Swift names "a Lawyer, a Pickpocket, a Colonel, a Fool, a Lord, a Gamester, a Politician, a Whore-master, a Physician, an Evidence, a Suborner, an Attorney, a Traitor, or the like." One sees here the irresponsible violence of the powerless. The list lumps together those who break the conventional code, and those who keep it. For instance, if you automatically condemn a colonel, as such, on what grounds do you condemn a traitor? Or again, if you want to suppress pickpockets, you must have laws, which means that you must have lawyers. But the whole closing passage, in which the hatred is so authentic, and the reason given for it so inadequate, is somehow unconvincing. One has the feeling that personal animosity is at work [Orwell's footnote].

the most essential thing in Swift is his inability to believe that life—ordinary life on the solid earth, and not some rationalised, deodorised version of it—could be made worth living. Of course, no honest person claims that happiness is *now* a normal condition among adult human beings; but perhaps it *could* be made normal, and it is upon this question that all serious political controversy really turns. Swift has much in common—more, I believe, than has been noticed—with Tolstoy, another disbeliever in the possibility of happiness. In both men you have the same anarchistic outlook covering an authoritarian cast of mind; in both a similar hostility to Science, the same impatience with opponents, the same inability to see the importance of any question not interesting to themselves; and in both cases a sort of horror of the actual process of life, though in Tolstoy's case it was arrived at later and in a different way. The sexual unhappiness of the two men was not of the same kind, but there was this in common, that in both of them a sincere loathing was mixed up with a morbid fascination. Tolstoy was a reformed rake who ended by preaching complete celibacy, while continuing to practise the opposite into extreme old age. Swift was presumably impotent, and had an exaggerated horror of human dung: he also thought about it incessantly, as is evident throughout his works. Such people are not likely to enjoy even the small amount of happiness that falls to most human beings, and, from obvious motives, are not likely to admit that earthly life is capable of much improvement. Their incuriosity, and hence their intolerance, spring from the same root.

Swift's disgust, rancour and pessimism would make sense against the background of a "next world" to which this one is the prelude. As he does not appear to believe seriously in any such thing, it becomes necessary to construct a paradise supposedly existing on the surface of the earth, but something quite different from anything we know, with all that he disapproves of—lies, folly, change, enthusiasm, pleasure, love and dirt—eliminated from it. As his ideal being he chooses the horse, an animal whose excrement is not offensive. The Houyhnhnms are dreary beasts—this is so generally admitted that the point is not worth labouring. Swift's genius can make them credible, but there can have been very few readers in whom they have excited any feeling beyond dislike. And this is not from wounded vanity at seeing animals preferred to men; for, of the two, the Houyhnhnms are much liker to human beings than are the Yahoos, and Gulliver's horror of the Yahoos, together with his recognition that they are the same kind of creature as himself, contains a logical absurdity. This horror comes upon him at his very first sight of them. "I never beheld," he says, "in all my Travels, so disagreeable an Animal, nor one against which I naturally conceived so strong an Antipathy." But in comparison with what are the Yahoos disgusting? Not with the Houyhnhnms, because at this time Gulliver has not seen a Houyhnhnm. It can only be in comparison with himself, i.e. with a human being. Later, however, we are to be told that the Yahoos *are* human beings, and human society becomes insupportible to Gulliver because all men are Yahoos. In that case why did he not conceive his disgust of humanity earlier? In effect we are told that the Yahoos are fantastically different from men, and yet are the same. Swift has over-reached himself in his fury, and is shouting at his fellow-creatures; "You are filthier than you are!" However, it is impossible to feel much sympathy with the Yahoos, and it is not because they oppress the Yahoos that the Houyhnhnms are unattractive. They are unattractive because the "Reason" by which they are governed is really a desire for death. They are exempt from love, friendship, curiosity, fear, sorrow and—except in their feelings towards the Yahoos, who occupy rather the same place in their community as the Jews in Nazi Germany—anger and hatred. "They have no Fondness for their Colts or Foles, but the

Care they take, in educating them, proceeds entirely from the Dictates of *Reason.*" They lay store by "Friendship" and "Benevolence," but "these are not confined to particular Objects, but universal to the whole Race." They also value conversation, but in their conversations there are no differences of opinion, and "nothing passed but what was useful, expressed in the fewest and most significant Words." They practise strict birth control, each couple producing two offspring and thereafter abstaining from sexual intercourse. Their marriages are arranged for them by their elders, on eugenic principles, and their language contains no word for "love," in the sexual sense. When somebody dies they carry on exactly as before, without feeling any grief. It will be seen that their aim is to be as like a corpse as is possible while retaining physical life. One or two of their characteristics, it is true, do not seem to be strictly "reasonable" in their own usage of the word. Thus, they place a great value not only on physical hardihood but on athleticism, and they are devoted to poetry. But these exceptions may be less arbitrary than they seem. Swift probably emphasises the physical strength of the Houyhnhnms in order to make clear that they could never be conquered by the hated human race, while a taste for poetry may figure among their qualities because poetry appeared to Swift as the antithesis of Science, from his point of view the most useless of all pursuits. In Part III he names "Imagination, Fancy, and Invention" as desirable faculties in which the Laputan mathematicians (in spite of their love of music) were wholly lacking. One must remember that although Swift was an admirable writer of comic verse, the kind of poetry he thought valuable would probably be didactic poetry. The poetry of the Houyhnhnms, he says—

> must be allowed to excel (that of) all other Mortals; wherein the Justness of their Similes, and the Minuteness, as well as

> exactness, of their Descriptions, are, indeed, inimitable. Their Verses abound very much in both of these; and usually contain either some exalted Notions of Friendship and Benevolence, or the Praises of those who were Victors in Races, and other bodily Exercises.

Alas, not even the genius of Swift was equal to producing a specimen by which we could judge the poetry of the Houyhnhnms. But it sounds as though it were chilly stuff (in heroic couplets, presumably), and not seriously in conflict with the principles of "Reason."

Happiness is notoriously difficult to describe, and pictures of a just and well-ordered Society are seldom either attractive or convincing. Most creators of "favourable" Utopias, however, are concerned to show what life could be like if it were lived more fully. Swift advocates a simple refusal of life, justifying this by the claim that "Reason" consists in thwarting your instincts. The Houyhnhnms, creatures without a history, continue for generation after generation to live prudently, maintaining their population at exactly the same level, avoiding all passion, suffering from no diseases, meeting death indifferently, training up their young in the same principles—and all for what? In order that the same process may continue indefinitely. The notions that life here and now is worth living, or that it could be made worth living, or that it must be sacrificed for some future good, are all absent. The dreary world of the Houyhnhnms was about as good a Utopia as Swift could construct, granting that he neither believed in a "next world" nor could get any pleasure out of certain normal activities. But it is not really set up as something desirable in itself, but as the justification for another attack on humanity. The aim, as usual, is to humiliate Man by reminding him that he is weak and ridiculous, and above all that he stinks; and the ultimate motive, probably, is a kind of envy, the envy of the ghost for the living, of the man who knows he cannot be happy for the others who—so he fears—may be a little happier than himself. The political expression of such an outlook must be either reactionary or nihilistic, because the person who holds it will want to prevent Society from developing in some direction in which his pessimism may be cheated. One can do this either by blowing everything to pieces, or by averting social change. Swift ultimately blew everything to pieces in the only way that was feasible before the atomic bomb—that is, he went mad—but, as I have tried to show, his political aims were on the whole reactionary ones.

From what I have written it may have seemed that I am *against* Swift, and that my object is to refute him and even to belittle him. In a political and moral sense I am against him, so far as I understand him. Yet curiously enough he is one of the writers I admire with least reserve, and *Gulliver's Travels,* in particular, is a book which it seems impossible for me to grow tired of. I read it first when I was eight—one day short of eight, to be exact, for I stole and furtively read the copy which was to be given me next day on my eighth birthday—and I have certainly not read it less than half a dozen times since. Its fascination seems inexhaustible. If I had to make a list of six books which were to be preserved when all others were destroyed, I would certainly put *Gulliver's Travels* among them. This raises the question: what is the relationship between agreement with a writer's opinions, and enjoyment of his work?

If one is capable of intellectual detachment, one can *perceive* merit in a writer whom one deeply disagrees with, but *enjoyment* is a different matter. Supposing that there is such a thing as good or bad art, then the goodness or badness must reside in the work of art itself—not independently of the observer, indeed, but independently of the mood of the observer. In one sense, therefore, it cannot be true that a poem is good on Monday and bad on Tuesday. But if one judges the poem by the appreciation it arouses, then it can certainly be true, because appreciation, or enjoyment, is a subjective condition which cannot be commanded. For a great deal of his waking life, even the most cultivated person has no aesthetic feelings whatever, and the power to have aesthetic feelings is very easily destroyed. When you are frightened, or hungry, or are suffering from toothache or sea-sickness, *King Lear* is no better from your point of view than *Peter Pan.* You may know in an intellectual sense that it is better, but that is simply a fact which you remember: you will not *feel* the merit of *King Lear* until you are normal again. And aesthetic judgment can be upset just as disastrously—more disastrously, because the cause is less readily recognised—by political or moral disagreement. If a book angers, wounds or alarms you, then you will not enjoy it, whatever its merits may be. If it seems to you a really pernicious book, likely to influence other people in some undesirable way, then you will probably construct an aesthetic theory to show that it *has* no merits. Current literary criticism consists quite largely of this kind of dodging to and fro between two sets of standards. And yet the opposite process can also happen: enjoyment can overwhelm disapproval, even though one clearly recognises that one is enjoying something inimical. Swift, whose world-view is so peculiarly unacceptable, but who is nevertheless an extremely popular writer, is a good instance of this. Why is it that we don't mind being called Yahoos, although firmly convinced that we are *not* Yahoos?

It is not enough to make the usual answer that of course Swift was wrong, in fact he was insane, but he was "a good writer." It is true that the literary quality of a book is to some small extent separable from its subject-matter. Some people have a native gift for using words, as some people have a naturally "good eye" at games. It is largely a question of timing and of instinctively knowing how much emphasis to use. As an example near at hand, look back at the passage I quoted earlier, starting "In the Kingdom of Tribnia, by the Natives called Langdon." It derives much of its force from the final sentence: "And this is the anagrammatic Method." Strictly speaking this sentence is unnecessary, for we have already seen the anagram deciphered, but the mock-solemn repetition, in which one seems to hear Swift's own voice uttering the words, drives home the idiocy of the activities described, like a final tap to a nail. But not all the power and simplicity of Swift's prose, nor the imaginative effort that has been able to make not one but a whole series of impossible worlds more credible than the majority of history books—none of this would enable us to enjoy Swift if his world-view were truly wounding or shocking. Millions of people, in many countries, must have enjoyed *Gulliver's Travels* while more or less seeing its anti-human implications: and even the child who accepts Parts I and II as a simple story gets a sense of absurdity from thinking of human beings six inches high. The explanation must be that Swift's world-view is felt to be *not* altogether false—or it would probably be more accurate to say, not false all the time. Swift is a diseased writer. He remains permanently in a depressed mood which in most people is only intermittent, rather as though someone suffering from jaundice or the after-effects of influenza should have the energy to write books. But we all know that mood, and something in us responds to the expression of it. Take, for instance, one of his most characteristic works, *The Lady's Dressing Room*: one might add the kindred poem, *Upon a Beautiful Young Nymph Going to Bed.* Which is truer, the viewpoint expressed in these poems, or the viewpoint implied in Blake's phrase, "The naked female human form divine"? No doubt Blake is nearer the truth, and yet who can fail to feel a sort of pleasure in seeing that fraud, feminine delicacy, exploded for once? Swift falsifies his picture of the world by refusing to see anything in human life except dirt, folly and wickedness, but the part which he abstracts from the whole does exist, and it is something which we all know about while shrinking from mentioning it. Part of our minds—in any normal person it is the dominant part—believes that man is a noble animal and life is worth living: but there is also a sort of inner self which at least intermittently stands aghast at the horror of existence. In the queerest way, pleasure and disgust are linked together. The human body is beautiful: it is also repulsive and ridiculous, a fact which can be verified at any swimming pool. The sexual organs are objects of desire and also of loathing, so much so that in many languages, if not in all languages, their names are used as words of abuse. Meat is delicious, but a butcher's shop makes one feel sick: and indeed all our food springs ultimately from dung and dead bodies, the two things which of all others seem to us the most horrible. A child, when it is past the infantile stage but still looking at the world with fresh eyes, is moved by horror almost as often as by wonder—horror of snot and spittle, of the dogs' excrement on the pavement, the dying toad full of maggots, the sweaty smell of grown-ups, the hideousness of old men, with their bald heads and bulbous noses. In his endless harping on disease, dirt and deformity, Swift is not actually inventing anything, he is merely leaving something out. Human behaviour, too, especially in politics, is as he describes it, although it contains other more important factors which he refuses to admit. So far as we can see, both horror and pain are necessary to the continuance of life on this planet, and it is therefore open to pessimists like Swift to say: "If horror and pain must always be with us, how can life be significantly improved?" His attitude is in effect the Christian attitude, minus the bribe of a "next world"—which, however, probably has less hold upon the minds of believers than the conviction that this world is a vale of tears and the grave is a place of rest. It is, I am certain, a wrong attitude, and one which could have harmful effects upon behaviour; but something in us responds to it, as it responds to the gloomy words of the burial service and the sweetish smell of corpses in a country church.

It is often argued, at least by people who admit the importance of subject-matter, that a book cannot be "good" if it expresses a palpably false view of life. We are told that in our own age, for instance, any book that has genuine literary merit will also be more or less "progressive" in tendency. This ignores the fact that throughout history a similar struggle between progress and reaction has been raging, and that the best books of any one age have always been written from several different viewpoints, some of them palpably more false than others. In so far as a writer is a propagandist, the most one can ask of him is that he shall genuinely believe in what he is saying, and that it shall not be something blazingly silly. Today, for example, one can imagine a good book being written by a Catholic, a Communist, a Fascist, a pacifist, an anarchist, perhaps by an old-style Liberal or an ordinary Conservative: one cannot imagine a good book being written by a spiritualist, a Buchmanite or a member of the Ku Klux Klan. The views that a writer holds must be compatible with sanity, in the medical sense, and with the power of continuous thought: beyond that what we ask of him is talent, which is probably another name for conviction. Swift did not possess ordinary wisdom, but he did possess a terrible intensity of vision, capable of picking out a single hidden truth and then magnifying it and distorting it. The durability of *Gulliver's Travels* goes to show that, if the force of belief is behind it, a world-view which only just passes the test of sanity is sufficient to produce a great work of art.

Lear, Tolstoy and the Fool

Polemic, 7, March 1947

Tolstoy's pamphlets are the least-known part of his work, and his attack on Shakespeare* is not even an easy document to get hold of, at any rate in an English translation. Perhaps, therefore, it will be useful if I give a summary of the pamphlet before trying to discuss it.

Tolstoy begins by saying that throughout life Shakespeare has aroused in him "an irresistible repulsion and tedium." Conscious that the opinion of the civilized world is against him, he has made one attempt after another on Shakespeare's works, reading and re-reading them in Russian, English and German; but "I invariably underwent the same feelings; repulsion, weariness and bewilderment." Now, at the age of seventy-five, he has once again re-read the entire works of Shakespeare, including the historical plays, and

> I have felt with even greater force, the same feelings—this time, however, not of bewilderment, but of firm, indubitable conviction that the unquestionable glory of a great genius which Shakespeare enjoys, and which compels writers of our time to imitate him and readers and spectators to discover in him non-existent merits—thereby distorting their aesthetic and ethical understanding—is a great evil, as is every untruth.

**Shakespeare and the Drama.* Written about 1903 as an introduction to another pamphlet, *Shakespeare and the Working Classes,* by Ernest Crosby [Orwell's footnote].

Shakespeare, Tolstoy adds, is not merely no genius, but is not even "an average author," and in order to demonstrate this fact he will examine *King Lear,* which, as he is able to show by quotations from Hazlitt, Brandes and others, has been extravagantly praised and can be taken as an example of Shakespeare's best work.

Tolstoy then makes a sort of exposition of the plot of *King Lear,* finding it at every step to be stupid, verbose, unnatural, unintelligible, bombastic, vulgar, tedious and full of incredible events, "wild ravings," "mirthless jokes," anachronisms, irrelevancies, obscenities, worn-out stage conventions and other faults both moral and aesthetic. *Lear* is, in any case, a plagiarism of an earlier and much better play, *King Leir,* by an unknown author, which Shakespeare stole and then ruined. It is worth quoting a specimen paragraph to illustrate the manner in which Tolstoy goes to work. Act III, Scene 2 (in which Lear, Kent and the Fool are together in the storm) is summarized thus:

> Lear walks about the heath and says words which are meant to express his despair: he desires that the winds should blow so hard that they (the winds) should crack their cheeks and that the rain should flood everything, that lightning should singe his white head, and the thunder flatten the world and destroy all germs "that make ungrateful man"! The fool keeps uttering still more senseless words. Enter Kent: Lear says that for some reason during this storm all criminals shall be found out and convicted. Kent, still unrecognized by Lear, endeavours to persuade him to take refuge in a hovel. At this point the fool utters a prophecy in no wise related to the situation and they all depart.

Tolstoy's final verdict on *Lear* is that no unhypnotized observer, if such an observer existed, could read it to the end with any feeling except "aversion and weariness." And exactly the same is true of "all the other extolled dramas of Shakespeare, not to mention the senseless dramatized tales, *Pericles, Twelfth Night, The Tempest, Cymbeline, Troilus and Cressida.*"

Having dealt with *Lear* Tolstoy draws up a more general indictment against Shakespeare. He finds that Shakespeare has a certain technical skill which is partly traceable to his having been an actor, but otherwise no merits whatever. He has no power of delineating character or of making words and actions spring naturally out of situations, his language is uniformly exaggerated and ridiculous, he constantly thrusts his own random thoughts into the mouth of any character who happens to be handy, he displays a "complete absence of aesthetic feeling," and his words "have nothing whatever in common with art and poetry." "Shakespeare might have been whatever you like," Tolstoy concludes, "but he was not an artist." Moreover, his opinions are not original or interesting, and his tendency is "of the lowest and most immoral." Curiously enough, Tolstoy does not base this last judgment on Shakespeare's own utterances, but on the statements of two critics, Gervinus and Brandes. According to Gervinus (or at any rate Tolstoy's reading of Gervinus) "Shakespeare taught . . . that one *may be too good,*" while according to Brandes "Shakespeare's fundamental principle . . . is that *the end justifies the means.*" Tolstoy adds on his own account that Shakespeare was a jingo patriot of the worst type, but apart from this he considers that Gervinus and Brandes have given a true and adequate description of Shakespeare's view of life.

Tolstoy then recapitulates in a few paragraphs the theory of art which he had expressed at greater length elsewhere. Put still more shortly, it amounts to a demand for dignity of subject matter, sincerity, and good craftsmanship. A great work of art must deal with some subject which is "important to the life of mankind," it must express something which the author genuinely feels, and it must use such technical methods as will produce the desired effect. As Shakespeare is debased in outlook, slipshod in execution and incapable of being sincere even for a moment, he obviously stands condemned.

But here there arises a difficult question. If Shakespeare is all that Tolstoy has shown him to be, how did he ever come to be so generally admired? Evidently the answer can only lie in a sort of mass hypnosis, or "epidemic suggestion." The whole civilized world has somehow been deluded into thinking Shakespeare a good writer, and even the plainest demonstration to the contrary makes no impression, because one is not dealing with a reasoned opinion but with something akin to religious faith. Throughout history, says Tolstoy, there has been an endless series of these "epidemic suggestions"—for example, the Crusades, the search for the Philosopher's Stone, the craze for tulip-growing which once swept over Holland,[1] and so on and so forth. As a contemporary instance he cites, rather significantly, the Dreyfus case, over which the whole world grew violently excited for no sufficient reason. There are also sudden shortlived crazes for new political and philosophical theories, or for this or that writer, artist or scientist—for example, Darwin, who (in 1903) is "beginning to be forgotten." And in some cases a quite worthless popular idol may remain in favour for centuries, for "it also happens that such crazes, having arisen in consequence of special reasons accidentally favouring their establishment, correspond in such a degree to the views of life spread in society, and especially in literary circles, that they are maintained for a long time." Shakespeare's plays have continued to be admired over a long period because "they corresponded to the irreligious and immoral frame of mind of the upper classes of his time and ours."

As to the manner in which Shakespeare's fame *started,* Tolstoy explains it as having been "got up" by German professors towards the end of the eighteenth century. His reputation "originated in Germany, and thence was transferred to England." The Germans chose to elevate Shakespeare because, at a time when there was no German drama worth speaking about and French classical literature was beginning to seem frigid and artificial, they were captivated by Shakespeare's "clever development of scenes" and also found in him a good expression of their own attitude towards life. Goethe pronounced Shakespeare a great poet, whereupon all the other critics flocked after him like a troop of parrots, and the general infatuation has lasted ever since. The result has been a further debasement of the drama—Tolstoy is careful to include his own plays when condemning the contemporary stage—and a further corruption of the prevailing moral outlook. It follows that "the false glorification of Shakespeare" is an important evil which Tolstoy feels it his duty to combat.

This, then, is the substance of Tolstoy's pamphlet. One's first feeling is that in describing Shakespeare as a bad writer he is saying something demonstrably untrue. But this is not the case. In reality there is no kind of evidence or argument by which one can show that Shakespeare, or any other writer, is "good." Nor is there any way of definitely proving that—for instance—Warwick Deeping is "bad."[2] Ultimately there is no test of literary merit except survival, which is itself merely an index to majority opinion. Artistic theories such as Tolstoy's are quite worthless, because they not only start out with arbitrary assumptions, but depend on vague terms ("sincere," "important" and so forth) which can be interpreted in any way one chooses. Properly speaking one cannot *answer* Tolstoy's attack. The interesting question is: why did he make it? But it should be noticed in passing that he uses many weak or dishonest arguments. Some of these are worth pointing out, not because they invalidate his main charge but because they are, so to speak, evidence of malice.

To begin with, his examination of *King Lear* is not "impartial," as he twice claims. On the contrary, it is a prolonged exercise in misrepresentation. It is obvious that when you are summarizing *King Lear* for the benefit of someone who has not read it, you are not really being impartial if you introduce an important speech (Lear's speech when Cordelia is dead in his arms) in this manner: "Again begin Lear's awful ravings, at which one feels ashamed, as at unsuccessful jokes." And in a long series of instances Tolstoy slightly alters or colours the passages he is criticizing, always in such a way as to make the plot appear a little more complicated and improbable, or the language a little more exaggerated. For example, we are told that Lear "has no necessity or motive for his abdication," although his reason for abdicating (that he is old and wishes to retire from the cares of State) has been clearly indicated in the first scene. It will be seen that even in the passage which I quoted earlier, Tolstoy has wilfully misunderstood one phrase and slightly changed the meaning of another, making nonsense of a remark which is reasonable enough in its context. None of these misreadings is very gross in itself, but their cumulative effect is to exaggerate the psychological incoherence of the play. Again, Tolstoy is not able to explain why Shakespeare's plays were still in print, and still on the stage, two hundred years after his death (*before* the "epidemic suggestion" started, that is); and his whole account of Shakespeare's rise to fame is guesswork punctuated by outright misstatements. And again, various of his accusations contradict one another: for example, Shakespeare is a mere entertainer and "not in earnest," but on the other hand he is constantly putting his own thoughts into the mouths of his characters. On the whole it is difficult to feel that Tolstoy's criticisms are uttered in good faith. In any case it is impossible that he should fully have believed in his main thesis—believed, that is to say, that for a century or more the entire civilized world had been taken in by a huge and palpable lie which he alone was able to see through. Certainly his dislike of Shakespeare is real enough, but the reasons for it may be different, or partly different, from what he avows; and therein lies the interest of his pamphlet.

At this point one is obliged to start guessing. However, there is one possible clue, or at least there is a question which may point the way to a clue. It is: why did Tolstoy, with thirty or more plays to choose from, pick out *King Lear* as his especial target? True, *Lear* is so well known and has been so much praised that it could justly be taken as representative of Shakespeare's best work; still, for the purpose of a hostile analysis Tolstoy would probably choose the play he disliked most. Is it not possible that he bore an especial enmity towards this particular play because he was aware, consciously or unconsciously, of the resemblance between Lear's story and his own? But it is better to approach this clue from the opposite direction—that is, by examining *Lear* itself, and the qualities in it that Tolstoy fails to mention.

One of the first things an English reader would notice in Tolstoy's pamphlet is that it hardly deals with Shakespeare as a poet. Shakespeare is treated as a dramatist, and in so far as his popularity is not spurious, it is held to be due to tricks of stagecraft which give good opportunities to clever actors. Now, so far as the English-speaking countries go, this is not true. Several of the plays which are most valued by lovers of Shakespeare (for instance, *Timon of Athens*) are seldom or never acted, while some of the most actable, such as *A Midsummer Night's Dream,* are the least admired. Those who care most for Shakespeare value him in the first place for his use of language, the "verbal music" which even Bernard Shaw, another hostile critic, admits to be "irresistible." Tolstoy ignores this, and does not seem to realize that a poem may have a special value for those who speak the language in which it was written. However, even if one puts oneself in Tolstoy's place and tries to think of Shakespeare as a foreign poet it is still clear that there is something that Tolstoy has left out. Poetry, it seems, is *not* solely a matter of sound and association, and valueless outside its own language-group: otherwise, how is it that some poems, including poems written in dead languages, succeed in crossing frontiers? Clearly a lyric like "Tomorrow is Saint Valentine's Day" could not be satisfactorily translated, but in Shakespeare's major work there is something describable as poetry that can be separated from the words. Tolstoy is right in saying that *Lear* is not a very good play, as a play. It is too drawn-out and has too many characters and sub-plots. One wicked daughter would have been quite enough, and Edgar is a superfluous character: indeed it would probably be a better play if Gloucester and both his sons were eliminated. Nevertheless, something, a kind of pattern, or perhaps only an atmosphere, survives the complications and the *longueurs*. *Lear* can be imagined as a puppet show, a mime, a ballet, a series of pictures. Part of its poetry, perhaps the most essential part, is inherent in the story and is dependent neither on any particular set of words, nor on flesh-and-blood presentation.

Shut your eyes and think of *King Lear,* if possible without calling to mind any of the dialogue. What do you see? Here at any rate is what I see: a majestic old man in a long black robe, with flowing white hair and beard, a figure out of Blake's drawings (but also, curiously enough, rather like Tolstoy), wandering through a storm and cursing the heavens, in company with a Fool and a lunatic. Presently the scene shifts, and the old man, still cursing, still understanding nothing, is holding a dead girl in his arms while the Fool dangles on a gallows somewhere in the background. This is the bare skeleton of the play, and even here Tolstoy wants to cut out most of what is essential. He objects to the storm, as being unnecessary, to the Fool, who in his eyes is simply a tedious nuisance and an excuse for making bad jokes, and to the death of Cordelia, which, as he sees it, robs the play of its moral. According to Tolstoy, the earlier play, *King Leir,* which Shakespeare adapted

> terminates more naturally and more in accordance with the moral demands of the spectator than does Shakespeare's: namely, by the King of the Gauls conquering the husbands of the elder sisters, and by Cordelia, instead of being killed, restoring Leir to his former position.

In other words the tragedy ought to have been a comedy, or perhaps a melodrama. It is doubtful whether the sense of tragedy is compatible with belief in God: at any rate, it is not compatible with disbelief in human dignity and with the kind of "moral demand" which feels cheated when virtue fails to triumph. A tragic situation exists precisely when virtue does *not* triumph but when it is still felt that man is nobler than the forces which destroy him. It is perhaps more significant that Tolstoy sees no justification for the presence of the Fool. The Fool is integral to the play. He acts not only as a sort of chorus, making the central situation clearer by commenting on it more intelligently than the other characters, but as a foil to Lear's frenzies. His jokes, riddles and scraps of rhyme, and his endless digs at Lear's high-minded folly, ranging from mere derision to a sort of melancholy poetry ("All thy other titles thou hast given away; that thou wast born with"), are like a trickle of sanity running through the play, a reminder that somewhere or other, in spite of the injustices, cruelties, intrigues, deceptions and misunderstandings that are being enacted here, life is going on much as usual. In Tolstoy's impatience with the Fool one gets a glimpse of his deeper quarrel with Shakespeare. He objects, with some justification, to the raggedness of Shakespeare's plays, the irrelevancies, the incredible plots, the exaggerated language: but what at bottom he probably most dislikes is a sort of exuberance, a tendency to take—not so much a pleasure, as simply an interest in the actual process of life. It is a mistake to write Tolstoy off as a moralist attacking an artist. He never said that art, as such, is wicked or meaningless, nor did he even say that technical virtuosity is unimportant. But his main aim, in his later years, was to narrow the range of human consciousness. One's interests, one's points of attachment to the physical world and the day-to-day struggle, must be as few and not as many as possible. Literature must consist of parables, stripped of detail and almost independent of language. The parables—this is where Tolstoy differs from the average vulgar puritan—must themselves be works of art, but pleasure and curiosity must be excluded from them. Science, also, must be divorced from curiosity. The business of science, he says, is not to discover what happens, but to teach men how they ought to live. So also with history and politics. Many problems (for example, the Dreyfus case) are simply not worth solving, and he is willing to leave them as loose ends. Indeed his whole theory of "crazes" or "epidemic suggestions," in which he lumps together such things as the Crusades and the Dutch passion of tulip-growing, shows a willingness to regard many human activities as mere ant-like rushings to and fro, inexplicable and uninteresting. Clearly he could have no patience with a chaotic, detailed, discursive writer like Shakespeare. His reaction is that of an irritable old man who is being pestered by a noisy child. "Why do you keep jumping up and down like that? Why can't you sit still like I do?" In a way the old man is in the right, but the trouble is that the child has a feeling in its limbs which the old man has lost. And if the old man knows of the existence of this feeling, the effect is merely to increase his irritation: he would make children senile, if he could. Tolstoy does not know, perhaps, just *what* he misses in Shakespeare, but he is aware that he misses something, and he is determined that others shall be deprived of it as well. By nature he was imperious as well as egotistical. Well after he was grown up he would still occasionally strike his servant in moments of anger, and somewhat later, according to his English biographer, Derrick Leon, he felt "a frequent desire upon the slenderest provocation to slap the faces of those with whom he disagreed." One does not necessarily get rid of that kind of temperament by undergoing religious conversion, and indeed it is obvious that the illusion of having been reborn may allow one's native vices to flourish more freely than ever, though perhaps in subtler forms. Tolstoy was capable of abjuring physical violence and of seeing what this implies, but he was not capable of tolerance or humility, and even if one knew nothing of his other writings, one could deduce his tendency towards spiritual bullying from this single pamphlet.

However, Tolstoy is not simply trying to rob others of a pleasure he does not share. He is doing that, but his quarrel with Shakespeare goes further. It is the quarrel between the religious and the humanist attitudes towards life. Here one comes back to the central theme of *King Lear,* which Tolstoy does not mention, although he sets forth the plot in some detail.

Lear is one of the minority of Shakespeare's plays that are unmistakably *about* something. As Tolstoy justly complains, much rubbish has been written about Shakespeare as a philosopher, as a psychologist, as a "great moral teacher," and what-not. Shakespeare was not a systematic thinker, his most serious thoughts are uttered irrelevantly or indirectly, and we do not know to what extent he wrote with a "purpose" or even how much of the work attributed to him was actually written by him. In the Sonnets he never even refers to the plays as part of his achievement, though he does make what seems to be a half-ashamed allusion to his career as an actor. It is perfectly possible that he looked on at least half of his plays as mere pot-boilers and hardly bothered about purpose or probability so long as he could patch up something, usually from stolen material, which would more or less hang together on the stage. However, that is not the whole story. To begin with, as Tolstoy himself points out, Shakespeare has a habit of thrusting uncalled-for general reflections into the mouths of his characters. This is a serious fault in a dramatist, but it does not fit in with Tolstoy's picture of Shakespeare as a vulgar hack who has no opinions of his own and merely wishes to produce the greatest effect with the least trouble. And more than this, about a dozen of his plays, written for the most part later than 1600, do unquestionably have a meaning and even a moral. They revolve round a central subject which in some cases can be reduced to a single word. For example, *Macbeth* is about ambition, *Othello* is about jealousy, and *Timon of Athens* is about money. The subject of *Lear* is renunciation, and it is only by being wilfully blind that one can fail to understand what Shakespeare is saying.

Lear renounces his throne but expects everyone to continue treating him as a king. He does not see that if he surrenders power, other people will take advantage of his weakness: also that those who flatter him the most grossly, i.e. Regan and Goneril, are exactly the ones who will turn against him. The moment he finds that he can no longer make people obey him as he did before, he falls into a rage which Tolstoy describes as "strange and unnatural," but which in fact is perfectly in character. In his madness and despair, he passes through two moods which again are natural enough in his circumstances, though in one of them it is probable that he is being used partly as a mouthpiece for Shakespeare's own opinions. One is the mood of disgust in which Lear repents, as it were, for having been a king, and grasps for the first time the rottenness of formal justice and vulgar morality. The other is a mood of impotent fury in which he wreaks imaginary revenges upon those who have wronged him. "To have a thousand with red burning spits Come hissing in upon 'em!," and:

> "It were a delicate stratagem to shoe
> A troop of horse with felt: I'll put't in proof;
> And when I have stol'n upon these sons-in-law,
> Then kill, kill, kill, kill, kill!"

Only at the end does he realize, as a sane man, that power, revenge and victory are not worth while:

> "No, no, no, no! Come, let's away to prison . . .
> . . . . and we'll wear out
> In a wall'd prison, packs and sects of great ones
> That ebb and flow by the moon."

But by the time he makes this discovery it is too late, for his death and Cordelia's are already decided on. That is the story, and, allowing for some clumsiness in the telling, it is a very good story.

But is it not also curiously similar to the history of Tolstoy himself? There is a general resemblance which one can hardly avoid seeing, because the most impressive event in Tolstoy's life, as in Lear's, was a huge gratuitous act of renunciation. In his old age he renounced his estate, his title and his copyrights, and made an attempt—a sincere attempt, though it was not successful—to escape from his privileged position and live the life of a peasant. But the deeper resemblance lies in the fact that Tolstoy, like Lear, acted on mistaken motives and failed to get the results he had hoped for. According to Tolstoy, the aim of every human being is happiness, and happiness can only be attained by doing the will of God. But doing the will of God means casting off all earthly pleasures and ambitions, and living only for others. Ultimately, therefore, Tolstoy renounced the world under the expectation that this would make him happier. But if there is one thing certain about his later years, it is that he was *not* happy. On the contrary, he was driven almost to the edge of madness by the behaviour of the people about him, who persecuted him precisely *because* of his renunciation. Like Lear, Tolstoy was not humble and not a good judge of character. He was inclined at moments to revert to the attitudes of an aristocrat, in spite of his peasant's blouse, and he even had two children whom he had believed in and who ultimately turned against him—though, of course, in a less sensational manner than Regan and Goneril. His exaggerated revulsion from sexuality was also distinctly similar to Lear's. Tolstoy's remark that marriage is "slavery, satiety, repulsion" and means putting up with the proximity of "ugliness, dirtiness, smell, sores," is matched by Lear's well-known outburst:

> "But to the girdle do the gods inherit,
> Beneath is all the fiends';
> There's hell, there's darkness, there's the sulphurous pit,
> Burning, scalding, stench, consumption," etc., etc.

And though Tolstoy could not foresee it when he wrote his essay on Shakespeare, even the ending of his life—the sudden unplanned flight across country, accompanied only by a faithful daughter, the death in a cottage in a strange village—seems to have in it a sort of phantom reminiscence of *Lear.*

Of course, one cannot assume that Tolstoy was aware of this resemblance, or would have admitted it if it had been pointed out to him. But his attitude towards the play must have been influenced by its theme. Renouncing power, giving away your lands, was a subject on which he had reason to feel deeply. Probably, therefore, he would be more angered and disturbed by the moral that Shakespeare draws than he would be in the case of some other play—*Macbeth,* for example—which did not touch so closely on his own life. But what exactly *is* the moral of *Lear*? Evidently there are two morals, one explicit, the other implied in the story.

Shakespeare starts by assuming that to make yourself powerless is to invite an attack. This does not mean that *everyone* will turn against you (Kent and the Fool stand by Lear from first to last), but in all probability *someone* will. If you throw away your weapons, some less scrupulous person will pick them up. If you turn the other cheek, you will get a harder blow on it than you got on the first one. This does not always happen, but it is to be expected, and you ought not to complain if it does happen. The second blow is, so to speak, part of the act of turning the other cheek. First of all, therefore, there is the vulgar, commonsense moral drawn by the Fool: "Don't relinquish power, don't give away your lands." But there is also another moral. Shakespeare never utters it in so many words, and it does not very much matter whether he was fully aware of it. It is contained in the story, which, after all, he made up, or altered to suit his purposes. It is: "Give away your lands if you want to, but don't expect to gain happiness by doing so. Probably you won't gain happiness. If you live for others, you must live *for others,* and not as a roundabout way of getting an advantage for yourself."

Obviously neither of these conclusions could have been pleasing to Tolstoy. The first of them expresses the ordinary, belly-to-earth selfishness from which he was genuinely trying to escape. The other conflicts with his desire to eat his cake and have it—that is, to destroy his own egoism and by so doing to gain eternal life. Of course, *Lear* is not a sermon in favour of altruism. It merely points out the results of practising self-denial for selfish reasons. Shakespeare had a considerable streak of worldliness in him, and if he had been forced to take sides in his own play, his sympathies would probably have lain with the Fool. But at least he could see the whole issue and treat it at the level of tragedy. Vice is punished, but virtue is not rewarded. The morality of Shakespeare's later tragedies is not religious in the ordinary sense, and certainly is not Christian. Only two of them, *Hamlet* and *Othello,* are supposedly occurring inside the Christian era, and even in those, apart from the antics of the ghost in *Hamlet,* there is no indication of a "next world" where everything is to be put right. All of these tragedies start out with the humanist assumption that life, although full of sorrow, is worth living, and that Man is a noble animal—a belief which Tolstoy in his old age did not share.

Tolstoy was not a saint, but he tried very hard to make himself into a saint, and the standards he applied to literature were other-worldly ones. It is important to realize that the difference between a saint and an ordinary human being is a difference of kind and not of degree. That is, the one is not to be regarded as an imperfect form of the other. The saint, at any rate Tolstoy's kind of saint, is not trying to work an improvement in earthly life: he is trying to bring it to an end and put something different in its place. One obvious expression of this is the claim that celibacy is "higher" than marriage. If only, Tolstoy says in effect, we would stop breeding, fighting, struggling and enjoying, if we could get rid not only of our sins but of everything else that binds us to the surface of the earth—including love, in the ordinary sense of caring more for one human being than another—then the whole painful process would be over and the Kingdom of Heaven would arrive. But a normal human being does not want the Kingdom of Heaven: he wants life on earth to continue. This is not solely because he is "weak," "sinful" and anxious for a "good time." Most people get a fair amount of fun out of their lives, but on balance life is suffering, and only the very young or the very foolish imagine otherwise. Ultimately it is the Christian attitude which is self-interested and hedonistic, since the aim is always to get away from the painful struggle of earthly life and find eternal peace in some kind of Heaven or Nirvana. The humanist attitude is that the struggle must continue and that death is the price of life. "Men must endure. Their going hence, even as their coming hither: Ripeness is all"—which is an un-Christian sentiment. Often there is a seeming truce between the humanist and the religious believer, but in fact their attitudes cannot be reconciled: one must choose between this world and the next. And the enormous majority of human beings, if they understood the issue, would choose this world. They do make that choice when they continue working, breeding and dying instead of crippling their faculties in the hope of obtaining a new lease of existence elsewhere.

We do not know a great deal about Shakespeare's religious beliefs, and from the evidence of his writings it would be difficult to prove that he had any. But at any rate he was not a saint or a would-be saint: he was a human being, and in some ways not a very good one. It is clear, for instance, that he liked to stand well with the rich and powerful, and was capable of flattering them in the most servile way. He is also noticeably cautious, not to say cowardly, in his manner of uttering unpopular opinions. Almost never does he put a subversive or sceptical remark into the mouth of a character likely to be identified with himself. Throughout his plays the acute social critics, the people who are not taken in by accepted fallacies, are buffoons, villains, lunatics or persons who are shamming insanity or are in a state of violent hysteria. *Lear* is a play in which this tendency is particularly well-marked. It contains a great deal of veiled social criticism—a point Tolstoy misses—but it is all uttered either by the Fool, by Edgar when he is pretending to be mad, or by Lear during his bouts of madness. In his sane moments Lear hardly ever makes an intelligent remark. And yet the very fact that Shakespeare had to use these subterfuges shows how widely his thoughts ranged. He could not restrain himself from commenting on almost everything, although he put on a series of masks in order to do so. If one has once read Shakespeare with attention, it is not easy to go a day without quoting him, because there are not many subjects of major importance that he does not discuss or at least mention somewhere or other, in his unsystematic but illuminating way. Even the irrelevancies that litter every one of his plays—the puns and riddles, the lists of names, the scraps of *reportage* like the conversation of the carriers in *Henry IV*, the bawdy jokes, the rescued fragments of forgotten ballads—are merely the products of excessive vitality. Shakespeare was not a philosopher or a scientist, but he did have curiosity: he loved the surface of the earth and the process of life—which, it should be repeated, is *not* the same thing as wanting to have a good time and stay alive as long as possible. Of course, it is not because of the quality of his thought that Shakespeare has survived, and he might not even be remembered as a dramatist if he had not also been a poet. His main hold on us is through language. How deeply Shakespeare himself was fascinated by the music of words can probably be inferred from the speeches of Pistol. What Pistol says is largely meaningless, but if one considers his lines singly they are magnificent rhetorical verse. Evidently, pieces of resounding nonsense ("Let floods o'erswell, and fiends for food howl on," etc.) were constantly appearing in Shakespeare's mind of their own accord, and a half-lunatic character had to be invented to use them up. Tolstoy's native tongue was not English, and one cannot blame him for being unmoved by Shakespeare's verse, nor even, perhaps, for refusing to believe that Shakespeare's skill with words was something out of the ordinary. But he would also have rejected the whole notion of valuing poetry for its texture—valuing it, that is to say, as a kind of music. If it could somehow have been proved to him that his whole explanation of Shakespeare's rise to fame is mistaken, that inside the English-speaking world, at any rate, Shakespeare's popularity is genuine, that his mere skill in placing one syllable beside another has given acute pleasure to generation after generation of English-speaking people—all this would not have been counted as a merit to Shakespeare, but rather the contrary. It would simply have been one more proof of the irreligious, earthbound nature of Shakespeare and his admirers. Tolstoy would have said that poetry is to be judged by its meaning, and that seductive sounds merely cause false meanings to go unnoticed. At every level it is the same issue—this world against the next: and certainly the music of words is something that belongs to this world.

A sort of doubt has always hung round the character of Tolstoy, as round the character of Gandhi. He was not a vulgar hypocrite, as some people declared him to be, and he would probably have imposed even greater sacrifices on himself than he did, if he had not been interfered with at every step by the people surrounding him, especially his wife. But on the other hand it is dangerous to take such men as Tolstoy at their disciples' valuation. There is always the possibility—the probability, indeed—that they have done no more than exchange one form of egoism for another. Tolstoy renounced wealth, fame and privilege; he abjured violence in all its forms and was ready to suffer for doing so; but it is not so easy to believe that he abjured the principle of coercion, or at least the *desire* to coerce others. There are families in which the father will say to his child, "You'll get a thick ear if you do that again," while the mother, her eyes brimming over with tears, will take the child in her arms and murmur lovingly, "Now, darling, *is* it kind to Mummy to do that?" And who would maintain that the second method is less tyrannous than the first? The distinction that really matters is not between violence and non-violence, but between having and not having the appetite for power. There are people who are convinced of the wickedness both of armies and of police forces, but who are nevertheless much more intolerant and inquisitorial in outlook than the normal person who believes that it is necessary to use violence in certain circumstances. They will not say to somebody else, "Do this, that and the other or you will go to prison," but they will, if they can, get inside his brain and dictate his thoughts for him in the minutest particulars. Creeds like pacifism and anarchism, which seem on the surface to imply a complete renunciation of power, rather encourage this habit of mind. For if you have embraced a creed which appears to be free from the ordinary dirtiness of politics—a creed from which you yourself cannot expect to draw any material advantage—surely that proves that you are in the right? And the more you are in the right, the more natural that everyone else should be bullied into thinking likewise.

If we are to believe what he says in his pamphlet, Tolstoy had never been able to see any merit in Shakespeare, and was always astonished to find that his fellow-writers, Turgenev, Fet and others, thought differently. We may be sure that in his unregenerate days Tolstoy's conclusion would have been: "You like Shakespeare—I don't. Let's leave it at that." Later, when his perception that it takes all sorts to make a world had deserted him, he came to think of Shakespeare's writings as something dangerous to himself. The more pleasure people took in Shakespeare, the less they would listen to Tolstoy. Therefore nobody must be *allowed* to enjoy Shakespeare, just as nobody must be allowed to drink alcohol or smoke tobacco. True, Tolstoy would not prevent them by force. He is not demanding that the police shall impound every copy of Shakespeare's works. But he will do dirt on Shakespeare, if he can. He will try to get inside the mind of every lover of Shakespeare and kill his enjoyment by every trick he can think of, including—as I have shown in my summary of his pamphlet—arguments which are self-contradictory or even doubtfully honest.

But finally the most striking thing is how little difference it all makes. As I said earlier, one cannot *answer* Tolstoy's pamphlet, at least on its main counts. There is no argument by which one can defend a poem. It defends itself by surviving, or it is indefensible. And if this test is valid, I think the verdict in Shakespeare's case must be "not guilty." Like every other writer, Shakespeare will be forgotten sooner or later, but it is unlikely that a heavier indictment will ever be brought against him. Tolstoy was perhaps the most admired literary man of his age, and he was certainly not its least able pamphleteer. He turned all his powers of denunciation against Shakespeare, like all the guns of a battleship roaring simultaneously. And with what result? Forty years later, Shakespeare is still there, completely unaffected, and of the attempt to demolish him nothing remains except the yellowing pages of a pamphlet which hardly anyone has read, and which would be forgotten altogether if Tolstoy had not also been the author of *War and Peace* and *Anna Karenina.*

Writers and Leviathan

Politics and Letters, Summer 1948

The position of the writer in an age of State control is a subject that has already been fairly largely discussed, although most of the evidence that might be relevant is not yet available. In this place I do not want to express an opinion either for or against State patronage of the arts, but merely to point out that *what kind* of State rules over us must depend partly on the prevailing intellectual atmosphere: meaning, in this context, partly on the attitude of writers and artists themselves, and on their willingness or otherwise to keep the spirit of Liberalism alive. If we find ourselves in ten years' time cringing before somebody like Zdhanov, it will probably be because that is what we have deserved. Obviously there are strong tendencies towards totalitarianism at work within the English literary intelligentsia already. But here I am not concerned with any organised and conscious movement such as Communism, but merely with the effect, on people of good will, of political thinking and the need to take sides politically.

This is a political age. War, Fascism, concentration camps, rubber truncheons, atomic bombs, etc., are what we daily think about, and therefore to a great extent what we write about, even when we do not name them openly. We cannot help this. When you are on a sinking ship, your thoughts will be about sinking ships. But not only is our subject-matter narrowed, but our whole attitude towards literature is coloured by loyalties which we at least intermittently realise to be non-literary. I often have the feeling that even at the best of times literary criticism is fraudulent, since in the absence of any accepted standards whatever—any *external* reference which can give meaning to the statement that such and such a book is "good" or "bad"—every literary judgement consists in trumping up a set of rules to justify an instinctive preference. One's real reaction to a book, when one has a reaction at all, is usually "I like this book" or "I don't like it," and what follows is a rationalisation. But "I like this book" is not, I think, a non-literary reaction; the non-literary reaction is "This book is on my side, and therefore I must discover merits in it." Of course, when one praises a book for political reasons one may be emotionally sincere, in the sense that one does feel strong approval of it, but also it often happens that party solidarity demands a plain lie. Anyone used to reviewing books for political periodicals is well aware of this. In general, if you are writing for a paper that you are in agreement with, you sin by commission, and if for a paper of the opposite stamp, by omission. At any rate, innumerable controversial books—books for or against Soviet Russia, for or against Zionism, for or against the Catholic Church, etc.—are judged before they are read, and in effect before they are written. One knows in advance what reception they will get in what papers. And yet, with a dishonesty that sometimes is not even quarter-conscious, the pretence is kept up that genuinely literary standards are being applied.

Of course, the invasion of literature by politics was bound to happen. It must have happened, even if the special problem of totalitarianism had never arisen, because we have developed a sort of compunction which our grandparents did not have, an awareness of the enormous injustice and misery of the world, and a guilt-stricken feeling that one ought to be doing something about it, which makes a purely aesthetic attitude towards life impossible. No one, now, could devote himself to literature as single-mindedly as Joyce or Henry James. But unfortunately, to accept political responsibility now means yielding oneself over to orthodoxies and "party lines," with all the timidity and dishonesty that that implies. As against the Victorian writers, we have the disadvantage of living among clear-cut political ideologies and of usually knowing at a glance what thoughts are heretical. A modern literary intellectual lives and writes in constant dread—not, indeed, of public opinion in the wider sense, but of public opinion within his own group. As a rule, luckily, there is more than one group, but also at any given moment there is a dominant orthodoxy, to offend against which needs a thick skin and sometimes means cutting one's income in half for years on end. Obviously, for about fifteen years past, the dominant orthodoxy, especially among the young, has been "left." The key words are "progressive," "democratic" and "revolutionary," while the labels which you must at all costs avoid having gummed upon you are "bourgeois," "reactionary" and "Fascist." Almost everyone nowadays, even the majority of Catholics and Conservatives, is "progressive," or at least wishes to be thought so. No one, so far as I know, ever describes himself as a "bourgeois," just as no one literate enough to have heard the word ever admits to being guilty of anti-semitism. We are all of us good democrats, anti-Fascist, anti-imperialist, contemptuous of class distinctions, impervious to colour prejudice, and so on and so forth. Nor is there much doubt that the present-day "left" orthodoxy is better than the rather snobbish, pietistic Conservative orthodoxy which prevailed twenty years ago, when the *Criterion* and (on a lower level) the *London Mercury* were the dominant literary magazines. For at the least its implied objective is a viable form of society which large numbers of people actually want. But it also has its own falsities which, because they cannot be admitted, make it impossible for certain questions to be seriously discussed.

The whole left-wing ideology, scientific and utopian, was evolved by people who had no immediate prospect of attaining power. It was, therefore, an extremist ideology, utterly contemptuous of kings, governments, laws, prisons, police forces, armies, flags, frontiers, patriotism, religion, conventional morality, and, in fact, the whole existing scheme of things. Until well within living memory the forces of the left in all countries were fighting against a tyranny which appeared to be invincible, and it was easy to assume that if only *that* particular tyranny—capitalism—could be overthrown, Socialism would follow. Moreover, the left had inherited from Liberalism certain distinctly questionable beliefs, such as the belief that the truth will prevail and persecution defeats itself, or that man is naturally good and is only corrupted by his environment. This perfectionist ideology has persisted in nearly all of us, and it is in the name of it that we protest when (for instance) a Labour government votes huge incomes to the King's daughters or shows hesitation about nationalising steel. But we have also accumulated in our minds a whole series of unadmitted contradictions, as a result of successive bumps against reality.

The first big bump was the Russian Revolution. For somewhat complex reasons, nearly the whole of the English left has been driven to accept the Russian régime as "Socialist," while silently recognising that its spirit and practice are quite alien to anything that is meant by "Socialism" in this country. Hence there has arisen a sort of schizophrenic manner of thinking, in which words like "democracy" can bear two irreconcilable meanings, and such things as concentration camps and mass deportations can be right and wrong simultaneously. The next blow to the left-wing ideology was the rise of Fascism, which shook the pacifism and internationalism of the left without bringing about a definite restatement of doctrine. The experience of German occupation taught the European peoples something that the colonial peoples knew already, namely, that class antagonisms are not all-important and that there is such a thing as national interest. After Hitler it was difficult to maintain seriously that "the enemy is in your own country" and that national independence is of no value. But though we all know this and act upon it when necessary, we still feel that to say it aloud would be a kind of treachery. And finally, the greatest difficulty of all, there is the fact that the left is now in power and is obliged to take responsibility and make genuine decisions.

Left governments almost invariably disappoint their supporters because, even when the prosperity which they have promised is achievable, there is always need of an uncomfortable transition period about which little has been said beforehand. At this moment we see our own government, in its desperate economic straits, fighting in effect against its own past propaganda. The crisis that we are now in is not a sudden unexpected calamity, like an earthquake, and it was not caused by the war, but merely hastened by it. Decades ago it could be foreseen that something of this kind was going to happen. Ever since the nineteenth century our national income, dependent partly on interest from foreign investments, and on assured markets and cheap raw materials in colonial countries, had been extremely precarious. It was certain that, sooner or later, something would go wrong and we should be forced to make our exports balance our imports: and when that happened the British standard of living, including the working-class standard, was bound to fall, at least temporarily. Yet the left-wing parties, even when they were vociferously anti-imperialist, never made these facts clear. On occasion they were ready to admit that the British workers had benefited, to some extent, by the looting of Asia and Africa, but they always allowed it to appear that we could give up our loot and yet in some way contrive to remain prosperous. Quite largely, indeed, the workers were won over to Socialism by being told that they were exploited, whereas the brute truth was that, in world terms, they were exploiters. Now, to all appearances, the point has been reached when the working-class living-standard *cannot* be maintained, let alone raised. Even if we squeeze the rich out of existence, the mass of the people must either consume less or produce more. Or am I exaggerating the mess we are in? I may be, and I should be glad to find myself mistaken. But the point I wish to make is that this question, among people who are faithful to the left ideology, cannot be genuinely discussed. The lowering of wages and raising of working hours are felt to be inherently anti-Socialist measures, and must therefore be dismissed in advance, whatever the economic situation may be. To suggest that they may be unavoidable is merely to risk being plastered with those labels that we are all terrified of. It is far safer to evade the issue and pretend that we can put everything right by redistributing the existing national income.

To accept an orthodoxy is always to inherit unresolved contradictions. Take for instance the fact, which came out in Mr. Winkler's essay in this series, that all sensitive people are revolted by industrialism and its products, and yet are aware that the conquest of poverty and the emancipation of the working class demand not less industrialisation, but more and more. Or take the fact that certain jobs are absolutely necessary and yet are never done except under some kind of coercion. Or take the fact that it is impossible to have a positive foreign policy without having powerful armed forces. One could multiply examples. In every such case there is a conclusion which is perfectly plain but which can only be drawn if one is privately disloyal to the official ideology. The normal response is to push the question, unanswered, into a corner of one's mind, and then continue repeating contradictory catchwords. One does not have to search far through the reviews and magazines to discover the effects of this kind of thinking.

I am not, of course, suggesting that mental dishonesty is peculiar to Socialists and left-wingers generally, or is commonest among them. It is merely that acceptance of *any* political discipline seems to be incompatible with literary integrity. This applies equally to movements like Pacifism and Personalism, which claim to be outside the ordinary political struggle. Indeed, the mere sound of words ending in -ism seems to bring with it the smell of propaganda. Group loyalties are necessary, and yet they are poisonous to literature, so long as literature is the product of individuals. As soon as they are allowed to have any influence, even a negative one, on creative writing, the result is not only falsification, but often the actual drying-up of the inventive faculties.

Well, then, what? Do we have to conclude that it is the duty of every writer to "keep out of politics"? Certainly not! In any case, as I have said already, no thinking person can or does genuinely keep out of politics, in an age like the present one. I only suggest that we should draw a sharper distinction than we do at present between our political and our literary loyalties, and should recognise that a willingness to *do* certain distasteful but necessary things does not carry with it any obligation to swallow the beliefs that usually go with them. When a writer engages in politics he should do so as a citizen, as a human being, but not *as a writer*. I do not think that he has the right, merely on the score of his sensibilities, to shirk the ordinary dirty work of politics. Just as much as anyone else, he should be prepared to deliver lectures in draughty halls, to chalk pavements, to canvass voters, to distribute leaflets, even to fight in civil wars if it seems necessary. But whatever else he does in the service of his party, he should never write for it. He should make it clear that his writing is a thing apart. And he should be able to act co-operatively while, if he chooses, completely rejecting the official ideology. He should never turn back from a train of thought because it may lead to a heresy, and he should not mind very much if his unorthodoxy is smelt out, as it probably will be. Perhaps it is even a bad sign in a writer if he is not suspected of reactionary tendencies to-day, just as it was a bad sign if he was not suspected of Communist sympathies twenty years ago.

But does all this mean that a writer should not only refuse to be dictated to by political bosses, but also that he should refrain from writing *about* politics? Once again, certainly not! There is no reason why he should not write in the most crudely political way, if he wishes to. Only he should do so as an individual, an outsider, at the most an unwelcome guerrilla on the flank of a regular army. This attitude is quite compatible with ordinary political usefulness. It is reasonable, for example, to be willing to fight in a war because one thinks the war ought to be won, and at the same time to refuse to write war propaganda. Sometimes, if a writer is honest, his writings and his political activities may actually contradict one another. There are occasions when that is plainly undesirable: but then the remedy is not to falsify one's impulses, but to remain silent.

To suggest that a creative writer, in a time of conflict, must split his life into two compartments, may seem defeatist or frivolous: yet in practice I do not see what else he can do. To lock yourself up in the ivory tower is impossible and undesirable. To yield subjectively, not merely to a party machine, but even to a group ideology, is to destroy yourself as writer. We feel this dilemma to be a painful one, because we see the need of engaging in politics while also seeing what a dirty, degrading business it is. And most of us still have a lingering belief that every choice, even every political choice, is between good and evil, and that if a thing is necessary it is also right. We should, I think, get rid of this belief, which belongs to the nursery. In politics one can never do more than decide which of two evils is the less, and there are some situations from which one can only escape by acting like a devil or a lunatic. War, for example, may be necessary, but it is certainly not right or sane. Even a general election is not exactly a pleasant or edifying spectacle. If you have to take part in such things—and I think you do have to, unless you are armoured by old age or stupidity or hypocrisy—then you also have to keep part of yourself inviolate. For most people the problem does not arise in the same form, because their lives are split already. They are truly alive only in their leisure hours, and there is no emotional connection between their work and their political activities. Nor are they generally asked, in the name of political loyalty, to debase themselves as workers. The artist, and especially the writer, is asked just that—in fact, it is the only thing that politicians ever ask of him. If he refuses, that does not mean that he is condemned to inactivity. One half of him, which in a sense is the whole of him, can act as resolutely, even as violently if need be, as anyone else. But his writings, in so far as they have any value, will always be the product of the saner self that stands aside, records the things that are done and admits their necessity, but refuses to be deceived as to their true nature.

Review of *The Heart of the Matter* by Graham Greene

The New Yorker, July 17, 1948

A fairly large proportion of the distinguished novels of the last few decades have been written by Catholics and have even been describable as Catholic novels. One reason for this is that the conflict not only between this world and the next world but between sanctity and goodness is a fruitful theme of which the ordinary, unbelieving writer cannot make use. Graham Greene used it once successfully, in "The Power and the Glory," and once, with very much more doubtful success, in "Brighton Rock." His latest book, "The Heart of the Matter" (Viking), is, to put it as politely as possible, not one of his best, and gives the impression of having been mechanically constructed, the familiar conflict being set out like an algebraic equation, with no attempt at psychological probability.

Here is the outline of the story: The time is 1942 and the place is a West African British colony, unnamed but probably the Gold Coast. A certain Major Scobie, Deputy Commissioner of Police and a Catholic convert, finds a letter bearing a German address hidden in the cabin of the captain of a Portuguese ship. The letter turns out to be a private one and completely harmless, but it is, of course, Scobie's duty to hand it over to higher authority. However, the pity he feels for the Portuguese captain is too much for him, and he destroys the letter and says nothing about it. Scobie, it is explained to us, is a man of almost excessive conscientiousness. He does not drink, take bribes, keep Negro mistresses, or indulge in bureaucratic intrigue, and he is, in fact, disliked on all sides because of his uprightness, like Aristides the Just. His leniency toward the Portuguese captain is his first lapse. After it, his life becomes a sort of fable on the theme of "Oh, what a tangled web we weave," and in every single instance it is the goodness of his heart that leads him astray. Actuated at the start by pity, he has a love affair with a girl who has been rescued from a torpedoed ship. He continues with the affair largely out of a sense of duty, since the girl will go to pieces morally if abandoned; he also lies about her to his wife, so as to spare her the pangs of jealousy. Since he intends to persist in his adultery, he does not go to confession, and in order to lull his wife's suspicions he tells her that he has gone. This involves him in the truly fearful act of taking the Sacrament while in a state of mortal sin. By this time, there are other complications, all caused in the same manner, and Scobie finally decides that the only way out is through the unforgivable sin of suicide. Nobody else must be allowed to suffer through his death; it will be so arranged as to look like an accident. As it happens, he bungles one detail, and the fact that he has committed suicide becomes known. The book ends with a Catholic priest's hinting, with doubtful orthodoxy, that Scobie is perhaps not damned. Scobie, however, had not entertained any such hope. White all through, with a stiff upper lip, he had gone to what he believed to be certain damnation out of pure gentlemanliness.

I have not parodied the plot of the book. Even when dressed up in realistic details, it is just as ridiculous as I have indicated. The thing most obviously wrong with it is that Scobie's motives, assuming one could believe in them, do not adequately explain his actions. Another question that comes up is: Why should this novel have its setting in West Africa? Except that one of the characters is a Syrian trader, the whole thing might as well be happening in a London suburb. The Africans exist only as an occasionally mentioned background, and the thing that would actually be in

Scobie's mind the whole time—the hostility between black and white, and the struggle against the local nationalist movement—is not mentioned at all. Indeed, although we are shown his thoughts in considerable detail, he seldom appears to think about his work, and then only of trivial aspects of it, and never about the war, although the date is 1942. All he is interested in is his own progress toward damnation. The improbability of this shows up against the colonial setting, but it is an improbability that is present in "Brighton Rock" as well, and that is bound to result from foisting theological preoccupations upon simple people anywhere.

The central idea of the book is that it is better, spiritually higher, to be an erring Catholic than a virtuous pagan. Graham Greene would probably subscribe to the statement of Maritain, made apropos of Léon Bloy, that "there is but one sadness—not to be a saint." A saying of Péguy's is quoted on the title page of the book to the effect that the sinner is "at the very heart of Christianity" and knows more of Christianity than anyone else does, except the saint. All such sayings contain or can be made to contain, the fairly sinister suggestion that ordinary human decency is of no value and that any one sin is no worse than any other sin. In addition, it is impossible not to feel a sort of snobbishness in Mr. Greene's attitude, both here and in his other books written from an explicitly Catholic standpoint. He appears to share the idea, which has been floating around ever since Baudelaire, that there is something rather distingué in being damned; Hell is a sort of high-class night club, entry to which is reserved for Catholics only, since the others, the non-Catholics, are too ignorant to be held guilty, like the beasts that perish. We are carefully informed that Catholics are no better than anybody else; they even, perhaps, have a tendency to be worse, since their temptations are greater. In modern Catholic novels, in both France and England, it is, indeed, the fashion to include bad priests, or at least inadequate priests, as a change from Father Brown. (I imagine that one major objective of young English Catholic writers is not to resemble Chesterton.) But all the while — drunken, lecherous, criminal, or damned outright — the Catholics retain their superiority, since they alone know the meaning of good and evil. Incidentally, it is assumed in "The Heart of the Matter," and in most of Mr. Greene's other books, that no one outside the Catholic Church has the most elementary knowledge of Christian doctrine.

This cult of the sanctified sinner seems to me to be frivolous, and underneath it there probably lies a weakening of belief, for when people really believed in Hell, they were not so fond of striking graceful attitudes on its brink. More to the point, by trying to clothe theological speculations in flesh and blood, it produces psychological absurdities. In "The Power and the Glory," the struggle between this-worldly and other-worldly values is convincing because it is not occurring inside one person. On the one side, there is the priest, a poor creature in some ways but made heroic by his belief in his own thaumaturgic powers; on the other side, there is the lieutenant, representing human justice and material progress, and also a heroic figure after his fashion. They can respect each other, perhaps, but not understand each other. The priest, at any rate, is not credited with any very complex thoughts. In "Brighton Rock," on the other hand, the central situation is incredible, since it presupposes that the most brutishly stupid person can, merely by having been brought up a Catholic, be capable of great intellectual subtlety. Pinkie, the racecourse gangster, is a species of satanist, while his still more limited girl friend understands and even states the difference between the categories "right and wrong" and "good and evil." In, for example, Mauriac's "Thérèse" sequence, the spiritual conflict does not outrage probability, because it is not pretended that Thérèse is a normal person. She is a chosen spirit, pursuing her salvation over a long period and by a difficult route, like a patient stretched out on the psychiatrist's sofa. To take an opposite instance, Evelyn Waugh's "Brideshead Revisited," in spite of improbabilities, which are traceable partly to the book's being written in the first person, succeeds because the situation is itself a normal one. The Catholic characters bump up against problems they would meet with in real life; they do not suddenly move onto a different intellectual plane as soon as their religious beliefs are involved. Scobie is incredible because the two halves of him do not fit together. If he were capable of getting into the kind of mess that is described, he would have got into it years earlier. If he really felt that adultery is mortal sin, he would stop committing it; if he persisted in it, his sense of sin would weaken. If he believed in Hell, he would not risk going there merely to spare the feelings of a couple of neurotic women. And one might add that if he were the kind of man we are told he is—that is, a man whose chief characteristic is a horror of causing pain—he would not be an officer in a colonial police force.

There are other improbabilities, some of which arise out of Mr. Greene's method of handling a love affair. Every novelist has his own conventions, and, just as in an E. M. Forster novel there is a strong tendency for the characters to die suddenly without sufficient cause, so in a Graham Greene novel there is a tendency for people to go to bed together almost at sight and with no apparent pleasure to either party. Often this is credible enough, but in "The Heart of the Matter" its effect is to weaken a motive that, for the purposes of the story, ought to be a very strong one. Again, there is the usual, perhaps unavoidable, mistake of making everyone too highbrow. It is not only that Major Scobie is a theologian. His wife, who is represented as an almost complete fool, reads poetry, while the detective who is sent by the Field Security Corps to spy on Scobie even writes poetry. Here one is up against the fact that it is not easy for most modern writers to imagine the mental processes of anyone who is not a writer.

It seems a pity, when one remembers how admirably he has written of Africa elsewhere, that Mr. Greene should have made just this book out of his wartime African experiences. The fact that the book is set in Africa while the action takes place almost entirely inside a tiny white community gives it an air of triviality. However, one must not carp too much. It is pleasant to see Mr. Greene starting up again after so long a silence, and in postwar England it is a remarkable feat for a novelist to write a novel at all. At any rate, Mr. Greene has not been permanently demoralized by the habits acquired during the war, like so many others. But one may hope that his next book will have a different theme, or, if not, that he will at least remember that a perception of the vanity of earthly things, though it may be enough to get one into Heaven, is not sufficient equipment for the writing of a novel.

Reflections on Gandhi

Partisan Review, January 1949

Saints should always be judged guilty until they are proved innocent, but the tests that have to be applied to them are not, of course, the same in all cases. In Gandhi's case the questions one feels inclined to ask are: to what extent was Gandhi moved by vanity—by the consciousness of himself as a humble, naked old man, sitting on a praying-mat and shaking empires by sheer spiritual power—and to what extent did he compromise his own principles by entering into politics, which of their nature are inseparable from coercion and fraud? To give a definite answer one would have to study Gandhi's acts and writings in immense detail, for his whole life was a sort of pilgrimage in which every act was significant. But this partial autobiography,* which ends in the nineteen-twenties, is strong evidence in his favor, all the more because it covers what he would have called the unregenerate part of his life and reminds one that inside the saint, or near-saint, there was a very shrewd, able person who could, if he had chosen, have been a brilliant success as a lawyer, an administrator or perhaps even a business man.

At about the time when the autobiography first appeared I remember reading its opening chapters in the ill-printed pages of some Indian newspaper. They made a good impression on me,

***The Story of my Experiments with Truth,* by M. K. Gandhi. Translated from the Gujarati by Mahadev Desai. Public Affairs Press, $5.00 [Orwell's footnote].

which Gandhi himself, at that time, did not. The things that one associated with him—homespun cloth, "soul forces" and vegetarianism—were unappealing, and his medievalist program was obviously not viable in a backward, starving, over-populated country. It was also apparent that the British were making use of him, or thought they were making use of him. Strictly speaking, as a Nationalist, he was an enemy, but since in every crisis he would exert himself to prevent violence—which, from the British point of view, meant preventing any effective action whatever—he could be regarded as "our man." In private this was sometimes cynically admitted. The attitude of the Indian millionaires was similar. Gandhi called upon them to repent, and naturally they preferred him to the Socialists and Communists who, given the chance, would actually have taken their money away. How reliable such calculations are in the long run is doubtful; as Gandhi himself says, "in the end deceivers deceive only themselves"; but at any rate the gentleness with which he was nearly always handled was due partly to the feeling that he was useful. The British Conservatives only became really angry with him when, as in 1942, he was in effect turning his non-violence against a different conqueror.

But I could see even then that the British officials who spoke of him with a mixture of amusement and disapproval also genuinely liked and admired him, after a fashion. Nobody ever suggested that he was corrupt, or ambitious in any vulgar way, or that anything he did was actuated by fear or malice. In judging a man like Gandhi one seems instinctively to apply high standards, so that some of his virtues have passed almost unnoticed. For instance, it is clear even from the autobiography that his natural physical courage was quite outstanding: the manner of his death was a later illustration of this, for a public man who attached any value to his own skin would have been more adequately guarded.

Again, he seems to have been quite free from that maniacal suspiciousness which, as E. M. Forster rightly says in *A Passage to India,* is the besetting Indian vice, as hypocrisy is the British vice. Although no doubt he was shrewd enough in detecting dishonesty, he seems wherever possible to have believed that other people were acting in good faith and had a better nature through which they could be approached. And though he came of a poor middle-class family, started life rather unfavorably, and was probably of unimpressive physical appearance, he was not afflicted by envy or by the feeling of inferiority. Color feeling, when he first met it in its worst form in South Africa, seems rather to have astonished him. Even when he was fighting what was in effect a color war, he did not think of people in terms of race or status. The governor of a province, a cotton millionaire, a half-starved Dravidian cooly, a British private soldier, were all equally human beings, to be approached in much the same way. It is noticeable that even in the worst possible circumstances, as in South Africa when he was making himself unpopular as the champion of the Indian community, he did not lack European friends.

Written in short lengths for newspaper serialization, the autobiography is not a literary masterpiece, but it is the more impressive because of the commonplaceness of much of its material. It is well to be reminded that Gandhi started out with the normal ambitions of a young Indian student and only adopted his extremist opinions by degrees and, in some cases, rather unwillingly. There was a time, it is interesting to learn, when he wore a top hat, took dancing lessons, studied French and Latin, went up the Eiffel Tower and even tried to learn the violin—all this with the idea of assimilating European civilization as thoroughly as possible. He was not one of those saints who are marked out by their phenomenal piety from childhood onwards, nor one of the other kind who forsake the world after sensational debaucheries. He makes full confession of the misdeeds of his youth, but in fact there is not much to confess. As a frontispiece to the book there is a photograph of Gandhi's possessions at the time of his death. The whole outfit could be purchased for about £5, and Gandhi's sins, at least his fleshly sins, would make the same sort of appearance if placed all in one heap. A few cigarettes, a few mouthfuls of meat, a few annas pilfered in childhood from the maidservant, two visits to a brothel (on each occasion he got away without "doing anything"), one narrowly escaped lapse with his landlady in Plymouth, one outburst of temper—that is about the whole collection. Almost from childhood onwards he had a deep earnestness, an attitude ethical rather than religious, but, until he was about thirty, no very definite sense of direction. His first entry into anything describable as public life was made by way of vegetarianism. Underneath his less ordinary qualities one feels all the time the solid middle-class business men who were his ancestors. One feels that even after he had abandoned personal ambition he must have been a resourceful, energetic lawyer and a hardheaded political organizer, careful in keeping down expenses, an adroit handler of committees and an indefatigable chaser of subscriptions. His character was an extraordinarily mixed one, but there was almost nothing in it that you can put your finger on and call bad, and I believe that even Gandhi's worst enemies would admit that he was an interesting and unusual man who enriched the world simply by being alive. Whether he was also a lovable man, and whether his teachings can have much value for those who do not accept the religious beliefs on which they are founded, I have never felt fully certain.

Of late years it has been the fashion to talk about Gandhi as though he were not only sympathetic to the Western leftwing movement, but were even integrally part of it. Anarchists and pacifists, in particular, have claimed him for their own, noticing only that he was opposed to centralism and State violence and ignoring the otherworldly, anti-humanist tendency of his doctrines. But one should, I think, realize that Gandhi's teachings cannot be squared with the belief that Man is the measure of all things, and that our job is to make life worth living on this earth, which is the only earth we have. They make sense only on the assumption that God exists and that the world of solid objects is an illusion to be escaped from. It is worth considering the disciplines which Gandhi imposed on himself and which—though he might not insist on every one of his followers observing every detail—he considered indispensable if one wanted to serve either God or humanity. First of all, no meat-eating, and if possible no animal food in any form. (Gandhi himself, for the sake of his health, had to compromise on milk, but seems to have felt this to be a backsliding.) No alcohol or tobacco, and no spices or condiments, even of a vegetable kind, since food should be taken not for its own sake but solely in order to preserve one's strength. Secondly, if possible, no sexual intercourse. If sexual intercourse must happen, then it should be for the sole purpose of begetting children and presumably at long intervals. Gandhi himself, in his middle thirties, took the vow of *bramahcharya,* which means not only complete chastity but the elimination of sexual desire. This condition, it seems, is difficult to attain without a special diet and frequent fasting. One of the dangers of milk-drinking is that it is apt to arouse sexual desire. And finally—this is the cardinal point—for the seeker after goodness there must be no close friendships and no exclusive loves whatever.

Close friendships, Gandhi says, are dangerous, because "friends react on one another" and through loyalty to a friend one can be led into wrong-doing. This is unquestionably true. Moreover, if one is to love God, or to love humanity as a whole, one cannot give one's preference to any individual person. This again is true, and it marks the point at which the humanistic and the religious attitude cease to be reconcilable. To an ordinary human being, love means nothing if it does not mean loving some people more than others. The autobiography leaves it uncertain whether Gandhi behaved in an inconsiderate way to his wife and children, but at any rate it makes clear that on three occasions he was willing to let his wife or a child die rather than administer the animal food prescribed by the doctor. It is true that the threatened death never actually occurred, and also that Gandhi—with, one gathers, a good deal of moral pressure in the opposite direction—always gave the patient the choice of staying alive at the price of committing a sin: still, if the decision had been solely his own, he would have forbidden the animal food, whatever the risks might be. There must, he says, be some limit to what we will do in order to remain alive, and the limit is well on this side of chicken broth. This attitude is perhaps a noble one, but, in the sense which—I think—most people would give to the word, it is inhuman. The essence of being human is that one does not seek perfection, that one *is* sometimes willing to commit sins for the sake of loyalty, that one does not push asceticism to the point where it makes friendly intercourse impossible, and that one is prepared in the end to be defeated and broken up by life, which is the inevitable price of fastening one's love upon other human individuals. No doubt alcohol, tobacco and so forth are things that a saint must avoid, but sainthood is also a thing that human beings must avoid. There is an obvious retort to this, but one should be wary about making it. In this yogi-ridden age, it is too readily assumed that "non-attachment" is not only better than a full acceptance of earthly life, but that the ordinary man only rejects it because it is too difficult: in other words, that the average human being is a failed saint. It is doubtful whether this is true. Many people genuinely do not wish to be saints, and it is probable that some who achieve or aspire to sainthood have never felt much temptation to be human beings. If one could follow it to its psychological roots, one would, I believe, find that the main motive for "non-attachment" is a desire to escape from the pain of living, and above all from love, which, sexual or non-sexual, is hard work. But it is not necessary here to argue whether the other-worldly or the humanistic ideal is "higher." The point is that they are incompatible. One must choose between God and Man, and all "radicals" and "progressives," from the mildest Liberal to the most extreme Anarchist, have in effect chosen Man.

However, Gandhi's pacifism can be separated to some extent from his other teachings. Its motive was religious, but he claimed also for it that it was a definite technique, a method, capable of producing desired political results. Gandhi's attitude was not that of most Western pacifists. *Satyagraha,* first evolved in South Africa, was a sort of non-violent warfare, a way of defeating the enemy without hurting him and without feeling or arousing hatred. It entailed such things as civil disobedience, strikes, lying down in front of railway trains, enduring police charges without running away and without hitting back, and the like. Gandhi objected to "passive resistance" as a translation of *Satyagraha*: in Gujarati, it seems, the word means "firmness in the truth." In his early days Gandhi served as a stretcher-bearer on the British side in the Boer War, and he was prepared to do the same again in the war of 1914–18. Even after he had completely abjured violence he was honest enough to see that in war it is usually necessary to take sides. He did not—indeed, since his whole political life centered round a struggle for national independence, he could not—take the sterile and dishonest line of pretending that in every war both sides are exactly the same and it makes no difference who wins. Nor did he, like most Western pacifists, specialize in avoiding awkward questions. In relation to the late war, one question that every pacifist had a clear obligation to answer was: "What about the Jews?

Are you prepared to see them exterminated? If not, how do you propose to save them without resorting to war?" I must say that I have never heard, from any Western pacifist, an honest answer to this question, though I have heard plenty of evasions, usually of the "you're another" type. But it so happens that Gandhi was asked a somewhat similar question in 1938 and that his answer is on record in Mr. Louis Fischer's *Gandhi and Stalin.* According to Mr. Fischer, Gandhi's view was that the German Jews ought to commit collective suicide, which "would have aroused the world and the people of Germany to Hitler's violence." After the war he justified himself: the Jews had been killed anyway, and might as well have died significantly. One has the impression that this attitude staggered even so warm an admirer as Mr. Fischer, but Gandhi was merely being honest. If you are not prepared to take life, you must often be prepared for lives to be lost in some other way. When, in 1942, he urged non-violent resistance against a Japanese invasion, he was ready to admit that it might cost several million deaths.

At the same time there is reason to think that Gandhi, who after all was born in 1869, did not understand the nature of totalitarianism and saw everything in terms of his own struggle against the British government. The important point here is not so much that the British treated him forbearingly as that he was always able to command publicity. As can be seen from the phrase quoted above, he believed in "arousing the world," which is only possible if the world gets a chance to hear what you are doing. It is difficult to see how Gandhi's methods could be applied in a country where opponents of the regime disappear in the middle of the night and are never heard of again. Without a free press and the right of assembly, it is impossible not merely to appeal to outside opinion, but to bring a mass movement into being, or even to make your intentions known to your adversary. Is there a Gandhi in Russia at this moment? And if there is, what is he accomplishing? The Russian masses could only practice civil disobedience if the same idea happened to occur to all of them simultaneously, and even then, to judge by the history of the Ukraine famine, it would make no difference. But let it be granted that non-violent resistance can be effective against one's own government, or against an occupying power: even so, how does one put it into practice internationally? Gandhi's various conflicting statements on the late war seem to show that he felt the difficulty of this. Applied to foreign politics, pacifism either stops being pacifist or becomes appeasement. Moreover the assumption, which served Gandhi so well in dealing with individuals, that all human beings are more or less approachable and will respond to a generous gesture, needs to be seriously questioned. It is not necessarily true, for example, when you are dealing with lunatics. Then the question becomes: Who is sane? Was Hitler sane? And is it not possible for one whole culture to be insane by the standards of another? And, so far as one can gauge the feelings of whole nations, is there any apparent connection between a generous deed and a friendly response? Is gratitude a factor in international politics?

These and kindred questions need discussion, and need it urgently, in the few years left to us before somebody presses the button and the rockets begin to fly. It seems doubtful whether civilization can stand another major war, and it is at least thinkable that the way out lies through non-violence. It is Gandhi's virtue that he would have been ready to give honest consideration to the kind of question that I have raised above; and, indeed, he probably did discuss most of these questions somewhere or other in his innumerable newspaper articles. One feels of him that there was much that he did not understand, but not that there was anything that he was frightened of saying or thinking. I have never been able to feel much liking for Gandhi, but I do not feel sure that as a political thinker he was wrong in the main, nor do I believe that his life was a failure. It is curious that when he was assassinated, many of his warmest admirers exclaimed sorrowfully that he had lived just long enough to see his life work in ruins, because India was engaged in a civil war which had always been foreseen as one of the by-products of the transfer of power. But it was not in trying to smoothe down Hindu-Moslem rivalry that Gandhi had spent his life. His main political objective, the peaceful ending of British rule, had after all been attained. As usual, the relevant facts cut across one another. On the one hand, the British did get out of India without fighting, an event which very few observers indeed would have predicted until about a year before it happened. On the other hand, this was done by a Labor government, and it is certain that a Conservative government, especially a government headed by Churchill, would have acted differently. But if, by 1945, there had grown up in Britain a large body of opinion sympathetic to Indian independence, how far was this due to Gandhi's personal influence? And if, as may happen, India and Britain finally settle down into a decent and friendly relationship, will this be partly because Gandhi, by keeping up his struggle obstinately and without hatred, disinfected the political air? That one even thinks of asking such questions indicates his stature. One may feel, as I do, a sort of aesthetic distaste for Gandhi, one may reject the claims of sainthood made on his behalf (he never made any such claim himself, by the way), one may also reject sainthood as an ideal and therefore feel that Gandhi's basic aims were anti-human and reactionary: but regarded simply as a politician, and compared with the other leading political figures of our time, how clean a smell he has managed to leave behind!

NOTES

Charles Dickens

1. In *Charles Dickens: The Progress of a Radical* (1937).

2. *The Scarlet Pimpernel* was a romantic novel and play (1905), the first of several stories featuring the adventures during the French Revolution of the suave English aristocrat Sir Percy Blakeney, who rescued those destined for the guillotine. Their author, Baroness Orczy (Mrs. Montagu Barstow, 1865–1947), was born in Hungary.

3. Carmagnole was a worker's jacket originating in Carmagnola, Piedmont. It became fashionable among French revolutionaries and was then used to describe a song and a wild dance. The first verse of the song pilloried "Madame Veto"—Queen Marie Antoinette—who was accused of influencing Louis XVI to exercise this right.

4. Samuel Smiles (1812–1904) was the author of a number of works of self-improvement; the best known is *Self-Help: with Illustrations of Conduct & Perseverance* (1859). By far the most successful of many such books of its time, it and the attitudes it represented have been much castigated.

5. On his return from a visit to the Soviet Union, André Gide (1869–1951), prolific French author and editor, wrote a somewhat disillusioned account of his experiences there, *Retour de l'URSS* (1936).

6. Bartram wrote novels and folklore verses. *The People of Clopton: A Poaching Romance* was published in 1897.

7. *Orley Farm* (1862) by Anthony Trollope (1815–1882).

8. "Ye Mariners of England," by Thomas Campbell (1777–1844); "The Charge of the Light Brigade," by Alfred, Lord Tennyson (1809–1892).

9. Orwell probably had in mind Bransby Williams (1870–1961), the "Hamlet of the Halls," whose impersonations of Dickens's characters and incidents were popular in music halls and on records; they anticipated the one-man Dickens recitals by legitimate actors in the latter part of the twentieth century.

10. *Frank Fairleigh, or Scenes from the Life of a Private Pupil* (1850) was by Francis Edward Smedley (1818–1864). *Mr Verdant Green* is a trilogy by Cuthbert Bede (Edward Bradley, 1827–1889), made up of *The Adventures of Mr Verdant Green, an Oxford Freshman* (1853), *The*

Further Adventures of Mr Verdant Green, an Oxford Undergraduate (1854), and *Mr Verdant Green Married and Done For* (1857). The books were frequently reprinted, with illustrations by the author. *Mrs Caudle's Curtain Lectures* (1846; reprinted from *Punch*) was by Douglas Jerrold, a prolific dramatist (1803–1857).

Boys' Weeklies

1. *Boy's Own Paper* (not *Boys'*, as sometimes printed), founded in 1879 by the Religious Tract Society, was a weekly to 1912, then monthly. It outlived Orwell. *Chums,* founded in 1892, was published by Cassell as a rival to *Boy's Own Paper.*

2. In fact, the stories were *not* all the work of "Frank Richards" (Charles Hamilton, 1876–1961). He is credited with 1,380 of the 1,683 stories in *Magnet;* there were some twenty-five substitute writers. Nevertheless, he wrote some 5,000 stories, "created" more than a hundred schools, used two dozen pen names (including Hilda Richards, for girls-school stories, and Martin Clifford). He probably published some 100 million words.

3. John Edward Gunby Hadath (c. 1880–1954), author of *Schoolboy Grit* (1913), *Carey of Cobhouse* (1928), and other school stories.

4. Desmond Francis Talbot Coke (1879–1931), author of *The House Prefect* (1908) and other books for children.

5. Officers' Training Corps, the army cadet force maintained in many public schools.

6. "Hilda Richards" is Frank Richards.

7. Mons, in Belgium, marked the limit of a British advance in August 1914. The German army under von Kluck was badly mauled, but success was short-lived. In what became a famous fighting retreat, the British II Corps held the Germans at the costly battle of Le Cateau.

8. Air Raid Precautions.

9. Ruby M. Ayres (1883–1955) was a prolific and popular romantic novelist and short-story writer, many of whose novels were made into films. Despite writing in this vein, she gave down-to-earth advice in her column in *Oracle,* the more convincing, perhaps, because her stories were so widely read.

10. The Navy League was founded in 1895 to foster national interest in the Royal Navy. Orwell was a member when he was seven years old.

11. Sapper was Herman Cyril McNeile (1888–1937), adventure-story writer and creator of the popular hero Bulldog Drummond. Ian Hay (John Hay Beith) (1876–1952) was a Scottish author and dramatist. His *The First Hundred Thousand* (see "Inside the Whale," *367, n. 35*) gave a propagandist account of Kitchener's First Army in France at the beginning of World War I and was widely read.

12. William Ewart Berry (1879–1954; Baron Camrose, 1929; Viscount, 1941) began his working life as a reporter and rose to control (with his brother, Lord Kemsley) a newspaper and periodical empire that included the *Sunday Times, Daily Telegraph, Financial Times,*

twenty-two provincial newspapers, and some seventy periodicals, including *Women's Journal* and *Boxing*. He was controller of press relations at the Ministry of Information for a short time in 1939.

13. *Chapaiev* (1935) was directed by the Vassiliev Brothers.

Inside the Whale

1. *Tarr*, by Percy Wyndham Lewis (1882–1957), was first serialized in the *Egoist*, April 1916–November 1917. It was expanded and published as a book in 1918.

2. A series of books by Ernest William Hornung (1866–1921), novelist and journalist, featured Raffles, an elegant, socially acceptable "amateur cracksman," as Orwell described him in his essay "Raffles and Miss Blandish," *Horizon*, October 1944; see *232*.

3. *The House with the Green Shutters* (1901) was the only novel of George Douglas (1869–1902), pen name of George Douglas Brown.

4. *Voyage au Bout de la Nuit* (1932), by Louis-Ferdinand Céline (Louis-Ferdinand Destouches; 1894–1961), was published in English as *Journey to the End of the Night* (1934).

5. *Little Women* (1868–69) was by Louisa M. Alcott (1832–1888); *Helen's Babies* (1876), by John Habberton (1842–1921). "Riding Down from Bangor" (Bangor, Maine) is an American folk song.

6. Charles Bedaux (1887–1944), U.S. efficiency engineer, devised the "Bedaux unit" or point system to assess the amount of work an individual should do in a specific time. The resultant speed-up of industry in the 1930s on both sides of the Atlantic was opposed by the unions. In London, it led to a major bus strike in 1937. Bedaux, who had been born in France, returned there in 1937, collaborated with the Nazis, was arrested by U.S. troops, and charged with treason. He committed suicide.

7. *Max and the White Phagocytes*, by Henry Miller (1891–1980), was published in 1938. *Tropic of Cancer* was published in 1934; *Black Spring*, in 1936; and *Tropic of Capricorn*, in 1939.

8. *All Quiet on the Western Front* (1929), by Erich Maria Remarque (1898–1970). *Le Feu: journal d'une escouade* (1916), by Henri Barbusse (1873–1935), was published in English as *Under Fire: Story of a Squad* (1917). It won the Prix Goncourt. *A Farewell to Arms* (1929) was by Ernest Hemingway (1899–1961); *Death of a Hero* (1929, expurgated; 1965, unexpurgated), by Richard Aldington (1892–1962); *Good-bye to All That, an Autobiography* (1929), by Robert Graves (1895–1985); *Memoirs of an Infantry Officer* (1930), by Siegfried Sassoon (1886–1967); *A Subaltern on the Somme in 1916* (1927), by Mark VII (Max Plowman). Plowman was among those who encouraged Orwell in his early days as a writer.

9. *The Booster*, a monthly magazine in French and English, was edited by, among others, Alfred Perlès, Lawrence Durrell, Henry Miller, and William Saroyan, September 1937–Easter 1939 (as *Delta* from April 1938). One of those who assisted was Anaïs Nin; see *n. 29* below. Orwell had reviewed *The Booster in New English Weekly* in 1937.

10. A. E. Housman (1859–1936), classical scholar and poet. *A Shropshire Lad* was published in 1896. The text printed in this essay is that of *The Collected Poems* (1939).

11. Richard Jefferies (1848–1887), a naturalist and writer, drew his inspiration from rural England. William Henry Hudson (1841–1922), travel and fiction writer.

12. "The Old Vicarage, Grantchester," by Rupert Brooke (1887–1915), was published twice in 1912, in *Basileon* and in *Poetry Review*.

13. Sheila Kaye-Smith (1887–1955) wrote novels associated with rural England, especially Sussex.

14. John Masefield (1878–1967), poet and dramatist, also wrote about the war. *The Everlasting Mercy* (1911) tells how a Quaker, Miss Bourne, saves the soul of the debauched Saul Kane, to whom Orwell refers a few lines below.

15. Orwell quotes this stanza from *Last Poems* (1922) by A. E. Housman; see *n. 10*.

16. George Norman Douglas(s) (1868–1952), novelist and travel writer. In fact, much of his small output of fiction was published *after* the outbreak of war in 1914, notably *South Wind* (1917), considered shocking in its day.

17. John Squire (1884–1958), literary editor of *The New Statesman*, 1913–1919, founded the monthly *London Mercury* (1919–1939), which he edited from 1919 to 1934. Philip Gibbs (1877–1967), prolific novelist and journalist, also wrote much on national issues, including the war, and was a war correspondent for the *Daily Telegraph* and the *Daily Chronicle*. Hugh Walpole (1884–1941), popular novelist, was the author of *Mr Perrin and Mr Traill* (1911) and *The Herries Chronicle*, in five volumes (1930–1940).

18. The reference to "eagles and of crumpets" is obscure. Possibly Orwell had in mind Psalm 103, 5, in the version in *The Book of Common Prayer:* "Who satisfieth thy mouth with good things: making thee young and lusty like an eagle."

19. *Told by an Idiot* (1923), by (Dame Emilie) Rose Macaulay (1881–1958), a prolific novelist.

20. *Of Human Bondage* (1915), by W. Somerset Maugham (1874–1965).

21. Louis MacNeice (1907–1963), a poet, dramatist, and critic.

22. See *The Road to Wigan Pier*.

23. The first line of "Poem No. 10" in *The Magnetic Mountain* (1933), by Cecil Day Lewis (1904–1972).

24. Stephen Spender (1909–1995, Kt. 1983), poet, novelist, critic, and translator.

25. Edward Falaise Upward (1903–), a novelist.

26. Cyril Connolly (1903–1974) was with Orwell at St. Cyprian's and Eton. They met again in 1935, and were associated with a number of literary activities, particularly *Horizon*, which Connolly edited.

27. By Matthew Arnold (1822–1888), published in 1853.

28. James M. Barrie (1860–1937), a popular Scottish novelist and dramatist. George Warwick Deeping (1877–1950), a popular novelist, is, with Ethel M. Dell (1881–1939), the object of Gordon Comstock's contempt in *Keep the Aspidistra Flying,* chapter I. (See also *n. 2, 374.*)

29. Anaïs Nin (1903–1977), novelist and diarist, with a special interest in psychology, was born in Paris, where she assisted in editing *The Booster* (see *n. 9* above). Her diary was published 1966–1974.

30. This essay, "Meditation on El Greco," by Aldous Huxley (1894–1963), appeared in his *Music at Night* (1931).

31. Job, xxiii, 15, though it continues, "but I will continue my own ways before him."

32. "Sketch of a Marxist Interpretation of Literature," in *The Mind in Chains* (1937), edited by C. Day Lewis.

33. *Minuit* (*Midnight* in English) (1936) by Julian Green (1900–1999). Green was born in Paris of American parents and became a prolific French novelist. Orwell reviewed his *Personal Record 1928–1939.*

34. E. M. Forster (1879–1970) broadcast for Orwell on a number of occasions in the BBC's service to India. Among his novels were *Where Angels Fear to Tread* (1905; New York, 1920), *A Room with a View* (1908; New York, 1911), and *Howards End* (1910). His critical works include *Aspects of the Novel* (1927), *Abinger Harvest* (1936), and *Two Cheers for Democracy* (1951). After the war, Forster supported the Freedom Defence Committee, of which Orwell was vice chairman.

35. *The First Hundred Thousand, Being the Unofficial Chronicle of a Unit of "K(I)"* (Kitchener's First Army, 1915) by Ian Hay; see "Boys' Weeklies," *364, n. 11.* Horatio Bottomley (1860–1933), politician, entrepreneur, and swindler, founded the *Financial Times* in 1888 and the popular weekly *John Bull* (1906–1958), and was its first editor. He was a Liberal MP, 1906–1912 and 1918–1922. He recruited vigorously and unscrupulously for the services during the war and raised money, ostensibly to further the conduct of the war and to provide for those who suffered in its cause, through War Savings Certificates. These certificates proved fraudulent. He was tried and sentenced to seven years' penal servitude in 1922.

36. Lawrence Durrell (1912–1990), poet, novelist, and critic. Michael Fraenkel (1896–1957) was a novelist.

37. Jack Kahane (1887–1939), author and publisher, lived in Paris between the wars and founded Obelisk Press there. He fostered the work of authors regarded as commercially risky either for fear of censorship or because of limited appeal. Among those he published were Henry Miller, Cyril Connolly, James Joyce (poetry and excerpts from *Finnegans Wake*), and Lawrence Durrell. Many of his choices became classics.

Film Review: The Great Dictator

1. Alain (735–804), theologian, adviser to Charlemagne: "The voice of the people is the voice of God."

Wells, Hitler and the World State

1. Viscount Sankey (1866–1948) was a judge of the King's Bench, 1914–1928; Lord Chancellor, 1929–1935. In 1919 he had chaired a Parliamentary Commission into the state of the coal industry that recommended its nationalization. H. G. Wells, in his *Guide to the New World: A Handbook of Constructive World Revolution* (1941), wrote: "There has been a worldwide need for some formula upon which mankind can unite against Air Terrorism and the present frantic waste of the world's resources. Such a Declaration was drawn up last year [1940] after a world debate, by a committee of responsible British people under the presidency of that great lawyer, Lord Sankey. It stands available today. It could be adopted as a universal fundamental law so soon as war conditions cease" (chapter 12, "Declaration of Rights," 48). He then outlined the propositions of the Sankey Declaration: 1. Right to Live; 2. Protection of Minors; 3. Duty to the Community; 4. Right to Knowledge; 5. Freedom of Thought and Worship; 6. Right to Work; 7. Right in Personal Property; 8. Freedom of Movement; 9. Personal Liberty; 10. Freedom from Violence; 11. Right of Law-Making.

2. Hermann Rauschning (1887–1982) was author of *The Revolution of Nihilism* (1939) and *Hitler Speaks* (1939). Alfred Rosenberg (1893–1946) provided Hitler with a quasi-philosophical basis for his racist practices in *Der Mythus des 20 Jahrhunderts* (1930). He was hanged following the Nuremberg war crimes trial. Ignazio Silone (1900–1978) was an Italian novelist. Dr. Franz Borkenau was an Austrian sociologist whom Orwell held in high esteem. Arthur Koestler (1905–1983) was a novelist and essayist.

The Art of Donald McGill

1. *Horizon* reproduced two of McGill's cards, but these have not been reprinted since. In one, a soap-box orator advocating temperance is concluding his oration with "Now I have just one tract left. What shall I do with it?" A wife is depicted with her hand over a fat man's mouth, stopping his answering, and the caption is: "Don't say it George!" In the other, a vastly overweight man who might be a bookie, accompanied by a shapely young lady, is seen telling a hotel receptionist, "I and my daughter would like adjoining bedrooms!"

2. Donald McGill (1875–1962) *was* a real person; compare Orwell's doubts about the existence of a Frank Richards in his essay "Boys' Weeklies." He began his career in 1904 when he sketched a drawing on the back of a postcard to cheer up a nephew in the hospital. By December 1905, *Picture Postcard Magazine* "picked him out as a designer whose cards would become 'widely popular.'" One card, no. 1772, designed in 1916, sold over three million copies. It was not of the kind described by Orwell, but showed a little girl in a nightdress at which a puppy was tugging; the caption read: "Please, Lord, excuse me a minute while I kick Fido!!" He fairly claimed that his cards were not obscene but depicted situations with honest vulgarity, and he was depressed by the way his art form was allowed to degenerate. See Tonie and Valmai Holt, *Picture Postcards of the Golden Age* (1971), 91–93, Arthur Calder Marshall, *Wish You Were Here* (1966). Orwell, in commenting that McGill was "a clever draughtsman," could not have known that, from 1897 to 1907, McGill worked as an engineering draughtsman.

3. Air Raid Precautions.

4. An air-raid shelter built in the gardens of individual houses, capable of holding four to six people in modest discomfort. It was designed by Sir William Paterson (1874–1956) at the instigation of Sir John Anderson (1882–1958; Viscount, 1952) in 1938. More than three million Andersons were built, and they are credited with saving many lives. A few have survived as makeshift garden sheds.

5. Winston Churchill, in addressing the House of Commons, May 13, 1940, said, "I would say to the House, as I said to those who have joined this Government, 'I have nothing to offer but blood, toil, tears, and sweat.'"

6. Ecclesiastes VII:15–17.

No, Not One

1. Ernst vom Rath (as "Vom" in the original) was Third Secretary at the German Embassy in Paris. A Jewish youth, Herschel Grynszpan, shot him there on November 7, 1938, and he died of wounds on November 9. Violent attacks on Jews and Jewish property—"Kristallnacht"—followed.

2. The *Arandora Star* was sunk in the Atlantic by a U-boat on July 2, 1940. It was carrying 1,500 German and Italian internees from Britain to Canada; 613 were drowned.

3. Matthew XVIII:7 and Romans III:10.

Rudyard Kipling

1. This essay took as its starting point the publication of *A Choice of Kipling's Verse,* made and introduced by T. S. Eliot (December 1941).

Orwell here, as elsewhere, does not always quote exactly. He doubtless relied on memory, having a good knowledge of what he was quoting. These errors are treated in two ways. The original is corrected if the error does not seem significant, however slightly, to Orwell's argument or to the impression the words might have made upon him. Thus "Hosts" is given its initial capital, as in Kipling. If the form Orwell uses might have been important to him, the quote is left uncorrected; the proper reading is in the notes.

The sources and page references of Kipling's poems quoted by Orwell are from *Rudyard Kipling's Verse: Definitive Edition* (1940; abbreviated to *RKV*). Dates of poems are provided where given in *RKV.* Reference is also made to Kipling's posthumous autobiography, *Something of Myself* (1937), and to Charles Carrington's *Rudyard Kipling: His Life and Work* (1955; Penguin, 1970, to which edition reference is made as "Carrington").

2. "Recessional," *RKV,* 328–29, was written after Queen Victoria's Jubilee and published in *The Times,* July 17, 1897.

3. London and Philadelphia, 1891. The U.S. edition has a happy ending. Kipling maintained in his preface that the English edition is "as it was originally conceived and written."

4. Although Singapore did not surrender until February 15, 1942, most of Malaya had already been overrun.

5. Strictly, a peddler, but in the context applied derogatively to those working in commerce in India.

6. "Tommy," *RKV,* 398–99.

7. "The Islanders" (1902), *RKV,* 301–4; Orwell has "and" for "or" and "goal" for "goals."

8. *RKV,* 477–78, which has this note: "The more notoriously incompetent commanders used to be sent to the town of Stellenbosch, which name presently became a verb." Kipling tells how the General "got 'is decorations thick" and "The Staff 'ad D.S.O.'s till we was sick / An' the soldier—'ad the work to do again!"

9. "'Follow Me 'Ome,'" *RKV,* 446–47.

10. "The Sergeant's Weddin'," *RKV,* 447–49.

11. From "For England's Sake" by W. E. Henley (1849–1903), who has "you" for Orwell's "thee." Kipling had "the greatest admiration for Henley's verse and prose" (*Something of Myself—SoM* hereafter—82), and it was Henley who encouraged Kipling by publishing his verse in *The Scots Observer,* beginning with "Danny Deever," February 22, 1890.

12. "Drums of the Fore and Aft" in *Wee Willie Winkie* (Centenary Edition, 1969, 331). It occurs in a story that is a parallel to the poem "That Day" (see *n. 15* below) and concerns an occasion when, contrary to popular belief, British soldiers fled in terror. Kipling teases out why soldiers don't follow "their officers into battle" and why they refuse to respond to orders from "those who had no right to give them" (330). The context of these words, which may be significant, is: "Armed with imperfect knowledge, cursed with the rudiments of an imagination, hampered by the intense selfishness of the lower classes, and unsupported by any regimental associations . . ." It is not surprising, argues Kipling, that such soldiers falter before a native attack if surrounded only by similarly raw soldiers and if poorly and uncertainly led.

13. *SoM,* 56. Kipling continued by saying he endured "on account of Christian doctrine which lays down that 'the wages of sin is death.'"

14. He was, however, a close observer. See *SoM,* chapter VI, "South Africa," and his account of the (slightly ironically titled?) "Battle of Kari Siding" (157–61).

15. "That Day," *RKV,* 437–38.

16. "The 'Eathen," *RKV,* 451–53. "They" are the NCOs—"the backbone of the Army is the Non-commissioned Man."

17. Tennyson, "The Charge of the Light Brigade."

18. Orwell probably refers to Karel Čapek (1890–1938), novelist and dramatist, whose play *R.U.R.* (1920) features Rossum's Universal Robots and is usually thought to have introduced the word "robot" into general use. However, according to William Harkins's *Karel Čapek* (1962), it was Karel's brother Josef (1887–1945) who introduced the word, in a story published in 1917. *OED* gives Czech *robota*—statute labor; *robotnik*—serf. Possibly forced labor aptly conveys the sense.

19. "East is East, and West is West": "The Ballad of East and West" (1899), *RKV,* 234–38. "The white man's burden": from the poem of that title (1899), *RKV,* 323–24, significantly subtitled "The United States and the Philippine Islands." The poem was first published in the United States, in *McClure's Magazine.* The appeal was initially to Americans, to take responsibility for the less fortunate, to assume a colonial burden. "What do they know of England who only England know?": "The English Flag" (1891), *RKV,* 221–24; Kipling has "What should they know. . . ." "The female of the species is more deadly than the male": from a poem of that title (1911), *RKV,* 367–69. "Somewhere East of Suez": "Mandalay," *RKV,* 418–20; Kipling has "somewheres." "Paying the Dane-geld": "Dane-geld," *RKV,* 712–13.

20. "The Absent-Minded Beggar," *RKV,* 459–60. Published October 31, 1899 in the *Daily Mail;* with music composed by Sir Arthur Sullivan, it raised some £250,000 for servicemen and their dependents. Kipling refused to admit the poem to his collected verse for many years. See *SoM,* 150; Carrington, 363–64.

21. Tennyson, "The May-Queen."

22. The poem concludes, in italic: *"No doubt but ye are the People . . . / On your own heads, in your own hands, the sin and the saving lies!"* (*RKV,* 304). Kipling records in *SoM* that "after a few days' newspaper correspondence" these verses "were dismissed as violent, untimely and untrue" (222).

23. *RKV,* 406–8 and 397–98.

24. "Mandalay," *RKV,* 418–20, hyphenation and punctuation corrected.

25. Harriet Beecher Stowe (1811–1896), ardent abolitionist, was the author of *Uncle Tom's Cabin* (1852), which brought her fame and aided the antislavery cause. She later started another storm, at home and in England, with her article "The True Story of Lady Byron's Life."

26. The authors of these poems are: Thomas Hood ("The Bridge of Sighs"); Charles Kingsley ("When all the world is young, lad" from "Young and Old"); Alfred, Lord Tennyson ("The Charge of the Light Brigade"); Charles Wolfe ("The Burial of Sir John Moore after Corunna"); Leigh Hunt ("Jenny kissed me" from "Rondeau"); Sidney Dobell ("Keith of Ravelston" from "A Nuptial Eve"); and Felicia Hemans ("Casabianca," which includes the line, "The boy stood on the burning deck").

27. Arthur Hugh Clough (1819–1861) wrote no poem entitled "Endeavour." Churchill quoted the last two stanzas of his lyric "Say not the struggle naught availeth" in his broadcast of May 3, 1941. The last line quoted was obviously directed at the United States, then providing much aid but still seven months away from becoming a combatant: "But westward, look, the land is bright"; see Churchill, *The Second World War,* III, 209–10; U.S.: *The Grand Alliance,* 237. It is possible that the title "Endeavour" comes from a reprint of the poem in an anthology.

28. "The God of the Copybook Headings" (1919), *RKV,* 793–95. In the last line Kipling has them "with terror and slaughter return!"

T. S. Eliot

1. The quotation from "The Dry Salvages," *Poetry* (London) omitted the comma after "us" in line 3. In the second and fourth stanzas from "Whispers of Immortality" (written about 1918), "his eyes" was printed for "the eyes"; "how thought" for "that thought"; a semicolon appeared for a full stop after "luxuries," and a colon for a semicolon after "skeleton."

2. Sir J. C. Squire (1884–1958), journalist, essayist, and poet.

3. Alan Patrick Herbert (1890–1971; Kt., 1945; Order of the Companions Honour, 1970), humorist, novelist, dramatist, and author of much light poetry.

4. *Poetry* (London) did not hyphenate "sea-girls"; it added a comma after "brown."

Can Socialists Be Happy?

1. Orwell wrote this essay under the pseudonym "John Freeman."

2. Henry Fitz Gerald Heard (1889–1971), author, broadcaster, and lecturer. Orwell may be referring to Heard's *Pain, Sex and Time* (1939).

Propaganda and Demotic Speech

1. Wallington, near Baldock, Hertfordshire.

2. Army Bureau of Current Affairs and (Women's) Auxiliary Territorial Service, 1938–1948.

3. From "Sweeney Agonistes: Fragment of an Agon." Orwell is probably quoting from memory and the quotation is not quite accurate. Eliot's text reads:

> This went on for a couple of months
> Nobody came
> And nobody went
> But he took in the milk and he paid the rent.

Raffles and Miss Blandish

1. *No Orchids for Miss Blandish* was James Hadley Chase's first book and was written when he was working for a book wholesaler. It was published in May 1939, and by the time Orwell wrote his essay had sold over a million copies. Chase's real name was René Brabazon Raymond (1906–1985); he wrote some eighty books, using various pseudonyms.

2. Charles Peace (1832–1879), petty criminal and murderer. In 1876 he killed Police Constable Cook, but another man was charged and found guilty of murder. In 1878 he murdered Alfred Dyson. Arrested in the act of burglary, he was tried for Dyson's murder and found guilty. He confessed to having killed Cook, and the man originally charged, William Habron, was given a free pardon. Peace was executed in 1879. His exploits entered popular myth and he was the subject of an early silent film.

3. *Zingari*] properly, I Zingari (Italian, the Gypsies); an exclusive English cricket club founded in 1845 that has no home ground and so travels away to all its matches.

4. The two lines, from *Barrack-room Ballads* (1892 or 1893), should be printed as a single line as "Yes, a trooper of the forces who has run his own six horses,"—no exclamation point. "[C]ohorts of the damned" is quoted from *Gentleman Rankers.*

5. *M.C.C.*] Marylebone Cricket Club, then the ruling body of English and international cricket, responsible for the rules of the game and situated at Lord's Cricket Ground, the "headquarters of cricket." Membership is restricted.

Politics and the English Language

1. "*rift within the lute*" is given after "fishing in troubled waters" in Orwell's list of metaphors in his notes. Not all the metaphors in this list are in the essay, but in his next sentence Orwell asks "what is a 'rift,' for instance?" He must have intended to include this metaphor, since his question does not make sense without it; it has therefore been added here in square brackets. The line comes from Tennyson's *Idylls of the King,* "Merlin and Vivien." Vivien sings to Merlin a song she heard Sir Launcelot once sing. It includes these two stanzas, which make the meaning plain:

> It [want of faith] is the little rift within the lute,
> That by and by will make the music mute,
> And ever widening slowly silence all.
>
> The little rift within the lover's lute,
> Or little pitted speck in garner'd fruit,
> That rotting inward slowly moulders all. [Lines 388–93]

2. Stuart Chase (1888–1985), economist who investigated the U.S. meat-packing industry and served with the Labor Bureau Inc. Orwell probably refers to his *The Tyranny of Words* (1938).

Politics vs. Literature: An Examination of Gulliver's Travels

1. Sir Alan P. Herbert (1890–1971; Knight, 1945), humorist, novelist, dramatist, represented Oxford University as an Independent MP, 1935–1950. G. M. Young (1882–1959), civil servant until his resignation after World War I; then author, historian, and editor. Godfrey Elton, 1st Baron Elton (1892–1977), author and broadcaster.

2. W. H. Mallock (1849–1923), author of *The New Republic* (1877) and *The New Paul and Virginia* (1878).

3. "Timothy Shy" was D. B. Wyndham Lewis, who wrote this column in the *News Chronicle;* "The Brains Trust" was a popular BBC program in which a panel discussed questions submitted by listeners.

4. Monsignor Ronald Knox (1888–1957), Roman Catholic priest and, for many people, an unofficial spokesman for that church. Bertrand Russell (1872–1970; 3rd Earl Russell,

1931), philosopher and mathematician, joint author, with A. N. Whitehead, of *Principia Mathematica* (1910–1913). A pacifist during World War I (he was imprisoned for six months), he renounced pacifism in 1939 because of the growth of Fascism. He was awarded the Nobel Prize for Literature in 1950.

Lear, Tolstoy and the Fool

1. Tulips seem to have originated in Turkey. A mania for them struck Holland in the seventeenth century with devastating financial results. In Alkmaar, in 1639, 120 tulip bulbs were sold for 90,000 florins; a single bulb, the Viceroy, fetched 4,203 guilders. In the eighteenth century, such was the economic damage being caused, the government stopped the tulip traffic. Orwell may have known the novel, *La Tulipe Noire* (1850) by Alexandre Dumas. An abridged version was often set for schoolboys to read (in French).

2. George Warwick Deeping (see *n. 28, 367.*), prolific and popular novelist. Perhaps his best-known work is *Sorrell and Son* (1925; New York, 1926). In *Keep the Aspidistra Flying* it looks as if Orwell originally intended to have Gordon Comstock call the novels of Warwick Deeping and of Ethel M. Dell "garbage." This was, however, suppressed on legal advice.